1980

# A CINEMA
# OF LONELINESS

# A CINEMA OF LONELINESS

## Penn, Kubrick, Coppola, Scorsese, Altman

## Robert Phillip Kolker

New York          Oxford
OXFORD UNIVERSITY PRESS
1980

Copyright © 1980 by Oxford University Press, Inc.

Library of Congress Cataloging in Publication Data
Kolker, Robert Phillip.
   A cinema of loneliness.
   Includes bibliographical references and index.
   1.  Moving-pictures—United States.  2.  Moving-
picture plays—History and criticism.  I.  Title.
PN1993.5.U6K57    791.43′0973    79-978
ISBN 0-19-502588-1

Printed in the United States of America

**for my
Parents**

# PREFACE

American film begs us to leave it alone. From its beginnings, it has presented itself as an entertainment, as an escape; it is made to give pleasure, to excite, to offer us a surrogate reality. On occasion it offers examination of a social or political problem. But rarely has it taken itself very seriously, and it has not, until quite recently, been taken very seriously by its critics. But in recent years many people have stopped leaving it alone. We understand now that film is not temporary, not fleeting, that it has had—particularly in those years from the early twenties to the middle fifties, when movies were the most popular form of entertainment—a cumulative effect, giving the culture a way of looking at itself, articulating its ideology, reflecting and creating its physical appearance and gestures, teaching and confirming its shared myths. We understand and we want to know why and how. The deeper we probe, the more we discover the ingenuity (and the disingenuousness) of our cinema, the ways it has used the intricacies of its formal structure to hide that structure and present itself as an unmediated presentation of reality, even when it was offering itself as an escape from reality. The more we look and the more we discover about our film, the more we discover about the methods of our looking, about the ways film works upon us and we upon it.

The growth of serious critical inquiry into American cinema began as that cinema went into a decline. Beginning in the late fifties production dropped, the studios collapsed, the economic system of filmmaking degenerated into chaos. Television took over as the cultural image-maker, inheriting many of the attitudes, and few of the successes, of the major period of American filmmaking. These events permitted a space for inquiry, a convenient cleavage in cinema history. They also provided opportunities for some filmmakers to break out of the old production methods, the old assumptions of cinematic form and content, and to begin looking, along with some critics, at the nature of their medium, its history, its methods and effects. Their works began to move in more than one direction. Their films were, and are still, primarily entertainments, and the concern for making a profit determines all phases of their work. But despite, or even in the face of, this overriding and often crippling concern, some filmmakers are seriously attempting to confront and examine the form and content of their work. They make detours into their cinematic past, they reflect upon the films that preceded them, they self-consciously call upon the formal elements at their disposal to build a narrative and control audience participation with it. There has been no direct joining of forces of critic and filmmaker, but there has been an occasional paralleling of inquiry and a knowledge on both sides that film is a serious business: financially, formally, culturally.

Five of these filmmakers—Arthur Penn, Stanley Kubrick, Francis Ford Coppola, Martin Scorsese, and Robert Altman—are the subjects of this study. They are part of a group that has been referred to as "the new Hollywood," "the Hollywood Renaissance," the "American New Wave," phrases that suggest that they and others somehow changed or revitalized our cinema. Would that were the case. The status of these new filmmakers—their ability to function more independently than those who came before them, their effect on filmmaking in general—is rather compromised. The essays that follow attempt to reach an understanding of that independence, that compromise, of the effect of their work on American film, and the effect of that film on ourselves.

R.P.K.

COLUMBIA, MD.
JUNE 1979

# ACKNOWLEDGMENTS

Writing a book on film requires a great deal of help, especially when it comes to gaining access to prints long since gone from movie theaters. Special thanks goes to the Motion Picture Section of the Library of Congress, Joe Balian, Barbara Humphrys, and Kathy Wise in particular. Wally Dauler and Clyde Norton, of MacMillan Audio Brandon, were of particular help with prints unavailable at the Library, as were Emily Green at Corinth Films and Charles Feiner at Twyman Films. Joseph Weill, Harry Ufland, and Jamie Glauber made it possible to screen an early film of Martin Scorsese. Scorsese's assistant, Donna Gigliotti, was also of great help on many matters, and Scorsese himself gave permission to use the long dialogue quotation from *Mean Streets* on pp. 218–20.

Gene Robinson, Stephen Prince, and Stephen Bernstein read parts of the manuscript, and their suggestions and corrections were invaluable. J. Douglas Ousley originally suggested that I write a book on Robert Altman; it was from his idea that the present work emerged, a work he read in its early form and to which his comments helped give shape and coherency. Joe Miller also read the manuscript, but his influence goes beyond suggestions: our long-term discussions about film have resulted in many of his ideas laying the groundwork for my own thought.

My students Mary Louise Rubacky and John Pacy helped me make my time a little less crowded while I was working on the manuscript. The American Film Institute, Preston Fray of Twentieth-Century Fox, and Gary Arnold supplied me with helpful information. Margot and Michael Kernan gave special support and encouragement through the many months of writing. David Parker, a man of extraordinary knowledge of American film, had more of an influence on this book than he knows.

Gene Robinson prepared the index. Myra Robinson typed a manuscript from a mess of smudges, crossed-out lines, red arrows, and illegible scribbles. Through it all they have remained wonderful friends, helping the book as much by their friendship as by their work on it.

My thanks to the Department of Communication Arts and Theater of the University of Maryland for a semester off that allowed me to do the major writing, and to *Sight and Sound* and the *Journal of Popular Film* for permission to use some material that I had originally published in their pages.

All stills in this book appear courtesy of the Museum of Modern Art Film Stills Archive.

Sheldon Meyer of Oxford University Press liked my idea for the book from the beginning and saw it through until the end. Stephanie Golden edited the manuscript vigorously and meticulously.

Linda Saaty, my wife, did a great deal of the boring work a manuscript needs to get it into shape. She provided as well some of the basic ideas for the book, guided its form and structure, and guided its writer. Without her it would not have been.

# CONTENTS

# A CINEMA
# OF LONELINESS

# INTRODUCTION

When the studios, as independent corporate bodies, fell apart in the late fifties and early sixties, assembly-line film production ended. Previously each of the major studios was a self-contained filmmaking factory with its own labor pool of producers, directors, writers, players, and technicians, turning out many films a month during the years of peak production. This self-containment and mass production created mediocrity to be sure, as well as an arrogance that comes with security of product and market. But out of the arrogance and the mediocrity came also a body of work of formal skill and contextual complexity unmatched by the cinema of any other country. If the films produced were not intended to be taken seriously as enduring examples of individual artistic worth, they often enough overcame the intent of their makers to stand as enduring examples of *filmmaking,* and all the collective energy that implies. They came as well to stand for us; they created the images in which we consented to see ourselves.

The studios were places where support and security were offered to those who could work within their order, and when they fell that security and assuredness fell with them. The reasons for their fall were many and varied. Television, of course, was the major cause. In the late forties and early fifties, population patterns shifted. People moved to the suburbs and watched television rather than going out to the movies once or twice a week. But even before the impact of television was fully felt, movie attendance began falling from its 1946 peak. Studio executives met this falling-off by tightening budgets, firing production staff (mainly in their story and publicity departments), and in general lessening the production values of their films. An attitude of self-defeat seemed to be in operation, an attitude that was reinforced by two other events that occurred between 1947 and 1949 and further contributed to the studios' change and ultimate collapse. The hearings of the House Un-American Activities Committee made production heads fearful and timid, uncertain as to what kind of content might be branded as subversive, what kind of creative person—director, writer, player—would be frowned upon as un-American. HUAC managed to damage irrevocably any courage the old studios might have had. The courts managed to damage their economic power. The divestiture rulings of the late forties separated the studios from the theaters they had previously owned. They could no longer count upon a guaranteed market for their films and had to seek out exhibition outlets on an individual basis. On top of this, foreign markets began placing quotas on American film. The confidence and self-sufficiency that had supported the studios since the twenties fell apart.

Uncertain as to what they could say in their films, uncertain as to whom they could say it, the studios floundered. They squandered their efforts on technical experiments—Cinerama, CinemaScope, 3D—and on overblown biblical and Roman epics. This is not to say that important films were not made in the fifties—they were, and it is a decade of films in need of study—only that the focal point of Hollywood filmmaking became diffuse, and by the end of the decade the "product," once controlled by a studio from inception to exhibition, was controlled and executed by different hands and from different sources. The "studios," most of which are now subsidiaries of enormous corporations, exist mainly as distributors, sometimes as backers, rarely as controlling entities.

Filmmakers no longer have a centralized community of administrators and craftsmen who can be drawn upon from production to production. Instead each film has to be developed, financed, and produced as an individual entity: its sole support is itself; its sole security is itself. Instead of the studio producer reigning over a production, the agent, the talent broker, now has powerful control. The "deal" and the contract loom over the production, affecting it perhaps more perniciously than any boorish old studio head ever could.[1] The "new Hollywood" is in fact the old Hollywood without security and without community. Money is still the beginning, middle, and end of its existence, and therefore fear of formal and contextual experiment in its creations reigns as strongly as ever. The audience for its product is unstable and, worse, unknown. Worse still it is too often a small audience (though increasing in recent years). In an attempt to attract greater attendance, more and more films are made to be blockbusters, to gross millions and perhaps create a formula to be followed by like films in sequel after sequel, or spin-off after spin-off. Huge amounts of money are spent in hopes of making huge amounts of money. The shaky independence gained by some filmmakers when the studios fell is now often compromised by the fact that many films are made as part of a complex economic structure that is created with the expectation that the individual film will spawn not only large financial returns, but offspring that will further those returns even more. I will have more to say on the sequel phenomenon in my discussion of Francis Ford Coppola. But it is important to note how the promise of "artistic freedom" offered when the old Hollywood structure collapsed has turned into something of an economic nightmare where costs, salaries, profits, and reputations are ruthlessly juggled and manipulated, with the film itself all but disappearing in a mass of contracts and bookkeeping.

Therefore, to speak of a group of filmmakers who have emerged to use their talents in a critical, self-conscious way, examining the assumptions and forms of commercial narrative cinema, is to speak

5

also of a context in which their experimentation is being carried out: an economic structure that permits experimentation only if it creates a profit, and thereby limits it. American cinema remains what it always has been, a cinema of compromise, and the directors to be considered here have had to deal, in one way or another, with the fact that without profitable returns on their work, they could not work at all. "Studio interference" has been replaced by the interference of backers or distributors, or of the individual filmmaker's own judgment—or fears.

Robert Altman and Stanley Kubrick have best accommodated themselves to this situation. Altman has created about him a ministudio within which he can work with a minimum of interference. He seems able to get backing for his films on his own terms, even though he has not had a "hit" since *M.A.S.H.* Kubrick has divorced himself from the chaos of contemporary American production. He works in England, and his films have been successful enough so that he can command both money and independence (an independence great enough to allow him to have made a demanding and uncommercial film, *Barry Lyndon*). Arthur Penn seemed able to work happily within the confusing bounds of post-studio production in the mid and late sixties. His films were popular, but their popularity derived from an inherent sense of defeat that seems to have undone their creator. As a filmmaker, Penn has just barely survived into the seventies. Coppola and Scorsese present a set of contrasts within the current economic system. One has created two enormous money-makers which are also two of the best-made films of the seventies. The other has made more modest films, thoughtfully constructed, inquiring deeply into the nature of cinematic perception. Coppola, for the moment, seems caught up in giganticism, in enormous budgets and enormous projects. Scorsese seems content to continue a somewhat more contained investigation of film forms and an examination of his cinema heritage.

But we must be careful here. Although the economic situation of contemporary film production determines a great deal of what an individual filmmaker can and will do—and although I will spend some

6

time in discussing this situation—dwelling upon it can become critically counterproductive. In American filmmaking (and not only in American filmmaking) the economic situation is only one of many factors that determine what a film will be. The "sense of defeat" briefly alluded to in regard to Arthur Penn's films is not a problem of film finance, but a problem of the way Penn views, and communicates his view of, American culture. That Coppola has gotten himself caught up in enormous projects, while Scorsese is content with smaller, more experimental works, may be as much a matter of personal inclination as anything else. What Coppola has to say in the *Godfather*s and what Scorsese has to say in *Mean Streets* or *Taxi Driver* is determined by the economic necessities of filmmaking, but it is determined as well by the ways these filmmakers perceive and respond to our culture and the ways film has delineated that culture.[2]

But to repeat, although the collapse of the studios has allowed filmmakers to confront cultural and aesthetic problems in ways that would not have been possible under the determining control of the old Hollywood, they have had to undertake their confrontations alone—not only without secure financial support, but without creative support, without a community among which ideas and concerns might be shared. In the true spirit of American individualism they work in a creative vacuum. And this leads to another paradox in the phenomenon of the "new Hollywood." The "old Hollywood" studio was a guild of craftsmen, individuals who worked together on film after film, sharing, influencing each other. The much-overpraised freedom of the new filmmakers often turns out a freedom to be alone. While attempts have been made to confront this problem, most notably by Coppola's American Zoetrope and Director's Company, little advance in the cause of creative community has been made. It is this problem that makes any comparison of new American filmmakers with, for example, the French New Wave or the short lived British "Free Cinema" impossible.

The French, and Europeans in general, never had a studio system comparable to ours. At the same time, they never had an intellectual condescension toward film comparable to ours. Unlike their

American counterparts, French intellectuals have not considered film a substandard form of entertainment, but rather a form of expression to be taken seriously. They have loved film, and American film in particular, loved it both intellectually and emotionally. In the fifties, a particularly obsessed group of Frenchmen, among them Jean-Luc Godard, François Truffaut, Claude Chabrol, Eric Rohmer, and Jacques Rivette, formed a group around Henri Langlois's Paris Cinémathèque and André Bazin's journal *Cahiers du Cinéma*. They glorified American film to the detriment of French film; they perceived the ability of the individual filmmaker to rise above studio uniformity. They recognized the visual strength of American film (partly because, knowing little English and seeing unsubtitled prints, they were unencumbered by dialogue), and they recognized the strength of American film's generic patterns. They used their understanding to fashion an approach both to their own and to American cinema in a concerted critical effort. They reevaluated the role of the screenwriter and the director, they explored film genres; in short, they celebrated and analyzed film as a special narrative form with a voice, a text, and an audience deeply interrelated.[3] Their critical perceptions were passed on to American film critics. They themselves turned to filmmaking, with an organized knowledge of what they wished to do. Their films were small, personal, and inexpensive. Early on they worked together (for *Breathless,* Truffaut supplied the story, Chabrol the technical assistance, and Godard, of course, the direction), and even after they went their own ways a sense of communal origins, and certainly a sense of commitment to cinema, continued.[4]

The influence of the French New Wave on both American film criticism and filmmaking is enormous. But no "new wave" in America occurred, no movement. The changes that have been made, the experiments that have been undertaken, have been individual and within the tradition of Hollywood film. The filmmakers discussed here have used these traditions and the basic patterns of American filmmaking to make us more aware of them, to interrogate them, to determine their further usefulness as narrative tools. They have, most importantly, attempted in various ways to come to terms with narrative itself, the story and its telling, and to realize the possibilities inherent in *refusing* the classical American approach to film, which is to make the formal structure of a work erase itself as it creates its content. These directors delight in making us aware of the fact that it is film we are watching, an artifice, something made in special ways, to be perceived in special ways.

But the paradoxes and the contradictions inherent in all this are painful. Influenced by a group of French intellectuals, some American filmmakers have become thoughtful about their films. But the films they make rarely explore ideas and rarely explore their own ramifications. As delighted as they are in the formal possibilities of their medium, as conscious as they are of the genres they emulate or attack, they do not go very far beyond the tradition and never present real alternatives to that tradition. Although their films carry on an ideological debate with the culture that breeds them, they never confront that culture with another ideology, with other ways of seeing itself, with social and political possibilities that are new or challenging. These are films made in isolation and, with few exceptions, about isolation. For without challenging the ideology many of them find abhorrent, they only perpetuate the passivity and aloneness that have become their central image.

A critical approach to these films gets caught up in the conflicts and contradictions. These filmmakers have created a body of exciting work, formally adventurous, structurally coherent and challenging. But for all the challenge and adventure, their films speak to our continual impotence in the world, our inability to change and to create change. It is important, therefore, to deal with them by examining the contradictions, keeping them present, in the foreground, confronting them formally and contextually, aware that, no matter how much separation is made for the sake of discussion, form and content are inseparable.

To this end, the essays that make up this study will attempt to address the filmmakers and their works from a variety of perspectives. They will not constitute a complete history of recent American film, nor an economic survey, though both history and economics will support the discussions. There will not be a film-by-film analysis of each director's output. Not all films are of equal interest or of equal worth, and where a filmmaker's output is large, it is not practical to give every film equal attention. I have attempted to avoid, wherever possible, the director's own analysis of his work. The interview has become a major critical tool in film studies, but it seems to me that it serves as a means of getting closer to the creator of a work rather than to the creation. My preference is to concentrate on the film itself, that organized series of images and sounds that have meaning, that exist in a carefully delimited time and space that is created when they are projected on a screen and perceived by a viewer. Films are initiated by individuals, who put the images and sounds together in specific ways, and who are influenced by their own perceptions of the world and by previous films. The films are perceived (and it is the act of perceiving that completes them) by individuals who are also influenced by their perceptions of the world and by previous films. It is this complex of relationships that will be my major subject.

The process of discussing these films will be, partly, a process of demystification (and demythification as well). There will be no assumptions that what constitutes a film is merely a story with interesting and well-motivated characters that either succeeds or fails to entertain us for a few hours. On the contrary, the "story" is constituted by the formal structure of the film, which is in turn constituted by other films and the history of our reactions to them. Given the fact that the filmmakers under discussion already know this, one of my tasks will be to extend that knowledge further, to explain how they put it to use and how we then use it or are used by it. For this reason there will be digressions along the way, detours into the past of American cinema, discussions of its genres, some of its major directors and their influences, some of the formal attributes of film that the new directors perpetuate, reflect upon, or change.

The major questions to be raised and, hopefully, answered in this study are "How?" and "Why?" How and why do filmmakers con-

struct their works? How and why do we react to them? In answering
these questions I must reaffirm the fact that film, by virtue of the
popularity and the immediacy of its fictions, by the nature of its
means of production and consumption, is profoundly tied up with
our cultural, social, and political being. In other words, we cannot
merely study the formal and thematic elements of individual works
or genres. Films are seen and understood (in various ways) by a
great many people. They have an effect, calculated or uncalculated;
the conventions and myths they have built and continue to build go
beyond them and are deeply embedded in our culture.

Film is a major carrier of our ideology. To define more precisely what I mean by this, it is necessary to back up and recover
some ground. American film, from its beginnings, has attempted to
hide itself, to make invisible the telling of its stories and to downplay
or deny the ways in which it supports, reinforces, and even sometimes subverts the major cultural, political, and social attitudes which
surround and penetrate it. Film is "only" entertainment. Film is "realistic," true to life. These contradictory statements have supported
American film throughout its history, hiding some basic facts about
its existence. American film, like all fiction, is a carefully crafted lie.
It is make-believe. It processes "reality" into the forms of fiction,
which allude to, evoke, substitute for, and alter "reality." This proc-
essing involves the active creation of ideas, feelings, attitudes, points
of view, fears, and aspirations that are formed into images, gestures,
and events that we either assent to or oppose. Any given film is an
organization, on the level of fictional narrative, of aspects of ourselves and the world we inhabit, substituting for our daily experience
characters and action, in a cinematically determined space and time.
This organization is not innocent (not since the early part of the
century, at least). Choices are made as to subject and as to the way
that subject will be realized, manifested—created, ultimately—in the
forms of cinema. If it is decided that those forms are to be invisible,
that the act of substitution will not appear to be an act of substitution, that the form of the fiction will recede behind the fiction and
therefore create the illusion that the fiction is somehow "real" and
unmediated, then a very specific relationship is set up with the audi-

11

ence. It is a relationship based upon the assumption and assertion that what is seen is real and cannot be questioned.[5] There are enormous implications to this phenomenon, implications that some of the filmmakers discussed here are aware of and respond to in their own work. As indicated, they have begun to take cognizance of the cinematic forms at their disposal and make that cognizance apparent. They have begun to question the ideology, formal and contextual, of their cinematic heritage, and to make their questions visible.

Yet I imagine many of them would hesitate if they were told they were involved in an explicit ideological endeavor, for the term itself is fraught with connotations of manipulation, of single-mindedness, of unyielding adherence to a political point of view. In our culture, it is often demanded by critics and artists alike that art be free of any specific political attitudes. But film, of any period, by any filmmaker, speaks to us about specific things in specific ways. Its form and content, its fictional mode and the ways we accept it, are part of and reflect the larger social, cultural, psychological, and political structure that is itself determined by the way we perceive ourselves and our existence in the world. This is what I mean by "ideology": the complex of images and ideas we have of ourselves, the ways we assent to or deny our time, place, class, the political structure of our society. "Ideology is not a slogan under which political and economic interest of a class presents itself. It is the way in which the individual actively lives his or her role within the social totality; it therefore participates in the construction of that individual so that he or she can act."[6]

Every culture has a dominant ideology, and as far as we assent to ours, it becomes part of our means of interpreting ourselves in the world, and we see it reflected continually in our popular media. But an ideology is never, anywhere, monolithic. It is full of contradictions, perpetually shifting and modifying itself as struggles within the culture continue and as contradictions and conflicts develop. American film is both the carrier of the dominant ideology and a reflector, occasionally even an arbitrator, of the changes and shifts within it.[7] It tends to support the dominant ideology when it presents itself as unmediated reality, entertaining us while reinforcing accepted notions of love, heroism, domesticity, class structure, sexuality, history. More recently it has questioned our assumptions, as some directors have become more independent and more in control of their work, and, equally as important, as television has taken over the dominant role of entertainer to the culture.[8]

An essential point in the analysis that follows is that narrative film is *fiction,* not reality. It substitutes images and sounds for "real" experience, and with those images and sounds communicates to us and manipulates particular feelings, ideas, and perspectives on reality. Film is not innocent, not *merely* entertainment, and most especially not divorced from the culture out of which it comes and into which it feeds. This is why I find it impossible to talk about the events and the characters of films as if they had an existence separate from the formal apparatus that creates the fiction they inhabit. While I will discuss conventional notions of motivation and character psychology, these discussions should always be seen in the context of the various structures and conventions of the cinematic fiction and our perception of them. It is the nature of fiction to present us with a clean and concentrated view of life. Even if this view is made to include ambiguities and questions, it is always neater than anything we can perceive in the loose and open narratives that are our own lives. I want to return the fiction to its proper place as artifice, as something made, and to reduce the emotional aura that most American film narratives create in the viewer, in an attempt to understand the sources of that aura.

A few further things by way of methodology. Most of the films discussed here have been viewed, closely, on an editing table. I have therefore been able to look at them somewhat in the manner of reading a book, stopping, starting, going back and forth at will. This is, of course, not the way the films are seen by an audience. One of the many powers the film narrative exercises over us is contained in the inexorability of its telling. We have no control over it at all. By creating for myself a privileged viewing situation I have put back some of that control. But this method of viewing, I find, is no perfect guarantee of visual acuity and accurateness of description. A limited warranty, perhaps, but the task of creating a complete verbal description of a complex visual space is basically impossible. At best, the descriptions may recall or allude to what exists in the film for the purposes of analysis; they may occasionally evoke; they will never take the place of. The verbal description is always tenuous and subject to correction. I had always assumed, for example, that in the first post-credit sequence of *Taxi Driver,* where Travis Bickle is asking the cab owner for a job, two figures could be seen arguing in a mirror. I elaborated a detailed analysis of this fairly complex shot. On a subsequent viewing, it was pointed out to me that I was seeing not a mirror, but a sort of window to the next room through which those arguing characters could be seen. I had somewhat to revise my analysis. I would be overly optimistic if I assumed that this was the only such error of visual interpretation.

There are two textual components of film that do not receive here the attention they should. One is music; the other is film acting. The reason for their slight treatment is, frankly, a feeling of inadequacy on my part to deal with them in any but a cursory way. We have not yet developed, as part of the language of film criticism, an analytic vocabulary appropriate to the complexity of music's interaction with the narrative, or its function in helping to create the narrative. (Eisenstein made a start many years ago, but doubtless the difficulties involved in learning music theory have prevented film critics from carrying his work forward.) Nor have we developed a vocabulary to help us talk accurately and objectively about film acting: what it is and how it affects us, how an individual creates a presence on the screen, what that presence is, and what our relationship is to it. Part of the problem lies in the difficulty of overcoming the Hollywood cult of personality. The critic may talk about the director, but the publicist still sells the picture by the star. This phenomenon tends to pull us away from the film itself and forces us to examine the individual—who, more often than not, is a person built up by the accretion of his or her roles and publicity (Bogart,

Wayne, Marilyn Monroe are examples)—rather than look closely at what is being created within the particular film under discussion. When we do examine a character in the particular film, we tend to fall into the trap of psychological realism I noted earlier and begin discussing the character as if he or she had an existence rather than a function within the total narrative structure. Between these extremes fall the adjectives: such and such a player gave an "edgy" or "nervous" performance, was "brilliant," was "absorbed" in the role. And, that final refuge of unexamined assumptions, was "believable."

I have no alternatives to these problems. We will be observing a few actors who move through more than one film under discussion: Gene Hackman, who appears in *Bonnie and Clyde, Night Moves,* and *The Conversation;* Robert De Niro, in *Mean Streets, Taxi Driver, New York, New York,* and the second *Godfather;* Marlon Brando, who starts his career in the fifties and is "reborn" in the seventies. Discussion of the characters they play may give some indication of their style and through this some indication of the changing forms of acting styles in recent film. But much work remains to be done in this area.

Finally, all of the filmmakers given major attention in this study are currently working. Their careers are in progress and their future films may prove or deny what is said about their work to date. Because of this I have avoided anything like a grand summary or an overall evaluation of what they have done. This book is deeply opinionated, but hardly final.

# CHAPTER ONE

# BLOODY LIBERATIONS, BLOODY DECLINES

## Arthur Penn

Where do the self-consciousness, the questioning of the form and content of established film genres, the realignment of the relationship between audience and film that mark so much of our recent film have their beginning? The temptation to nominate "firsts" or "beginnings" in the history of film is as difficult to avoid as it is to carry off confidently. Can we point to a film, a director, and say here is where "contemporary" American film has its origins? If I were to create a proper historical context for the growth of modernism, I would have to go back at least to Buster Keaton's *Sherlock Jr.* (1924). If it were just the history of sound film that concerned us, *Citizen Kane* (1941) would offer itself as a major break with the conventions of "realism" and the seamless narrative construction that marked the development of film in the thirties. If I were looking for a more recent point of entry, Hitchcock's *Psycho* (1960) could be considered the first "modern" American film. Its coldness and distance; its unsympathetic characters; its insistence that the audience be aware of what is being done to them, and how; its refusal to provide a comforting and final conclusion to its text—all these characteristics radically alter the generally complacent and often banal narrative structure of fifties cinema. (Care must be taken, though, in generalizing about fifties film: this was the decade that produced Aldrich's *Kiss Me Deadly,* Ford's *The Searchers,* Welles's *Touch of Evil,* and Hitchcock's *Vertigo,* each of which contains the elements that I will be defining in the works under consideration here.)

*Citizen Kane* and *Psycho* are major influences on the directors who are the subjects of this study. *Psycho* in particular is the source from which so much of the blood in recent film has flowed. But they do remain influences rather than initiators, and will be referred to as such throughout. What we need to locate is a filmmaker who moves out of the mainstream of American production and looks at it, even for a moment, with foreign eyes—because it is the foreign perspective on American film, the French perspective in particular, that, along with economic changes in production, influenced the major changes in recent films. Welles, Hitchcock—even John Ford, who also figures as a major influence on the filmmakers discussed here—might have gone unnoticed by American filmmakers and film critics alike, were it not for their recognition by the French. By no means am I suggesting that American film in the sixties and seventies is a direct result of the French New Wave of the late fifties. But the French are responsible for our ability to reflect seriously on our own cinema. They offered the intellectual means, through their criticism, and the practical means, through their films, for some of our filmmakers to stand back from their own tradition in order to reenter it with different points of view.

With this in mind, it is still incumbent to find a place of entry, a figure who conveniently offers an example of this standing back and whose films offer a reexamination of the conventions of American cinema. John Cassavetes comes immediately to mind as a director who very early on recognized some things that could be done in American film in response to the New Wave. In *Shadows* (1960)* he attempts to create a narrative structure that parallels the impro-

---

* In most instances, the date given for a film is its release date.

visatory nature of early Godard; he takes a direction away from the tidily plotted narrative of heroic endeavor and melodramatic longings, so much the core of American film, toward a more loosely observed structure in which the director, his players, and his *mise-en-scène* create a process in which the telling of a story becomes subordinate to the moment-to-moment insights into character and situation. It is a direction that Cassavetes follows unflinchingly in all his work, sacrificing consistent and planned narrative development to microscopic observation of his characters' attempts to articulate their pain. It is precisely because of this sacrifice that I find Cassavetes's work difficult to watch and even more difficult to talk about. In a book dedicated to the study of formal strategies and the realization of expression through the structure of expression, a detailed examination of Cassavetes's films would run the risk of being more judgmental than critical. But, because the work of Scorsese and of Altman would be different without the influence of Cassavetes, and because his films so defy the dimensions of commercial American cinema, he will lurk as my bad conscience over much of what is written here.[1]

I turn to Arthur Penn as an initiating figure, but with some ambivalence. Penn came to film in the fifties from television, as did many of his colleagues (though unlike many of his colleagues, from the theater as well). His first work, *The Left-Handed Gun* (1958), was part of the cycle of fifties westerns that began reexamining and shifting some of the accepted conventions of the genre, psychologizing its hero and scrutinizing the myth of the hero itself. After that Penn moved in and out of various genres and various means of production, filming *The Miracle Worker* (1962), which he had originally directed on the stage; producing and directing *Mickey One* (1964); working for Sam Spiegel in an old-style studio production, *The Chase* (1966); finally achieving a major formal and financial success with *Bonnie and Clyde* (1967), which, indicative of the changing patterns of Hollywood production, was produced by its star, Warren Beatty. These, and the films that followed—*Alice's Restaurant* (1969), *Little Big Man* (1970), *Night Moves* (1975), and *The Missouri Breaks* (1976)—make up a patchwork of generic experiments, ideological reflections, and guides to our social malaise. Penn's sixties films, particularly *Little Big Man* and *Alice's Restaurant,* are so acutely barometers of the moment that, the moment gone, the films have receded, becoming not so much filmic as cultural artifacts. His most recent film, *The Missouri Breaks,* fell victim to its stars, Jack Nicholson and Marlon Brando, and appears to have had five directors: the two actors, scriptwriter Thomas McGuane, and the United Artists production accountant, as well as Penn. While the film carries through some favorite Penn oppositions—particularly that of the individual who lives on the fringes of the legal order and confronts the guardians of that order—and while Penn introduces, for the first time and without much success, a woman of some strength and independence, it is a fairly lifeless work, unable to locate itself within a point of view or a consistent method of telling its tale. It is possible that Penn has been unable to survive the transition out of the sixties, that the cultural conflicts and cinematic experimentation that marked the decade gave a strength and urgency to his work that diminished as those conflicts diminished.

*Night Moves* is a strong and bitter film, but its bitterness comes from anxiety rather than anger, from a loneliness that exists as a given, rather than a loneliness fought against, a fight that marks most of Penn's best work. *Night Moves* is a film of impotence and despair. More than *The Missouri Breaks* it marks the end of a cycle of films. It is, for Penn, almost a declaration that the ideological struggles of the sixties are over and an announcement of the withdrawal and paranoia of the seventies.

But this ought not to be an elegy. Penn's decline may be quite temporary. It is indeed possible that he is not a great filmmaker, but rather an important indicator of what is happening in film, particularly in terms of its response to immediate cultural situations. If popular enthusiasm for his work diminishes (and there was little for *Night Moves* and *The Missouri Breaks*), the best of that work—particularly *Left-Handed Gun, Mickey One, Bonnie and Clyde,* and *Night Moves*—retains its importance as a guide to the changes in American cinema in the sixties and seventies.

*Mickey One* marks the first major guidepost. For if we accept my initial premise, that French criticism and filmmaking of the late fifties and early sixties created a noticeable change in our own films, then *Mickey One* stands out, even more than *Shadows,* as being the film most influenced by the work of the New Wave, so much so that Robin Wood condemned Penn for denying his American heritage.[2] Penn himself dismisses the film as a work made in anger (he had just been fired by Burt Lancaster from *The Train* and replaced by John Frankenheimer) and in a spirit of obscurity. It cannot be so dismissed. Not only is it a work of great energy and visual imagination, but it performs those operations on narrative structure that Godard and Truffaut were themselves performing in their early work. It undoes the closed and stable story-telling devices that American film depends upon. It suppresses direct statement, clear transitions, an objective, neutral point of view. It makes its central character almost inaccessible. And does not attempt to hide its formal devices, but rejoices in them. In sum it writes, as Alexandre Astruc instructed his French colleagues to do, with the *caméra-stylo,* inscribing the director's imagination into the film and allowing the audience to meet it actively and inquisitively.

Another operation performed by *Mickey One* is a probing into a particular genre of American film, a questioning of the conventions of that genre, its assumptions and points of view. The genre in question—and there is some controversy over whether it is in fact a genre—is *film noir. Mickey One* is a film of paranoia, of a man trapped and isolated by fear, who perceives his world in terms of that fear. The film of entrapment, of individuals caught in a dark and foreboding world that echoes their vulnerable state of being, began in the early forties and expanded into the major dramatic style of the decade. Its prevalence was matched only by the lack of consciousness of its prevalence, for it seems no one making *film noir* in the forties, and no one viewing it, was aware of precisely what was going on. The French, seeing our forties films in concentrated viewings after the war, recognized the change in form and content and brought it to our attention.[3] It was not until the late sixties that American film critics began looking at the phenomenon in a concentrated way and not until the early seventies that American filmmakers began seriously to consider the applicability of *noir* to their own work. *Mickey One* stands at a mid-point, coming some time after the initial cycle of *noir* films was over and before the *noir* revival began. An understanding of *noir* is crucial not only for Penn's film, but for so many of the films discussed here that I want to digress for a moment to discuss something of its history and implications.[4]

The move to darkness in the forties—both a visual darkness in *mise-en-scène* (the ways in which the narrative *space* of a film is articulated) and a darkness in the narrative itself—was a result of cultural and technological forces operating simultaneously. At the end of the thirties, a faster film stock was developed, which meant lower light levels could be used and a greater contrast of light and dark within a shot achieved. As a result of this and other technological factors, Orson Welles and Gregg Toland could create the deeply shadowed and deeply focused space in *Citizen Kane* which became the basis of the *noir* style. They not only availed themselves of the new lighting possibilities of the time but reached back before the thirties to employ the largely dormant forms of German Expressionism and its chiaroscuro.* The result was that a decade of a particular lighting style was put to rest. The bright, even illumination and shallow focus that had prevailed in the thirties (with some major exceptions, such as the Universal horror films, which were heirs to the German style, and the films of Josef von Sternberg) gave way to a deeper focus and a deeper sense of the effect of light and shadow.

The formal qualities of Welles's *mise-en-scène* exist as profound manifestations of the film's narrative thrust. *Citizen Kane* is an attempt to grasp the personality of an enigma and to prove the impossibility of such an attempt. The combination of depth of field, in

---

* The history of film is never simple. Toland photographed *The Grapes of Wrath* and *The Long Voyage Home* for John Ford in 1940. Many of the visual strategies that would be further developed in *Kane* can be seen in them, particularly in *The Long Voyage Home,* though they stand very much apart from the content. It took Welles to integrate technology and narrative.

which many details throughout the shot are visible, and the intense darkness that encloses these details, creates a tension between what is seen and what we, and the surrogates for our point of view in the film, want to see, or even think we see. The effect is, finally, to leave us and the characters within the fiction rather alone and unfulfilled, or filled with the sense of Kane's mystery and isolation.

*Citizen Kane* altered the visual and narrative conventions of American film. In the years immediately following it, the darkness of its *mise-en-scéne* began to inform much of Hollywood's output, particularly those films involving detectives, gangsters, and lower-middle-class men oppressed by lust and the sexuality of destructive women. The key year was 1944. Edward Dmytryk's *Murder My Sweet* (made at RKO, the studio of *Citizen Kane*) and Billy Wilder's *Double Indemnity,* the first from Raymond Chandler's *Farewell My Lovely,* the second scripted by Chandler, introduced the major subjects and formal structures of *film noir,* beginning a cycle that would continue through Robert Aldrich's *Kiss Me Deadly* (1956) and achieve a self-conscious conclusion, most fittingly by the man who started it, in Orson Welles's *Touch of Evil* (1958).

Throughout the forties and into the fifties, *film noir* played upon basic themes of aloneness, oppression, claustrophobia, and emotional and physical brutality, manifested in weak men, gangsters, detectives, and devouring women who lived—or cringed—in an urban landscape that defied clear perception and safe habitation. The appearance of these figures and their landscape became so insistent that they must have been responses to some profound, if unconscious, shifts in the way the culture was seeing itself. Was *noir* merely reflecting, as many critics have suggested, a post-war depression so prevalent that the audience merely assented quietly and passively to images of its own fear? Was the vicious *noir* woman somehow a response to the fears of returning soldiers that the sweethearts they left at home were busy betraying them? (*The Blue Dahlia* [1946] directly addresses these fears.) It seems likely that *noir* was a response to a complex of societal and cinematic phenomena (to which we will return). But as much as we can speculate about the culture and the ideology of the high forties and how they were imaged forth in *film noir,* we can also speak of *noir* as a dialectical response to the cinematic conventions of the thirties. Formally, the high-keyed, shallow-focus *mise-en-scène* is replaced by darkness and depth. The heroic male is replaced by the vulnerable, anxiety-ridden male. The bright, subservient, domesticated woman is replaced by the dark, manipulative, uncontrollable woman.

None of these forms of expression or character traits are new. The dark, brooding lighting of *noir* is present in German Expressionism. The dangerous woman has her origins in the twenties vamp and in the persona created for Marlene Dietrich by Josef von Sternberg. The *noir* male has his origins in the Peter Lorre character of Fritz Lang's *M* and in Professor Rathaus of Sternberg's *The Blue Angel,* as well as in the gangster films of the early thirties. The fact that these figures of the dark appear so strongly in the forties and were so readily accepted bespeaks an ideological shift, but seemingly a temporary one. The *noir* style and themes slowly disappeared by the mid fifties. The two most self-conscious examples of the form, *Kiss Me Deadly* and *Touch of Evil,* indicate the decline by their very self-consciousness. They recognize the formal properties of *noir* in a way its earlier practitioners did not, creating brutal, exaggerated worlds which, originating in actual locations rather than studio sets, go beyond the accepted conventions of cinema realism and become subjective visions of entrapment and threat. Their characters are bizarre to the point of madness and realize to an extraordinary pitch the hysteria inherent in most inhabitants of the *noir* universe. They are the climax of the genre, or perhaps its coda.

It has been suggested that the decline of black-and-white cinematography contributed to the decline of *noir,* but more likely the viability of its conventions had worn down, and a change in the ideology demanded a change in the films that embodied it. Rather than the bourgeois man undone, a favorite theme of forties *noir,* the fifties were fond of portraying the bourgeois man at bay, threatened but triumphant. It seems the anxieties of the fifties needed a different expression from those of the forties; reassurance became more important than reinforcement of uncertainties. Anti-Communism, for example, occasionally received a *noir* treatment, as in Samuel Fuller's *Pickup on South Street* (1953), but that and other cold war subjects came to be more comfortably treated in science fiction. Anxiety, despair, and isolation returned as fit subjects in the late sixties and early seventies, and as they did, *noir* began to make a fitful return.

Coming as it does after the major period of *film noir,* but before the *noir* revival (of which his own *Night Moves* is a major part), Penn's *Mickey One* stands in a sort of generic limbo, foreshadowing the paranoia films of the early seventies, reevaluating the narrative structure of the *noir* films that preceded it. Forties *noir* focused upon a world of entrapment, isolation, and moral chaos, often by observing this world from the perspective of one character. Yet despite the attempts at first-person narrative, and despite the inherent isolation of the *noir* universe, the story-telling structures of the films were traditional. The plots may have been complex (it is still difficult to figure out who committed one of the murders in *The Big Sleep*), but their form followed a basic expository style, directing the viewer through a causal series of events. *Mickey One* fractures causality, suppresses motivations, and not merely draws us into an observation of the central character but forces us to share his perception, a perception that is confused, paranoid in the extreme, and unable to comprehend the world in anything but a jagged, fragmented manner. The *noir* world is internalized, and we see it the way the character sees it—not *through* his eyes, but *with* his sensibility.

The story told by the narrative is in fact more simple than that of most forties *noir:* Mickey (Warren Beatty)* is a second-rate night-club comic who gets involved with the mob in Detroit. He runs away in terror and comes to Chicago, living like a bum. He meets a girl, impresses a local night-club impresario (Hurd Hatfield in a very bizarre role, menacing and friendly at the same time; his club, in obvious homage to Welles's *Citizen Kane,* is called the Xanadu)

---

* Names of major players, or those whose recognition is important, will be given in parentheses. For a complete list of characters for each film, see the filmography.

who auditions him. He attempts again to flee, gets viciously beaten in a fight in Chicago's tenderloin, and, unable to clarify for himself who, if anyone, is pursuing him, assumes his paranoia as a permanent condition and takes again to the stage, open, vulnerable, yet with a renewed freedom. The telling of the narrative presents this information obliquely, withholding so much in the way of discursive information and giving so much in the way of disconnected and grotesque images (photographed in a sharp-edged black and gray by Ghislain Cloquet and edited by Aram Avakian) that we are as affected with an opaque and fractured perception, and an attendant anxiety, as is the character in the fiction. This is not to say that we "identify" with the character, but that seeing a world in distorted pieces distances and confuses us so that our experience is analogous to that of the inhabitant of the fiction. The credit sequence, for example, is a seemingly disconnected series of surreal images: Mickey sits in a steam bath in a derby and overcoat with turned-up collar; behind him a group of fat men in towels look on and laugh (one wears a gun). Mickey and a girl swim under water in a pool. A girl is draped on the hood of a car, face pressed to the window as the wipers turn back and forth. Mickey and a girl make love while, in deep focus behind them, a man is beaten up. The sequence comes to a close as Mickey runs in the dark from a man yelling at him, "There's no place you can hide from them. You'll have to be an animal." There follow quick shots of Mickey burning his identification papers and sleeping on a coffin in a railroad car.

Midway through the film, in what almost amounts to a failure of nerve on Penn's part, this sequence is explained in a flashback. Mickey tells his lover about his past; we see his former employer, Ruby Lapp (an old and puffy Franchot Tone), who explains to him his obligations to the mob. Mickey runs in panic, and we are given a repeat of Ruby yelling after him, "You'll have to be an animal." It is a moment of reversion to conventional narrative procedure, in which the character's past is explained and his present—his love affair—offered in melodramatic terms (although the images in the flashback do retain a bizarre and menacing presence—Ruby's warning to Mickey is given in a meat locker, slabs of beef on hooks providing a background). It may be unfair to criticize a film that does take so many chances just because it hedges at one point. Penn is a melodramatist, a creator of large emotions through dramatic excess, and in this he is firmly within the great tradition of American film. In *Mickey One* he attempts to counter the melodramatic comfort of easy emotions, slips back into them, and then pulls away again.[5] The romantic interlude comes almost as a relief to the jarring world that otherwise surrounds and reflects the character (it is intended precisely as such a sanctuary for the character himself), a world in which Mickey is implicated but also detached from what he sees.

The body of the film retains this perspective. Mickey's wanderings in Chicago are marked by threat and provocation: in an automobile graveyard (a favorite image of Penn's, occurring again in *The Chase* and in *Bonnie and Clyde*) he is pursued by a crane as the police demonstrate death by car crusher. The high- and low-angle shots of the crane turn it into a palpable and purposive menace and a reflection of Mickey's fears. A strange oriental figure beckons to him from the junk yard, a figure who reappears throughout the film, finally revealing himself as an artist who creates, out of junk, a self-destroying machine (a bit of heavy-handed symbolism, perhaps, but visually effective). Mickey goes to a derelicts' mission for shelter. The man who runs the place can barely speak and painfully stutters words that occur over and over throughout the film: "Is there any word from the Lord?" The words connote a fashionable (for the time) religious angst, yet their irony and, finally, their poignancy in relation to Mickey's loneliness and fear are undeniable.

Loneliness and fear pursue Mickey in images of himself throughout the film. One sequence in particular indicates how clearly the world perceived by Mickey enfolds and reflects him. He flees the automobile graveyard and, as he flees, turns to watch a car that is bursting into flames. The camera is positioned behind him, and as he moves to screen left away from the fire, the shot begins to dissolve to another shot of Mickey, now on screen right and to the rear of the frame, walking as if through the fire, down a street toward the camera, drinking from a bottle. These images are held together briefly so that it appears as if Mickey were observing himself in flames. As both superimposed shots begin to dissolve out, a third is dissolved in under them, showing Mickey walking along a row of storefronts, his image reflected in the windows. For a brief moment there are three—actually four—images of Mickey on the screen at once. The entire sequence lasts only about thirteen seconds, but long enough to indicate the fragmented and inward nature of the character. It is a bit of thoroughly self-indulgent cinematic bravura which indicates how cinematic conventions can be exploited and invigorated. The dissolve is conventionally used to indicate a change in place and/or time. But in this sequence its use for simple transition is made subordinate to its ability to signify an entrapment of the character by himself and to make manifest to us as observers the extent to which the images of the film reflect the character's state of mind.

*Mickey One* is a self-indulgent film, and self-indulgence is a quality not looked kindly upon in American cinema, where self-effacement is a traditional value. The breaking of the tradition has a liberating effect, on the film, on ourselves as viewers, on Penn himself. As a fiction, *Mickey One* celebrates a frightened individual who finally overcomes his fear, finding strength to perform in a threatening and incoherent world. At the end of the film, a beaten and still paranoid Mickey goes before an audience. As he sits down at the piano to do his act, the camera pulls back to reveal him in the middle of Chicago's lakefront, exposed, vulnerable, but carrying on. It is the most liberating moment in Penn's films. And I suspect there is something allegorical in it, a reflection of the American filmmaker's allowing himself to become vulnerable and to perform counter to the cinematic conventions of the moment. Penn survived the film, absorbed what he learned from it, and realigned himself within the commercial cinema, going on in three years to create the most influential film of the decade.

The films that follow *Mickey One* owe very little to it directly. The jagged and abrupt editing of Aram Avakian is replaced by the more rhythmic and cohesive style of Dede Allen, which depends on rapid and dynamic associations of image and movement within the image, as opposed to the dissociations that mark the editing in *Mickey One* (and which can be seen again in the film that Avakian cuts for Francis Ford Coppola, *You're a Big Boy Now*). The subjective intensity of *Mickey One,* the projection of an inner fear onto the outer world which is so much responsible for the discomfort and disparities of the film, is replaced by more tangible quasi-historical and political forces: southern reactionism in *The Chase,* white brutality toward the Indians in *Little Big Man,* rebellion versus societal order in *Bonnie and Clyde,* threats to middle-class order in *Alice's Restaurant.* But *Mickey One* remains an intriguing and exciting film as well as an important document. The narrative experiments of the French were inimical to traditional American cinema and for critic and audience to accept them had to be realized more quietly, more unobtrusively than they were in Penn's film. But they were realized, and *Mickey One* acts as a kind of pointer, a direction sign for Penn and other American filmmakers to follow.

Penn's films are all marked by a tension between vitality and oppression, by a desperate need for the self to extend itself into the world, to assume a measure of control and direction, no matter how illusory and how temporary that control is. *Mickey One* expresses this tension in an oblique and suggestive form. It expresses as well a way for the tension to be resolved and the individual to endure. But in his major films, Penn refuses to allow resolution or compromise, or even endurance. He assumes the position of "realist" (or is it pessimist?) too thoroughly to allow alternatives, to allow liberation to survive, to indicate that there are political and social possibilities other than the repressive order he seems to see as inevitable. This tension exists in the form of his films as well. Although, after *Mickey One,* he turns away from open, experimental narrative forms, he cannot entirely forget the opportunities they offer, so that the conventional melodramatic structures of his films are often altered by a distancing, an attention to their existence as film and as responses to existing film genres. Like the characters in Penn's fictional worlds, the filmic construction of these worlds threatens to free itself from the conventions and authority of accepted narrative procedures, only to yield to those procedures in the end, just as his characters are forced to yield to the social order.

*Bonnie and Clyde* is the film in which all these tensions and contradictions are played out fully and to great advantage. It attempts, with varying degrees of success, to achieve a structural integrity, and it becomes a social phenomenon and a major influence on many films and filmmakers who follow it. It uses a narrative form that appears straightforward and "realistic" in its detail, but is in fact highly manipulative, carefully forging a relationship between viewer and central characters without hiding the fact that it is doing this. *Bonnie and Clyde* is a conscious act of myth-making and extends this consciousness within the fiction and outside it simultaneously. We feel a sympathy with and an admiration for its central characters, a joy in their lives and a fear for their survival, and at the same time realize they are larger than life, fictional beings in a fictional realm. We want to emulate them; they themselves attempt to create a version of themselves to be emulated. Like characters in the conventional gangster film, a genre which *Bonnie and Clyde* reflects upon and updates—like Rico in *Little Caesar* and Tony Camonte in *Scarface*—Bonnie and Clyde are concerned about their image, about how they look to the world. They photograph each other and send the pictures to the newspapers. Bonnie's doggerel verse about their exploits so thrills Clyde that his potency returns (the impotence motif in the film, the substitution of gun for penis, is its most banal element, which still manages to work despite its obviousness and banality). The attempts of the early film gangsters to boost themselves, to create their own legends, were observed by us coolly and disparagingly as another sign of their pride, which we knew would lead to their fall. But in *Bonnie and Clyde* we do not observe it coolly: we share the characters' joy in their exploits and their notoriety. We still know it will lead to their fall and agonize over this fact, even more because we know that their destruction will be a response to the very joy they take in their lives.

The myth-making that occurs within the narrative is doubled by the myth-making that is carried on *by* the narrative itself. As audience, we wind up watching both processes as well as our own reactions to them, a phenomenon Penn takes cognizance of in the film. After they commit their first murder, Bonnie and Clyde go to the movies to hide. The film they see is *Golddiggers of 1933,* and the particular sequence—in ironic parallel to their first successful bank robbery—is the number "We're in the Money." In the film they (we) watch, people are watching the song and dance number. We are therefore placed in the situation of an audience watching a movie in which the characters watch a movie in which other people watch a song and dance number. The song and dance number comments upon events in our movie, and was itself filmed at the time when the events in our movie are meant to be taking place. Penn does not permit us to linger over this distancing device, for nowhere is it his intention to force us away from the fiction, in the manner of Godard. Yet the levels of involvement are clearly marked and there for us to observe if we will. We are forced, on some level, to take cognizance of the fact that we are watching a film, that we are observing, intruding, being intruded upon. We are invited into total participation and warned away from participation at the same time, forced, finally, as Jack Shadoian says, into an observation of our own emotions.[6] The complexity of points of view within the film creates conflicts within us and within our relationship to it. And although these conflicts do not force us to perceive a moral structure as they do in Hitchcock's films (on the contrary, they make us question moral structures), they permit us to understand why we are so engaged with the characters and their exploits and to examine that engagement.

The opening sequences of the film provide us briefly with conflicting points of view. The credit sequence, with its photographs and printed biographies of the characters, creates a distance, a provocation of curiosity. This is enforced by the graphics of the titles themselves, the letters turning to red on the screen, a premonition of the violence we know is coming. (It is impossible to underestimate the power of foreknowledge that is brought to the film. *Bonnie and Clyde* was a matter of such controversy upon its release that there could have been few people who went to see it without knowing, and therefore expecting, the outcome. Even without that foreknowledge, red is a fairly universal sign of blood, and a dissolving of the titles to it from a neutral color disrupts the continuity and creates discomfort.)[7] The titles set up a conflict, which is aggravated by the first shot of the film that follows: an enormous closeup of Bonnie's lips. Normally the first shot of a film is an establishing shot, situating the audience in a defined space that the characters inhabit, so that the filmmaker can begin his cutting pattern without confusing the audience. Here, as in the fragmented opening of *Mickey One,* we are given no spatial coordinates, no secure situating of the character, and, indeed, no character at all.

We see Bonnie's lips; we see her at her mirror and, in a succession of abrupt shots, see her flouncing about her room. The cutting is very swift and arhythmical; many of the shots are terminated before the physical action contained within them is finished. We are given, in a brief time, an unlocalized place and a barely determined figure. John Cawelti, in his excellent visual analysis of the film, states that the opening gives us a sense of Bonnie's imprisoned sensuality, and certainly Bonnie's abrupt movements indicate frustration, a feeling of being trapped.[8] Even more, they give us, as audience, a sense of immediate, if confused, attachment to the character. In *Bonnie and Clyde* no time is lost and no space between us and the characters is allowed. No sooner do we begin attempting to make sense of who and what Bonnie is than Clyde is introduced. We see him in the street, in a shot inserted amid Bonnie's moving about and dressing. She immediately notices him from her window, and the next shot we see of him is from her point of view. When he responds to her question "Hey, boy, what you doin' with my mama's car?" he makes eye contact with her (his glance up at the window providing the shot that responds to her observation of him).* The two are immediately

---

* The shot/reverse shot that links one character to another and to our observation of them is a major structuring principle in American film. In the chapter on Francis Ford Coppola, I will examine in more detail the theory of this cutting procedure and its effect on our perception of the filmic event.

linked and are not separated for the rest of the film. We are immediately linked to them, and are rarely allowed to be separated from
them for the rest of the film, until we are violently wrenched away
by their slaughter.

Bonnie trundles downstairs to meet Clyde, in that amazing low
shot which allows us to look up her dress while giving us the figure
in a distorting tilt. The two walk down a sunlit, deserted street and
the camera tracks along with them, keeping them together in the
shot. We remain close as they walk into an apparently abandoned
town (the only other figure to be seen is a black man sitting in a
chair, and throughout the film Penn will continually link Bonnie and
Clyde with the disenfranchised). They talk, drink Cokes, Clyde does
his engaging trick with a matchstick in his mouth and boasts of his
outlaw prowess. Bonnie caresses his gun and urges him to "use it."
At this point, Penn gives us an establishing shot: he cuts to a long
shot of the street as Clyde enters a store to rob it. This occurs a good
ten to fifteen minutes into the film, and it is the first time since the
credit sequence that we are permitted some distance from the characters. But it is a contradictory distance. We are given a physical separation, but we have been made emotionally close to them because of
what has gone before and because of our curiosity as to whether
Clyde will pull off the robbery. The bravura and bantering of the two
and their complete isolation allow us, literally, no emotional room.
When the camera does finally give us visual space, we do not want it.
Penn, as if realizing that this new distance is unwanted, cuts immediately to Bonnie's point of view, with a shot from behind her, looking
at the store Clyde has entered. He cuts from this to a closeup of her
looking concerned, mirroring our emotions and thereby reestablish-
ing the characters' link with each other and ours with them.

From this point on our connection with the characters is not
allowed to diminish. We are occasionally permitted to side with one
or the other: early in the film Bonnie taunts Clyde about his impotence, shifting our sympathies to him; later on Bonnie shows her
loneliness, allowing us an understanding of her pain. But in each of
these instances the siding is only temporary. Bonnie and Clyde's

attachment to each other assures our attachment to them equally. As the violence of the film increases—and it does in a very measured progression—as the threats to their well-being become greater, they become increasingly isolated from their world. It is just the combination of our attachment to them and their own growing isolation that helps the film's myth-making mechanism to operate. Their need to be free of their society's restrictions, its economic and emotional poverty, the pleasure they take in their freedom, the tenuousness of their freedom and our sympathies with it and fears for its outcome—all these create a complex of emotions that makes the characters, finally, surrogates for our own basic social and personal desires and anxieties.

But herein lies a flaw in the film. We are too easily manipulated into this emotional complex. The myth-making process, apparent as it is, is directionless; the voice that speaks the discourse of the film is unclear. Why should we invest our emotions in these two figures and make of them surrogates for our fears and desires? Why are we given pleasure in their exploits, in their vitality, only to have that pleasure brutally attacked? Who are the enemies in the film? Why do they win? Why must we lose? Heroism in American film conventionally displays an individual who can conquer oppressive odds and adversity; if the hero loses, the struggle of his fight (and with the exception of some romantic melodramas it is usually a man who struggles heroically in American film) transcends the victory of his adversaries. The Hollywood heroic melodrama is, of course, naive and simplistic, but in attempting to overcome it Penn and screenwriters Robert Benton and David Newman sacrifice dialectical clarity for emotional entanglement. The adversary in *Bonnie and Clyde* is intangible. It is "society," an oppressive and denying society but one without detail. We are given little to see of it; the barrenness, the empty, dusty towns, one failed bank and one dispossessed farmer, some Roosevelt posters signify The Depression. But this historical moment is not fleshed out. The connotations of dearth and poverty are present, but unaccounted for. (One need only recall the sequence in Ford's *The Grapes of Wrath* where Muley rages against the in-

Clyde (Warren Beatty) attacked during a robbery as Bonnie (Faye Dunaway) looks on.

justice of losing his farm to understand how direct a definition of Depression politics and economics can be rendered.)

The people with whom Bonnie, Clyde, and their gang come in contact are defined only as scared, compliant, or mean. And they are usually silly or ugly. The man in the store who takes a meat cleaver to Clyde, who is only trying to steal a few groceries, is enormous and gross. His violence is greater than what Clyde's robbery calls for. He scares not only Clyde but us, and we thoroughly approve Clyde's pistol-whipping him. When the teller of the Mineola bank leaps onto the window of the escaping car and gets his face shot, we are appalled but realize that, like the fat man with the cleaver, he didn't have to attack. These people who emerge from the empty, sun-baked, Depression-ridden Midwest to attack Bonnie, Clyde, Buck, Blanche, and C. W. are the ones trying to be heroes. The gang are only trying to rob banks. Banks rob us, don't they? Bonnie and Clyde don't want to hurt anyone; they are lonely people trying to escape their loneliness, their sexual dysfunction, their economic oppression. They themselves become heroes almost despite themselves.. The pleasure they take in their exploits, the part they take in the making of their own legend grow from the success they have in the face of these unattractive opponents, a success that continues until these single attackers begin to join into groups and become represented by the police. This is a successful maneuver on the part of Penn. It keeps the film focused on the main characters and our point of view steady. Social and political realities are present by suggestion only. We know there is something amiss in the world, but not what it is. We are only certain that our heroes make the world come alive. The individuals who try to stop them are foolish and misdirected. When the police appear, they are as abstract and uncomprehending as the landscape.[9]

The police first appear as a faceless group of Keystone Kops. The initial shootout is presented as slapstick. The gang bulldoze their way out, Blanche is hysterical (which annoys not only the rest of the gang but us as well, for we do not want any real upset at this point, nor anyone to make us aware that this is a desperate situation); the gang retain their control. The police are harmless until they themselves become realized in a single person, Texas Ranger Frank Hamer, who is humiliated by the gang. The sequence with Hamer tests and confirms our devotion to the main characters. The scene is once again one of isolation. The gang's car is shown in a far shot by a lake. Another car quietly glides into the frame in front of it. The policeman, serpent-like, insinuates himself into the gang's place of rest. They jump him, they take his picture, and he is roundly taunted. The group seems to be in control, but once again Blanche's hysteria threatens our mood and our enjoyment, provoking us to consider the consequences of their actions and our reactions. When C. W. suggests, half-seriously, that they shoot Hamer, Blanche screams a very serious "No!" And on that scream there is a quick cut to Frank looking over at her, sizing up her weakness and her future usefulness in trapping the gang.

Even though, after the Hamer episode, the gang go on to rob successfully and with even greater pleasure and confidence, the memory of Hamer's unblinking seriousness during his captivity, the ferocity with which he spits in Bonnie's face when she teases him, stay with us. Opposition to Bonnie and Clyde is beginning to consolidate itself into something more serious than the Keystone Kops. The world is not as receptive to the gang's exploits as we had hoped; it is certainly not as receptive as we are. When they are attacked again (an attack in which, significantly, the first bullet hits a mirror, shattering Bonnie and Clyde's reflected image, their closeness, their inviolability, and their protective isolation), blood flows: Blanche is blinded and Buck is shot in the head. The gang, in wretched shape, escape and huddle by their car. The scene dissolves to morning, and we discover them surrounded by a posse. The people, who with a few exceptions were friendly to Bonnie and Clyde when alone, are violent toward them when in a crowd and under the aegis of the police. But their violence is strangely impotent. The police do the serious shooting. Buck dies horribly. Bonnie and Clyde are wounded. The bystanders shoot the gang's car to pieces, whooping around it like Indians.

This is a particularly awful moment for the audience. Obviously we are guaranteed a strong reaction to the violence committed upon the people to whom we've grown attached; but, added to this, the impotent destructiveness of the crowd is a curious punctuation. Throughout the film the relation of Bonnie and Clyde to the people surrounding them is tentatively good. They are attacked only twice by ordinary people (the grocery man with the cleaver and the bank teller); otherwise "folks" maintain a respectful, even cynical, distance from them. After their last robbery, Penn inserts two "interviews" with people involved, contrasting a melodramatic policeman— "There I was, staring square into the face of death"—and a bystander who prophesies their end: "They did right with me, I'm bringin' me

The Barrow gang and Frank Hamer (left to right: Michael J. Pollard, Warren Beatty, Gene Hackman, Denver Pyle).

a mess of flowers to their funeral." The people touched by Bonnie and Clyde understand them within the fiction better than we do outside it. Except for the police, they do not seem to embrace them as myths or to accept them as liberated surrogates for their repressed lives. We hope that "folks" will remain as respectful of and awed by Bonnie and Clyde as we are; that they will, in fact, protect them. Penn, of course, not missing a chance to play further with our emotional dependency on his heroes, shocks us with the frustrated and maddening violence of the crowd at the ambush, but then turns to give us almost what we hoped for all along. In their painful escape from the ambush, Bonnie, Clyde, and C. W. find a white car, which will finally be the place of their death. They drive all night, coming finally to an Okie camp. The crowd of poor people huddle around the car, whispering, "They famous? . . . Is that really Bonnie Parker?" A man touches Clyde. A bowl of soup is offered. The scene ends on a long shot of the car, isolated, surrounded by a group of curious, wondering people.

Like most of the bystanders with whom Bonnie and Clyde come into contact, the Okies are distant. They cannot join with the robbers; they cannot really help them, for the key to Bonnie and Clyde's success and fame is their isolation from the world in which everyone else is caught up—the people in poverty, the police in the poverty of law and order. Bonnie and Clyde are not revolutionaries, for they cannot give the people anything, save some money at a bank robbery; they offer no opportunity for people to join them. The Okies' reaction demonstrates Bonnie and Clyde's success and their failure. They gain fame, even a recognition of sorts, but they fail because people are merely in awe of them. The result of that awe is isolation. The far shot that ends the Okie sequence sums up their situation within the film; they are alone and wounded, trapped in the car, surrounded by people with a distant and wondering attitude toward them but ultimately unconcerned, for our heroes do not touch their lives. The only ones still connected to them with concern are the audience, and we are forced to share their isolation.

Note must be taken of one of the central images of the characters' isolation. The car is the place of Bonnie and Clyde's existence, of their freedom, and of their entrapment. The car functions often as part of a double frame: it encloses the characters as it itself is enclosed within the screen. Penn makes a special point of this. In the first murder, the bank teller leaps at the car, pressing his face against the window. Our point of view is inside, looking through the window with the characters, and we are made to share the act of violence against this man. But we are also made to share the feeling of intrusion. The man is attempting to violate the car, the safe place. Clyde shoots him in response to this violation. In the Frank Hamer episode there is a particularly pointed repetition of this. Clyde grabs Hamer, pins his arms, and throws him down on the back of the car, against the rear window. As he hits the glass, there is a cut to inside the car looking out the rear window as Hamer hits it. But Dede Allen, Penn's editor, chooses to break continuity slightly. We see and hear Hamer hit the window in the exterior shot, we see and hear him hit the window again in the interior.[10] It happens quickly and is easy to miss, but it has a definite function. It emphasizes the action, of course. It also emphasizes the outside/inside structure that the car creates. There is no one in the car when we pick up Hamer from its interior. The gang is outside and in control of the intruding Texas Ranger (who Clyde, ever the good Populist, insists should be looking after poor people and not chasing them). The sudden shift to a point of view from inside the car reveals to us a heretofore unexpected vulnerability, of which the gang themselves are as yet unaware.

The Hamer episode is the turning point of the Barrow gang's fortune. After this, the car will become a target, as in the ambush discussed earlier (which begins as the gang is huddled by their car, proceeds as they attempt an escape, driving in circles, and ends with the car being shot to pieces), and the place of their isolation, as in the Okie episode.[11] Its security is tenuous and it becomes the place of Bonnie and Clyde's failure. The hilarious episode with Eugene and Velma, in which the car becomes a sort of living room on wheels, filled with camaraderie and an attempt on everyone's part to convince themselves they are "just folks," ends abruptly when Eugene tells them he's an undertaker. The sequence focuses the conflict of security-vulnerability-isolation signified by the car throughout the film. The Barrow gang first surround Eugene and Velma's car, pressing their faces against the window. Our point of view is from the inside, and we are permitted to share the couple's anxiety and our own superiority to that anxiety, for we know the gang mean them no harm. (Compare this to the feeling of foreboding when the bank teller presses his face against the car window and is shot and when Frank Hamer is pushed against the window of the empty car.) After the gang join Eugene and Velma inside, pleasure and relaxation are mutual, until Eugene reveals his occupation. Bonnie has the couple thrown out, and we are left with them on the outside observing the car disappear down the dark road. It is a rare moment of separation and distance from the main characters. Coming as it does after the Hamer episode and before the sentimental meeting of Bonnie with her mother and the bloody ambush, it allows us to consider our feelings. Bonnie and Clyde are essentially alone, their vitality and their pleasures are attractive, but tentative, and we share them at the risk of ourselves being made isolated and alone. Our separation from them at this point serves as a warning.

The warning is borne out by the end of the film, when our perspective on the characters and our emotional relationship to them are violently shattered. Again the car plays an important role. As Frank Hamer teases information out of the blind Blanche, Bonnie and Clyde sit in their white car in the rain. Bonnie reads Clyde her doggerel on their life and death, and their faces reflect the rain on the car windshield. The car is again their refuge, their place of protection, and now, at the same time, their trap. There is a cut to the outside of the car and a dissolve to Hamer, reading the poem Bonnie has sent to the papers. There follows a dissolve back to Bonnie and Clyde, sitting by their car in a sunlit field. Bonnie reads the end of her poem, its celebration of their life giving Clyde a shot of potency. As they make love, the newspapers blow across the field (significantly, and perhaps heavy-handedly, two sheets of newspaper blow apart and separate). At this point an abrupt change in the visual form of the film occurs. By means of a panning telephoto shot we observe, simultaneously at a distance and in proximity, C. W.'s father walk down a street to rendezvous with Frank Hamer and betray our heroes. Penn has placed us first in the most intimate proximity with the central characters and their new-found sexuality. He then moves as far as possible from intimacy with a shot whose focal length disrupts our perspective and presents us with the point of view of a spy. We now know the end is near, but we also know that, as close as we have been allowed to come to the characters, we remain only observers and are as helpless as they in averting their destruction.

Their deaths occur as their car is blocked in the road by C. W.'s daddy. Clyde is outside, Bonnie in the car. Their safe place is violated. Before the bullets fly, and as the two of them realize what is occurring, there is a rapid series of shots in which each looks at the other. In the course of the film, Penn has attempted to keep Bonnie and Clyde closely together in the frame. Now that they are to die, he separates them physically, but at the same time associates them by the glances they exchange, glances that indicate their affection for each other and their resignation.[12] Bonnie is ripped apart by bullets as she sits helplessly behind the wheel. Clyde is killed just outside the car. The very last shot of the film is from behind the car, observing through its window the police moving about the scene of carnage in quiet and awe. The camera almost cowers in reaction to what has happened. And what has happened is not merely the death of the characters in the film, but the destruction of the point of view that has been so carefully forged. The car violated, its inhabitants dead, we have no one to look at and look with; no secure and mobile isolation. We are alone and lost. The bad guys have won, and the film has nothing more to tell us about our heroes. Since there is, as far as Penn is concerned, nothing more to see, the screen unceremoniously and anticlimactically goes black.

In *Bonnie and Clyde* Penn has created an extreme inversion of the structure and iconography of early gangster films. The car functioned as an instrument of protection, aggression, and ostentation in the gangster film of the early thirties, and entered the mainstream of American film narrative thereafter (how many dramatic films do not contain at least one major dialogue sequence in a car?).[13] But no gangster used the car as a surrogate world the way Bonnie and Clyde do. Penn has changed the gangster environment. The gangster film, in its beginnings and through its metamorphosis into *film noir* in the forties, was radically urban in its setting. Gangsters were creatures of the city, which provided them with protection for as long as possible.[14] Bonnie and Clyde are country gangsters (a type that offers very little cinematic tradition—Nicholas Ray's *They Live by Night* and Joseph H. Lewis's *Gun Crazy,* both 1949; perhaps also Fritz

41

Lang's *You Only Live Once,* 1937) and as such they require the mobility of a car and, more important, protection from the openness, the vulnerability that is paradoxically created by the sunlight. In *Bonnie and Clyde* Penn is, in a way, extending the investigation of *film noir* that he began in *Mickey One.* It is an extension by contrast, placing the hunted characters in the open daylight rather than in an enclosing urban darkness. They are as vulnerable and ultimately as trapped as their *noir* relatives, but it is a vulnerability and entrapment countered by an openness and innocence that only the country can provide. In American film the country is conventionally a place whose inhabitants are untouched by corruption, a place that offers security and comfort.*

This is of course another of the film's paradoxes. I have pointed out that the world Bonnie and Clyde inhabit is insecure, barren, and lifeless; they give it life by their activity in it; they in fact energize it. Unlike their thirties and forties progenitors, these two gangsters have nothing mean-spirited about them. They do not share the attractive repulsiveness of their thirties ancestors nor the depressed paranoia of their *noir* cousins, and we are not allowed to have the mixed feelings toward them that we have toward Rico in *Little Caesar* or Tony Camonte in *Scarface* or even Tommy Powers in *Public Enemy.* The morality of the thirties gangster films does not permit a whole-hearted endorsement of their heroes. The brutality and stupidity of the inhabitants of *Little Caesar, Scarface, Public Enemy* and their like always stand in the way of an unmodified admiration of these small men who made it big. It is up to us to separate the gross charm of these characters from their sordid urban background, their viciousness, the ugly people who surround them, and the morally platitudinous police who always look for a way to get them. When the gangster film was transformed into *film noir,* the characters became even more unreachable; they became small, mean figures scurrying

---

* *Noir* gangster films such as Jacques Tourneur's *Out of the Past* (1947) and John Huston's *The Asphalt Jungle* (1950) clearly present the conventional contrast of city and country and the frustrated desire of their gangster heroes to find comfort in the pastoral world.

about in the dark. Nicholas Ray attempted to redeem the gangster in *They Live by Night* but only managed to create a passive couple trapped by circumstance, and their own innocence. The attraction of Bonnie and Clyde is that they are neither passive nor innocent. They are active and know perfectly what they are doing. They are attractive to us—as are their thirties forebears—precisely because of their energy and the way they give life to their barren world. The very isolation that undoes them is part of their attraction. Unlike most other movie robbers and gangsters, Bonnie and Clyde are without any peers to pressure them or threaten them. The only people they have to overcome, other than the police, are themselves. To be sure, Blanche and her hysteria help give them away, but Blanche is a sort of negative force. Her failing is that she does not share the vitality and joy of her companions.

Bonnie and Clyde are self-made crooks. This is a basic trait of movie gangsters, to be sure. Our admiration of them is rooted in the ideology of the individual who succeeds by dint of personal effort, the man or woman who distinguishes him or herself by energetically circumventing normal societal patterns. The thirties movie gangster embodied this ideology to curious ends. He started as a member of the lumpen proletariat, an economically disenfranchised individual who began working his way up in an urban "business" organization. As he did so, he gathered to himself the tangible properties of a man of means: a fancy lady, clothes, cars, a penthouse, hangers-on, and a reputation. The gangster is a parody of the bourgeois on the make, every working man's dream of leaving his class and getting to the top. The working man had, after all, always been told he could get there— at least that he had the opportunity to—but somehow class, education, and economic situation never quite made it apparent how that opportunity could be realized. The myth of the gangster provided a reasonable surrogate (all myths are surrogates) for his own desires. It also provided a certain caution. If a poor man violently works his way to the top and remains unregenerate when he gets there, he will be destroyed.

*Bonnie and Clyde* reworks this ideology for the sixties, generalizes it and depoliticizes it even more than did the early gangster films, appealing to the cultural discomfort growing at the time, the ripening of a rebelliousness that was just beginning to find the Vietnamese war an object for rebellion. Penn sketches in a world that is unhappy and repressive, sketches it in just enough to make us uncomfortable with it, but not enough to give us the details of that repression. We are left free to generalize, to make it analogous to the repression many people were experiencing in the sixties. He makes his heroes young, appealing, and oddly classless (though, in the traditional style of Hollywood heroes, very classy: Warren Beatty takes on the appearance of Robert Kennedy more than once in the film, and Faye Dunaway's Bonnie looks more like a woman's magazine model than a poor southwestern bank robber). Officially, the characters, like their ancestors, are "lower class": Bonnie is a waitress, Clyde a petty thief. But they have no essential class accouterments and do not seem to want them. Their robberies seem to advance their status not one whit: they gain no power, and they gain no things. What they do gain is a certain tentative freedom and happiness, self-esteem, and each other's love, qualities more immediately attractive to a young mid-sixties audience.

Romantic love plays almost no part in the early gangster genre, whereas *Bonnie and Clyde* can be read, on one level, as being mainly about romantic love. Clyde is a powerful and dominating figure. He tells Bonnie how to wear her hair; he offers her an exciting life. He can't make love, but somehow that is made to appear more Bonnie's fault than Clyde's. Early in the film she is portrayed as being too demanding and too insulting of Clyde's impotence. Clyde's self-deprecating acceptance of his problem makes us sympathize with him. Besides, both we and Bonnie know he's a man, because of his gun and his readiness to use it. Clyde's substitute phallus serves for Bonnie until the end of the film, at which point they have reached a closeness with each other that allows them to make love. That they die soon after this gives the film a perfect melodramatic structure. Try as he may, Penn cannot bring himself to reverse certain fundamental cultural themes that are imbedded in our cinema and the ideology that informs it. One of the most fundamental of these is that love is not simple and triumphs only by great sacrifice. Sacrifice is the key element of melodrama, and Penn makes it a structural principle of his film.

Love is never free. Neither, Penn would lead us to believe, is freedom. Bonnie and Clyde are shot down, as was every gangster in every film before them. (Only recently have we had the odd film in which the criminal escapes: Peckinpah's *The Getaway* [1972] is a major example.) The very mythologizing process of *Bonnie and Clyde* demands that the characters, whose point of view we share, be sacrificed so that they may transcend themselves. In that sense, Penn moves far from his generic starting point. The death of the thirties gangster had, of course, a moral necessity.[15] If such an individual survived, our societal order would have little meaning; and anyway, according to Hollywood, everyone has to suffer for their sins. But Penn is not merely creating gangsters who go against the social order —all gangsters, by generic definition, do—he is using them to make us uncomfortable with that order. By their ability to enjoy their criminal life, by their camaraderie, by the ease with which we are allowed to share their point of view and therefore share their momentary triumph over the desolation that surrounds them, Penn allows Bonnie and Clyde to generate themselves as figures of freedom. As they proceed, they suffer loneliness and an awareness of their fate, and we begin to fear for them. But they are unyielding: they do not wish to change, nor do we wish them to. At the same time, we are allowed to understand that they will not prevail, and this makes us angry with the society that we know will undo them.

It is left finally to us to come to terms with them, with our relationship to them, with the brutal world that destroys them. For the first part of the film we are in thorough support of Bonnie and Clyde's activities. When their fortune changes and we realize they will die, we still support them and want them to survive. When they are destroyed, we are left, as I indicated earlier, suddenly on our own. The structure of the film is ruptured, and we have nowhere to turn. The crucial element of *Bonnie and Clyde* is its closure. The punishment we receive by watching the grotesque, slow-motion, bullet-punctured destruction of the two characters is immense. Are we being told we were wrong to admire them? Are we being told that *they* were wrong? If they were wrong, if these fictional characters are to be disapproved of, then surely such pains to make us admire them should not have been taken. Were they too free? Were they having too much fun? Is Penn assuming the melodramatic directive that we must pay for our pleasures? Are we meant somehow to share the death agonies? If we have been asked, indeed commanded, to share the main characters' perspectives and, by sharing, to admire them and feel for them, then perhaps we are also asked to share the agonies of their deaths.

But of course we cannot share a screen death. And as the attack begins, a great distance is created between us and the characters, not only by means of camera placement, but because of the use of slow motion and the very horror of the sequence. We watch agony and (simulated) dying; we certainly do not share it. But we do react to it and so are left finally to consider Penn's own intentions and our own reactions. It is well known that in Benton and Newman's original script Bonnie and Clyde's death was to be swift and indeed only alluded to, using stills to replace action. But Penn felt that a drawn-out, slow-motion death would enlarge the characters, seal them in our memories, enforce their mythic dimensions.[16] It succeeds. I do not think the film would have entered our contemporary mythology or have had the influence on American film it had without the characters dying the way they do.

The end of the film makes manifest its inherent contradictions. In order to mythologize his characters, Penn makes us love them and then removes them from us violently. The result is that the film leaves us desolate: shattered and alone with our feelings. We have been punished for enjoying the characters and their exploits too much. As I said, it is the nature of melodrama to deny unalloyed pleasure and freedom: the form regards them as attractive sins for which penance must be paid. *Bonnie and Clyde* merely extends this pleasure-pain, profit-and-loss phenomenon further than it had been extended before.

The real changes it makes in the conventions of melodrama involve the extent to which we are made to suffer and the extent of the violence that provokes that suffering, both our own and the characters'.

In *Bonnie and Clyde,* Penn breaks for good and all a major cinematic contract between viewer and filmmaker which held that violent death on the screen would be swift and relatively clean. A bloodstain was permissible, a recoil from the force of the bullet, perhaps; but little more. He introduces a new convention: violent death is now to have an immediacy and to create a physical reverberation; it is to have a sense of anatomical detail. No doubt this new element resulted from certain historical anxieties. The Kennedy assassination and the Vietnamese war, the two American traumas of the sixties, made the culture acutely aware of the details of physical suffering and placed those details within a profoundly emotional context. Penn is concerned in all his films with examining that context, with forcing us to examine our responses to violence in terms of our feelings toward the characters against whom the violence is committed. He begins the examination in his earlier films. In *The Chase* (written by Lillian Hellman), a liberal sheriff (Marlon Brando) of a Texas town is beaten to a pulp by the bored, bigoted, frightened bourgeoisie because of their resentment of him. This same awful bunch, a kind of liberal's nightmare of contemporary southern reactionary degeneracy, assassinate the town's free spirit (Robert Redford), who has escaped from prison and whose return aggravates their repression and frustration. The film is a sort of miniaturized and overheated allegory of the Kennedy assassination. It speaks of a violence born of hate, jealousy, ennui, and emotional impotence. No one is ennobled in the film: the middle class is seen as vulgar and destructive; its opponents, the sheriff and the escaped convict, capable only of helpless rebellion.

In *The Chase,* our response to the violence is itself impotent. We are outraged and helpless in the face of it. Earlier, in *The Left-Handed Gun,* Penn attempts a different balance: Billy the Kid kills out of revenge, a sense of loyalty to a man who befriended him and was, in turn, shot down. But Billy is larger than his revenge. He is portrayed as a force, as the young vitality of the West; his high spirits puzzle him as much as they threaten the society around him. Penn deals differently with our attitudes toward Billy than with our attitudes toward Bonnie and Clyde. Billy is a creature, ironically, of the fifties, rather than of the old West. He is the misunderstood, misunderstanding adolescent. Paul Newman's Billy is a relative of James Dean in *Rebel Without a Cause,* an orphan with two surrogate fathers. One is murdered; the other is Pat Garrett, who murders Billy because he believes the anarchic sense must be contained.

When Billy kills, it is out of a sense of righteousness and occasionally regret. The violence has an extraordinary (for the fifties) deliberateness. If, in *The Chase,* violence is overwhelming and revolting, in *The Left-Handed Gun* it is stylized and exaggerated. We are given measured images of violence, more detailed and analytic than had usually been presented in American film and intended to demonstrate both the suffering and the banality of the violence up to then taken so much for granted. One sequence in the film foreshadows the ritualized violence that the Italian westerns of the late sixties (particularly those of Sergio Leone) would develop almost as a parodic response to the intensity of violence by that time rampant in American film. Billy and his friend Tom confront a deputy, one of the people Billy needs to kill to finish his revenge. The space they inhabit is expanded and strained: they are forward and on the left of the frame, while the deputy, in deep focus, is across the western street. The deputy in an hysterical attempt to get help rings a triangle. Billy almost relents, and another friend does the shooting. As the deputy is hit, we cut to a shot from a room behind him, and he falls with his face pressed against the glass, smudging the window as he slides to the street (the face on the glass is a favorite image of Penn's; it occurs in *Mickey One* and, of course, in the murder of the bank teller in *Bonnie and Clyde*). There is a sense of pain in these sequences, of suffering. When Billy's friend is shot in an ambush he cries: "I feel my blood." Penn is inquiring into the physicality of shootings and beatings and the ways that physicality can be expressed

48

on the screen, experienced by his characters, and understood by his audience. In *The Left-Handed Gun,* Penn's concern is with a boy whose feelings are too large and too primitive, who suffers and causes suffering despite his attempts to do otherwise. In *The Chase,* suffering is a result of meanness and cruelty and a repressive intolerance. In *Bonnie and Clyde,* a sort of combination and transformation is achieved. Billy the Kid and Bubber Reeves of *The Chase* become the Barrow Gang, though the gang lack the psychological motivation of the earlier characters. The townspeople of *The Chase* become the generalized and oppressive authority that must destroy the gang.

The violence increases throughout these films as the oppressive forces and those attempting to liberate themselves from them become stronger; and it begins to get out of hand. *The Left-Handed Gun* inquires into the ways violence is depicted. *The Chase* portrays the cruelty of violence blindly and fearfully directed at those who only want to avoid it. (Between these two films, *The Miracle Worker* deals with violence as a therapeutic instrument, as a way of demonstrating how, by emotional and physical strength, a determined woman deals with the primitive, blind child she attempts to civilize; the violence of *Mickey One*—in particular the vicious beating of Mickey—grows out of the bizarre and perceptually distorted world the character dwells in.) In *Bonnie and Clyde,* Penn begins to show signs of enjoying the presentation of violent events for its own sake and playing with the attraction-repulsion the audience feels with respect to these events, leading them to bloodshed and then punishing them when they get there. It is another contradiction that emerges from the film: the violent activities of Bonnie and Clyde have a liberating effect. The violence done to them disrupts our pleasure, shocks and indeed brutalizes us. The violence and its violent play upon our emotions begin to reveal a certain amount of cynicism.

It is a cynicism that did not go undetected and unexploited. Violence is an easy way to command emotional response. Penn showed the way: *Bonnie and Clyde* opened the bloodgates, and our cinema has barely stopped bleeding since. One of the filmmakers most responsible for the flow is Sam Peckinpah, and it is of interest to consider him in relation to Penn in order to see how the violence of *Bonnie and Clyde* becomes distorted and mismanaged, and how Penn's attempt to understand the relation of that violence to the moral situation of the audience (however uncertain or cynical that understanding is) becomes the tool of a rather vicious sensibility. If Penn's films, at least until *Night Moves,* are concerned with the losing battle of freedom against oppression, then Peckinpah's films see the battle as always already lost. Peckinpah can only elegize over a fantasy time when men enjoyed each other's companionship in an open frontier, before politics and civilization and order turned them into enemies. He indulges in a curious populism that excludes everyone but rugged men who laugh at women and abuse them and who embrace death as the final proof of their lives' worth. *The Wild Bunch* (1968), his best film, works on the level of its fascination with the body exploding in blood and falling in slow motion. But "works" is a terribly neutral verb. The visual splendor of the film is undeniable, its celebration of death surprising, if nothing else. It remains a film to admire and to despise simultaneously. Were it the only one of its kind, it would stand as an important example of one way cinema deals with physicality, one way it can create visions of the violent end of life. But it does not stand alone: Peckinpah (and others) have gone on endlessly repeating variations on the theme of male identity and male bonding (but never with an insight into its fragility or its homosexual subtext) in narratives that require more and more exploding flesh to prove that this male bond cannot succeed.

An excellent contrast with Penn is offered by *Pat Garrett and Billy the Kid* (1973), Peckinpah's version of the Billy the Kid myth. In *The Left-Handed Gun,* Penn examines the construction of the myth and how it creates violent tensions between its subject and those that surround him. Peckinpah assumes the given of the myth and allows his narrative to encompass its demise. His Billy (Kris Kristofferson) is a tired remnant in a world that can no longer contain him and whose politics need a corrupt law and order without the anarchy Billy represents. And so his friend Pat (James Coburn) is sent out to kill him. This—the transition of the frontier into civilization—is an interesting subject, and one that John Ford handled, in *The Searchers* and *The Man Who Shot Liberty Valance,* with a great deal of passion and sensitivity (though, unfortunately, with a great deal of racism as well). Peckinpah handles it with a smugness that debases any power the subject might have and so flattens the moral landscape of his narrative that violence becomes the only way to give it shape.

There is a sequence in both *The Left-Handed Gun* and *Pat Garrett and Billy the Kid* in which Billy escapes prison by shooting his jailor. Penn treats it, as he does the film's other violent sequences, in a stately, almost ceremonial fashion. Billy is up on the roof of the jail; the jailor, Ollinger (Denver Pyle, who will become Frank Hamer

The violent end of life: Peckinpah's **The Wild Bunch.** Thornton (Robert Ryan) gazes at the bodies of Bishop (William Holden) and Dutch (Ernest Borgnine).

in *Bonnie and Clyde*), is in the street, looking up. There is a rapid switch of point-of-view shots, from Ollinger to Billy, out of focus against the sun, and the reverse, from Billy down to Ollinger. Billy aims his gun. Before he shoots, Ollinger begins falling back. Billy fires and we cut to a slow-motion shot of Ollinger continuing his fall. This is one of the earliest uses of slow motion for violent death and therefore serves to introduce a major new element into contemporary cinema. From this slow-motion fall, we cut to a lower shot of Ollinger hitting the ground at normal speed. The sequence ends with a far shot of the body and a boot lying next to it. The man has been blown out of his shoe. A child enters and laughs at this peculiar juxtaposition, and gets slapped by its mother.

It is tempting to speculate how much this film influenced Peckinpah. The use of slow-motion violence is an obvious element that Peckinpah adopted and made his own. But the shot of the child laughing at the death tableau may very well have helped form a central Peckinpah motif, one which informs the opening images of almost every film he makes: children and death. The laughing child in *Left-Handed Gun* is indicative of the surprise Penn means us to have in the face of sudden violence. We, as observers, are amazed at the enormity of Billy's action; we are amazed that a child can laugh at such a grotesque tableau; at the same time, we are aware of that very grotesqueness. A multiple perspective is achieved. Before he allows things to get out of hand in *Bonnie and Clyde,* Penn is always concerned with the contradictions inherent in the presentation of violence: the physical destruction of one human being by another is always traumatic and always amazing, repellent, and attractive. For Peckinpah, however, violence is reduced to an attractive necessity. Children are not merely drawn to it, they learn it early. Death and mutilation are part of their nature and therefore part of ours. When Peckinpah repeats the murder of the jailor in *Pat Garrett and Billy the Kid,* the child does not laugh with innocent incomprehension at the body; an adult has to restrain the child's eagerness to run out to it. The killing itself shows the juicy expansion of bloodiness that so many years of cinematic violence have allowed. The set-up is the same: Billy on the roof, the sheriff on the street. Their recognition of each other is done not merely through a series of reverse shots, but through cross-cut zooms. The stately sense of surprise and awe with which Penn prepares us for violence in *The Left-Handed Gun* is replaced by movements of anticipation and eagerness. A zoom forward moves our perception forward, directing us to the action. And the action itself, in good Peckinpah fashion, is thrown at us. Billy's rifle blasts at the camera; the jailor, who has been made into an unsympathetic religious fanatic, explodes in blood. Like the child who runs out to greet the spectacle, we are excited by it. The reaction required from us is very simple.

Bloodiness is part of the material texture of Peckinpah's cinematic world. His violence is not "realistic." The notion that late sixties cinematic killing is "real" is real nonsense. Most of us have not and never will see a person blown apart by a shotgun. What we have seen so often on the screen since *Bonnie and Clyde* has become just one more cinematic convention, which through repetition we have accepted as a norm. Therefore, to say violence is a given for Peckinpah is to say that in his cinematic universe it is a given, but not a necessary reflection of some cultural or psychological need. His violence does allow us to be excited by dynamic movement and gives us, to use some old-fashioned language, a vicarious thrill. But the thrill is short-lived. His narratives become repetitive spectacles of independence and individuality lost. They give no real indication of why these qualities are lost or why they should be lamented; his male-centered, female-hating trial-by-blood situations become finally *only* hymns to death. There is something, as many have noted, vaguely fascistic about them. They are oppressive and humiliating.*

* My opinion of Peckinpah has altered considerably over the past few years. In "Oranges, Dogs, and Ultra-Violence" (*Journal of Popular Film* 1 [Summer 1972], 159–72), I argued that Peckinpah, in *Straw Dogs,* was condemning the violence of his characters and the audience's positive reaction to it. I was dead wrong. If he reflects upon his work at all, it is only manifested in the grossest kind of confusion. *Cross of Iron* (1977) is a celebration of the death spirit of war, focusing on a battalion of Nazi soldiers on the Russian front. There are the "good" German soldiers and a martinet. (The Russian soldiers are never

The violence that spread through American cinema in the late sixties and early seventies indicates the extent of the miscalculation made by Penn in *Bonnie and Clyde.* Despite his effort to create a special context for the slaughter, to understand it and attempt to make us consider it as well as react to it, the obvious audience thrill it created was taken by filmmakers as a signal that audiences wanted and would pay for more extended killings. The intensity and detail of the violence in *Bonnie and Clyde,* though tame in retrospect, was at the time unlike anything that had been done before. The various and conflicting messages Penn had hoped to generate—the massive overreaction of authority to individuals who try to defy it; the radical fracture of audience point of view; the impossibility of vitality and freedom; the glorification in death of two martyrs to that vitality and freedom—are lost in the spectacle of two characters who, having earned our affection and admiration, are slowly shot to pieces. Form took precedence over meaning, and the formal trend of violence started by *Bonnie and Clyde* has been irresistible. American filmmakers in the last ten years have been ready to leap for the veins more quickly and easily than for the intellect. The sight of blood

---

personalized, except for a battalion of women who are degraded.) At the end of the film, as the two German antagonists go off laughing together, accepting each other's faults, Peckinpah suddenly launches into a montage of stills depicting war atrocities, ending with an extraordinary epilogue from Bertolt Brecht about the end of Hitler: "Don't rejoice in his defeat, you men. For though the world stood up and stopped him, the bitch that bore him is in heat again." I expect that Peckinpah meant this ironically to reverse everything he had developed in the film. But since the narrative proper has more weight than the epilogue, the effect is shock and disbelief over his almost schizophrenic attempt to dissociate himself from his film and inject the notion that war can be admired for what it does to men's characters, but hated for what it does to other people. *Cross of Iron* is the dead end to which Peckinpah's death hymns lead.

A similar, if less grotesque, confusion occurs in *The Wild Bunch.* Bishop and his gang aid the brutish *Federale* troops, yet admire Villa's revolutionaries. Peckinpah treats the revolutionaries with romantic awe and allows Sykes (a member of the original Bunch) and Thornton (Bishop's past friend who has become his enemy) to join them after the Bunch are destroyed in their suicidal attack on Mapache. But his sympathies remain with the self-centered group of men whose vitality only embraces death.

guarantees an instant response. Blood-letting in American film, whether caused by repressive authority or by an individual seeking revenge, speaks to some immediate needs and fantasies which grow out of fear or a desire to see our enemies easily disposed of. They may grow as well from a desire for action in an otherwise passive existence, a desire, finally, to see in film the otherwise unseeable, to partake from a distance in acts that would be inconceivable in actuality.

It will be necessary to return to this point. For even the filmmakers under discussion in this book, as conscious as they are of the forms they use and the problems they deal with, find it difficult to distance themselves from received ideas and cultural clichés. Although they are less likely than Peckinpah to fall into the gruesome and violent clichés of masculine camaraderie, and unwilling to assume, like Don Siegel, that a fearless individual like Dirty Harry Callahan can cleanse a world made prey to the lawless because of liberal laws, they will yield often enough to elements that are guaranteed a ready-made response. Violence is an integral part of all their work and it is often difficult to separate it as a device to exploit the audience from its presence as a means to demonstrate or analyze important cinematic or cultural phenomena.

After *Bonnie and Clyde,* Penn tones down the violence in his own films. It still appears, but briefly and pointedly. The destructiveness of fear and anxiety remains his most pertinent subject, realized in the hopeless cycle of liberty gained at the price of failure. Like his earlier films, *Alice's Restaurant* plays the disenfranchised against the established order of society. It goes a bit further, though, in its depiction of part of this order, embodied in Alice and Ray, who attempt to embrace the communal yearnings of free-spirited teenagers. The film was made at the high point of the antiwar movement, when many of a left-liberal frame of mind had visions of a sharing communal world withdrawn, somehow, from the larger, repressive society. Arlo Guthrie, son of an old freedom singer, was one of the many spokespersons of this group, and his narrative song, "Alice's Restaurant," about a Thanksgiving dinner that ended in jail when he was caught dumping garbage in an empty lot, and about the army's refusal to draft him because he had a prison record as a litterer, became something of a rallying point. Penn attempts to flesh out the song, give it a setting and a larger narrative. The result is a fantasy of communal life fraught with the frictions of jealousies and sexual tensions of the bourgeois world.

Unlike his procedure in *Bonnie and Clyde,* Penn keeps a distance from his characters in *Alice's Restaurant,* examining their attitudes, his own, and ours. In the first part of the film, as Arlo moves in the straight world, we often observe him through a window, separated from us. The sexual insecurity that was at that time aroused by long hair on males is turned upon us as we are made to observe Arlo forced to be the butt of many jokes about his hair and his sex. As we watch the film, we too are made the butts. In the first scene at the draft board we hear an offscreen, masculine voice questioning Arlo. When we see the speaker, it turns out to be a woman clerk. Later, at Arlo's school, we hear a female voice talking to him. It turns out to be a male guidance counselor. Penn teases us about our inability to comprehend and accept otherness, contrasting continually the gentle, unassuming Arlo with the bullying people around him. But the gap is breached. Arlo, running away from college, stops at a diner. He is taunted by the local rednecks and hurled through a window. This is the only violent scene in the film, and it quite literally breaks the distance and pushes Arlo into the audience's sympathies.

The film works wholeheartedly on Arlo's side. It is less than wholehearted about Alice and Ray, surrogate parents to the commune. They are self-conscious about their role as protectors of hippiedom, mediators between the straight, middle-class world and their young communards. They are caught up in the old codes of behavior, of male supremacy and sexual exclusiveness. By the end, Alice is isolated, emotionally and physically, from her surroundings, as was Arlo at the beginning. Unlike the earlier films, no one wins at the end of *Alice's Restaurant*—not oppressive authority, not the liberated hippies. The commune breaks up, and Alice is left alone. A film that wishes, with all its heart, to celebrate community ends by observing isolation. The last shot is a long, complicated track and zoom around Alice, approaching her and retreating at the same time, giving us movement and stasis and, finally, uncertainty.

In retrospect, *Alice's Restaurant* seems to be a melodramatic dirge to the youth culture that Penn had a part in creating with *Bonnie and Clyde*. But then *Bonnie and Clyde* is itself a dirge to the impossible spirit of the rebellion that it celebrates. Unable to offer alternatives to the rebellion-repression cycle of American culture, Penn can merely create various manifestations of it, and by so doing begins to set a trap for himself. From the myth-making of *Bonnie and Clyde* to the withdrawal and uncertainties of *Alice's Restaurant* to the positive demythifications of *Little Big Man*, Penn can be seen tracing a pattern of uncertainty and disillusion just slightly ahead of what is occurring in the culture at large. *Little Big Man* attempts to forestall the disillusion. Penn moves back into history, or more accurately into the myth of history created by film, in an attempt to account for the origins of the rebellion-repression cycle. The film, first, acts to undo the conventions of the western by exposing them as pompous frauds and inhuman gestures. It refutes Peckinpah's bloody lamentations over the loss of simple times and simple camaraderie by ignoring such lies and showing the West as merely another arena for the establishment of personal and political advantage. The only inhabitants of the West who offer a stable, ordered culture are the Indians, the "human beings," as they refer to themselves. And here a second revision of convention occurs.

The western has taught us that the white man brought civilization to a savage land. Penn tells us the opposite: the white man was the active destroyer of a culture that was established, passive, and benevolent, that wished only to pursue a very human and life-promoting civilization. He is also presenting a variation on his own usual narrative structure. The admirable figures here are not, as in *Bonnie and Clyde*, active and rebellious, but quiet and conservative. The opposition to them is not an established order, but an *establishing* order.

The gentle old chief, Old Lodge Skins, is placed against the bluster-ing egomaniac, General Custer. Between them and their worlds is the narrative voice of the film, Jack Crabb (Dustin Hoffman), who lives out the conflicts of both worlds and clearly marks the hypocrisy of one and the stability and honesty of the other.

Once again a trap is sprung. The initial anger that informs the film slowly changes to nostalgia and special pleading. Penn's Indians are irresistible (it is important to note that the film was made at the time when a new consciousness—or guilt, perhaps—with respect to the Indians and what had been done to them was developing in the country), but, like all his irresistible characters, they are doomed. No hope is offered (except a lesson to be learned from the Indian way of life—an unlikely prospect), and the Indians of *Little Big Man* sud-denly become part of a myth older than those created by the western, the myth of the noble savage. They are installed within Penn's pan-theon of lost causes and destroyed lives.

Robert Altman, in *Buffalo Bill and the Indians* (1976), attempts to come to terms with this aspect of the western myth without revert-ing to sentimentality and nostalgia. But at the turn of the seventies, Penn seemed to be unable to come to terms with his culture in any other way. For whatever reasons, he withdrew from filmmaking for five years, contributing only a documentary on pole-vaulting to a film on the Munich Olympics. He returned with a bleak and despairing film.

*Night Moves* returns to the *noir* world of *Mickey One,* yet with-out that film's energy and delight in its exploits and its offer of vic-tory in the face of anxiety. To situate it properly, it is necessary to return to the discussion of *film noir* begun earlier. In 1964, the *noir* cycle over, Penn could elaborate upon it, reinvestigate its milieu and characters and its relationship to the audience. By the mid-seventies, something of a *noir* revival was taking place. Altman's *The Long Goodbye,* the two *Godfather*s, Scorsese's *Mean Streets* and *Taxi Driver* (and to a certain extent Roman Polanski and Robert Towne's *Chinatown*) were investigating again the dark, barren, angst-ridden world that had enveloped crooks, detectives, and simple men of the middle class in the forties.

That the *noir* spirit should reassert itself is not strange, given the consciousness of our cinematic past on the part of recent film-makers, coupled with the historical and cultural events of the sixties. The first appearance of *noir* in the mid forties has been explained, as I mentioned, by the war and an almost dialectic response to victory. It reflected an anxiety attendant upon our expansion of power away from home, the separation of families, the new economic status of women, and, perhaps, a knowledge that the culture (and the country) was not as secure and as innocent as had been thought. It took the whole of the fifties—McCarthy and the atomic bomb and the cold war—to convince us once again of our insular strength (or convince us that we had to be convinced of this strength) and the necessity of retaining a reactionary and protective innocence about the world at large. In the sixties came domestic assassinations, an incredible war, a rebellion within the middle class of its children, the collapse of that rebellion; in the seventies, some understanding of how corrupt our political and economic institutions are. As if in response to all this, we seem, as a culture, to be suffering from something like a depressive reaction, a helpless withdrawal from the political and social difficulties of our situation as those difficulties press upon us. Feelings of powerlessness in our daily lives have become realized in our recent film with images and themes of paranoia and isolation stronger than forties *film noir* could have managed.[17]

These images and themes take various forms. There are Peckinpah's male death songs. There are revenge and vigilante films, such as Peckinpah's *Straw Dogs,* Michael Winner's *Death Wish,* Phil Karlson's *Walking Tall,* Don Siegel's *Dirty Harry* and its sequels, and the almost unending list of black exploitation films, all employing the Hollywood convention of the lone hero who takes upon himself the task of cleansing corruption. The revenge film implies potency, an ability to act and to correct oppressive situations, but it implies it on a local level only; the society is unchanged when the hero is finished "blowing away" a few villains.

The reverse side of the heroic venture is the paranoia film, such as Sidney Pollack's *Three Days of the Condor,* Alan J. Pakula's *The Parallax View* and *All the President's Men,* Stanley Kramer's *The*

*Domino Principle,* Paul Schrader's *Blue Collar,* Coppola's *The Conversation,* films spawned by assassinations, the Vietnamese war, and Watergate which reinforce our fears that we have no control over our political and social destinies, that no matter what efforts are made, an unknowable presence—governmental, corporate, both—will have its way and exert its ineluctable power.* These films exemplify impotence and despair and signal disaster, a breakdown of community and trust so thorough that it leaves us with images of lonely individuals, trapped, in the dark, completely isolated. And whether the films offer us the myth of a violent hero or tell us that no heroes are available to conquer the threat, they affirm our passivity and by reiteration soothe and comfort it.

Not all of these films fit comfortably within the category of *noir.* Some, like the vigilante films, are urban westerns, others are chase thrillers. But many of them are informed with a *noir* sensibility, and when that sensibility overtakes the entire film, the sense of desolation is tremendous. *Night Moves* is such a film. Like many of its forties predecessors, it has as its subject a detective, a film figure who has been a continually responsive image of our ideas of control and authority, of potency, and of success. During the Depression the urbane William Powell held the Thin Man series together, operating with the ease of the dilettante, detached and disinterested, so much in control that detection became another upper-class amusement, a pursuit only momentarily dangerous and barely serious. There was little sense, in these films, of being in touch with the danger they hinted at, and it took the entrance into film of Dashiell Hammett's and Raymond

* In 1978 a film called *Capricorn One* appeared. It followed the by now well-trod paranoia path: NASA decides to fake a space flight to protect its standing and its funding. When the simulated flight fails, the powerful forces involved in the sham attempt to kill off the astronauts forced to take part, so no one will know it was a fake. But there is a twist: the investigative reporter who discovers the cover-up (in the mid-seventies this figure briefly replaced the private eye as the moral quester after the truth, and in this film he is played, in one of the more improbable bits of casting, by Elliott Gould) succeeds in saving one of the men. They triumphantly return to confront the perpetrators of the plot. Perhaps audiences are now ready for the notion of victory over the politically omnipotent.

Chandler's fiction, and the simultaneous development of *film noir,* to establish the detective as a lower-middle-class working man, morally committed to his work, willing to enter a dark, amoral world to find reasons and answers. Humphrey Bogart, as Sam Spade in *The Maltese Falcon* and as Philip Marlowe in *The Big Sleep,* became the archetype against whom all succeeding film detectives were measured. The sense of assurance, the willingness to descend into the dark world and return, sullied perhaps but with morality intact and order seemingly restored, turned the Bogart persona into the image of calm strength and persistence that would yield success. (The fact that this persona also manifested the opposite qualities—a dis-ease and insecurity, a control that was always tenuous at best and non-existent at worst—is something I will examine further when discussing Altman and *The Long Goodbye.*)

*Night Moves* consciously plays against the idea of the forties Bogart detective by retaining the world he inhabited, brought up to date in the seventies but still filled with the dark streets, the fancy homes, and the labyrinthine plotting that marked the *noir* world of Spade and Marlowe. The difference lies in the detective himself. Gene Hackman's Harry Moseby is a figure of contemporary anxiety, with none of the wit and bluff that Bogart brought to his roles, none of the security in self-preservation, indeed, none of the sense of self and its endurance that allowed the forties detective to survive. Harry is not the neurasthenic that Elliott Gould's Marlowe is in Altman's *The Long Goodbye;* quite the contrary, he feels very deeply and sees in a limited way the world around him. What he does see, however, fills him with an almost paralyzing unhappiness, an inability to move in a way that will make things clear and give them order. "Who's winning?" asks Harry's wife as he watches a football game on television. "Nobody," he answers. "One side's just losing slower than the other."

Detective films are about seeing, about perceiving and discerning. The success of the detection depends upon how clearly things are seen and how secure the point of view of the perceiver is. Harry sees, but he has no point of view, no moral position from which to act upon what he sees. Images in the film are continually reflected, often by distorting surfaces; Harry is observed, or observes, through screens and windows. Much of the central part of the film, Harry's visit to Florida, where he attempts to find and return his client's runaway daughter, Delly, and discovers a complex smuggling operation, is filmed in darkness and empty spaces. The cutting of the film does not permit sequences to complete themselves. A new scene may be entered with the dialogue of the previous one carried over, so that no comfortable continuity between narrative units is allowed. As viewers, we are given no more security of structure in what we perceive than is the fictional character (a strategy similar to what Penn attempts in *Mickey One*).

However, the form does not function merely to make us share Harry's darkness and despair, but to indicate the difficulties of seeing and knowing clearly anything about anyone. This perceptual murkiness extends to the character's insights about himself and our understanding of him. At one point a psychological explanation for Harry's anomie seems to be offered. His father ran away when Harry was young and Harry felt the need to find him. He tells his wife that he tracked his father down once, found him on a park bench in Baltimore and walked away. This information could offer a touching bit of understanding for the character and a typical screen-writing ploy: when in doubt, explain the character's personality by giving him or her trouble with parents. But here it serves a different function. What appears to be psychological explanation is not. No explanation is given for Harry's refusal to greet his long-sought-for father. It is offered as the expression of one more emotional dead end, one more provocation of anxiety and hopelessness. In *Night Moves,* interior and exterior states are the same: fearful and insoluble. The act of detection creates an anxiety in Harry that does not permit him to bring the act to an end. Or perhaps the ending and the possibility of revelation that endings bring are too painful, or simply impossible. The question, and it saturates the film, is that, if the end of the search is painful, how much more so can it be than the search itself, which proceeds as a series of stumblings and humiliations, deaths and personal agonies?

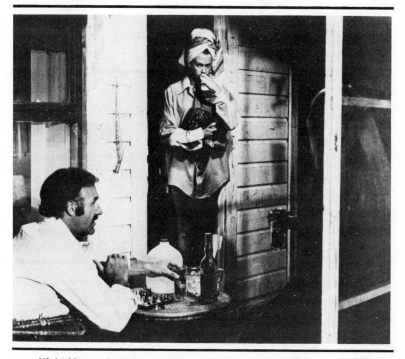

**Night Moves:** darkness, empty spaces, and screens. Harry Moseby (Gene Hackman), Delly (Melanie Griffith), Paula (Jennifer Warren).

Impotent anger, impotent actions, impotent anxiety permeate *Night Moves*. Sexuality is a thing of loathing and a weapon. Harry follows his wife and discovers his own cuckolding. When he confronts the man, a physical cripple (complementing Harry's emotional state), he is insulted with his own movie origins. "C'mon, take a swing at me, Harry, the way Sam Spade would." And when he confronts his wife, he must let out his rage by grinding a glass down the disposal. The child Delly, one of the objects of Harry's search, is promiscuous to the point of destruction of herself and others. She sleeps with everyone, including her stepfather. "She's pretty liberated, isn't she?" asks Harry. "When we all get liberated like Delly," he is

"C'mon, take a swing at me, Harry, the way Sam Spade would." Marty
Heller (Harris Yulin) and Harry Moseby. Note the distorting glass.

told, "there'll be fighting in the streets." Paula, the woman Harry
meets during his Florida quest and who joylessly makes love to him,
and betrays him, is saddened by her sexuality. In *Bonnie and Clyde,*
sexuality is displaced into violence and its momentary triumph over
that violence becomes a prelude to death. In *Alice's Restaurant* it is
a source of jealousy and conflict. In *Little Big Man* it is reduced to
sniggering chauvinism. Penn is never very comfortable with it (but
then none of the filmmakers discussed here are); in *Night Moves* it is
manifested as one more weight upon his characters' spirits, a depress-
ing activity good only for betrayal and for further anxiety.

The emotional paralysis and moral corruption that permeate the film render any attention to the details of its plot useless. Partly in the tradition of the *noir* detective film, the complications arising from the entanglements of the film's characters with each other indicate the difficulties of detection and the almost impossible labyrinths the detective must follow. Ultimately, the plotting becomes less important than the searching itself, which is a contest between the moral strength of the detective and the potently amoral state of the world he encounters. This strength is vitiated in *Night Moves* by the fact that Harry has himself no moral center and no faith in discovering one. As his "case" widens; as the search for Delly expands to a search for a ring of antique smugglers, and this ring widens to include his friends and, though it is never stated, his wife (who works in an antique store); as the deaths build up; and as clues are missed or aborted, the possibilities for success disappear. Harry's job becomes not so much detecting as confirming the existence of a moral swamp, an unclear, liquid state of feelings and relations in which the drowning of the spirit is perpetual. Paula tells Harry how the films of the Kennedy assassination appear to have been taken under water, and this metaphor for the opaqueness of our political and cultural condition spreads over the film, literally—in the vague, swimming quality of the films Harry views showing Delly's death, of the scene of the discovery in Florida of an airplane under water, its pilot's corpse being eaten by fishes, and of the climactic sequence of the film.[18]

At the end of his quest Harry goes out on a boat named, with perfect irony, the *Point of View*. As Paula dives in an attempt to discover the sunken plane, we see Harry from her point of view, looking through the glass bottom of the boat, out of reach and out of touch. A plane buzzes Harry and shoots him in the leg. A Mexican antique surfaces on the water, an ugly statue similar to one Harry was looking at in a friend's office earlier in the film. Paula comes up, only to be hit by the plane, which goes under in its attempt to destroy them all. Through the glass bottom, Harry sees the drowning pilot, a friend from L.A., a stunt man whose only implication heretofore was his involvement in the "accident" that killed Delly. Each looks helplessly at the other through the water. Finally the camera withdraws, dissociating itself from anybody's point of view. It assumes the high, downward angle that Hitchcock loves to assume when a character is in moral or physical danger. We are left to observe, helplessly, Harry, crippled in the *Point of View,* going around and around in the water.

*Night Moves* seems almost inevitable in Penn's career. In film after film he has attempted to maneuver the spirit of life against the repressive order and laws of society that bring death to those who move against them. He has contented himself not with an attempt to understand the politics of repression in America and the attempts to struggle against it, but with the emotional power of the struggle itself, and has reaped from his audience the emotional profit that seems always to come from being witness to the death of vitality, from the reaffirmation that we are lost and helpless. But in *Night Moves* the profit of loss seems to have run out. Harry Moseby is emotionally dead from the beginning. He does not so much entangle himself in the oppression of others as merely sink deeper into his own and their moral vacuum. There is not even the external force of authority to fight against as there is in the earlier films. As in *Mickey One,* the outside is a reflection of the inside, but in *Night Moves* there is no triumph, and both interior and exterior worlds remain squalid and empty. The destroyers seem to have won; they have become us.

Penn has trapped himself within the cycle of advance and retreat, liberation and inevitable repression, that has marked all his films. His attempt to break out of it in *The Missouri Breaks* is unconvincing. When Jack Nicholson's Tom Logan cuts Brando's throat, thereby destroying the landowner's hired gun, it is only a local act of revenge (it is also little more than Nicholson "killing" Brando, which may be a symbolic act of a young actor transcending an older one but not of one character or situation transcending another). Logan kills the landowner as well, but not ownership; and while the film offers another response to the myth of the western frontier, it has little of the political and emotional insight into its lies that Altman's *McCabe and Mrs. Miller* has, or even Penn's own *Little Big Man.* I believe

The destruction of the **Point of View.**

that *Night Moves* must stand, for the moment, as Penn's statement: a dark reflection on a dark cultural moment, and, like so many American films, a reflection only, rather than an alternative or at least a question as to why the moment must be the way it is.

Early in the film, Harry's wife asks him if he wants to see an Eric Rohmer film. "I saw a Rohmer film once," Harry answers. "It was kinda like watching paint dry." This is a curious statement, and it offers an indication of Penn's predicament. Rohmer's films are inimical to the conventions of American cinema. They are quiet, witty, and without violence. They depend on dialogue, and any given sequence is built upon two people talking to each other within a carefully defined and visually simple—but acute—setting. And the talk that goes on involves moral problems: choices, feelings, and thoughts, and the appropriateness of those feelings and thoughts; the intricate decisions about how and why one person acts toward him or herself and others. People lose in Rohmer's films; they make mistakes and wrong judgments; but they do not suffer inordinately, and they all have a strength that enables them to endure. My intention here is not to set up an invidious comparison, but to indicate alternatives that Moseby and his creator seemingly know about and deny. The talk that goes on in *Night Moves* is divisive and sniping; it has no center of care or of understanding. The characters are locked within mutually exclusive anxieties and secrets; no community of thought and feeling is possible. Penn could not make a Rohmer film, for he is too caught up in the conventions of contemporary American cinema. He must define his characters by action and, inevitably, by violence. But it seems that these conventions have turned on him and caught him up. He seems to insist that, at a moment in our history when action seems fruitless and violence aimless and total, reliance on these modes of behavior only result in death, paralysis, or at best, an endless cycle in which one side just loses slower than the other.

It is impossible to see where Penn can go from here. But it is not difficult to see that he is not alone in the trap. Isolated and impotent characters populate many of our films, and their despair is sometimes overwhelming. Harry Moseby himself survives his crippled circlings in the ocean. Again in the person of Gene Hackman, he emerges, older, more frightened, and even more lonely, as Harry Caul in Francis Ford Coppola's *The Conversation.**

* I am not suggesting any conscious relationship between the two films. *The Conversation,* in fact, appeared before *Night Moves,* in 1974. However, the sense of continuity of character is intriguing enough to allow a suppression of chronology for the sake of imagining the relationship of the fictions.

# CHAPTER TWO

## TECTONICS OF
## THE MECHANICAL MAN

# Stanley Kubrick

If some of Arthur Penn's problems as a filmmaker can be attributed to his desire to embrace the form and content of commercial American cinema and his getting caught up in its contradictions in the process, Stanley Kubrick's success can be attributed to his total divorce from these contradictions. Of all American filmmakers, he works in the most non-American fashion. He has eschewed American production methods; he has in fact eschewed America. Only four of his ten films—*Fear and Desire* (1953), *Killer's Kiss* (1955), *The Killing* (1956), and *Spartacus* (1960)—have been made in the United States (one of the distracting delights of *Lolita* [1961] and *Dr. Strangelove* [1963] is seeing how British exteriors are made to stand for American), and Kubrick himself has lived in a kind of isolation in England, traveling little and immersing himself in his projects. He is close to the European standard of the film *auteur,* in complete control of his work, overseeing it from beginning to end.

But with this control and his almost total independence, one contradiction does arise. Instead of creating "personal" and "difficult" works, of the kind European filmmakers are supposed to make,

Kubrick seemed destined to be recognized as a great popularizer.[1] The films of his trilogy—*Dr. Strangelove, 2001: A Space Odyssey* (1968), *A Clockwork Orange* (1971)—were commercially successful and demonstrated an unerring ability to seize upon major cultural concerns and obsessions—the cold war, space travel, the ambiguities of violence—and realize them in images and narratives so powerful and appropriate that they became touchstones, reference points for these concerns: myths. *2001* is not only a narrative of space travel, but a way of seeing what space travel *should* look like. It is a design for our imagination and a notion of modernity. It creates the lineaments of a modern environment and enunciates the metamorphosis of human into machine. *Dr. Strangelove* is the complete text of politics as a deadly joke, a text that has become more and more accurate in the years since its first appearance. *A Clockwork Orange* holds in suspension, in the cold light of its cinematography, the outrageous contradictions of freedom and repression, libido and superego, the death of the other in the name of liberation of the self.

These films offer us insight while they offer immediate pleasure; they are beautiful to watch, funny, and spectacular. The "youth culture" of the late sixties and early seventies embraced *2001* and *A Clockwork Orange* for reasons of their immediacy and their spectacle. Kubrick was in danger of being seen as the panderer of contemporary film. Until he did something rather amazing. After three films that structured a mechanics of the modern age, he made a costume drama. *Barry Lyndon* (1975), based on a largely unread Thackeray novel published in 1844, about an eighteenth-century rogue, was the most unlikely and proved to be the most uncommercial film that an artist who had seemed so able to gauge the needs of his audience could have made. Had Kubrick abandoned his audience? After a decade of successful filmmaking, was he becoming self-indulgent or losing his judgment? Or was he not as calculating and cold about filmmaking as some critics have thought? It is well known that Kubrick plans his films by computer and solves production problems as if he were playing chess with a machine. There is a notion that this is perhaps somehow responsible for the popular success of the trilogy—that Kubrick calculates his narrative and its effects, perhaps even our response. But now the great calculator, the independent popularizer, had erred.

Or had he? Kubrick's films have far outlived their popularity of the moment. His best films—*Paths of Glory* (1957), *Dr. Strangelove, 2001,* and the unpopular *Barry Lyndon*—yield up more and more information on each viewing, revealing themselves as meticulously made and carefully considered. Kubrick *is* very much a calculator: his films are very cold and have strong designs upon us—emotional, intellectual, and commercial. The latter does not cancel out the first two, and it is a happy coincidence when all three are offered to and met by the filmgoer. It is quite possible to say then that with *Barry Lyndon* it was not Kubrick who failed but his audience. The film is an advanced experiment in cinematic narrative structure and design. It attests both to the strength of Kubrick's commercial position (no other director could have received the backing for such a project) and to the intensity of his interest in cinematic structures. That he will, in his next film, have to consider more carefully commercial viability is certain. The state of contemporary film financing does not tolerate large commercial failures. That he will continue to explore the nature of his medium is certain as well.

I want to concentrate on *Paths of Glory, Dr. Strangelove, 2001, A Clockwork Orange,* and *Barry Lyndon.* This means the earlier works will be slighted. They make up an interesting body of generic experiment and indicate something of the direction in which Kubrick was to move.[2] *Killer's Kiss* and *The Killing* are gangster films in the *noir* tradition. The sense of entrapment and isolation they offer is visually acute, and the hard black-and-white photography, the glaring lights, and a sense of exaggerated, even distorted space were to be developed and refined until Kubrick became a master of organizing large and expressive cinematic spaces. The nightmare sequence in *Killer's Kiss,* in which the camera rushes through a claustrophobic city street, photographed in negative, is a source for all the major tracking shots in the films to come, shots which integrate a subjective point of view within an environment that encloses and determines the character who inhabits it. The structure of *The Killing,* in which Sterling Hayden's Johnny Clay attempts to organize a foolproof race-track robbery, only to be undone by a dismal accident, creates a concatenation of events that points the way to the typical situation of the Kubrick character, entangled and destroyed in systems of his own creation, systems that turn upon him and take him over.[3] These two films provide a base for the future work, but this work was not to be as generically oriented as they are.

Unlike the other directors discussed here, Kubrick became essentially uninterested in cinematic genres, in the interplay of convention and response, expectation and satisfaction that generic patterns allow. His sources are literary. The complexities of *2001,* for example, are much closer to science fiction literature than to the science fiction films of the fifties. And by literary sources I mean two things: that most of his films come from pre-existing works, and that they have an intellectual complexity associated more with the literature of words than with that of film. It is the second of these characteristics that I want to examine. Rather than Kubrick's use of literary sources, his translations from verbal to visual and aural text, what I find of most interest in his work is the way he organizes a complex spatial realm that encloses his characters and expresses their state of being. For in Kubrick's films we learn more about a character from the way that character inhabits a particular space than (with the exception of *Dr. Strangelove*) from what that character says. Kubrick's is a cinema of habitations and rituals, of overwhelming spaces and intricate maneuvers, of the loss of human control, of defeat.

But before entering these spaces, we must approach them from two different directions. Kubrick's influences emerge from the work of two seemingly opposite filmmakers, Orson Welles and John Ford. Every filmmaker of the last twenty years, American or European, will admit to the influence of *Citizen Kane;* but very few, perhaps only Kubrick and Bernardo Bertolucci (and Coppola via Bertolucci), indicate they have learned from *Kane* and Welles's subsequent films in the sense of understanding the Wellesian *mise-en-scène* and realizing it in terms of their own visual needs. The Wellesian cinema is a cinema of space and spatial relationships. The camera, for Welles and for Kubrick, is an inscriber of a deep and complex visual field. It creates an intricate space and then begins to investigate it, building a labyrinthine narrative structure that is a reflection of its investigations.[4] *Kane* is a study of the inviolability of personality, an inviolability that is proven when other people attempt to break it. A newspaper reporter provokes four people to re-create the character of Charles Foster Kane. The narrative that results is made up of the interlocking points of view of these people, points of view that create various spatial relationships between perceiver and perceived and between the audience and their perception of the narrative. The camera functions as creator and mediator of the entire structure, and the result is an extreme formal and thematic complexity. For all the discussion of Wellesian deep focus, moving camera, and long takes, and how these cinematic elements allow us a greater freedom to observe spatial relationships, not many observers have noted that the more we see in Welles's films, the more opaque and intractable what we see becomes. For so intricate are these relationships, so complete and closed the world they create, that they become ambiguous and abstract. The worlds Welles creates, especially in his later films—in *Touch of Evil* and *The Trial* (1962)—are so radically dislocated that they become mental landscapes. Knowable structures and the spatial relationships between human figures and those structures are distorted by lighting and camera placement to the point of straining the perceptions of the audience. Until *Chimes at Midnight (Falstaff,* 1966), the Wellesian *mise-en-scène* becomes more and more complex, overwhelming, and subjective.

Kubrick assumes many of Welles's attitudes toward the articulation of cinematic space. His composition in depth is almost as extreme, as is his use of the moving camera. But where Welles tends to move his camera to investigate the intractability of the space he is creating, Kubrick most often uses it to traverse that space, to control it and understand it. He is much more inclined to use the moving

Wellesian space (Tony Perkins in **The Trial**).

camera as a surrogate or parallel for the point of view of a character
than is Welles. Compare the fleeing backward-moving camera retreating in front of Joseph K. in *The Trial* with the stately backward-
moving camera that tracks Alex into the record boutique in *A Clockwork Orange*. In the first instance the camera shares K.'s panic, it
emphasizes his entrapment, and by retreating through a corridor of
extreme dark and light it combines the need to escape with an indication of the impossibility of ever really emerging from the psycho-
physical cage K. inhabits. In Welles the moving camera often de-
scribes a double perspective, that of the character and that of the
environment, and the two are almost always at odds. By contrast the
sequence quoted from *Clockwork Orange* links us to the character in
a different way. His movement, the camera's, the synthesized version
of the march from the fourth movement of Beethoven's Ninth Symphony, the bright metallic colors, the assuredness of the entire struc-

ture indicate total control: Alex's control of the situation and our pleasure in acknowledging that control. Much the same can be said for the celebrated tracking shot of Commander Poole in the centrifugal hall of the spaceship *Discovery* in *2001*. It is a shot indicative of peace and comfort with the character's surroundings.

But this is greatly oversimplified. The comfort Kubrick affords his characters is always ironic. The control Alex manifests in the sequence referred to is temporary. And while we marvel at the nonchalance of the inhabitants of the spaceship, we marvel as well at how they can be so nonchalant in such a strange and awesome place. Kubrick, like Welles, creates a double perspective with his moving camera. The difference lies in the fact that, where Welles investigates the awesomeness and fearsomeness of the space he creates, Kubrick is superior to it. He can allow us to share a character's point of view and remove us from it, thereby defining it in many ways simultaneously. Where Welles implicates us in his spatial labyrinths, Kubrick allows us greater room to observe and judge his characters' situation. Colonel Dax's march through the trenches in *Paths of Glory* is an excellent example: as a tracking shot, a technical accomplishment, it is powerful and assured; as a point-of-view shot, communicating Dax's control of his situation and what that control must lead to, his sending his men out to be slaughtered, it becomes more complicated. The physical space and the emotional space comment upon each other. We observe rapid, assured movement, but that movement is contained by the trenches, their filth and smoke, and their purpose: to hold the soldiers until they leave for the battlefield and death. Later in the film, as the three soldiers condemned to die march to their place of execution, the camera both observes them and assumes their point of view, tracks toward the sandbags, past onlookers (a photographer, the generals responsible for their deaths). In this case, the characters are not in control of their space; quite the contrary, they are controlled by it, surrounded and impelled by the mechanism of their destruction. When we see Dax in this sequence it is by means of a cutaway to him in the crowd, photographed through a telephoto lens, isolating him, demonstrating his impotence and in fact answering the seeming assurance of movement and control ironically expressed in his earlier walk through the trenches. All through the film, the camera creates and then observes a world in which the characters manipulate and are manipulated, depending on who and where they are.

This act of description, here and in all of Kubrick's films, is done on a cooler and calmer level than in Welles's films. There is a level of hysteria in Welles that Kubrick abjures. Even *Dr. Strangelove,* a film about hysteria, observes that hysteria from a distance that makes it all the more odious and horrifying. Welles pulls, distorts, amplifies space; Kubrick distances himself from it, observes it, peoples it often with wretched human beings, but refuses to become involved with their wretchedness. The penultimate sequence of *2001,* astronaut Bowman in the Jupiter room, the human cage, offers an example in contrast. Welles would diminish the human figure and indicate his inferior position. The space would be deeply sculpted in light and shadow. But Kubrick chooses to create this environment in bright, clean lines. We observe the character as the intelligence that has "captured" him observes. At the same time we share Bowman's own detachment and curiosity about himself. As he passes the stages of his age and youth (having entered the whirlpool), we look over his shoulder as he sees himself at different points in his life (this is a rare time in his later films when Kubrick uses this most conventional of shots, the over-the-shoulder shot; but its use here is most unconventional, since Bowman sees not another, but himself—and, of course, there is no true reverse shot possible, for there is no one looking at him). Like Welles, Kubrick has created a visual realm and proceeds to explore it. But unlike Welles's worlds, his is mysterious not because of its intricacy and darkness but because of its clarity and simplicity, a simplicity that belies the complexities it contains.

Both filmmakers are concerned with the ways humans inhabit environments, and both use cinematic structures to observe this. Welles is a humanist, one of the last in the classic sense of the word. He is deeply aware of the power, the inviolability, and the fragility of the human spirit. The spatial fractures and distortions he inflicts on his characters, the extremes of light and dark through which he sees them, the narratives of power and impotence, gain and loss in which he sets them, all attest to the moral battles of mortal men and women, whose worlds reflect their struggle. Kubrick is an anti-humanist. He sees men (his films are rarely concerned with women, except in a peripheral and usually unpleasant way) mechanistically, as determined by their world, sometimes by their passions (as is Humbert Humbert in *Lolita*), always by the rituals and structures they set up for themselves. Forgetting that they have set these structures up and have control over them, they allow the structures to control them. Like William Blake, Kubrick perceives individuals and groups assuming a helpless and inferior position with respect to an order they themselves have created. But Kubrick does not go beyond anti-humanism to embrace another social or philosophical order, for he does not see the possibility of men or women regaining control over their selves and their culture. He sees rather a dwindling of humanity and its destruction, apocalyptically in *Dr. Strangelove,* through a transformation at the mercy of other-wordly intelligences in *2001,* or, less dramatically, via domestic politics in *Barry Lyndon.*

As complex as the design and the spatial manipulations in Kubrick's films may be, their narrative structure (with the exception of *The Killing* and *Barry Lyndon*) is usually very simple and direct. This marks another difference between Kubrick and Welles, whose narratives are as complex as the visual realm in which they are articulated. In this simplicity, Kubrick is allied with John Ford, though it is a strange and perverse alliance, and one that must be approached via Welles. One of the most tantalizing statements by a filmmaker about his work and his influences was made by Welles early in his career: "John Ford," said Welles, "was my teacher. My own style has nothing to do with his, but *Stagecoach* was my movie textbook. I ran it over forty times."[5] Ford's *Stagecoach* (1939) in fact does contain some stylistic elements that Welles expanded upon: deep-focus shots, low-angled shots that take in a room's ceilings, an occasional capturing of light and dust, textures that Welles would find attractive. Just a few months before working on *Kane,* Gregg Toland,

77

Welles's cinematographer, photographed *The Long Voyage Home* for Ford. The chiarascuro in this film was expanded upon in *Kane,* and, as I noted in the discussion of *film noir,* it is possible to see these two films, with Toland as mediator, profoundly influencing the photographic style of forties cinema. But besides these visual attributes, which Ford pretty much abandoned in the later forties when he did more exterior shooting and worked in color, but which Welles went on to refine and expand, there is apparently little that Ford and Welles have in common. What I think we find in Welles's statement is a wish, a desire, not to have emulated Ford, but somehow to have absorbed his narrative facility. The characters, events, and surroundings in Ford's films have a connection one to the other, an integration that allows his narratives to move with immense ease. Ford's films are about communities: families or a group of men or women who survive by resorting to an integral strength among themselves (or the memory of such strength, should the community die or be proved false).[6] The thematics and the formal structuring of these communities in Ford's films work in a harmony of cause and effect, action and reaction that goes beyond the normal narrative felicity of Hollywood's classical period. Ford never hides his effects: his compositions are bold and rich in information, his editing precise, and the dramatic confrontations of his characters open and direct. Yet in his best work all is contained in a simplicity of structure that is full of tension.

Welles's films are about individuals in decline. Families and other groups barely exist in his work, or if they do, as in *The Magnificent Ambersons,* they exist to show their decay. The narrative structure of Ford's films, with its tight, seamless, closed construction, the perfect congruity of its parts, embodies his concern with the relationship of people in a closed unit. Welles's complex, jarred, and fragmented narratives reflect the struggle and defeat of his characters. His admiration of Ford is the admiration of an opposite, a desire to attain what he knows he is incapable of attaining because of the nature of his insight and the cinematic necessities of realizing that insight. The moral struggles of Welles's characters are shattering; those of Ford's are healing.

If the relation of Welles and Ford is dialectical, the relationship of Kubrick and Ford is diabolical. Kubrick, on his own terms, attempts to pursue the narrative linearity that Ford developed to perfection. But his narratives achieve an intellectual richness Ford could not and would not aspire to. What occurs, then, in Kubrick's work is a realization of cinematic space directly influenced by Welles, a narrative structure that is close to Ford's, and a narrative content that responds to Ford's by denying its insights and the myths it draws upon and re-creates. Kubrick, like Ford, is concerned with individuals in groups; but his groups are almost always antagonistic or exclusionary. The Kubrick community is cold, as cold as Kubrick's own observation of it. There is rarely any feeling expressed, other than antagonism, and certainly no integration.

An interesting example in comparison occurs between Ford's *Fort Apache* (1948) and Kubrick's *Paths of Glory.* Ford's film concerns the antagonism between an Indian-beleaguered cavalry outpost and a martinet commander, Lt. Col. Owen Thursday (Henry Fonda). Thursday is presented as an intrusion into the composed and ordered community of the men at the fort. He hates his assignment there and acts out his hatred by demanding a strictness of military procedure that the men have never found necessary. Their order is one of fellowship and gentleness, and they integrate their family with their military lives. As a result, Thursday is an irritant and in his attempt to intrude upon them he is isolated from them.*

The result of the conflict is the massacre of Thursday and his men by the Apache, a massacre that results from Thursday's inability to recognize the Indians as men to whom understanding and courtesy must be given. The violent differences in situation and attitude are

---

* On his arrival at the fort, Thursday interrupts a dance, that primary Fordian sign of civilized community. (In *Paths of Glory,* the dance is a sign of a rigid and heartless community.) He is stiff and alone compared with the ease and movement of the men and their wives. The central conflict occurs between Thursday and Capt. Kirby York (John Wayne), who emerges not quite as the mediator between Thursday and his men (that role is taken on by Thursday's daughter, who provides the domesticating softness absent from her father), but more as a leader whose sensitivity provides a practical contrast to Thursday's unyielding behavior.

presented in the visual configurations of the battle with the Indians. They are seen situated within the hills and rocks, secure and inhabiting an enclosed space. Thursday and his soldiers are isolated on the plain, vulnerable and open. The spaces Ford's characters inhabit and the way they comport themselves within them are, as in Kubrick's films, a key to their emotional state. Thursday is always removed and isolated, first from his own men, then from an understanding of his opponents in battle. His separation and his inability to resolve the tensions between self-sufficiency and community, rules of order and emotional freedom lead to his fall and the fall of his men. But these tensions also lead to the terrible ambiguity of the film as a whole. In the body of the film Thursday is roundly condemned: his inability to yield leads to catastrophe. In the epilogue, however, John Wayne's Captain York insists that the catastrophe and its cause must be ignored. Thursday has been celebrated in the press as a hero, and York (and by implication Ford) upholds this myth. The army must be accepted as the advance guard of American civilization, and as a harmonious community in its own right. It must be believed that Thursday and his men worked together for a common good.

In *Fort Apache,* Ford suffers a major conflict between some truths of human behavior and the need for historical myth. It is as if the myth-making possibilities of his narrative stopped working when it was forced to deal with a character it couldn't contain, and he had to add a coda convincing us everything was all right after all. *Paths of Glory* makes no pretense of examining legends. Rather, it deconstructs the Fordian notion of community and replaces it with a radical isolation of individuals who, though they are part of a large organization, are forced to be alone. Their desolation is created, in part, by the form of the narrative itself. Earlier I said that Kubrick was in the Fordian narrative tradition in that he usually employs a simple linear structure. This observation must be modified by noting that, though linear, the narratives are often foreshortened and condensed. A great deal of information is presented in a short period of time.

Even in his early work—predating the French New Wave experiments in narrative discontinuity—Kubrick leaves out transitional elements and linking passages. Ford worked to perfection the Hollywood tradition of seamless story construction. His narratives have a kind of centripetal action, drawing all their elements into a relationship with one another and finally (with the possible exception of *Fort Apache*) into a stable center.* Kubrick's narratives work centrifugally. Parts of the whole are delineated and then set outside a center never seen or defined, and therefore non-existent. Kubrick's narratives are about the lack of cohesion, center, community. They are about people caught up in a process that has become so rigidified that it can be neither escaped nor mitigated.

*Paths of Glory* is precisely about such a process, or rather the processes that make up military organization, an organization given, predetermined, and so absolutely exclusionary that each human element within it is separated from the next. It is a matter not, as in *Fort Apache,* of one misguided individual disrupting an established community, but of antagonistic individuals, each out for his own aggrandizement or protection. The essential struggle in the film is, as Alexander Walker and others have pointed out, between classes— the aristocratic leaders of the French army in World War I on one side and the proletarian troops, the scum, or the "children," as the general staff calls them, on the other.[7] In the middle is Colonel Dax (Kirk Douglas), loyal soldier, bad attorney, self-righteous and trapped within the military organization. Three entwined and opposing forces—the general staff, Dax, the troops—are set within two related but opposing spaces, two areas of activity which, knitted together, provide the narrative structure and rhythm of the film. The "story" is made by the way events occur within and are defined by these spaces. The generals inhabit a chateau of enormous rooms, flooding sunlight, and walls hung with the late seventeenth and early

---

* It can be argued that some of Ford's later films, like *The Searchers* and *The Man Who Shot Liberty Valance,* demonstrate a marked lack of stability and security within the old myths. But even these films, like *Fort Apache,* seek amelioration, an accommodation with order and certainty.

eighteenth-century paintings that so obsess Kubrick that they appear in one form or another in every film (except *Dr. Strangelove*) from *Paths of Glory* until *Barry Lyndon* (which in a sense becomes those paintings). Such a chateau, with all its accouterments, is itself an image of elegance and rigid formal structures. By emphasizing the spaces of the chateau, Kubrick demands that we understand and account for its associations and connotations, particularly within the given context. In this cold and elegant, inhumanly scaled habitation, the generals play a brutal and elegant game. "I wish I had your taste in carpets and pictures," says General Broulard (Adolf Menjou) to General Mireau (George Macready) when he first greets him, intending to cajole and bribe him to lead his troops to disaster.

The second space consists of the habitations of the troops: the dark and squalid trenches, the battlefield that looks like the surface of the moon turned into a garbage heap, the prison that holds the three men assigned to die for cowardice. The narrative moves between these spaces, climaxing at the firing squad (an extension of the chateau) and the cabaret (an extension of the trenches). There is no indication that anywhere else in the world exists. Unlike *Fort Apache,* where the fort, situated in the midst of the wilderness is seen as its embattled but self-sufficient focus, there is no indication of any physical connection between the front and the chateau, or between both places and anywhere else. Kubrick is creating a closed world, or rather closed worlds, since they are isolated from each other. Mireau visits the trenches, and Dax the chateau, but each is out of place in the other's realm. When Mireau and Broulard first meet in the chateau, they start as antagonists but end as happy and comfortable conspirators, circling about the great hall, the camera moving with them, insisting we look closely and share the rhythms of deceit and death. But Mireau in the trenches is completely out of place. When he inspects and brutalizes the troops, the camera flees in front of him, sharing our revulsion at his mechanical "Hello there, soldier, ready to kill more Germans?" Dax's walk through the trenches, as pointed out earlier, is comfortable and assured; the camera not only precedes him, but shares his point of view. In the chateau, Dax is either isolated or enclosed in the discomfort of its spaces.

But it is here that a question is raised. Dax is comfortable with his men and uncomfortable with, indeed antagonistic to, the general staff. Does that mean that his is the mediating and ameliorating voice of the film, speaking of humanity in the midst of the terrifying brutality that occurs around him, speaking reason as does the John Wayne character in *Fort Apache?* He clearly does not accommodate himself to the space of the generals, but his comfort with his men proves to be an illusion. He sends them to battle, knowing most will be killed; and though he joins them, he remains separate. In the complex tracking shot that accompanies the attack, the camera continually zooms in on Dax, picking him out, showing him with the men, but separate from them. For Dax is finally not the man of the trenches we would like him to be, upholder of the rights of the scorned and misused. He is a powerless creature of the high command. When the men retreat, and immediately after a closeup of a raving Mireau—"If those little sweethearts won't face German bullets, they'll face French ones"—the film cuts back to the chateau. Two soldiers are seen moving a large painting, expending energy shifting signs of a worn-out elegance. Dax, Mireau, and Broulard meet on the fate of the troops. Mireau is framed against a large, bright window, Dax and Broulard, the mean and cunning general who first ordered the attack, are framed together, beneath paintings—an odd pairing, but indicative of Dax's manipulated, used status. The three bargain over the men's lives, Broulard ordering that three be chosen, tried, and executed. Dax will defend the men in the trial, whose outcome is preordained.

In this sequence, as in others, Dax appears to reflect our anger at the generals and our sympathies for the troops. He seems to be the voice of reason against their cunning brutality. But he is not, and could not be if he wanted to. Kubrick is playing a cruel game here, as cruel as the generals'. Throughout the film we are sure that Dax will get the men off; more than that, our expectations of such a cinematic situation assure us that the men must get off (the film was made in 1957, when we had all the more reason to believe that a film fiction injustice would be righted). They don't. When Dax gives his impotent defense summary at the courts martial, stating, fatuously, that he can't believe compassion, "the noblest impulse in man," is dead, the camera tracks him from a low angle, behind the guards, who are situated behind the prisoners. Dax is trapped between the men and the judges, walking back and forth, seen through the legs of the guards. He is completely enclosed. The track is lateral, in contrast to the swift forward motion of his earlier walk through the trenches. The composition is sufficient to show that he is as imprisoned as the men he uselessly defends.[8] In a curious way, Dax has become Ford's Lieutenant Colonel Thursday—upholding rigid procedure, but here in the face of an even more rigid procedure. Unlike Thursday, Dax has no humane alternatives. He is trapped and doomed.

Kubrick refuses to see a way out and cannot find any justification for the presence of "noble impulses." After the firing squad, Dax is reduced to name-calling. In his last confrontation with Broulard in the chateau, he calls him "a degenerate, sadistic old man." And as Broulard comes to understand that in defending the men Dax was not acting out of a desire for a promotion he calls him an idealist and says, "I pity you as I would the village idiot." He proclaims his own proper behavior in the whole affair and asks where he went wrong (he is pleased with himself for having ordered a court of inquiry to investigate Mireau for ordering fire on his own men). Dax answers, "Because you don't know the answer to that question, I pity you." Mutual sarcasm and hatred, and a thorough impasse. Kubrick should have ended the film there, with two duty- and ritual-bound antagonists in impotent confrontation. Instead, like Ford in *Fort Apache,* he chooses to add a coda that might have a softening effect. Dax passes an inn where some of his troops are relaxing. A German girl sings to them. They first boo her, then sing along, weeping. Outside, Dax allows them "a few minutes more" to indulge themselves.

This bit of sentimentality runs against the grain of the film. What has been a close and tight structure of brutality, false hope, and greater brutality now seems to fizzle in a conventional audience-grabber, communal tears. In fact what Kubrick does here is the opposite of what Ford did. The coda to *Fort Apache* is very much military stiff upper lip: the army has its problems, but they all work out for the greater good. Kubrick is presenting us with an easier structure of meaning: the man who cries has feelings and is therefore somehow aware of his lot. Tears permit the audience to release pity and understanding, and they soften our feelings, particularly the moral frustrations we have suffered during the course of the film. Ultimately this coda takes us away from what has happened. It seems to deny the narrative by presenting conventional material, much easier to accept than what preceded. It is of course possible to read the last sequence ironically, concluding that these wretched souls only find relief weeping over another wretched soul on the stage, and that even this relief is short-lived, since they must return to the prison of the trenches. But even were this the intent it is done too quickly and too easily. Nothing before has given us much of a sense of the troops' individuality. The three men chosen for execution are little more than types. Yet now Kubrick demands that we see the men as having the emotions the generals do not.

If this sequence works, it does so by restating the entrapped condition of everyone concerned. The generals are trapped by their adherence to a military ritual of patriotism, place-gaining, and self-aggrandizement; the men are trapped by their inferior status and total passivity. (The only officer who actively attempts to save his men's lives does so passively. Lieutenant Roget, a drunken coward who caused a man's death on a night mission, refuses, out of fear, to send his troops out of the trenches to assault the Ant Hill.) Indeed Dax, caught between his duty to the military and allegiance to his men, is himself passive. He makes no move to take his case outside the military cage. No world exists beyond the trenches and the chateau; all behavior is dictated by the unyielding rules and rituals that belong to them. There is no indication that mutiny or an appeal to other powers is possible. Determination of behavior is complete.

One almost wishes another film had been made, one in which either Dax or the troops took some active role in saving themselves, some opportunity to indicate there might be an alternative to being manipulated or brutalized. But Kubrick is not a revolutionary filmmaker: quite the contrary. The force of his films grows out of their sense of frustrating inevitability, of men almost willfully submitting themselves to an ineluctable order of events. When in his next film Kubrick tries to create a revolutionary figure—transforming, through the person of Kirk Douglas, the impotent Dax into the heroic Spartacus—the result is considerable failure. And I am not sure that the failure of *Spartacus* is the result only of a bad script and of Kubrick's inability to exercise complete control over the production. Part of the film's problem may result from the fact that a human being attempting to escape or to correct an intolerable situation does not fire Kubrick's imagination as does an individual trapped in an intolerable situation. If Arthur Penn celebrates the attempt to overcome oppression, no matter how much he believes such attempts are doomed, then Kubrick mourns the doom that follows upon *no* attempt to overcome. Those wonderful tracking shots in his films lead, finally, but to the grave. There is for him no revolutionary spirit nor even a simple Fordian spirit of communal energy or sacrifice for the greater vitality of the community. His characters merely die or dwindle, isolated and trapped.

Kubrick's ideas seem responsive to the decade in which he began his creative work, and *Paths of Glory* is indeed a film of the fifties, that period in our history when passivity was looked upon as a virtue and opposition as treason. In that light, it is a deeply conflicted film. To have taken as strong a stand against military order as *Paths* does was itself remarkable for 1957—so remarkable that the film was banned in France for years. To have created such an unrelenting narrative (with no sexual or romantic interest), structured in such stark and demanding images, was, for the time, more remarkable still. But with these images to have created a narrative that stops with a revelation of lives trapped and not go on to suggest how they might be freed is itself an intellectual gambit typical of the decade. This was the period of "the end of ideology," a political dead center which declared useless, if not treasonous, any political-cultural structure other than the status quo. As a critical tool, it prescribed analysis without judgment, understanding without a declared point of view. *Paths of Glory* suffers from this ideological paralysis because it seems to attack an ideological stance—assumptions of hierarchical rule and the fitness of a given order—and then backs off. It shows us the ugliness of a situation and its propensity to destroy men; it demonstrates how a moral stance against the immorality of such a rigid structure turns to impotent self-righteousness. It provokes great anger at a ruthlessness that appears unassailable. But finally our anger is, like Dax's, useless. In offering us no possibility of altering the situation it portrays, it leaves us only to wallow in the self-pity of the men in the cafe, weeping at cruelty and at our seemingly natural and helpless passivity in its face.[9]

The result is frustration, a response that (to resume my earlier comparison) a filmmaker like John Ford would never permit. Perhaps because of his conservatism, his allegiance to the rightness of military and domestic order, and because of the clarity with which he sees the relationship of individual and group, Ford insists upon a harmonious reaffirmation of a healing order. The rule-bound, mean-minded Lieutenant Colonel Thursday of *Fort Apache* is an anomaly who, no matter what damage he causes, must be understood and absorbed, ameliorated within a larger historical myth. Passivity is never a problem for a Fordian character. When such a character can no longer act, he withdraws into heroic isolation from the group he once aided. Ford's characters are supremely secure in their place and, usually, are or become actively engaged in promoting concord within that place. The conflicts they suffer are the result not of ideological turmoil but of ideological certainty. Ford is secure in the belief that the American democracy he celebrates is the best of all social-political orders, and his characters act out narratives that confirm the fitness and security of that order. For Kubrick, fitness and security become traps to destroy his characters, traps from which they cannot extricate themselves. In Kubrick's fictions Fordian stability becomes a prison house and his characters are both—and often simultaneously —inmates and jailors. They do not lunge against the physical, emotional, and ideological spaces they inhabit, as do Welles's characters; they are not comfortable in them, as are Ford's. They are caught, they sometimes struggle, and they almost always lose.

Kubrick realized the error he made in *Paths of Glory,* the error

Military spaces: (**above**) Mireau (George Macready) and Dax (Kirk Douglas) in the chateau of **Paths of Glory;** (**opposite**) Thursday (Henry Fonda) and York (John Wayne) in **Fort Apache.**

of permitting his own anger and frustration to intermingle with those of a character in the fiction, thereby inviting the audience to assume a point of identification and ultimately be frustrated. Sentimentality and melodrama quickly vanish from his work. While he never moves far beyond the entrapment, impotence, and despair figured in *Paths of Glory* (and foreshadowed in *The Killing*), his narratives and their cinematic structures become more distant and abstract, and his characters less the psychologically motivated creations we are used to seeing in American film and instead more obsessive, maniacal ideas released in human form, expressions of aberrations in the human personality. More than in *Paths of Glory* they are functions of the spaces they inhabit, spaces that themselves create closed and inflexible worlds, predetermined and unalterable.

Discounting *Spartacus*—as do, with good reason, most commentators on Kubrick's work—*Lolita* is the last film in which he attempts the study of a character who demonstrates at least some awareness of who he is and what he does, even though, as always, that character has no control over himself or others. It is also the last film in which the human figure is foregrounded and observed against, rather than within, the space he inhabits. James Mason's Humbert Humbert attempts a quizzical posture before the bizarre characters and places he meets and journeys through, and the long takes by means of which Kubrick forces us to observe this figure decaying under the force of his sexual obsession serve to bring us uncomfortably close to pathos. Through it all, Kubrick is fascinated by the characters he is creating (particularly with Peter Sellers's Quilty), but apparently uncomfortable at the same time. *Lolita* does not achieve an identity: part adaptation of a celebrated book, part event (both novel and film received much publicity due to their content), part character study, part attempt to make England look like America, it remains a curiosity piece. In regard to the elements of Kubrick's work I am discussing here, it demonstrates his need to withdraw even further from the world he creates, to integrate his characters more fully with the total design of the film, to demonstrate how a world is formed by a personality and then re-forms and destroys the personality who made it. This is a process and a method that become fully realized in what may be Kubrick's best work: *Dr. Strangelove: Or, How I Learned To Stop Worrying and Love the Bomb.*

*Dr. Strangelove* is that rare film that serves the function of prophecy. In 1963, Kubrick perceived in the dominant political ideology certain modes of speech, figures of thought, and images of America's imagined place in the world that allowed him to set up a narrative of events so logical and unavoidable that the only possible result (in the fiction made up by the narrative) was the end of the world. The narrative, in its turn, has created a structure of explanation for our political behavior that becomes more valid and more chilling as we go on. In fact, our history in the years since *Dr. Strangelove* has tended to imitate the film even more than the film, at the time of its making, imitated history.

90

A number of elements work toward making the film a complex text of ideas and reflections and predictions. Not the least of these is the extreme simplicity of its narrative structure: there are (not counting a brief sequence in Buck Turgidson's bedroom) only three areas of action: the war room, an enormous black space ringed by fluorescent light, a dark version of the chateau in *Paths of Glory,* computerized maps replacing the paintings; the cockpit, control room, and bomb bay of a B-52; and the offices and exterior of Burpelson Air Force Base. There is no interrelationship between these locations, no communication.[10] Each operates on its own. Even within these areas, no one speaks to another, only to himself. No one listens, no one responds. Words are interchanged, but the words are, in the war room, only clichés; at the base, lunatic ravings; and in the plane, military jargon. These three areas of activity are intercut to form the narrative. The activities that occur in each area are caused by what goes on in the others and are independent of the others at the same time: a mad general declares an alert and seals off his base; SAC bombers, which are in the air all the time, proceed to their target, cutting themselves off from communication; the war room coordinates plans to cut off the attack by aiding Russian defense, by means of a hysterical American president talking on the telephone to a hysterical Russian premier. Everyone talks, or tries to talk, on the phone. The first line of dialogue in the film is delivered by General Ripper (Sterling Hayden) on the phone to his chief aide, Mandrake (Peter Sellers), asking, significantly, "Do you recognize my voice?" Everyone does indeed recognize everyone else's voice. No one understands a word that is being said.

*Dr. Strangelove* is that rarity among American films, a film in which verbal language plays a major role. In fact it is a film about language that creates its own destruction, its own death, and the death of the world. In a film that delineates a love of death, a *merkwürdigliebe* (Strangelove's German name), everything done and everything said manifests this love and hastens its consummation. What Kubrick, Terry Southern, and Peter George do in their script and what Kubrick does in his direction is create a series of linguistic and visual reductions and give the characters utterances which defeat meaning. Like the auto-destruct mechanism on the SAC bomber's radio, the characters' words undo and destroy themselves. The bomber, for example, is introduced by a very serious voice-over narration explaining the SAC system. When we cut to the interior of the plane, we see Major Kong (Slim Pickens) reading *Playboy* and the communications officer playing with a deck of cards, images which immediately undercut the seriousness of the introduction. When the attack plan is confirmed, drums and trumpets begin playing "When Johnny Comes Marching Home," music that will accompany all the sequences in the bomber, creating a music–image complex that ultimately contradicts itself. No one comes marching home from this battle.

Major Kong prepares for "nuclear combat, toe to toe with the Russkies." He pulls out a cowboy hat, which he wears through the rest of the flight. He tells his men, "I reckon you wouldn't even be human beings if you didn't have some pretty strong personal feelings about nuclear combat. . . . If this thing turns out to be half as important as I figure it just might be, I'd say that you're all in line for some important promotions and personal citations when this thing's over with. And that goes for every last one of you, regardless of your race, color, and your creed. . . ." Both image and words clash with the seriousness of purpose expected from the situation: a bomber about to start Armageddon. The words in particular reduce meaning to a level of banality and cliché. Roland Barthes, speaking of the linguistic structure in the works of Sade, writes that "he juxtaposes heterogeneous fragments belonging to spheres of language that are ordinarily kept separate by socio-moral taboo."[11] Kubrick's characters in *Dr. Strangelove* do precisely the same thing. The socio-moral taboos they break are those which attempt to keep expressions of serious connotation apart from those that are trivial. A drawling cowboy must not be associated with the commander of an aircraft carrying a nuclear bomb. When this cowboy begins speaking, we do not want to hear grammar-school commonplaces and locker-room psychologisms. When we do, it is very funny; but it is also very frightening. The serious is made light of and the ridiculous is made

Linguistic subversion: Major Kong (Slim Pickens) on the bomb (a production still from **Dr. Strangelove**).

serious. Of course "human beings" have "strong personal feelings" (are there impersonal feelings had by other than "human beings"?) about "nuclear combat." These men, however, seem to have no feelings about anything; feelings are supplied by utterances that express the obvious, the reductive, and the redundant, utterances that speak about feelings in ways that indicate their absence.

This linguistic subversion continues throughout the film, destroying meaning whenever it threatens to emerge. When the Russians discover we are entering their air space, says General Buck Turgidson, clutching his book, *World Targets in Megadeaths,* "they are gonna go absolutely ape . . ." Turgidson (George C. Scott) is particularly apt at laundering language of meaning, substituting jargon for information (hopes to recall the SAC bombers are "reduced to a very low order of probability") and speaking about the end of the world in the terms of a businessman ("I'm not saying we wouldn't get our hair mussed. But I do say no more than ten to twenty million killed. Tops. Depending on the breaks"). And the president himself, Merkin Muffley (Peter Sellers), a fussy little liberal, well-meaning and unable to comprehend the mechanisms set in operation, delivers himself of a line that encapsulates the refusal of these men to understand their actions or the distance between these actions and the words they use to describe them. To Turgidson and the Russian ambassador, wrestling over a spy camera, he says, "Gentlemen, you can't fight here, this is the war room."

At the center of this is Jack D. Ripper, the mad general ("he went a little funny in the head—you know, a little funny," says the president to Premier Kissoff on the hotline) who put all the mechanisms of doom into operation. It is his confusion of language, the psychotic ease with which he amputates and reconstructs meanings, that permits the entire structure of death to be erected, or, more appropriately, permits the structure, already erected, to work itself out to completion. He is a fundamentalist anti-Communist, filled with all the clichés that go with that ideology. He is also rather confused sexually, believing that post-coital relaxation and depression is really a loss of vitality (he is not, as many commentators claim, impotent; his radical misunderstanding of normal psycho-sexual reactions is much more horrifying than mere sexual dysfunction and is part of the transfer and breakdown of meaning that informs the film).

I said Ripper is at the center of this, but that is a completely false metaphor for the film. *Dr. Strangelove* is about the lack of center; it is about a multitude of tangents glancing off non-concentric circles. That Ripper sets the mechanisms in operation is a convenience of plot and evidences, perhaps, some need on Kubrick's part to present a "human factor" in the proceedings. The inhumanity of the cold war and its destructive potentials are somehow mitigated if we can point to an individual who is mad and triggers those potentials into action. Happily, in the following films, Kubrick tries with some success to eliminate this essentially melodramatic escape valve. However, the point is that Ripper is the most radical example in *Dr. Strangelove* of the dislocation of word and meaning. His great speech is a concentrated collapse from the somewhat shared clichés of reactionary discourse into the crazed, subjective discourse of someone who is creating his own meanings. "Mandrake," he asks his barely comprehending aide, "do you recall what Clemenceau once said about war?"

> He said war was too important to be left to the generals. . . . But today war is too important to be left to the politicians. They have neither the time, the training, nor the inclination for strategic thought. I can no longer sit back and allow Communist infiltration, Communist indoctrination, Communist subversion and the International Communist Conspiracy to sap and impurify all of our precious bodily fluids.

There is a perfectly logical movement to these words, just as there is perfectly logical movement to the mechanism of defense and retaliation that makes up the war machine. But the logic of both is internal only: the forms are correct, but what the forms signify is illogical and destructive. Ripper's speech ends in bathos, in perfect nonsense; the mechanisms of the war machine end with a different kind of anticlimax: the end of the world, the sapping of everyone's precious bodily fluids.

The appearance of Ripper as he makes his speech is a fine example of the way Kubrick creates an image that objectively comments on character and situation. He is in close-up, from a low angle, his face brightly lit from below, against a black background. He is smoking a long cigar. It is the image of a man isolated in his own madness, yet protruding from his entrapment, threatening our space (which is represented, in this sequence, by Mandrake, who attempts a facade of calm and sanity in the face of Ripper's ravings). This appearance of Ripper is similar to a shot of Norman Bates in Hitchcock's *Psycho*. At one point Norman leans over the camera, his face emerging from the dark in an unexpected, and therefore unsettling, angle. These two closeups of madness are similar in effect, but lead in different directions. The madness of Norman Bates is significant of a momentary, unknown, unpredictable terror, always lurking, seldom perceived. The madness of Ripper is the madness of the body politic. It should be easily perceived and perfectly predictable, for it results when individuals create a mock rationality based on language and gesture that appears logical and is in fact dead and deadly. Norman's madness is local, the momentary eruption of violence in an unexpecting world. Ripper's madness is global. He is, rather than the source of violence, its catalyst in a world geared and prepared for death.

*Dr. Strangelove* is a discourse of death: its language, its images, the movement of its narrative bespeak the confusion of life and death and the desire to see the one in terms of the other. The persistent sexual metaphor of the film emphasizes the reversal. From the copulating bomber that opens the film, to Ripper's confusion of sexual release with a subversive draining away of vitality, to the planned storage of sexually active men and women in mine shafts to await dissipation of the doomsday shroud, to Major Kong's riding his great, phallic H-bomb into the apocalyptic orgasm and the death of the earth,[12] sexuality in the film is turned to necrophilia, which in turn is part of a greater mechanism of destruction over which the individuals in the films are powerless. Dr. Strangelove is himself, even more than Ripper, the primary agent of this destruction. He is the fascist machine, aroused by the word "slaughter," drawing life from death, becoming fully activated just as the apocalypse occurs. When the men in the war room think that the bombers have been recalled, Turgidson says in a prayer: "Lord! We have heard the wings of the Angel of Death fluttering over our heads from the Valley of Fear. You have seen fit to deliver us from the forces of evil." On the words "Valley of Fear," Kubrick cuts to Strangelove sitting in his wheelchair, apart from the others, shrouded and crouching in darkness. The words of the prayer, like all the other words in the film, are undone: the image cancels their denotation, for everyone has been delivered into the Valley of Fear; and the Angel of Death becomes the figure around which all the others will cluster.

Through the creation of Dr. Strangelove, Kubrick allows us an important insight. At the peak of the cold war, at a time when the great, grim myth of Communist subversion was still the operative force in our ideology, Kubrick is suggesting that fascism is operating as the ghost in the machine. Its glorification and celebration of death feeds our politics, our need for power and domination, and it is resurrected in the body of Strangelove as death dominates the world. It is a chilling vision and difficult to comprehend for those who tend to look at fascism as a momentary historical aberration that died with Hitler. Kubrick is suggesting that its death was its disguise and that its strength is drawn from its ability to hide itself in the guise of anti-Communism and the cold war (it is important to note that Kubrick looks upon the Americans and the Russians in *Dr. Strangelove* as being equally idiotic). This was a brave insight for its time. Its validity remains undiminished.

I have been talking very seriously about a film that is, of course, very funny. Part of the complexity of *Dr. Strangelove* is that it presents its prophecy as comedy, that it makes us laugh while it makes us fearful, that it makes us look with bemused condescension at a situation that in fact shows our own powerlessness and potential destruction.

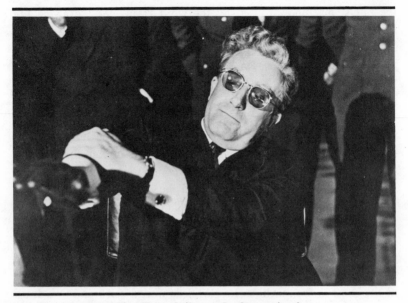

The fascist machine (Peter Sellers as Dr. Strangelove).

Kubrick manages this situation by applying, in this work of contemporary cinema, the specifically literary form of eighteenth-century satire. And to see how comfortable he is with this form, it is helpful to compare *Dr. Strangelove* with another film released in the same year and by the same studio (Columbia), Sidney Lumet's *Fail-Safe*. The "story" both films tell is identical, except that the bombers in *Fail-Safe* are sent to their targets by a mechanical error and, rather than ending the world, an even score is achieved. To make up for our planes bombing Moscow, the president (played by the American movie icon of presidents, Henry Fonda) sends a plane to bomb New York. The difference in the telling, however, is important. Lumet's film is straightforward melodrama: all the characters are given psychological motivation for their actions, and the narrative is developed out of basic cinematic conventions of human conflict. The film demonstrates Lumet's skill in developing overwrought situations through a tightly controlled *mise-en-scène* and cutting which tends to emphasize conflict and tension rather than transition.*

Where Lumet, in *Fail-Safe,* sees the cold war as an arena in which are played out various temperaments and the occasional neurosis, and fudges the political issue by blaming destruction on mechanical failure, Kubrick sees it as a massive breakdown of temperament and control, a surrender of conflict and struggle to uniform modes of thinking and acting that, once put into motion, cannot be stopped. It is not mechanical failure or even "human error" that causes Kubrick's apocalypse, but human activity imitating and surrendering itself to the mechanical. These different approaches to the same situation are therefore rendered in different forms: where Lumet finds melodrama the best structuring mode for conflict, Kubrick finds satire the best mode for structuring a narrative of the mechanical man and the death of language.[13] It gives him the distance needed to observe the process; it removes the barrier of psychological realism and the necessity of providing "motivation" for the characters. "Two things . . . are essential to satire," writes Northrop Frye; "one is wit or humor founded on fantasy or a sense of the grotesque or absurd, the other is an object of attack. . . . For effective attack we must reach some kind of impersonal level, and that commits the attacker, if only by implication, to a moral standard."[14] The world as portrayed in *Dr. Strangelove* does not exist. It is, rather, a grotesque amalgam of various elements, various ways of thinking and seeing that make up our political structure. The characters of Jack D. Ripper and Buck Turgidson are constructs, types of the right-wing general, or the nightmare vision of what the archetypal right-wing general would look and sound like. Strangelove is more than a parody of Edward Teller and Werner von Braun (with, in retrospect, a dash of Henry Kissinger); he is a terrifying fantasy of

---

* A partial list of Lumet's works from the late fifties through the seventies—*Twelve Angry Men, The Pawnbroker, The Group, Bye Bye, Braverman, The Seagull, Serpico, Murder on the Orient Express, Dog Day Afternoon, Network, Equus*—indicates a craftsman at work on a variety of genres, linked by a strong sense of the arrangement of conflicts among people in extreme situations.

resurrected fascism. And he is funny. All the characters in the film are funny, because they are exaggerated. But they are only funny to us as observers. No one in the film ever laughs.* It is not only the exaggeration of character and their absurd slaughter of language that makes them funny; it is the maniacal seriousness of their activities and their inability to perceive how wretchedly hilarious they are that makes them funnier still.

This demands a considerable separation, on our part, from what is occurring within the world of the fiction. The satirical mode demands that we be observers and not "identify" with the characters or even understand, in the conventional sense, why the characters are behaving the way they do. We must, as Frye says, reach an impersonal level, where we are guided by a controlling and moral "voice." In classical satire, this voice is often heard directly, setting out ideas of normative behavior against which the aberrations of the characters can be judged. In *Dr. Strangelove* we do not hear it directly, but rather feel it intuitively through our reaction to the discourse (the closest thing we can find to this voice in the film is Mandrake, who attempts to remain calm and rational amidst the lunacy). If we find the discourse funny it is because we understand, with Kubrick, that it is monstrous. If we are also appalled by it, then, with Kubrick, we have assumed a moral stand against it.[15] If we are, finally, terrified by Strangelove's emergence from his wheelchair as a fully organized body of death, then, with Kubrick, we assume what is often the final perspective of the satirist, a depressive pessimism, a certainty that what is seen and revealed as stupidity, arrogance, and knavery is unstoppable. Indeed, *Dr. Strangelove* owes so much of its vision and power to earlier literary modes that it can be seen through them and as part of them. It shares the anger and despair, as well as the energy, of Jonathan Swift and Alexander Pope (the link is recognized: the target of the SAC bomber is Laputa, one of the kingdoms visited by Gulliver in his travels, a world of scientists so inward-looking that

---

* After a number of viewings, if you look closely, you will see Peter Bull, who plays the Russian ambassador, smile at Peter Sellers's Strangelove antics; but this is one actor uncontrollably reacting to another's talent and is not meant to be noticed.

they must employ people to hit them on the head to bring them to consciousness of the external world). And the last lines of Pope's *Dunciad,* which sees the powers of dullness and rigidity and the death of the mind conquer the world, are quite applicable to the film:

> Lo! thy dread Empire, Chaos! is restor'd;
> Light dies before thy uncreating word:
> Thy hand, great Anarch! lets the curtain fall;
> And Universal Darkness buries All.

Film (as well as the other arts) has largely forgotten satire (or replaced it with parody or lampoon). Moral righteousness is outmoded, and the holding of a moral or political opinion is considered too often a personal fault and a liability in a creator. That Kubrick was able to rediscover the validity of satire and, more than that, make it work in a way that contemporary writers and filmmakers have not is important. Satire is an intensely social-political form which requires a close engagement with the world. This kind of engagement is rare in American filmmaking, and its presence in Kubrick's work is indicative of a scope not ordinarily found in our film.

*Dr. Strangelove* is the only film Kubrick has made in this mode. It is a work of certainty; it manifests a secure moral position and it attempts to create the same in the audience. The films that follow are more speculative and open. They do not offer the audience a determined response. The images with which they build their narratives achieve a great complexity and make the viewer come to terms with this complexity. But in so doing the force of anger that is present in *Paths of Glory* and *Dr. Strangelove* is diminished. The films remain cautionary in their response to the mechanization of human behavior, but Kubrick seems more willing to stand away and observe the spaces in which his mechanical men operate, and less willing to condemn them. Never a filmmaker to suggest alternatives to the world he creates, he structures his later films with a high level of uncertainty, allowing a latitude of interpretation that often, and particularly in the case of *A Clockwork Orange,* creates confusion and dissatisfaction.

But *2001* and *A Clockwork Orange* do continue Kubrick's engagement with immediate cultural and ideological problems. They are intimately tied to the time at which they appeared; and *2001* was influential not only on other films of the same genre but on our basic perceptions of the future and of our present in terms of the future. It also constitutes Kubrick's most radical break with film-narrative tradition, at least until *Barry Lyndon*. His early work was marked by conciseness and immediacy; *Paths of Glory* and *Dr. Strangelove* have a sharply rhythmical structure of sequences occurring in rapid progression.* This progression and the relationship of parts is clear. The films are closed narrative forms, in that at their end all action is concluded, all loose ends, all the events started within the narrative, are tied and explained. The narratives may be rich in connotation, but their denotative realm, the immediate meanings of what is seen and heard, is precise and accessible. In *2001* denotation is at a minimum; it is often withheld. The narrative structure refuses to explain itself through conventional means. Actions and events are not immediately motivated, while transitions are startling and minimal. There is little dialogue, and much of what exists is banal. The film has an open structure in which the viewer plays an operative role. We are denied a stance of passive observation in front of a predetermined set of meanings and are forced instead to engage ourselves with the forms and images presented to us and thus evolve a continual process of meaning, connotation, and suggestion. The very reason so much has been written on the film is because it is, to use Peter Wollen's words on the theory of open narrative construction, "the factory where thought is at work, rather than the transport system which conveys the finished product."[16]

This kind of openness is alien to American film, which traditionally operates according to conventions of narrative completeness. Even among the filmmakers discussed in this book, each of whom is aware of the formal possibilities of his medium, we rarely find a work practicing the kind of open-endedness present in Kubrick's

---

* A sequence is a complete narrative unit, usually encompassing one temporal and spatial area.

film. We have seen it in Penn's *Mickey One* and will see it in some of Altman's films, particularly *Three Women*. It is evident in an excellent work by Bob Rafelson, *The King of Marvin Gardens,* though not in his more popular and influential film *Five Easy Pieces*. It is a process that is not necessarily synonymous with ambiguity, an effect which offers uncertainty instead of plurality of meaning. Ambiguity presents no demands on the viewer. Quite the contrary, it relieves him or her of any real responsibility of decision or understanding. Ambiguity can mean nothing more than that we need not be concerned with what we see, for it is indefinite, unrealizable, unknowable. Ambiguity provokes passivity in an audience, whereas openness demands activity and integration—but not identification. This is another favored convention of American film: the phenomenon of forging an emotional bond between a character and the audience. It is part of the general process of erasing the barrier of form, so that the viewer becomes immersed in the film and experiences it as an extension of his or her own experience rather than as a special or specific experience that he or she must deal with on its own merits (we have seen how Penn plays with elements of audience identification in *Bonnie and Clyde* in order to make the audience aware of their relationship to the film and its characters). Perpetuating a confrontation between viewer and film is a different matter, for it involves participation, questioning, and working with the film's visual and aural structures. Paradoxically, this is brought about by emotionally distancing the viewer from the narrative. Closed narrative, invisible form, emotional identification force the viewer to enter into the work's predetermined structure. The less immediate and apparent the narrative links and meanings, and the more immediate and apparent the formal elements of the work, the more the viewer is allowed options. These options include ignoring the work altogether or confronting it intellectually and emotionally in an ongoing process.

Kubrick does slip into ambiguity at some crucial points in *2001,* and almost entirely in *A Clockwork Orange. 2001* does not play with temporal structure as much as modernist European and Third World film did in the sixties. Although it covers a span of time from pre-history to infinity, its structure is perfectly linear. There are great gaps in its temporal field, but no overlappings, no flashbacks or simultaneous actions (with two exceptions: as the ape "learns" how to use the bone as a weapon, there is an insert of the monolith, indicating his "thinking" about it and its influence on him; and as he begins using the bone, there is an insert of a felled animal). But the film's very linearity, its almost obsessive trajectory through time, with nothing but visual clues, and minimal clues at that, as to how parts of the trajectory are linked, helps create its open and inquisitive structure. The paucity of narrative information and explanation, the precision of its visual detail and the complexity of the images provide a wide-ranging field for inquiry. They also provide a field for no inquiry whatsoever. Its narrative is so sparse, its images so overwhelming, its theme of human submission to a higher force so insistent that it runs the risk of rendering rational engagement with it impossible.[17] Much of the initial reaction to the film, particularly on the part of young people, was of the "oh, wow" variety. It became, in the late sixties and early seventies, the drug-trip movie and was promoted as such. In this light it is easy to see it as a mindless bit of visual stimulation, and rather than grandly theorize about its narrative experimentation, decide that its structure is merely vague and therefore entirely undemanding. In short, the film may be as inducive to passivity and yielding acquiescence as any forties melodrama. John Russell Taylor sees it as indicative of a shift in sensibility, a change in audience demands and expectations that signals a willingness, even a desire, to accept minimal story, in the conventional sense, and maximum sensation. He believes that Kubrick sensed this shift and exploited it, creating an undemanding, because unarticulated, work.[18] In other words, because *2001* met with an uncritical response from many viewers, and because this response is made possible by its non-discursive form, it is possible to dismiss the film as a work that panders to the immediate needs of an undemanding and uncritical audience.

The problem as to whether the film is a complex experiment or a cheap thrill can be solved Solomon fashion. *2001* is two films. One is a work for its moment, a flashy, stimulating bombardment of visual stimuli that can accentuate a high or cause one. The other (particularly when seen in a 35-mm anamorphic print rather than the more awesome 70 mm), is a speculative, pessimistic inquiry into the forms of the immediate future.* It continues and enlarges upon Kubrick's attempt to observe the way men occupy space (both literally and figuratively), how that space is articulated, and how it both reflects and imposes upon human behavior. Seen this way, *2001* is an extension of *Dr. Strangelove,* a prophecy of things to come in light of things as they now are. But more than *Dr. Strangelove, 2001* is concerned with the appearance of things to come and the reaction to appearances by us and by the inhabitants of the fiction. It is, on an important level, a film about design—about size, texture, and light, about the ways that objects within a cinematic space are delineated, ordered, shaped, and colored, and about how human figures interact with those objects.

Earlier I said it would not be fruitful to talk about *2001* in generic terms, in its relation to other science fiction films. But one area of that relationship is important, namely the way Kubrick's film changes the genre's conventions about how the future will look. In the fifties—and earlier, if we wish to go back to William Cameron Menzies's *Things to Come* (1936)—the conventions that inform the cinematic design of our own future, or of "advanced" extra-terrestrial civilizations, are cleanliness, spareness, and order. These conventions are visually manifested in straight lines and severe geometric forms. The materials of the future world are metal, glass, and plastic. Wood is never seen. Clothing is uniform, smooth, close-fitting. Human habitations are never crowded: figures occupy areas

---

* All theatrical film, since the early sixties, has been exhibited in one version of wide screen or another. The anamorphic process (of which there are many, CinemaScope and, now, Panavision being the main ones) squeezes the image onto the 35-mm frame. When it is unsqueezed by the projector lens it yields a wide image of approximately 2.35 : 1. Standard wide screen is in a ratio of 1.85 or 1.66 to 1. (The standard ratio of film before the advent of wide screen was 1.33 to 1, or 4 x 3.) While the anamorphic image is wide, it is less overwhelming than the 70-mm format in which *2001* was originally released.

in a neat and orderly arrangement, and always in bright light. Except for the vastness of outer space, darkness does not exist.* Certainly all this is partially the result of literary influences. Utopian literature, from Plato's *Republic* on, presents its perfect world as the model of clean, rational order. But it is curious that in our century, when that model has been broken by the anti-utopian literature of Orwell and Huxley, it has persisted in film. This persistence can be explained by the very fact of convention: it is much easier to repeat old forms of expression than it is to invent new ones. The repetition is responsive as well to a seemingly profound need to mark progress by images of tidiness and cleanliness. An uncluttered, linear environment is better. (There is no "Than what?" implied: it is merely better.) The future means greater efficiency, doing things better with less effort. The future is progress, easy movement forward with no physical or emotional barriers. Neatness and spareness are its signs.

These equations do yield contradictions in fifties science fiction. In Robert Wise's *The Day the Earth Stood Still* (1951), a stream-lined messenger from space and his smooth-skinned robot come to warn the earth that its nuclear bombs threaten the universe. The visitor is clearly an admirable figure, but his rationality and calm are supported with an awesome power that will destroy the earth if it does not heed him. Fred M. Wilcox's *Forbidden Planet* (1956) shows the world of the Krel as the epitome of order, efficiency, and intellectual strength. Unfortunately, the Krel forgot about their unconscious drives, which became personified and destroyed them. The clean, ordered, and rational future was to be feared as well as desired. In Don Siegel's *Invasion of the Body Snatchers* (1956), the calm rationality achieved by those who have been taken over by the aliens seems to themselves desirable; to those not yet taken over it is horrifying.

---

* The convention is not immutable: Fritz Lang's *Metropolis* (1927) follows it in its depiction of the above-ground city of the elite, but the workers' underground city is crowded, dark, and noisome. Recently, Richard Fleischer's *Soylent Green* (1973), responding to the new ecological awareness, depicts a future foul and overcrowded, an inner-city slum extended and magnified.

These contradictions are troublesome because they go unquestioned. Images of order and spareness and light mean "future." The future is inevitable, often good, but sometimes threatening. But whether good or threatening, the images are basically the same. The creators of science fiction film seem for the most part unable to see a future that looks otherwise. Kubrick, in *2001,* looks closely at the conventions, at the assumptions about the look of the future, and considers their ramifications. The future and its automatic connotations of efficiency and progress must be questioned.

In *Dr. Strangelove,* the womb-like war room, with its halo of fluorescent light, its computerized wall maps, its faceless, unsmiling inhabitants, and the SAC bomber, with its multitude of neatly arranged buttons and switches and equally unsmiling inhabitants, are images of efficiency and progress that signify a breakdown of control and reason. The efficient structures of progress become efficient structures of death. In *2001* the principal images of the future present in so many science fiction films are extended much further than they are in *Dr. Srangelove,* so far in fact that they acquire new meaning. *2001* is as much about science fiction, or at least our reading of the conventions and meaning systems of science fiction film, as it is about the search for some extra-terrestrial force. It encourages us to confront the images of the future we have invented for ourselves. What makes the design of *2001* different from those of other cinematic visions of the future is the combination of the conventional components of linearity, cleanliness, and severe geometrical forms with an extraordinary sense of detail. The exteriors and interiors of Kubrick's spaceships seem to suffer from a *horror vacui.* Surfaces are intricately textured and articulated; the interiors are filled with screens and buttons that do not merely flash, but flash complex verbal, mathematical, and graphic messages. At times the screen we are watching is filled with screens, and these screens are filled with information (one of the most dramatic episodes in the film, the computer HAL's murder of the hibernating astronauts, is done entirely through words and graphs on a computer screen, flashing the stages of the astronauts' decline, ending with "Life Functions Terminated," a cold, mechanical machine message of death).* Many have commented on the minimal dialogue in the film, but they have failed to point out just how much language, via print, computer graphics, mathematical formulas, and configurations, does in fact appear. Visually these words and graphics are themselves clean and linear, presented (as are the credits of the film) in a typeface called Helvetica, a bold, uniform, sans-serif type introduced in 1952 and ever since used on posters, in road and building signs, and for other directional devices. It has been the favorite typeface for advertising and corporate communications. It is, in short, the typeface of the modern age and has achieved the status of having a meaning beyond what the words formed by it have to say. Helvetica, writes Leslie Savan, means "sanitized, neutralized, and authorized." "You see Helvetica," writes one designer, "and you perceive order."[19]

*2001* is a Helvetica film. Not merely the words, but the total design of the film predicates a clean authority, an order of total mechanical, electronic perfection. But, as I said, Kubrick is not merely assuming the equation clean equals future equals better. He is examining the assumption and returning a verdict. It is a verdict implicit in much utopian literature, explicit in anti-utopian fantasies of the twentieth century, and the cause of conflict in much American science fiction film: the future equals emotional and intellectual death. Perfect order and perfect function decrease the need for human inquisitiveness and control. A perfectly clean world is clean of human interference. But *2001* is no humanist's outcry against the diminution of the spirit, nor does it share the hysterical equation of alien mind control with the International Communist Conspiracy implicit in many fifties science fiction films. It does not even share the anger over human surrender explicit in its predecessor, *Dr. Strangelove.* The film exists as a long, distanced contemplation of technological advance and human retreat. It is the design of man accommodated to

---

* There are other important machine communications: we learn some of the details of the Jupiter mission from a television program viewed by Poole and Bowman in the spaceship. Bowman learns the final detail, the need to discover the source of the monoliths, from a videotape that is played just as he finishes dismantling HAL.

A Helvetica world (**2001**).

and owned by his machines, neat, ritualized, without awe, without response. Gene Youngblood tries to make a case for Kubrick's presenting a new consciousness in his bland, non-reacting scientists and astronauts, a sort of reverse nostalgia in which the future is reverie, "melancholy and nostalgia, not for the past, but for our inability to become integral with the present"[20]—in short, for our loneliness in the face of our progress. This, however, is wishful thinking; more appropriately, this is the late nineteen-sixties' wishful thinking, when passivity and withdrawal were regarded as one possible response to the irrationality of the corporate, technological State. Youngblood is right that Kubrick is presenting the human being as an outsider but wrong in implying that this is a psychological or metaphysical position. Kubrick's men are on the outside like the buttons and "read-outs" of their machines; which is to say they are not outside at all, but perfectly integrated into corporate technology, part of the circuitry. Every-

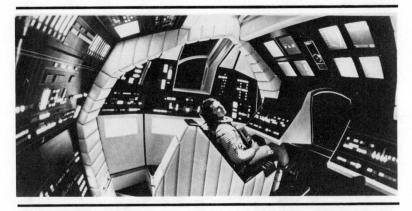

Screens and buttons **(2001)**.

thing—except, finally, the machine itself—works in perfect harmony. It is not humanity out in space, it is Pan Am, Conrad Hilton, ITT, Howard Johnson, Seabrook Frozen Foods, computers and their men and women. The people in the film lack expression and reaction not because they are wearing masks to cover a deep and forbidding anguish, as would be the case in a film by the French director Robert Bresson, for example; they are merely incorporated into a "mission" and are only barely distinguishable from the other components. They are sans-serif figures.

What then of the film's premise, the notion that the history of man has been guided by unknown, extra-terrestrial forces, represented by a dark version of a Helvetica character, the black, featureless monolith? It is here that the openness of the film is so great that there is a danger of falling through it. The only helpful way of dealing with it is in a dialectical fashion, seeing its contradictions clearly. History, one possible reading of the film will have it, is at the mercy of a god-like controlling power. The transmitters of this power, the monoliths, teach us to use weapons to kill; they lure us into technological per-

fection; they carry us to a transcendent stage of rebirth. Men, therefore, have a reason to be passive: they are the servants of a higher
order, slaves of a predetermined plan so precisely calculated that only
a precise calculator, the HAL 9000 computer, realizes its full meaning and gets, quite literally, emotional about it and goes crazy (I
don't mean to underplay this: I find the confrontation of HAL and
Bowman, the latter undoing the computer's thought patterns while it
cries "I can feel it," to be one of the most powerful and ironic sequences in the film—an agon between a man and a construction with
a human voice in which the latter wins our sympathies).

But suppose the monoliths do not literally represent an existent
higher intelligence? They may be read allegorically, as imaginary
markers of our own evolution, dark and featureless because one of
the valid connotations of the future is the unknown, a blindness to
possibilities. Extending this further, the monolith becomes not a
precipitator, but an obstacle to full development. After all, the first
result of contact with it is killing. The ape touches it and learns to
use a bone as a weapon. The wide-screen closeup of the ape's arm
crashing down his new-found club is a prophecy of human savagery
to come. The weapon may be a tool to control nature, indicated by
the shot of a beast being felled; but it is also used to hold territory
and to slay others. Kubrick attempts to present many mitigating
situations: the apes are being attacked; they need to defend themselves. But they also take an undeniable pleasure in the kill. Brutality
is aligned with pleasure, and the bone weapon is a mark of our
progress. In one of the most celebrated bits of editing in recent
American film, the bone becomes a spaceship. But this leap forward
is no great leap at all. Kubrick's vision of space travel is spectacular,
but deadly. The ape showed a manic joy in its discovery; the space
travelers show neither joy nor sorrow; they are mere receivers of the
data flashed on the various screens that surround them. The territory
they conquer seems to offer no excitement, no danger to them (until
one of the tools revolts). The ape used his tool; now the tools and
the men are hardly distinguishable.

When the boring Dr. Heywood Floyd touches the monolith discovered on the moon, the movement of his hand echoes that of the ape. The monolith emits a signal, and in the next shot we see the *Discovery* mournfully making its way toward Jupiter. The music, the deliberate track through the spaceship's centrifugal main hall, the quiet passivity of the astronauts give this sequence the air of a ceremonial: a detached, sad, and lonely aura. This is the end of man, alone in space, surrounded by the frozen, half-dead bodies of the other crewmen, and finally locked in combat with a machine of his own making. The isolation is complete, though Bowman and Poole take no cognizance of it. The situation is not unlike that in *Dr. Strangelove*. There the mechanisms of isolation were ideological. Here the ideology is not as apparent. It must be sought out by us in the deadpan faces and automatic reactions of the astronauts, in the red eye of HAL that watches over the proceedings and takes charge. As in *Dr. Strangelove,* the end is the death of the person; but here Kubrick allows a further step, an indication of rebirth, of change. The old Bowman in his bed in the Jupiter room, looking up at the monolith, calls to mind a statement by William Blake: "If the doors of perception were cleansed, everything would appear to man as it is, infinite." The point-of-view shot we are given, from Bowman's position looking at the tablet, presents it as an impenetrable mass, both promising something beyond it and enclosing that something at the same time. Once again, the monolith can be seen to signify something in the way, a perceptual block that must be transcended.

This puts us, of course, on the brink of the metaphysical, a place the film begs us to enter and a place I would like to avoid. It is important to note the suggestion of rebirth, how the film moves from the dawn of man through his senescence and back to before the dawn. The enormously evocative images that constitute the film's final sequences point to possibilities of renewed intelligence, a return to a sense of curiosity. The fetus moving through space is the only image in the film of a human being unencumbered by things and undiminished by surroundings. But it is, at the same time, an image of enormous solitude and powerlessness. Why is it there? Who is guiding events? We are back to the initial dilemma: we either assent to the power of the images and yield to sensation, or we assent to the suggestion of the narrative that some super-intelligence is guiding our destiny. In either case, we must assent, and the openness of the film is suddenly denied. The final sequences of *2001* are the most disturbing, for they are at once beautiful and overwhelming, vague and ambiguous, and suggestive of human impotence in the face of a higher authority. These images and their implications lead to some difficult and unpleasant conclusions.

A film that structures enormous images, and places the human figure in a passive role, that structures its narrative to indicate an inescapable destiny at the mercy of some super-human force, is a film that runs the risk of structuring itself upon a fascist model. Susan Sontag writes:

> Fascist aesthetics . . . flow from (and justify) a preoccupation with situations of control, submissive behavior, and extravagant effort: they exalt two seemingly opposite states, egomania and servitude. The relations of domination and enslavement take the form of a characteristic pageantry: the massing of groups of people; the turning of people into things; the multiplication of things and grouping of people/things around an all-powerful, hypnotic leader figure or force. The fascist dramaturgy centers on the orgiastic transaction between mighty forces and their puppets. Its choreography alternates between ceaseless motion and a congealed, static, "virile" posing. Fascist art glorifies surrender, it exalts mindlessness: it glamorizes death.[21]

She includes *2001* as a representative work.

But I do not agree completely with her assessment, for the reason that formally *2001* does not create the kind of insistence, the rhythmical structuring of assent, that is part of the fascist model. Perhaps, as I have indicated, the options offered by *2001* are what save it from falling into this trap. It does show us the condition of people turned into things, but shows this, as does *Dr. Strangelove,* from a cautionary perspective. It does not glamorize death, but rather points toward (a rather fantastical) rebirth. Yet it undeniably points toward surrender to a hypnotic force and suggests that this surrender is inevitable.

The film toys dangerously with images of assent and surrender.

113

If it manages to escape total commitment to a vision of human impotence and enslavement it does so through its narrative openness and the speculative nature of its images.[22] Yet the fact that it dallies with these issues, that it does offer a possibility of audience surrender to its spectacle, is indicative of a definite and troubling strain in American film of the late sixties and seventies. In content and form, often in both, a number of American films have indeed submitted to a fascist aesthetic, and it is necessary to digress a moment to see where Kubrick stands in relation to this unfortunate movement.

Part of the movement is represented by that run of reactionary revenge films already referred to, in which Don Siegel's *Dirty Harry* (1971) and Michael Winner's *Death Wish* (1974) are key entries. Imbued with the law-and-order fantasies of the time, these films present a strong-armed cop or an aroused bourgeois (sometimes a small-town sheriff, as in the *Walking Tall* series) who battles not only criminals but a caricatured liberal authority which seems to thwart his every move with irritating laws. These films carry forward the cinematic tradition of a powerful individual avenging a largely passive society. They speak to a strong societal frustration and a desire for expedient action. They are obsessed with the idea that a super-hero can do what the society as a whole cannot and, by default, encourage passivity by presenting fantasies of a virile and aggressive leader who will emerge to save us.

More disconcerting than these is a small group of films that do not so much suggest a quasi-fascist solution to societal problems as incorporate a formal pattern of assent and submission in their very structure. The paradigm for this is, of course, Leni Riefenstahl's famous documentary of Nazi Germany, *Triumph of the Will*. It is a work whose images and rhythm demand total involvement (or total divorcement). Fortunately it is no longer able to hypnotize anyone, but its intent is clear: to create a longing in the audience to partake in the faceless geometric mass of happy people, eyes upward, worshipping Hitler. Formally it not only points the way to the ideology, it *is* the ideology in action. And what *Triumph of the Will* now fails to do, films as seemingly antithetical as William Friedkin's *The*

*Exorcist* (1973) and Steven Spielberg's *Close Encounters of the Third Kind* (1977) succeed in doing. These films were not consciously made in the service of a greater political movement, to be sure; but they succeed, on a smaller scale, in inducing a state of irrationality, enveloping and absorbing the viewer, permitting no distance and no discrimination. *Close Encounters* provides the most immediate comparison to *2001,* and the differences are striking. Spielberg has created an update of the basic fifties science fiction film subject: the invasion of the earth by aliens. Fifties xenophobia rarely permitted these aliens to be friendly and never allowed passive acceptance of them. But in the seventies we seem to be more open to—perhaps more needful of—giving ourselves over to some greater protective and benevolent force. Therefore, Spielberg's spacemen are welcomed and revered. They are not a threat, but they are overwhelming and inescapable. As in fifties science fiction, the army still figures as the authoritative force. But whereas in the fifties it impotently attacks the aliens, now it is prepared to greet them and, indeed, employs a massive coverup operation to do so, a coverup infiltrated only by a few civilians who, controlled by the spacemen, fight their way to be present at their epiphanic appearance.

The structure of *Close Encounters* is such that we, as viewers, are allowed as little free will as the characters in the film. Extremes of dark and light, a predominance of low-angle shots and rapid dollies toward figures and objects, the incredible size of the space paraphernalia (the "size" of the sound track itself) continually reduces us to an accepting position. The film leaves us no place to move emotionally, and no place to think. We are made subordinate to lights in the sky, to the army, and finally to an elephantine spacecraft, so overwhelming and so intriguing that, like the characters in the film, we have no choice but to give in. I submit that the strategies employed by Spielberg are precisely analogous to those employed by Riefenstahl in *Triumph of the Will.* The descent of Hitler from the clouds to an adoring populace dwarfed by his presence and their own monumental, geometric configuration is echoed in *Close Encounters.* Here humans are dwarfed by their loneliness in the inhabited night-time sky, by lights, by obsessive geometric figures (the characters contacted by the aliens have implanted in their minds the shape of a mountain where the aliens will land); and finally by the enormous ship that descends from the clouds and reduces them to open-mouthed awe. *Close Encounters* is a fantasy, it may be argued, a work of the imagination that should not be submitted to ideological scrutiny. Spielberg could not have consciously intended such a structure, and, besides, what other reaction is possible but awe and submission to such awesome forces?

As I have insisted throughout, no work of cinema, or any other imaginative form, is ideologically innocent, and Spielberg is responsible for the formal construction of his film, whether or not he is aware of its parallels and heritage.* Spielberg, like Friedkin, is working, it can be argued, in the mainstream of American film, developing forms of audience involvement, giving a thrill, creating emotion. Alfred Hitchcock has said, "I feel it's tremendously satisfying for us to be able to use the cinematic art to achieve something of a mass emotion."[24] Hitchcock, though, always shows his hand, always gives the audience means to step back and observe what is being done to them and why. Hollywood film, at least before the late sixties, often attempted to demonstrate some respect for its audience: it was enticing, it played upon fantasies of melodrama, it induced passivity to a great degree, but rarely did it dehumanize or attempt to reduce the audience to a function of the sound and images confronting them. Kubrick, in *2001,* retains this respect. Spielberg (and not only Spielberg) does not. Where *Close Encounters* seals us inside its structure from the opening shot—a blast of light and sound from out of the darkness—and keeps us submissive for its duration, *2001* demands above all our attentiveness. It is open, where *Close Encounters* is closed; it is speculative, where *Close Encounters* is predetermined;

* Was George Lucas aware of what a number of critics have seen: that the final sequence of *Star Wars* is patterned directly after a sequence in *Triumph of the Will?* Here is a genuine case of confusion. The plot of *Star Wars* involves a red army in revolt against the black fascist forces of "The Empire." When the red army wins, it celebrates in a Nazi rally! It is just possible that most American science fiction, for a variety of reasons, is inherently reactionary.[23]

its images are detailed, where those in Spielberg's film are merely overwhelming. *2001* is, among other things, about the terror of dehumanization; *Close Encounters* is about our yearning to yield ourselves up to something more exciting than the merely human that will relieve us of responsibility. And where *2001* is occasionally bitter and always (with the exception of the "Stargate" sequence) calm, *Close Encounters* is sentimental and hyper-emotional. If Kubrick dallies with the notion of predetermination and ultimate control by a super-intelligence, it is as a speculation that is part of the total design of his film. It may not be a very palatable speculation; but we are at least given an open narrative and an intellectual space in which to consider it.

The concept of the open narrative is an attractive one because it places a task on the viewer, forcing him or her to be actively engaged in creating a meaning system from the film. But there is a danger: the form has the potential of removing a task from the film's initial creator. This can result in a yielding-up of responsibility, and the film, rather than being open, may become, as indicated earlier, merely ambiguous. *2001* demonstrates this danger when Kubrick's very acute observations of human passivity and ennui are mitigated by suggestions that this ennui is part of our ineluctable service to a master race. The danger is even greater in *A Clockwork Orange,* where Kubrick seemingly gets himself stuck in a thematic quandary: is the only alternative to passivity an individuality so brutal that many must suffer for one person to be free? Is our political future merely one of self-serving manipulations for power? Is our delight in viewing violence a reflection of a perverse need for it, at least in a safe and distanced form?

If *Dr. Strangelove* is satirical and *2001* contemplative, *A Clockwork Orange* is cynical. There are no honest or even responsible answers to the problems it poses. Formally, it is the least successful of Kubrick's later works: it is structurally loose and, visually, it more often resorts to being flashy than attempts to create an integrated *mise-en-scène*. It easily fits Sontag's description of a "choreography [that] alternates between ceaseless motion and a congealed, static, 'virile' posing." It seems to be the one film in which Kubrick makes easy choices and easy set-ups. Yet, for all its problems, it attempts at times to follow through on some patterns suggested in the preceding films and sporadically seems to deny the understandable reaction of some critics that it is a hollow pandering to audience desires for more and more violence.

In its design, *A Clockwork Orange* is the dialectic to *2001.* The clean lines and intricate detail of that film are here replaced by clutter and squalor. Only Mr. Alexander's house reflects the sterility of *2001;* but where the cold, clean space tools were fascinating in their detail, the writer's home is only arid and pretentious. The Korova Milkbar, where Alex (Malcolm McDowell) and his droogs get high, bears a resemblance to the Hilton space station in color and furnishings, but it has the added features of erotic sculpture and very un-Helvetica printing on the walls, advertising the various "moloko plus" drugs that Alex gets stoned on. In *2001,* decoration is at a functional minimum; on earth it has assumed an erotic obviousness and cheapness.[25] The sexuality that was repressed in *Strangelove* and disappeared in *2001* emerges in the world of *A Clockwork Orange* in graffiti, paintings, and sculptures and in the brutality of Alex and his comrades. Sexuality has become the mundane in art, the bestial in human behavior. And it is precisely the mundane and the brutal that informs the world created in the film. Passivity and a lack of human, communal integrity resulted in global destruction in *Strangelove* and the suggestion of slavery to super-human forces in *2001.* Here it results in a mindless brutality, a violence of one individual against another, and the state against all. The love, order, and gentleness of the humanist tradition that we dearly believe to be our goals Kubrick observes to be fantasies. Hate, manipulation, and cruelty are the dialectic to these fantasies, and the life of the mind and spirit becomes the caricatured target of the vitality of the libido and the club. The Cat Lady (whose home is festooned with animals and grotesque erotic art) does battle with Alex by wielding a bust of his beloved Ludwig van Beethoven (to whose music Alex has grotesque and violent fantasies), while he does her in with a bloated, white-sculpted penis.

When *2001* makes its transition from the ape's bone floating in the air to the spaceship, something important is left out: what happened to the violence, indeed the glee of violence that the bone represented? *2001* indicates it has been drained from humans and placed in their mechanical surrogates: HAL cleanly kills off all but one of the crewmen on the ship. *A Clockwork Orange* returns to examine the ape's heritage. The beating scenes are choreographed like the ape sequences in the earlier film. When Alex and his droogs beat up the hobo and Billy Boy's gang they use their clubs as did the ape when he killed the leader of the opposing tribe. When Alex beats up his own gang, his slow-motion antics are similar to those of the ape with his bone. The dawn of man has become the senility of man. Violence prophesied by the ape's discovery of a murdering weapon has become violence realized and ritualized, a force no longer to be examined or understood but to be used, either anarchically or under the control of the state. Kubrick seems to offer no other alternative than that aggression is an inherent component of human behavior (Kubrick is a great fan of Robert Ardrey and his "territorial imperative" ideas about human aggression); it must manifest itself in some form, controlled or uncontrolled. In *2001,* humans have delegated their responsibilities to their machines, and the machines become the aggressors. In *A Clockwork Orange* responsibility is not so much delegated as dissipated. Life is lived at such a low level of vulgarity that the only expression it seems able to achieve is destruction. It is a hopeless state.

At the end of *2001,* Old Mankind is catapulted by some force back into the cosmos as a wandering fetus, presumably ready to start anew. Toward the end of *A Clockwork Orange,* Alex catapults himself out of a window, driven to attempt suicide by his nemesis, Mr. Alexander, the liberal writer brought to madness by Alex's destruction of his wife. He tortures Alex with the music of Beethoven, to which Alex has been conditioned to react with horror. Like Bowman, Alex is sealed in a bare room. It is not the room of sanitized rococo splendor, the last plastic gasp of human civilization that marked man's end in *2001.* But it provides a similar enclosed and observed isolation, with this ironic difference: it does not constitute a way station to another form of existence. When Alex leaps to his death, he is indeed reborn, but only to his former violent self.

*A Clockwork Orange* is a dismally cyclic vision which seems unable to do anything but celebrate the violence it portrays, because it portrays only that as being alive. The death of feeling and response Kubrick depicted in the preceding films comes alive as its own opposite. Life only responds to death; love becomes the attraction to brutality. It is no longer a strange love. We are allowed to feel superiority to the characters of *Dr. Strangelove* because they are grotesque and ridiculous; their monomania is obvious. We can feel superiority to the characters of *2001,* because we experience the awesomeness of their world to which they are insensitive. But Alex is admirable. We cannot help but be fond of him. The narrative moves from a bravura celebration of Alex and his atrocities, which we observe with horror and excitement, to restrained observation of Alex's arrest and imprisonment, when he is treated so badly we can hardly avoid sympathy. The Ludovico treatment that subdues him is presented subjectively (to be accurate, the point of view throughout the film belongs to Alex: he narrates, there is hardly a scene in which he is not present, and we therefore share his perspective and attitudes). With the stage performance that demonstrates the success of the treatment, Alex's humiliation and our sympathies for him are complete. After his humiliation, the narrative duplicates the first part of the film almost incident by incident, only with Alex as the butt of the events (the hobo whom Alex beat up returns with his hobo friends to beat Alex up; Alex's parents take in a boarder who kicks Alex out; Alex's droogs have become policemen and turn on him; and of course the mad Mr. Alexander tries to send Alex to his death as earlier Alex sent Mrs. Alexander to hers). By the time Alex is reborn to his former self, we are so thoroughly on his side that it is hard to tell whether Kubrick is laughing at us or agreeing with us.

Is Alex's way of life to be admired? Is his animal aggression more admirable than the deviousness of the Minister of the Interior and the state? Or is everyone to be condemned, as in *Dr. Strangelove?*

One clue to Kubrick's position is the association made between three of the characters. Two of them share similar names: Alex and Frank Alexander, the writer whose wife Alex rapes. Along with Fred, the Minister of the Interior, they make a strange trio. It is as if the three— the loony liberal, Frank Alexander, first cold and sterile, then all chattering grimaces; Alex DeLarge, the violent child, virile killer, magnificent wielder of club, penis, and language, and pathetic victim; and Fred, the devious law-and-order politician, who first uses Alex to show how he can get crime off the streets and then uses him to get it back on the streets when it is politically advantageous to do so—are aspects of the same personality.* In the manner of William Blake, Kubrick divides up components of human behavior and places them in separate bodies. The joke, therefore, if joke it is, lies in placing these three social/emotional/political abstractions within the flesh of separate characters, playing them off against each other, and convincing us that they offer real alternatives, when in fact they represent aspects of the human personality that should be integrated. If we favor Alex over the others, it is because vitality is more attractive than deviousness and hypocrisy, even if that vitality is misdirected and distorted. This reading is indeed hard to come by, and it takes some strength of conviction to believe that Kubrick is laughing at both his characters and at us for refusing to see his joke. The film gives every indication that we must admire Alex and admire him with little hesitation. It therefore becomes exploitative of its audience in the worst way. If Kubrick has a satirical intent in artificially dividing components of the human personality into separate types but then builds for one of these types—Alex—a narrative that makes him so attractive and sympathetic that we lose sight of the schematic pattern, then the text becomes skewed and we become used. We are given no option but to sympathize with a vicious character.

Things are further complicated by the character of the chaplain

---

* Anthony Burgess, in his novel, makes the connection between Alex and Mr. Alexander explicit: "F. Alexander. Good Bog, I thought, he is another Alex." In the film, when Alex rings Mr. Alexander's doorbell, it sounds the opening of Beethoven's Fifth Symphony.[26]

in the film; his speech on the necessity of free will seems to be a thesis statement. Even in the formal satirical structure of *Dr. Strangelove,* Kubrick did not make a direct statement of position, allowing the audience to assume its own moral and rational perspective. But in creating a serious religious character, who proceeds to talk seriously and with feeling about an irresistible idea, the narrative and our attachments are further skewed toward a sympathy with poor Alex.* Coming as it does at the point of Alex's greatest humiliation and focusing our attention on what seems to be a central theme of the film, this speech gives us no choice but to assent to the chaplain's words. Kubrick's films are all to some extent concerned with failure of will, with a giving up of active participation in events and allowing those events to take control. *A Clockwork Orange* goes beyond this to indicate the threat of a direct manipulation of the will of one individual by others (no super-human powers here, only the state). But seen objectively, Alex has a will that needs manipulation; he is a killer, with no rationale for his acts but the general decadence of the society he lives in. We are faced, finally, with an old problem. No alternatives are offered. If a society exists in which humans are reduced to passive, quasi-erotic squalor, if the state exists only to manipulate the wills of its semi-conscious members, then certainly any one with initiative and some vitality, even if that vitality is directed toward death, must be appreciated. We are trapped in the cyclic nature of the film as much as are its characters.

*A Clockwork Orange* is, finally, a confused work. As an act of provocation, as a film that reveals to us how easily we submit and can be made to react favorably to images of violence, it is of major importance. "It's funny," says Alex, as he tells us his feelings during the Ludovico treatment, "how the colors of the real world only seem really real when you viddy them on the screen." Kubrick seems to ask

---

* In *Paths of Glory,* the priest is depicted as powerless and hypocritical. The unpleasantness of his character is pointed up by that fact that he is played by Emile Meyer, a singularly ugly individual most often associated in fifties film with roles of brutal, corrupt New York policemen. In *Barry Lyndon,* Murray Melvin's Reverend Runt is a priggish character who cannot be taken seriously.

us to assent to the ramifications of this statement. Whatever he may be telling us about the brutality of "civilization," he seems at the same time to want to demonstrate our willingness to accept and even enjoy the images of that brutality which are more powerfully "real" than anything we might see in the "real" world. And so a paradox emerges, one that we have already noted in Peckinpah's *The Wild Bunch.* The thematic confusion of the film is transcended by the kinetic delight we take in Alex's exploits. We are forced to assent to these exploits as images of life rather than images of death. Judgment is rendered difficult, and the film, finally, can be seen as a cynical manipulation of its audience. It is a cynicism that indicates Kubrick had become ready to allow his audience to wallow in its own worst instincts or that he simply did not have an adequate understanding of the problem. Or that he didn't care.[27]

Which brings us back to where we started, to the notion that Kubrick is a clever calculator of audience desires and able to satisfy those desires in slick and glossy images. As much as *A Clockwork Orange* indicates a struggle to justify those images and provide them with a narrative context, it does not allow the viewer to escape their initial power and attraction, their essential deviousness. It was as if in reaction to this problem and confusion that Kubrick made *Barry Lyndon,* a film that insists its audience remain distant and contemplative, observant and barely involved. *Barry Lyndon* is more open than *2001.* Slow, almost static, its images are of such painterly beauty that they seem to call for admiration on their own terms, apart from their narrative function. These images are peopled with characters whose actions and motives appear irrelevant to contemporary concerns. There is none of the kinetic frenzy of *A Clockwork Orange,* no invitation to admire individuals or assent to specific acts. The film demands only attentiveness and cooperation from the viewer, demands it more than anything of Kubrick's that precedes it. More, indeed, than almost any film by an American director one can think of.

The popular critics were absolutely incapable of dealing with the film, for it denied so many of the filmic conventions they could securely respond to. Its "story" or "plot" is minimal; the emotional reactions it calls forth are small and unclear; the characters do not exist as psychological entities. But it is pretty; more than one critic offered the comment that its images belonged in a museum (tantamount to saying the film was dead). The popular audience fared little better. Because of critical response the film got poor distribution, and many of those who did see it were no doubt bored or baffled.

In attempting to account for popular critical response to a film we often learn more about audience expectations than we do about the film itself. The reaction to *Barry Lyndon* was a reaction less to what that film is than to what it is not. Because it does not meet demands for action, clear motivation of characters, straightforward development of story in clear, dramatic terms and with a functional, unobtrusive style, it sets itself at odds with the traditions of American commercial filmmaking. It is true that *2001* suffers from these same "faults"—it has, in fact, a less dramatic structure than *Barry Lyndon*—yet it had a considerable popular success. The difference, of course, lies in the immediacy of its images, their technical fascination, and, finally, the awe created by its attractive mystical connotations. *2001* is a celebration of technology and an elegy to the end of man, but an elegy mitigated by the suggestion of rebirth that ends the film. *Barry Lyndon* is an elegy that is unmitigated, and rather than fantasize a future, it only evokes a past. The only technology it celebrates is that which makes its own cinematic construction possible: the refined use of the zoom lens, the candelight cinematography. But the joy and skill of the film's construction is played against the sadness and loss to which the film addresses itself. Kubrick structures a decline of vitality and a loss of individual power more severe and final than that seen in any of his other films. At the end of *Barry Lyndon* we see a date on a check: 1789. It is the year of the French Revolution. But there is no suggestion that a change in society, a change in the rituals of social behavior, is possible. Kubrick leaves us with an impression of permanent passivity and entrapment. In a peculiar way, *Barry Lyndon* can be seen as Kubrick's first film: it sets up historical patterns of obsession and impotence, ritual and retreat that inform all his other work. It is a ceremony of loneliness, and I wonder if the

sadness it evokes is as responsible for its unpopularity as is its unconventional form.

The pictorial aspect of that form continually calls for admiration. As we attempt to admire it, however, we are reminded that its
beauty is cold and the characters who dwell within are suffering from
the coldness and the very perfection of form and formality that we
are admiring. Formal beauty should give us pleasure; Kubrick makes
it communicate sadness. The film's images become charged with feelings of loss, an effect enhanced by the dirge-like quality of much of
its music. The more we try to come to terms with what we see and
what we feel, the more distanced and alone we feel.[28]

The dialectic of attraction and distance is carefully structured by
means of the way the images are controlled and the way the narrative
progresses. By giving us compositions that entice us and then distance
us, Kubrick generates in us a frustration and a longing that parallels
the experience of the character of Barry Lyndon (Ryan O'Neal) himself, who wishes to enter the world of grand society and is rendered
impotent by its formal rituals, rituals which are unable to accommodate his vitality. A major compositional strategy in the first part of
the film exemplifies this process. Kubrick will begin with a fairly
close shot of one or more individuals and then very slowly zoom
back until these individuals become part of a much larger composition, engulfed by the natural world that surrounds them. This
achieves a number of results. The repetition of the slow reverse
zoom creates a steady, somber rhythm. Visually, it tends to reduce
the importance of individuals by placing them within a greater natural design.[29] By doing this within the boundaries of a single shot,
rather than by cutting, Kubrick achieves an effect of continual change
of perspective, of point of view. A shot that begins close to human
figures whom, by all the rights of cinematic convention, we expect to
observe and listen to, and then removes us from them, forcing us to
observe a large, natural landscape, puts us off balance. Alan Spiegel
writes:

> . . . the motion of the camera begins in drama and ends in spec-
> tacle, starts off with an action and finishes with a design, converts
> human value to aesthetic value and a utilitarian image into a self-

> reflexive image. . . . Characters and situations are taken away from us even in the midst of their happening; the camera withdraws from that to which we would cleave close—and in this respect, our sorrow is collateral to Barry's: we too can never get what we want or keep what we get, and the motion of the camera is a measure of our bereavement.[30]

This reading may be a bit too literal. We cannot identify with a camera movement any more than we can with Barry himself. We can, however, be provoked into observing and, perhaps, responding to correspondences, to our frustration as spectators of a film which refuses to yield to us what we expect and to Barry's frustration (and destruction) in a world which refuses to yield to his desires.

Another sequence of shots in the film fulfills in a different manner the same function as the reverse zoom. These shots are static and they take place indoors. I refer to those sequences lit only by candlelight, which are at first very warm and intimate: Barry and Captain Grogan, the only friend he will ever have, talk in a dark candlelit tent about Barry's mother and about the ruse played upon him in the duel with Captain Quinn; Barry and the German girl he meets after his desertion talk of their love in a dark farmhouse made intimate by the golden yellow candlelight and the girl's baby, prominent in the composition and foreshadowing Barry's own child whom he will love to his own destruction. But the candlelit sequences soon begin to embrace larger numbers of people, in gambling halls and at banquets, where the yellow light and hideous make-up create a vision of the dead come to life. With the exception of one late sequence, in which Barry, his mother, and his son Bryan share a moment of intimacy and warmth, the candlelit shots diminish the human figure as they progress. They replace intimacy with distance, the human with the inhuman, or, more disturbing in these images, with the human made to look like death.

The candlelit sequences and the reverse zoom shots are only two of the compositional and structural devices used throughout the film that draw attention to themselves and make us reflect upon them. To an even greater extent than in his previous films, Kubrick

126

The human figure made to look like death: a candlelit scene in **Barry Lyndon**. Reverend Runt (Murray Melvin), Lady Lyndon (Marisa Berenson).

structures both images and narrative with deliberateness and certainty. He leaves us much space to observe and contemplate but guides this observation, commenting on what we see and how we see it, on his characters and their situation. By means of cutting, for example, and by playing on proximity and distance through montage, he can indicate Barry's precise social and emotional situation at a given moment. When Barry's banishment from polite society is complete, we see him in a closeup with Bryan, reading; a quiet, domestic, and tranquil shot. Immediately Kubrick cuts to an extreme long shot of the same scene so that the two figures appear dwarfed under a painting in an enormous room, isolated and barren. The effect is more striking than would have been achieved by zooming back from the figures to show their isolation in a large space. The rapid change isolates them and us from them, and exemplifies a refusal, throughout the film, to permit us intimacy with the characters, to give any hope that isolation can be overcome. In a potentially touching sequence, when Barry attempts to reconcile himself to his wife, Kubrick takes pains to minimize our emotions. Lady Lyndon (Marisa Berenson) sits almost naked in a tub, one of those curious, upright affairs, similar to the tub in which Marat sits in David's painting. As Barry stands over her, behind and between them can be seen a painting of a man kneeling to his lady. As the sequence continues Barry apologizes to Lady Lyndon for his indiscretions and assumes a kneeling position just like the man in the painting. There follows a closeup of the two kissing, which is immediately followed by a long shot of the castle in which they live (variations of this shot occur frequently in the latter part of the film, acting as punctuation, reinforcing the sad isolation of Barry as well as our isolation from him, his life, and his world). Everything in the sequence, Lady Lyndon's nakedness in the tub, the action of the characters echoed in the painting, the cutting into the embrace by the shot of the castle, forbids our closeness but assures our attention and our awareness of the rigidity of the characters' lives as embodied in the rigid formal structures through which Kubrick presents those lives.

Paintings are a primary means by which Kubrick creates these structures. Paintings appear throughout the film, and the film as a whole is made of painterly compositions. This phenomenon climaxes an almost obsessive concern throughout Kubrick's major work. Late seventeenth and early eighteenth-century paintings decorate the chateau in *Paths of Glory*. Humbert Humbert shoots Quilty through an eighteenth-century portrait in *Lolita*. A rococo landscape hangs over the interior of the derelict casino where two gangs fight in *A Clockwork Orange,* and a tapestry hangs over Mr. Alexander and his friends when they torment Alex later in the film. In each instance, the camera focuses on the painting and then moves down to pick up the action, the first one violent, the second sadistic (in the first instance, the painting appears immediately after one violent act and before another). The Jupiter room in *2001* is decorated with art similar to that in *Paths of Glory;* it is, in fact, a fluorescent-lit, antiseptic parody of the chateau in the earlier film. A rather amazing combination of

both appears in *Barry Lyndon* in the enormous chamber in which
Barry discovers the Chevalier of Balibari (Patrick Magee). Just as
we had observed Bowman in the earlier film, we see the Chevalier
from behind, at a table, eating in grand solitude, in an enormous
rococo room. The reverse shot reveals to us his grotesque made-up
face.[31]

In all instances, Kubrick uses paintings for ironic juxtaposition.
The quiet, civilized artifice of late seventeenth and early eighteenth-
century French art embodies a code of polite behavior in sharp contradiction to the brutal codes of military order and justice played out
in *Paths of Glory*. The pastoral landscape in *A Clockwork Orange*
is in complete contrast to the rubble in which the gangs fight. The
elegant seventeenth-century chamber–cum–motel room–cum–fishtank
in which Bowman moves from youth to old age in *2001* is a parody
of images of "civilization" that might be drawn from the humdrum
mind of an astronaut. The dream of order and politeness, the reality
of brutality and manipulation and death: these antinomies plague
Kubrick to the point where in *Barry Lyndon* he attempts to enter
the paintings themselves and, rather than merely use them as ironic
visual counterpoint, pierce these ritual signs of order and civility to
discover other rituals, to discover the dynamics of a civilization whose
rigid facade on canvas reveals other rigid and brutal facades when
these canvases are set in motion.

Kubrick is not making paintings come alive (like those wonderful opening sequences of certain films in which a sketch or painting
under the credits proceeds to dissolve into the "real" scene as the
film begins). He is using a painterly aesthetic to set his characters
within a design, to re-create the forms and formalities—the rituals—of
the past *as* rituals and to keep the viewer continually aware of the
external and internal rigidities of the images. "Each image," writes
Alan Spiegel, "seals off direct access to its content by converting content into an object of formal admiration; the formalism, that is, in-
sures the image as both visual enticement and proof against further
intimacy."[32] I would modify this in one important way: the images
do not convert content into form—form always precedes content.

Rather, the images in *Barry Lyndon,* these forms of light and color, human figures, natural landscapes, architectural surroundings, resist yielding a content. They point more to themselves than they do to any expected narrative event. No, Kubrick is not making paintings come alive; he is playing our perceptual expectations of painting against those of cinema. We come to painting to observe static design. We come to film prepared to see motion, drama, and narrative. *Barry Lyndon* continually threatens to deny us drama and narrative by emphasizing rigid composition and then threatens rigid composition with movement and narrative. In all instances our expectations are stymied. The conventions of eighteenth-century painting are reversed: instead of finding order and politeness we find ugliness and brutality. The conventions of contemporary American cinema are reversed: instead of finding action and a clever story, we find static, painterly images that require as much or more attention than any story they might be telling. Formally, contextually, the film keeps us alert, keeps us uncertain, keeps us at a distance. We are struck by the way its images look and wish to admire them. Our admiration is turned against us when we discover the sadness of events occurring within the images. When we try to approach this sadness and understand it, we are put off by the rigidity, the ugliness of the events that evoke the sadness. At no point are we permitted to indulge our aesthetic or our emotional desires. And, as if this were not enough, Kubrick adds yet another element which prevents our easy access to the characters and their world: a narrator whose words we wish to, but cannot, trust.

Kubrick has always favored voice-over narration. The temporal jigsaw puzzle of *The Killing* is fitted together by a narrator. Humbert Humbert narrates *Lolita,* and a narrator gives us the historical setting at the beginning of *Paths of Glory.* In *Dr. Strangelove* a voice tells us about the doomsday machine and explains the SAC system. *2001* replaces narration with titles at the beginning of each section. In *A Clockwork Orange,* Alex's voice reflects upon what we are seeing and what he is feeling. In most instances, the voice-over is a device of convenience, used to prepare us for the action, explain it, or, in the case of *Dr. Strangelove,* create a mock-serious tone. Only in *A*

*Clockwork Orange* is this voice an integral part of the discourse, helping to form it and our attitude toward it and the central character, to whom the voice belongs. Alex's voice, with its verbal vitality, its delight in its speaker's exploits, its self-pity and final triumph, both seals our sympathies and frightens us at the same time. The narrator in *Barry Lyndon* is a friendly, somewhat detached, always calm and completely anonymous voice (though it is, of course, the voice of Michael Hordern, immediately recognizable to anyone familiar with British film) that provides a variety of services for us. It tells us what has happened and what will happen; it tells us what is happening and what the characters are feeling. Often it tells us things we do not see and would not know had it not told us. In short, the narrator of *Barry Lyndon* is part of another discourse, the teller of another tale, often parallel to the narrative we see on the screen, though as often denying what we see or telling us a great deal more that contradicts what we see.

Sometimes, particularly in the battle sequences, the narrator will provide a moral and political perspective absent from the visual and dramatic narrative. He may merely be sadly cynical: "Though this encounter is not recorded in any history books," he says of the absurd suicidal march of British troops into stationary French lines, "it was memorable enough to those who took part." Memorable indeed, for in this battle Barry loses his friend, Captain Grogan. As we see the troops marching by a burning building, and as Barry, carrying a goat, walks into a closeup, the narrator, leaping far beyond the immediate implications of the scene, states: "Gentlemen may talk of the Age of Chivalry, but remember the plowmen, poachers, and pickpockets whom they lead. It is with these sad instruments that your great warriors and kings have been doing their murderous work in the world." We cut to a shot of Barry carrying a milk pail, at which point the narrator comments on Barry's low circumstances, though he assures us that he is fated for greater things. Just prior to his dissertation on warriors and kings, the narrator, over a shot of Barry standing by a fire, has commented upon Barry's desire to escape the army.

This brief series of images and voice-over comments manages to create three different narrative directions: one in the visuals, two in the narration. We see Barry thoughtful by the fire and are given something presumably close to his thoughts in the voice-over (he wants to desert). We then observe him involved in the low, humdrum life of a soldier, at which point the narrator takes off on his own speculations on the politics and meanness of war, comments almost more appropriate to *Paths of Glory* than to what we are seeing here (we know Barry is not a plowman, poacher, or pickpocket, those "sad instruments" who the narrator tells us fight the wars). The visual content remains the same until, having disburdened himself of his sadness over war's inhumanity, the narrator comments on Barry's particular state and assures us it will change, due to accidental circumstances. In the next sequence, Barry steals the uniform of one of the two homosexual soldiers bathing in the river (two characters, incidentally, who express a devotion to each other, unlike any of the "straight" characters in the film) and is off to the better things the narrator has promised. Barry's life as a soldier and his unhappiness with it; the narrator's philosophy of war; the narrator's assurance that Barry will go on to other things—none of these elements are contradictory; they simply provide us with more information than we see or hear within the film itself at this point. Most of all, they remove any immediate uncertainties as to where the narrative is going. Barry will get away from the army (though, as it turns out, only temporarily) and will do well in life (but again only temporarily).

However the narrator can and does present material contradictory to the visual narrative. He undercuts Barry's love affair with the German peasant girl by telling us, in elegant and humorous language, that she is little more than a whore. He tells us of the horrible recruitment of children by the Prussian army and how Frederick the Great stoops to kidnapping "to keep supplied those brilliant regiments of his with food for powder," while all we see is young soldiers marching. As he talks of the deplorable sadism, mutilation, and murder that go on among the ranks, we merely observe Barry leading a soldier through the gauntlet—unpleasant enough, but hardly the visual equal to the words. As we watch Barry marching with Prussian troops, the narrator tells us: "Thus Barry fell into the very worst of courses and company, and was soon very far advanced in the science of every kind of misconduct." We then observe Barry engaged in battle, saving the life of General Potzdorf (who first discovers his desertion and later becomes his protector). Except for the brief gauntlet scene, we have no visual evidence of Barry being anything but a proper soldier. Is it, as one writer suggests, that Kubrick was so sensitive to the criticism of violence in *A Clockwork Orange* that he spared us scenes to bear out the narrator's words? Or would such scenes have been totally opposed to the film's design? The violence we do see—the boxing match, the battles, the various duels—is ceremonial and distanced.[33] The one major explosion of violence, Barry's attack on Bullingdon, and the one time Barry is the subject of violence, in the duel with Bullingdon, are startling and effective because they are unusual in their immediacy and their expression of emotional and physical pain.

The distance between the narrative we hear and the narrative we see is as specifically determined as the differences in perspective we are given within the zoom shots. We are forced to take a double view—in this case of Barry the vicious wretch we hear about and Barry the sad, incompetent man of feeling we see. Kubrick has constructed a film strangely reminiscent of *Citizen Kane*. In Welles's film, different perspectives, different points of view on an individual, some friendly, some adverse, conflict with our own perception of a powerful man racked with loneliness and an inability to express his passion appropriately. In *Kane,* we are confronted with at least five distinct personalities whose points of view interlock to create the narrative. In *Barry Lyndon* we really have only ourselves and our own point of view to contend with. The contradictions set up by the narrator and the obstacles to emotional involvement set up by the composition and design of the images keep forcing us away from the film and into a confrontation with our own perceptions and attitudes. Kubrick is not playing the games he played in *A Clockwork Orange,* where he forced us to identify with a brutal killer. If Barry is vicious and dissolute, we only have someone's word for it; we see no proof.

We see no proof that makes valid any of Barry's suffering. He is unpleasant to his wife for a time: riding in a coach, she asks him not to smoke. He responds by blowing smoke in her face. The narrator comments that Lady Lyndon occupied a place "not very much more important than the elegant carpets and pictures which would form the pleasant background of [Barry's] existence." Later we and Lady Lyndon see him kissing Bryan's nurse. But Barry makes up with his wife, and the narrator never tells us whether his behavior is any different from that of any other male member of the society Barry wants to be part of. Once more we are disallowed any satisfactory accounting, within the film, for the contradictory and condemnatory information we hear. The ceremonials the film is about and the ceremony that the film *is* prevent us from fully accepting anything told us and many things shown us.

The result of all of this, as I said earlier, is to make our emotional situation vis-à-vis the film parallel to the emotional situation of Barry Lyndon, who cannot enter the rich, decaying world he so craves and whose moments of emotional satisfaction are undone even before they are finished. After Barry, provoked beyond endurance, beats Bullingdon in front of a proper gathering of gentlefolk and is properly ostracized from their proper company, we are given gentle scenes of Barry and Bryan playing: polite but happy family scenes. Over these are the sad melody of the Handel Sarabande and the voice of the narrator:

> Barry had his faults [a more moderate statement than the earlier reference to his viciousness and depravity], but no man could say of him that he was not a good and tender father. He loved his son with a blind partiality. He denied him nothing. It is impossible to convey what high hope he had for the boy and how he indulged in a thousand fond anticipations as to his future success and figure in the world. But fate had determined that he should leave none of his race behind him, and that he should finish his life poor, lonely, and childless.

The narrator undercuts the content of the visuals (the images of domestic pleasure) and assures us as to the outcome of the film. We need only wait to see how that outcome will be detailed. Soon Bryan dies from a fall from his horse, the horse Barry gave him and which the child rode with an enthusiasm that proved to be his undoing, as Barry's own enthusiasm in his undertakings undoes him. Bryan's deathbed sequence is the most sentimental thing Kubrick has ever filmed; it momentarily breaks the film's distance and makes us uncomfortable. Alan Spiegel condemns Kubrick for the conventionality of this sequence, as others have condemned him for not having more sequences like it in his films.[34] But the sequence does work, again in terms of the very frustration of audience point of view I have discussed. Suddenly we are allowed a direct emotional engagement, and just as suddenly the rigid formal structure of the film returns. We are once again not allowed any easy emotion or unquestioning identification with the character.

Soon after Bryan's death comes the duel between Barry and Bullingdon, a violent sequence but one that is also restrained and so structured as to deny its highly emotional content. It takes place in an abandoned building (possibly a church); the characters are isolated against walls (Bullingdon is composed so that the walls are clearly defined behind him; Barry is shot with a telephoto lens, similar to the way Dax is photographed during the execution sequence in *Paths of Glory*, so that he is slightly removed from the action, isolated both in it and from it). The sequence emphasizes Barry's aloneness more than any other in the film, trapping him in a final, perfectly ordered, unimpassioned ritual of proper conduct. Barry, as always, tries to bring some humanity to it: he refuses to kill Bullingdon and fires into the ground. But, as in every other instance when Barry attempts to humanize his world, he suffers for it. Bullingdon may be a revolting coward, but when given his chance, he shoots his stepfather, takes advantage of weakness, and triumphs.*

---

* Early in the film, Barry duels with the cowardly Captain Quinn. It is a faked duel; he thinks he has shot Quinn and is sent from his home. Here he duels with his cowardly and vicious stepson, whom he does not shoot; this time he gets shot and is sent from his home. It should be noted that in the first of those happy family scenes referred to earlier, Barry and Bryan play at dueling, thereby foreshadowing the serious duel with Bullingdon.[35]

135

No matter what Barry attempts, he loses and is isolated. No matter what attempts we make to join emotional ranks with the film, we lose and are isolated, forced into a contemplative stance before images and actions which invite us only to observe; settings and characters culturally distant from us; and an aura of sadness, painful to confront in the character of Barry Lyndon, more painful to confront in ourselves.

This may be the formal triumph of the film, but it raises a question about *Barry Lyndon* and about Kubrick's work in general. As much as the formal structures of his films force us to come to terms with our perceptions and engage us in an active role in determining narrative development and meaning, the result of the work is a reinforcement of our own passivity and impotence. Let me put it another way: struggling to emerge from the discussions of *Barry Lyndon,* and, to a lesser degree, of *Dr. Strangelove* and *2001,* is the adjective "Brechtian." The confrontation these films provoke between their structure and meaning and our perception of them, the way they insist upon a reconsideration of how we understand cinematic narratives and, subsequently, what those lonely narratives tell us, the way they inhibit stock emotional responses, would seem to indicate a realization of the Brechtian principles of distancing, of substituting intellectual for emotional response, of turning narrative into a process involving our continuing understanding, rather than a product demanding a predetermined reaction. Films like *Paths of Glory, Dr. Strangelove, 2001, A Clockwork Orange* separate us from our ideological assumptions and make us view objectively the forms and images of our culture which we take for granted. The corporate names that adorn the space station in *2001* and that film's entire treatment of technology allow us to question, to feel uncomfortable about our ordinarily unquestioning attitude toward the myth of progress and toward scientific and corporate hegemony. *A Clockwork Orange,* as uncertain as it seems to be of its own center, still confronts us with our attitudes toward violence, both of the cinematic and the day-to-day variety, visually enticing us with it while exposing the ease with which we allow ourselves to be enticed. More profoundly than *A Clockwork*

*Orange, Barry Lyndon* examines the easy clichés of "individual freedom" and societal necessities. Barry, somewhat like Alex, suffers from an attempt to exert his own vitality within a social structure too rigid to support it.[36] *Barry Lyndon,* however, extends to us less cynicism and more sad contemplation. It is Kubrick's most anti-Fordian film, representing the domestic unit as a composition not of security and comfort but of rigid economic ceremony, between whose members checks pass rather than affection.[37]

All of Kubrick's work seems an effort to wrench us away from satisfaction and acceptance; but it is always an effort meant to place us in a position of sadness or uncertainty. *Dr. Strangelove* is the only film which has the potential of arousing anger; it affirms our sanity in the face of madness. The others, and *Barry Lyndon* in particular, seem only to affirm our loneliness, an affirmation which denies the Brechtian premise of art as an instrument of intellectual and social engagement. If, for Brecht, the forms of art should deflect the spectator from those forms to the political and social realities of his or her world, then for Kubrick the forms of art deflect the spectator from those forms only to the individual self. This is a ticklish point. In discussing the troubling passivity inherent in *Paths of Glory* I said that Kubrick was hardly a revolutionary filmmaker. It would be misguided to demand of him that his work affirm viable possibilities of action, engagement, and change since these do not seem to be part of his artistic sensibility. More important, in American film these possibilities are usually realized in melodramatic, heroic fantasies, the very forms Kubrick eschews. At the same time, we cannot ask him to investigate our culture in the manner of, say, Jean-Luc Godard, a true Brechtian and an ironist whose restrained, self-interrogating films allow his characters and the cultural paraphernalia that surround them to do intellectual battle with each other, with an open invitation to the spectator to join. Kubrick is an ironist whose films are open and unrestrained in their formal grandeur. They invite emotional more than intellectual engagement (even though they are more intellectually rigorous than the work of any other American filmmaker), and they are considerably more declarative than are the films of Godard. They state more than they question, and even though *2001* and *Barry Lyndon* offer us room to observe and draw conclusions, the conclusions we draw are always the same. For in his films Kubrick's characters have either yielded to or become functions of their environment, or do emotional and physical battle with it and are subdued. We as spectators are invited to observe the losing and perhaps consider its ramifications, but little more. His powerful spectacles and intriguing, intricate formal structures open to us a cavern of mirrors which reflect either our own worst fears of ourselves or our most passive inclinations to remain as we are.

# CHAPTER THREE

## LEAVE THE GUN.
## TAKE THE CANNOLI.

# Francis Ford Coppola

The differences between the careers and working methods of Kubrick and Coppola are enormous. Kubrick, from the start, worked independently of the Hollywood studios. His first films were privately financed—money coming often from relatives—and he controlled every aspect of their production. With the success of *Dr. Strangelove, 2001,* and *A Clockwork Orange,* he was assured independence, and he was assured as well distribution for whatever he made. With the financial failure of *Barry Lyndon,* he is now assured of only one thing: that his next film must be successful, or his freedom might be lost. American film production and distribution does not permit failures in the marketplace, and indeed frowns upon films that make only a modest profit.

Francis Ford Coppola has a responsibility for creating this state of affairs. Unlike Kubrick, he started his career—after spending some time in film school (and a small amount of time making pornography films)—in the very midst of the Hollywood production system.[1] He has done a great deal of screenwriting: some of it, like his script for Franklin Schaffner's *Patton* (1970), successful; some of it, like his work for Jack Clayton's *The Great Gatsby* (1974), not very successful. In the sixties he made films of varying degrees of interest and success, films that played with various genres and cinematic styles, none of them indicating an individual approach or even—at least until *The Rain People* (1969)—a desire to do anything too different from the general run of Hollywood production. Perhaps the most important thing Coppola did in the late sixties was to attempt the creation of a filmmakers' cooperative. His American Zoetrope was to be a place that would help new filmmakers with equipment and with financing. George Lucas benefited greatly from it. His *THX1138* (1971) and *American Graffiti* (1973) were helped into being by Coppola. But American Zoetrope was a short-lived venture. With the two *Godfather* films (1972, 1974) Coppola was no longer on the fringes of American film, able to do good works and aid his colleagues. He became an event.

The *Godfather*s marked a change in American film production; not a radical change, but an important shift in the economic mentality that had always existed but was kept somewhat under control during the years of the studios. The total control the Hollywood studios exercised until the mid-fifties created something like a total security for those working within them. Careers did not need to rise and fall on the basis of one film, and one film did not place the financial situation of a given studio in peril. With the dissolution of that control, each individual production became enormously important, a focus of financial attention. As production fell off throughout the sixties and into the seventies, more and more stock was placed in a given film. When it was discovered, especially with *Godfather I,* that one film could make an incredible amount of money for everyone concerned, there arose in the minds of producer, distributor, agent, star, screenwriter, and director the fantasy of the blockbuster, the greatest money-maker of all time.[2] The result is that many filmmakers are now under extraordinary pressure to create a single work that will gain such profit as to make the successes of the past pale in comparison. No self-respecting business can be run like this, of course, and this phenomenon is a measure of the lack of respect that the businessmen in filmmaking have for their work and its product. It is capitalism gone madder than it already is: more and more money is spent on less and less output, so that the little that is put out bears the greatest amount of burden to make or break all concerned. Yet at the same time, most of the moneymen and the filmmakers have little notion of just what the audience will react to. Too much filmmaking is now based on an enormous gamble supported by enormous hype.

Coppola is certainly not to blame for this state of affairs. He could not have known just how popular the first *Godfather* would be. He may, however, in retrospect, be blamed for making the sequel. Even though it, too, was commercially successful, even though it is in many ways a superior and more demanding film than its predecessor, it set in motion a circular, self-defeating and repressive demand. A film now becomes too often the single monument upon which a filmmaker's reputation lives or dies. If all the advance publicity works, and the film is very successful, the filmmaker must do better next time. But, if in order to be successful, the original film must be enormous in size and expensive in budget, what can the filmmaker do to top it? The answer is, of course, a sequel. Sequels sometimes succeed, usually if done by the same director who did the original. *Godfather II* is a perfect example. But sequel-making merely extends the self-defeat inherent in the blockbuster fantasy.

George Lucas, once Coppola's protégé, and Steven Spielberg appear to be two directors who are most immediately vulnerable to the trap. Lucas's early science fiction film *THX1138,* expanding upon a work he did in film school, is a comfortably sized narrative of a repressive, underground future world, realized essentially through images of white, formless space, which manages to be claustrophobic through its very formlessness. *American Graffiti* deals with another kind of formlessness, psychological and social, manifested in the lives of Southern California teenagers in the early sixties who exist in the aimless isolation of their cars. It is a sad and genial work. *Star Wars,* the all-time blockbuster as of 1978, is also a genial if confused work, a great amalgam of film genres—western, war, swashbuckler, science fiction—a pubescent fantasy of bloodless slaughter and mysterious powers. It puts to use all the hardware nascent in Kubrick's *2001* and creates an escapist fantasy that would have been the envy of MGM in the thirties. But, ultimately, Lucas's films and Spielberg's *Jaws* and *Close Encounters of the Third Kind* are more than merely films. They are phenomena. Only a few people spoke to the social-aesthetic ramifications of these latest science fiction films—the one prophesying cosmic warfare, the other demanding passive assent to super-powers, both demanding perfect passivity in the face of their spectacle. This is simply because their very existence and the attention demanded by their existence (attention created by publicity and news coverage) outstripped their significance as imaginative constructs. It is within the context of event (as well as within the context of their own form and meaning) that these works are disturbing. Where will Lucas and Spielberg go from these films? They will probably make sequels (it is somewhat heartening that Spielberg did not make the sequel to *Jaws* and will not make a *Close Encounters* sequel immediately; Lucas is planning to "produce" the second *Star Wars*). But then what? I am not suggesting that they cannot make better films; that in itself would be easy, for they are talented filmmakers. But in a business that oppressively demands more and more returns, can they possibly make more popular films? And if not, will they be able to make any films at all?

It appeared that Coppola might escape this trap that he was partly responsible for setting. In between the two *Godfather*s he made *The Conversation* (1974), a smaller film, intelligently constructed, with an understanding of the morality of Nixonian America and its consequences much more perceptive than what is found in the majority of paranoia films that have been appearing since the late sixties. It seemed that Coppola was striking an enviable balance, creating a series of well-made films and varying their size and appeal, all in all using his talent and his money wisely. However, following *Godfather II* he embarked on *Apocalypse Now*, a film about Vietnam, structured on the narrative of Conrad's *Heart of Darkness*. The amount of pre-publicity and the millions of dollars being squandered on the project—which holds questionable promise of commercial success—

are appalling. Like *Close Encounters,* it is being pre-sold on the basis of its economic adventures and, like other huge projects before it, its production difficulties. It is being created on such a make-or-break basis that it could conceivably damage the progress of a major talent in contemporary American film. It may, perhaps, crack the block-buster syndrome and force filmmaking into something approaching a more rational means of production, although it is not pleasant to con-sider this as happening at Coppola's expense.

The lunatic state of current film production and its economics is a fascinating but frustrating area of investigation, and it is tempting to pursue it in a state of anger and lamentation. It needs to be set up as a context and as a constant reminder that American film is first and always a commercial venture. Nonetheless, my concern is primarily with what can be accomplished within this context. Therefore, the fact that Coppola seems to have ensnared himself within a system partly of his own creation becomes somewhat less important than the work he has managed to do within the snares. As it happens, *God-father I* and *II* and *The Conversation* are among the most important films of the early seventies and represent the work of a filmmaker fully aware of the possibilities and intricacies of his medium. They are, as well, works which encompass the contradictions of contempo-rary culture more than do many of their contemporaries; and they demonstrate the progress of a filmmaker learning his trade. Coppola's decade-long apprenticeship in commercial filmmaking provides an interesting look at an individual trying out the forms of his medium. Unlike the early films of Kubrick, which mark a talent almost fully formed, the early films of Coppola—*Dementia 13* (1963), *You're a Big Boy Now* (1967), *Finian's Rainbow* (1968), and *The Rain People*—exhibit a groping toward form, a trying out of genres. They are not very good films, and I do not wish to give them more than cursory attention. They will, more than anything, offer an opportu-nity to investigate some of the formal conventions of American film and indicate the various options open to the filmmaker and to the viewer, the one who uses them to create a narrative, the other who interprets them to understand the narrative.

Coppola was introduced to commercial film by Roger Corman and American International Pictures, an individual and an organization devoted to the low-budget drive-in movie. As he did for so many others—Martin Scorsese, Peter Bogdanovich, the actors Jack Nicholson and Bruce Dern, the cinematographer Laszlo Kovacs—Corman allowed Coppola to work, for little money, and to learn the craft. The Corman/AIP environment provided an entry into the film business; it also provided something to escape from. AIP produced horror films, beach-party films, bike films, and there is only so much room in these genres to move around in (as Dennis Hopper and Peter Fonda discovered when in *Easy Rider* they attempted to turn the AIP bike film into a grand generational statement). If Corman taught his pupils to work quickly and cheaply, he also taught them the necessity of finding a situation that provided more leisure and more room for imaginative growth.

*Dementia 13,* Coppola's first film, is an exercise in primitive filmmaking: characters talk to each other in wooden, halting dialogue; there is no point of view or coherent narrative structure. What there is of value is an occasional manifestation of a sense of composition, although this sense is itself dictated by the genre: a closeup track of faces moving down dark corridors; a couple embracing in an ancient dark room as the camera pulls back to reveal—unnoticed by them—the corpse of a little girl. Cutting, too, is of the basic horror variety: quick and shocking: a closeup of a terrified face intercut with the slashing blade of a knife; a sudden, loud insert of a hammer crashing down on an iron sculpture. There are scantily clad women, brutal murders, a weird doctor (Patrick Magee, the British actor who turns up in Corman's *The Masque of the Red Death* and then as Mr. Alexander in *A Clockwork Orange* and the Chevalier in *Barry Lyndon*). At one point, an example of Coppola's academic background appears, as he constructs a shot of a woman lying sick in bed. In the foreground is a bottle of medicine and a glass with a spoon in it. In the background another character is seen entering the room. The shot is a homage to Welles, echoing the sequence in *Citizen Kane* where Susan lies in bed after her attempted suicide (there is, in fact, a character in *Dementia 13* named Kane). Unfortunately, the time and facilities available to Coppola did not permit deep focus in the shot, and it stands only as a brief but important indication of a major influence on Coppola's future style.

Coppola may allude to Welles in *Dementia 13,* but the film as a whole is an obvious attempt to imitate *Psycho.* It fails in this attempt, but in its failure indicates what Coppola needs to learn about Hitchcock. *Psycho* is not a horror film; it uses some of the conventions of that genre, the old dark house, the lurking presence, the unexpected onslaught of violence, but uses them for the purpose of exploring the nature of irrationality, vulnerability, and complacency. The structure of *Psycho* is such that the audience becomes victim, though not in the way that a Friedkin or a Spielberg audience is victimized, for with Hitchcock there is always a sense of play, an ability to let the audience know they are being had while he is having them. There is in Hitchcock the ability to confront the audience with the very things that are thrilling them, to make them, on some level, question their own response. In the *Godfather* films, Coppola will discover methods of presenting an audience with different perspectives, different ways of reading his narrative and its characters. In *The Conversation* he will move close to a Hitchcockian treatment of points of view and moral argument. His first film remains merely an attempted imitation of exterior style (much in the way Brian De Palma's films imitate the more superficial aspects of Hitchcock). But as poor as *Dementia 13* is in itself, it points, weakly and perhaps by default, to areas Coppola will explore more fully in his later work.

The same cannot be said for his next two films, *You're a Big Boy Now* and *Finian's Rainbow.* The latter was Coppola's first big studio project (it was made for Warner Brothers) and turned out to be a minor exercise in a dead genre. The musical had been one of film's essential means of escape from the spatial restrictions imposed upon it by the conventions of narrative realism. It allowed filmmakers to break down narrative "logic" and expand the material world into flexible and fantastic areas of movement. But this sense of play and liberation that the musical offered broke down rapidly in the fifties. The musical written for film began to disappear, to be replaced by lavish, static adaptations of stage musicals.* As these adaptations became bigger and bigger, they had less and less vitality, so that by the time Coppola attempted an adaptation of a forties musical comedy he could do little more than exercise the conventions. He demonstrates a facility in organizing groups of people across the wide Panavision screen (a format he uses only here, preferring the less expansive non-anamorphic wide-screen ratio which he uses to perfection in the *Godfather*s) and creates some excellent comic sequences for Al Freeman, Jr., and Keenan Wynn, who plays a roaring southern reactionary. Otherwise, the song-and-dance sequences are indifferent, Fred Astaire is old and slow, and the main interest lies in the charm of the studio sets, which were becoming a rare occurrence in the late sixties. Coppola is not making a point of the artificial sets, as Martin Scorsese will in his musical, *New York, New York;* rather they come with the territory of a big-budget studio assignment. (By the late sixties a rather odd corollary had developed: the less expensive, independent production would be shot on location, the big studio piece would be shot indoors and look it; in a word, those who could not afford sets used the world; those who could afford to make the best use of the world went indoors.)

Prior to *Finian's Rainbow,* Coppola did make a small-budget location film. *You're a Big Boy Now* is so representative of a moment in the history of recent cinema that it is now almost unwatchable. The "youth film," started by Richard Lester with *A Hard Day's Night* and *Help* (the roots of which go back to the rock and roll and beach-party films of the fifties), climaxing with *The Graduate* and *Easy Rider,* and then dying swiftly with a string of films from MGM at the turn of the seventies, was part of a strange, touching, and cynical period for Hollywood. Producers thought they had discovered an audience, an age group from the mid-teens to the mid-twenties, who were

---

* The self-cannibalizing of the popular arts is amazing: as film began adapting stage musicals, stage writers began adapting film drama into musical comedies.

certified movie-goers and would react instantly with the price of admission to films directed at them and concerning them. This group did react undeniably to *Bonnie and Clyde* and to *The Graduate* and *Easy Rider,* both of which, like *Bonnie and Clyde,* played off the need for a myth of freedom against an equally strong need for its opposite, a warning that freedom inevitably brings doubt or death.

The Lester films, however, have no cautionary elements; they celebrate anarchy anarchically, drawing upon the narrative experiments of the French New Wave. *You're a Big Boy Now* is remarkably close to Lester, though a bit more anxiety-ridden in its approach to adolescent sexuality and the attempts of its hero, Bernard Chanticleer (Peter Kastner), to escape the clutches of his parents. It is closer still to Arthur Penn's *Mickey One,* particularly in its cutting pattern and some of its images. *Mickey One* is itself a film responsive to the new narrative structures that were being developed in France, so Coppola's film works out of a double or triple heritage (out of Lester via *Mickey One,* both with roots in early Godard, Truffaut, and Chabrol).

Like that of *Mickey One* (and the Lester films), the cutting of *You're a Big Boy Now* is rapid and oblique, done not so much for the sake of continuity as for the sake of rhythm and a desire to speed up the images and express vitality. While Coppola's film is not involved in the perceptual distortions of *Mickey One,* it is similarly concerned with the effect of a collage of images and their swift, even tenuous associations. There is one sequence that is almost identical in cutting and visual content in the two films: Mickey and Bernard each go to an amusement arcade and look into a porno peep-show machine. In each, the sequence is cut the same way, with tantalizing point-of-view shots of the film or flip cards going through the machine intercut with the surprised reactions of the viewer. In *Mickey One,* the sequence goes nowhere and is used as another fragment of the bizarre, subjective images that make up the film. In *You're a Big Boy Now* the sequence is played for comedy. Bernard gets his tie caught in the film loop and is rescued by Amy Partlett (a young and ever-pouting Karen Black), who cuts it off. Perhaps the similarity of the sequences is due to the fact that Aram Avakian was the editor of both films, and no doubt exerted influence on both Penn and Coppola. None of their other films indulge in such frantic cutting, and in fact Coppola will radically alter his cutting style in his later work.*

*You're a Big Boy Now* is an amalgam of styles and influences, and it cannot quite come to terms with them and emerge with a sense of its own identity. It is full of Lesterish romps through New York streets, and contains some fine visual and verbal free associations. Bernard comes across a bit of nasty graffiti in the subway: "Niggers Go Home." He stares at it and wonders where is home? "Home is where the heart is," he decides, and the graffiti rearranges itself accordingly. He continues his associations: "My heart is in the Highlands"—and there is a shot of a black man in kilts, playing a jazz riff on his bagpipes, leading a group of children through Central Park. Barbara Darling (Elizabeth Hartman), the rather bitchy, heartless free spirit to whom Bernard loses his heart, dictates her life story to a dwarf (Michael Dunn). The dictation takes place, in rapid succession and with no transitional links, in Barbara's room and in the street, intercut with flashbacks to the story itself (her childhood affair with an albino hypnotherapist with a wooden leg) that appear with the typed words of the story superimposed over the image. Elsewhere in the film Coppola indulges in some self-allusion and an acknowledgment of his mentor: on the walls of a disco are flashed images from *Dementia 13,* and in one of Barbara Darling's flashbacks she sees Roger Corman's *The Pit and the Pendulum* (in *Godfather II,* the acknowledgment will be even warmer, as Corman himself appears as one of the senators investigating Michael Corleone). Entwined with these clever devices is a tale of frustrated adolescence, a domineering mother and father, a chicken that hates young women, a character, played by Julie Harris, named Miss Thing, and a fine score by a late-sixties rock group, the Lovin' Spoonful.

---

* Of course it is just as possible that Avakian simply gave both Penn and Coppola what they wanted. *The Miracle Worker,* which Avakian cut for Penn before *Mickey One,* is, except for its credit sequence, more restrained in its montage than the two films mentioned here. Avakian does not, in the films he edits or those he directs, stay with one particular style.

In the late sixties this film looked and felt fine. Now it does not: it is awkward, it strains for effect; when the characters speak they sound like refugees from an AIP production. But there is something more: even looking at *A Hard Day's Night* and *Help* from the distance of these many years is like peering into a cinematic Garden of Eden. The vital innocence of these films looks a bit futile now, while their energy and their trying out of new narrative structures and editing patterns seem to have gone nowhere but into the style of television commercials (which should not be entirely underrated in terms of how they teach viewers to perceive and understand oblique and condensed narratives). As a Lester imitation, *You're a Big Boy Now* seems more nervous than vital, and not quite able to cover up its sense of sexual anxiety with its joyful rompings. Purely as an experiment in editing, it served Coppola well. He learned from Avakian how to cut a film in rapid, sometimes jarring fragments. He learned this and then abandoned it. In *The Rain People,* the first film in which Coppola seems to move toward a concise and workable style, he experiments with the possibilities and limitations of the long take. In the *Godfather*s he discovers a workable compromise in cutting style, combining aspects of the long take with the traditional cutting continuity of dialogue sequences. In *The Conversation,* he examines some basic assumptions inherent in the conventional cutting of shot/reverse shot (a look at a person and a cut to a look at what that person is seeing). From *You're a Big Boy Now* to *The Rain People* to *Godfather I,* he works through the many possibilities of how film editing affects our perception of the film narrative, and it will be useful here, before discussing *The Rain People* and his major films, to examine some of the problems and theories of editing that Coppola is dealing with.

The basic function of editing in American film is to achieve narrative movement, continuity, and unbroken audience participation in this movement. This function can be related to two "discoveries" (as always in the history of film, it is difficult to assign precise moments, individuals, or even intentions to the appearance of specific formal devices and strategies). One of these, always assigned to Edwin S. Porter and his 1903 film *The Great Train Robbery,* is the discovery that the narrative structure of a film could be determined by cutting various sequences together so that two bits of action meant to be occurring simultaneously could in fact occur one after the other on the image track. The images that are seen are sequential and have a temporal relationship to each other (first this occurs then that occurs). But what is interpreted is a simultaneous relationship between the two units. We recognize a difference in space, but accept these two spaces as containing actions and events occurring at the same moment. This, which Christian Metz and others have called alternate montage, has become the most fundamental of cinematic structures, and it can be seen operating in the baptism sequence of *Godfather I,* where the slaughter of Michael's enemies is intercut with the church service for Michael's godson.[3]

It is important to emphasize the illusionary aspect of this: what *appears* as sequential is *interpreted* as simultaneous. One thing that films like *You're a Big Boy Now* and its predecessors do is jar us out of this illusion a bit, make obvious the fragmented aspect of film editing and use this fragmentation to stimulate in the audience perceptions other than that of an unbroken flow of events, to challenge the conventions of continuity in film. But the alternate montage is not the only editing device by means of which a whole is signified by fragments. The other major component of cutting that has a similar effect involves the operation performed on a simple dialogue sequence. In solving the problem of how two people can be shown talking to each other, American filmmakers discovered what has become one of the most persistent of formal clichés. The strategy is to cut a dialogue sequence by dissecting it into a series of shots and reverse shots of the characters involved. Although many variations occur, the basic structure involves a number of separate shots: a two shot which establishes the characters' situation, occupying an intimate space, confronting each other; over-the-shoulder shots from one character to the other, in which each will be shown alternately listening and speaking; shots of each character alone, also used to show that character alternately listening and speaking. These shots are then combined in a way that establishes a proper rhythm for the sequence, emphasizing the appropriate importance of each character speaking and each character reacting to the other's words.

Two reasons for the firm establishment of the shot/reverse shot technique have been assumed: first, it is an easy and controllable production method. The best performances of each actor can be selected and cut in; both actors need not be present for the entire filming of the sequence. Second, it was hoped that rapid cutting of a dialogue sequence (indeed, of any sequence in American film from the early sound period through the fifties, when few shots are much longer than nine to fifteen seconds)[4] and rapid changes in point of view would prevent boredom for the viewer. Recently, Daniel Dayan and others have offered interpretations that have opened up these filmic conventions to reveal profound ideological currents. Besides avoiding boredom, the rapid cutting of numerous separate shots into a pattern that creates a smooth sense of continuity is a way of avoiding viewer objectivity. The illusion of wholeness that is obtained (as opposed to the sense of fragmentation created by a film like *Mickey One* or *You're a Big Boy Now*) renders the cutting process invisible. We are forced to attend to the events occurring within the narrative. The gaze of the spectator is directed beyond the formal structure of the film and into the "story," the surrogate reality of the characters and events on the screen. The shot/reverse shot sequence in particular does not permit the viewer to move beyond, or outside, the closed space of the characters. The gaze of the characters is never directed outward to the camera/audience (of all conventions in filmmaking this is the strongest: no character within a film may look at us, and by that look announce the existence of a medium, a mechanical, optical, aesthetic structure that stands between us and the people and events it creates). We, therefore, are ignored, but we may not ignore what we see: a fully articulated, inhabited world. Furthermore, the constant opening and closing of this world—one character looks to one side and in the next shot the other character answers the direction of his gaze—seals us within it. The editing structure of American

151

film is based on an extraordinary contradiction: many pieces rapidly linked together create a wholeness and completeness; the complexity of parts produces the illusion of an absence of parts, indeed, an absence of form. We see through the screen into a completely realized world we are given little choice but to accept as valid.[5]

This editing structure and its implications are certainly not the result of a conspiracy, although the filmmakers of the classical period of Hollywood production almost always thought in terms of "realism" and were quite conscious about not drawing audience attention to the means by which the filmic illusion of the real was created. But this editing is certainly not inherent or essential to the medium either. The theory and practice of Eisenstein demonstrate that editing can have a form and function that do not create an illusion of a real world. André Bazin, godfather to the French New Wave, was of the opinion that film did not need editing at all, at least not as a device for fragmenting space to create the illusion of wholeness. He observed that the shot itself was a sufficient unit of wholeness: it did, after all, incorporate a given, whole space. Bazin proposed this in the fifties, on the basis of a belief that the long take would somehow reveal a faithfulness to "reality," to the structure of the world, which, he felt, it was film's purpose to reveal.[6]

Reality, however, has nothing to do with it. After all, American film, with its dependence upon cutting, is supposed to be "realistic." Is the kind of film championed by Bazin, the film in the tradition of Murnau, Welles, and the neo-realists, indeed most European filmmakers from Renoir on, more "real" or differently "real" or constituent of another order of "reality"? It is in fact a matter only of filmmakers and film viewers building upon different sets of conventions and expectations, different ways of constructing and assembling images, and significant of the different ways we perceive these images and deal with them intellectually and emotionally. There is nothing more "real" or true to life about a dialogue sequence in which we watch two characters talking to each other unimpeded by cutting. There is, however, a major perceptual readjustment that we make. We are not directed in such a sequence to see one or another of the characters at a precisely determined instant; we are not sealed off within a space by the continuous correlation of the characters' glances. In fact, the major perceptual event in this type of shot—the sequence shot—is the awareness of our own gaze. Bazin is correct when he says that the long take gives us a freedom to observe that we do not have with the conventional pattern of cutting (whether or not this freedom makes the sequence shot a more "democratic" form is a moot question), and this very freedom can be used to remove us, if only slightly, from the action at hand. We have seen this effect radically employed in *Barry Lyndon,* where the shots are not only long in duration, but long in terms of the distance created between the viewer and the events on the screen. The result is that we are constantly forced to recognize our situation as observers of an artificial construct, and made to be what we always are when we watch a film—though conventional cutting obscures the situation: interpreters of form.

The long take is prominent in European filmmaking and, with the exception of Penn and Altman, evident in the work of the filmmakers I am discussing here. The ways they use it differ greatly, however. Kubrick, following Welles, uses long takes with a moving camera not only to observe—and make us observe—but to encompass and articulate large spaces and make those spaces contribute greatly to the information derived from the composition. Scorsese employs a moving camera to energize the space he articulates, to connote a sense of nervousness and repressed violence. Coppola, who works his way through many cutting styles from *Dementia 13* to *Finian's Rainbow,* comes to a contemplative stop in *The Rain People* and experiments with the possibilities of the long take and the ways it can direct us to an observation of characters and their interaction. In *Godfather I,* he will, as I said, integrate this method of observation with more conventional cutting and develop out of it—in a different way than Kubrick—a Wellesian concern with the ways characters are placed in the frame and the way the viewer is affected by this placement and the ways he or she is made to observe them.

*The Rain People* is a narrative of loneliness and despair, about a woman who attempts to break out of a domestic enclosure without

153

knowing precisely where or why she is going. The opening shots of the film set up a point of view that creates a distance between us and events which immediately places us in a position to observe a quiet sadness and detachment. We observe from a low, distant angle a gray, rainy, deserted suburban street. In the distance a garbage truck moves slowly down the block toward the camera; we see the figures of the garbage men and a few cars that pass by. The shot is quite long, both allowing the credits to play out over it and permitting us to situate ourselves in its rhythm and its emptiness. The next shot begins on an object not immediately identifiable: an iron bar dripping with water. The focus is pulled, and the chains (as we learn in the next shot) of a children's swing are brought into view; it is pulled again, and a suburban house appears.* The next shot is of the children's swings in the rain. There follow another shot of the house, from a bleak, low angle, and then a cut to an interior, and the main character, Natalie Ravenna (Shirley Knight), lying in bed, isolated in the morning dark, pulling herself away from under the arm of her sleeping husband.

I describe this sequence of shots to indicate Coppola's attempt—really for the first time in his films—to go beyond simple conventions to create a determining point of view, a mood, and a situation that is something more than can be created by the grimy shock cuts of an AIP horror film or the nervous cutting of a post-Beatles romp through the streets. The fact that this atmosphere does not last for long is a measure of the film's failure. The slow and measured rhythm set up by the opening does endure for the length of the film, but Coppola cannot decide whether he wishes to create by means of this rhythm a lower-middle-class melodrama in the loose intensive manner of John Cassavetes, or a road movie of the sub-genre that gained popularity after *Bonnie and Clyde* and *Easy Rider,* with roots going back to *It Happened One Night.* The subject of the film, a suburban housewife

---

* Focus pulling, or rack focus (in which points of focus are changed within the shot), appeared in the early sixties (Richard Lester was among the first to use it). It is a major device for calling attention to the cinematic process and for avoiding cutting. Unfortunately it was overused and rapidly became a cliché.

who must distance herself from her husband, her children and her pregnancy because she feels imprisoned by them, would have been treated by Cassavetes in terms of an intricate, swirling interchange of talk. Cassavetes defines his characters not so much by what they do or where they are, or even what they say, as by how they sound. Coppola does not have the facility for the sound of characters talking that Cassavetes has, and he has too much of a visual sense merely to leave his characters alone. The film does not develop a consistent attitude toward its characters or its viewers, and the long takes often go unsupported by the events being played out within them.

After the opening sequences there is a series of jump cuts (the only ones used in the film) rapidly depicting Natalie leaving her home, visiting her parents, recalling her wedding (an Italian wedding, in rich preparation for the opening sequence of *Godfather I*); shots of the bride and groom fleeing through a corridor are matched with shots of Natalie in her car, leaving the city through a tunnel. At this point the film loses its dramatic focus. Natalie is a character defined by her despair and her need for escape (she does not define herself very much, thereby keeping a kind of inarticulate sadness and anger about herself throughout); she is also defined by her urban (or at least suburban) origins. It would seem reasonable to allow this character a desire to escape her environment by driving out through the open country; but the disjuncture is too severe. The "road" sequences, complete with traveling shots of highway and countryside (another late-sixties film convention, of which Coppola seems conscious, for at one point Natalie's car passes a drive-in showing *Bonnie and Clyde*), seem to pull away from the rest of the narrative. Though the movement is intended to give an ultimately false sense of freedom and escape, it soon becomes merely movement through scenery and at best indicates Natalie's inability to act out her desires in any environment. All dramatic confrontation takes place within enclosures: the car, a motel room, a house, an animal farm, a trailer, a phone booth. One sequence in particular manifests the sense of enclosure she brings with her into any situation. Just after she leaves New York, Natalie makes a phone call to her husband from a booth in a gas station. The camera tracks slowly toward her, remaining, though, outside the booth as we hear her attempting to explain her leaving. The first shot of this sequence lasts almost five minutes. The second shot, from the same angle, lasts almost three minutes.

It doesn't work, for the simple reason that there is nothing of great interest happening in the narrative or in what we are seeing in the shot. We are made uncomfortable with Natalie's talking about herself in the third person, we have a sense of her neurosis and the terrible breaking-up of her personality, and we are allowed something of an observation of her entrapment. But the camera's remaining for so long outside the booth dissipates intensity rather than concentrating it, and we are left finally with an awareness only of our own looking, without a clear understanding of why we are looking and at whom. Finally, we do not become aware of a shot that forces us to come to terms with a formal presence, but merely, to use for once the most simple of critical judgments, we become bored.

The classic reference for a sequence like this is the eating scene in Welles's *The Magnificent Ambersons*. Here the camera is stock still, in a dark, cavernous kitchen. In the foreground, George Amberson Minafer (Tim Holt) sits stuffing himself with strawberry shortcake, teasing his Aunt Fannie (Agnes Moorehead) to the point of hysteria. The sequence lasts, uncut, for about four minutes, and the intensity both of what is happening within the shot and of our consciousness of the shot itself is enormous. Coppola cannot achieve that intensity, partially because we want no part of the character. She is too troubled and troubling, and we fight against having to look so closely at her for so long; paradoxically, she is also not very interesting. In addition, while in Welles's film the careful articulations of the Amberson kitchen, with its sharply focused background playing off the figures in the foreground, increase our attention, the endless gaze on the phone booth in *The Rain People* decreases it.

*The Rain People* is finally an insecure film interesting in parts and in the performances of its players. It never achieves a working relationship with the viewer, because Coppola still does not have a notion of what that relationship must be. He does not know just how

156

much distancing and how much melodrama are needed. What he does know, what becomes most obvious in this film, is his talent with actors. James Caan and Robert Duvall, who will figure largely in the *Godfather* films, respond well to his direction. Caan's Killer Kilgannon, an ex–college football player rendered simple and childish by an injury, and Duvall's Nebraskan policeman, curiously mixing redneck crudity with sentimentality, manage to maintain an independence and self-sufficiency in the face of the Shirley Knight character's grasping uncertainty. Coppola shows a specific talent for handling strong performers in ways that do not allow any one to dominate the others. Shirley Knight's sparse career has been devoted mainly to developing variations of the repressed, depressed woman she portrays here. It is an extraordinary persona, managing to be pitiable as it threatens to devour the men she comes into contact with. Caan and Duvall are best at portraying strong, almost unapproachable characters. In *The Rain People,* Caan inverts this strength into his simple-minded, dependent Kilgannon; but it is still there, for, as much as Natalie uses Kilgannon as the object of her spasmodic attempt at independence, he continually pushes back with a marked independence of his own. (That Coppola has him killed at the end, shot by the Duvall character's daughter as he tries to protect Natalie from the policeman's advances, only indicates the trap of melodrama that American filmmakers fall into whenever they suffer a failure of nerve or difficulties of closure. There is no reason for death in the film.) The characters, in their small loneliness, show remarkable abilities to survive, and the film works well when it depicts this ability. It is at its worst when, at the end, it attempts to pump up emotions and wring our hearts.

Perhaps what is most interesting about *The Rain People* is that Coppola does seem to learn from it that melodramatic puffery is counterproductive, and that strong characters can play against one another without stifling each other. An outstanding quality of the *Godfather* films is the precise development of each figure and the giving to each figure a presence that is undiminished no matter what occurs to him or her. Even John Cazale's Fredo, the weakest and saddest character in the films, is played strongly and distinctly. When he or any other major character is central to a given sequence, or even just part of a sequence, out of focus in the background, he or she is noticed and attended to both as an individual and as part of a group. The strength of the acting and of the characters created by the acting can be detected in *The Rain People;* but something remains missing. That is a clearly defined and coherent *mise-en-scène* for those characters to dwell in, a space for them and for us to share. This quality of *mise-en-scène* is so barely visible in the earlier films that its appearance with such power and presence in *Godfather I* is remarkable. Its presence can be partly accounted for by the care Coppola begins to give each image in the film. At a time when the visual component of American film is becoming weaker and weaker, due partly to the influence of filming for television (which, as the cinematographer Floyd Crosby has pointed out, requires speed, and for that speed flat, evenly lit sets so that multiple cameras can be used) and partly to laziness and a belief that audiences will not notice indifferent image-making, Coppola achieves a richness based on an ability to control light and dark, balance color patterns, and fill the space of a given composition with figures and objects in dramatic relationship to each other. In short, the *Godfather*s have a carefully realized visual texture so well controlled that any isolated shot from them is immediately recognizable.

Part of the responsibility for this precision and care certainly is shared by the cinematographer of the *Godfather* films, Gordon Willis, and their production designer, Dean Tavoularis. But in cases like this it is very difficult to assign individual contributions. Tavoularis, particularly as a re-creator of periods, manifests an excellent ability to arrange the appropriate physical detail. His work on *Bonnie and Clyde* established the appearance of all the thirties-evocation films to follow. In *Farewell My Lovely* (Dick Richards, 1975), a minor remake of *Murder My Sweet,* he does not so much "evoke" the forties as design a cinematic analogue to them, placing appropriate objects in the very configurations of the decade. A newsstand or a cluttered room becomes the articulation of an idea of the time rather than a mere imitation. He does this as well in the *Godfather*s, with a sense of detail that is not "realistic" (how many of us have seen the interior of the home of a mafioso in the forties?) so much as indicative and creative of a sense of place and of habitation. (Tavoularis can work in the detail of spareness as well: his design for *The Conversation* works on a principle of emptiness: sparely furnished rooms, the empty floor of a warehouse, an antiseptic office, a hotel room). Gordon Willis lights each scene so that the play of color and shadow becomes part of the narrative movement, creating dramatic structure as much as do the actors.

Coppola, of course, orchestrates the design and the cinematography into a narrative whole, and perhaps the need to account for contributors to the *mise-en-scène* of the *Godfather*s comes from the simple fact that it is so different from his previous work. Perhaps it is unnecessary to account for this difference at all and we can merely presume that the nature of subject and the pressure to create something special brought from him abilities previously untapped. Perhaps it is necessary to forget Coppola for a moment and attend to the cinematic texts that are *Godfather I* and *II*.


If *Barry Lyndon* is a film of impossibilities shared by audience and characters—impossibilities of tenderness, engagement, emotional sharing, acceptance—*Godfather I* is a film of possibilities: the possibility of protection, security, the loving closeness of a family, geniality, and the power and safety that come from the control of every aspect of the familial environment. Unlike *Barry Lyndon, Godfather I* invites its audience within the narrative, asks them to share its promise of security and power. This seems a contradiction when we realize that it is also a film of brutality, fear, loss, and treachery. But Coppola carefully controls the dialectic. The breakdown of familial closeness and security threatened in the first film is not completed until the second, where the myth of the protective family collapses and becomes only a memory in the face of a cold and fearful environment offering warmth and protection to no one and existing only as a ritual of destruction. Neither film is pure and untainted by elements from the other (I am taking a liberally synchronic view, assuming that *Godfather I* and *II* always co-existed; it is, of course, difficult to know how much of the second film was in Coppola's mind when he was making the first). They are of a piece and separate at the same time, separate enough so that their re-edited television version, in which a strict linear chronology was followed, did not work. The way the films play against each other is a measure of their dialectical strength and of their ability to manipulate our attitudes and sympathies, our fantasies and expectations.

Like *Bonnie and Clyde, Godfather I* is an exercise in the control of audience point of view. But in Coppola's film it is not so much characters to whom we are joined and from whom we are separated but situations, states of being, and places. The film is structured by our desire to move into a world portrayed as being warm, attractive, and protected. This needs clarification: the characters of the film—Marlon Brando's Don Corleone, Al Pacino's Michael, Robert Duvall's Tom Hagen, Diane Keaton's Kay Adams, Richard Castellano's Clemenza, James Caan's Sonny, and the rest—function less as individuals than as representatives of an attractive and dangerous world. They embody it, and it contains them. Our attraction to them, our fears for them, are controlled and are controllable because of the fact that they represent a situation we wish to be part of. The narrative structure of the film plays with their relationship to each other and to their world, and plays even more with our attitudes toward it.

The opening of the film sets up the structure in a form to be followed throughout, unquestioned until Part Two. The first shot begins in the dark as we hear a heavily accented voice say, "I believe in America. America's made my fortune . . ." As the voice speaks, an oldish, foreign man's face appears against the dark and the camera begins to move back. As the man tells a tale of his daughter's violation, the camera continues its movement back, slowly revealing a room colored in browns and lit in gold light. The movement continues until it passes behind the shoulder and head of Don Corleone, who is motionless, save for a gesture of the hand. After the old man whispers into the Don's ear, there is a cut to a reverse shot, looking at the Don, seated at his desk, playing with a cat. The opening tracking shot is about three minutes in length, but there is no discomfort experienced with it as there was with the lengthy takes in *The Rain People*. We are not merely made observers of a simple visual field, listening to simple dialogue. This long take is, more than anything else, enigmatic. It invites our questions and our anticipation: Where are we? Who is the man talking? What is the purpose of the frightful story he is telling? Where are we being taken by the slow pulling back of the camera? The motion itself is significant. A dolly forward tends, obviously, to move us into an action and toward a character or object. It is a motion of approach. A backward dolly usually indicates retreat, or, more mildly, withdrawal, and is conventionally used to end a film. Why, in an opening shot, would we be withdrawing? The opening of a film usually places us in an environment and defines a space, but the opening of *Godfather I* seems to make the space mysterious.*

We are not given a clear establishing shot of a conventional nature until the film moves outside to the wedding. And it is finally in the juxtaposition of these two scenes, the interior of the Don's office and the exterior wedding, which are intercut to create the first major sequence of the film, that the full strategy is clear. The movement of the camera that opens the film is not a withdrawal *from* but a withdrawal *into*. The camera is defining a dark area: at its periphery is the supplicating undertaker, pleading for vengeance against his injured daughter, and at its center is the Don, the majestic giver of favors, a thoughtful and humane old man, playing with his cat and asking the supplicant why he never invites him over for coffee. The Don is secure behind his desk, against the shuttered window, away from the light, in control. These opening shots give us an excellent example of the effect of the shot/reverse shot that I spoke of earlier. The

* Compare the opening shot of *Godfather I* with that of *A Clockwork Orange,* which begins on the bizarre, leering face of Alex and slowly withdraws to show him and his gang in the Korova Milkbar. The movement of the camera starts with a disconcerting image, which becomes more so as the camera pulls back. The more space is defined, the more uncomfortable, strange, and uninviting it becomes.

pull back from the undertaker opens up to us a mysterious and discomfiting space. As the shot pulls back behind the head and shoulders of the Don, introducing another figure, as yet unnamed and unrecognized, that space becomes highly charged with our expectation. The reverse shot closes the space, shows us the face of the man whose back we have just seen, and shows it as being old and rather kindly.

Some further questions quickly become apparent; the enigmatic situation is intensified.[7] Who are these mafiosi? Where do they live? How do they conduct their business? Are they monsters? We bring these questions with us to the film; they are set against the images we see: these people seem pleasant and genial, they occupy a secure environment. "We are not murderers, despite of what this undertaker says," says the Don, sniffing the rose on his lapel; at which point we cut to the wedding of the Don's daughter, Connie, taking place outside. A dark inner sanctum is set against the bright congenial world of familial happiness and security; while the familial world is set, as the narrative unfolds, against the adjacent world of the *other* families and opposing forces who threaten happiness and security. (This is just suggested in the wedding scene by the stern face of Barzini—Richard Conte—an old movie gangster, who refuses to have his picture taken, and by the police who attempt to copy down the license numbers of the cars parked outside.) As the opening sequence proceeds, we are invited to quiet our fears. The family is indeed a happy and secure world, and its inner sanctum, the Don's office, is the center of its activity, opening out to and enclosing all other areas. This sanctum is inviolate; even when it is attacked and casualties accrue to the family, its inner core of control remains. This is especially evident when Don Corleone is shot down. No chaos or breakdown occurs: power is passed first to Sonny and then to Michael, who eventually assures a control even greater than what preceded.

The opening sequence of the film sets up the film's basic structure, a structure that suggests the existence of three Corleone "families" operating one within another: the outer family of wives and children, weddings and meals, romances and marital disputes; the inner family, made up of men only, who run the "bus-i-ness," kill and get killed;

and the *myth* of the family, an overriding concept held by the Corleones of an integrated, self-perpetuating, self-controlling force, protective of its members, secretive in its operations, and exercising,
above everything else, power. A deep and fragile structure is formed
that might please Lévi-Strauss. Actions and deeds emanate from an
abstract concept of kinship and domestic ritual shared and adhered
to so strongly that the slightest breach of its inviolable status—as
when, during the crucial meeting with the Tattaglia family, Sonny
blurts out the family's concern about protection—assaults and threatens the structure. These assaults and threats are enough to keep us
concerned and engaged, anxious that the order be maintained. We,
as observers, are kept in a tenuous balance of comfort and fear and
in a state of awe. The powers the Corleones have to protect themselves with are almost magical. Their strength appears when needed,
easily and without resistance. They are continually threatened, yet
they continually maintain their control.

The sense of magic and the awe of their power emanate from the
fact that, with few exceptions—such as Michael's preparations for
the killing of Sollozzo and McCluskey—we are never permitted to see
the details of planning, of strategies being worked out, or the people
involved in executive power. The murderous or brutal acts that keep
the family alive occur with an immediacy that belies their complexity
and force. The sequence of Woltz and the horse is a striking example.
Johnny Fontane begs the Don to help him get a role in a film. Tom
Hagen is told to go to California to look into the problem. The wedding continues, Don Corleone dancing happily and with apparent
innocence. The scene fades to black (there are many such fades in
the film; Coppola employs an old filmic convention to indicate a time
and space transition, linking the film's numerous episodes together).

The transition to Los Angeles is made via light forties music on
the sound track and stock forties footage of a four-engine plane landing and a pan of the city, followed by a montage of film studio interiors and exteriors. When Tom and Woltz (John Marley) meet, the
former is very stiff and proper, the latter crude and arrogant. This
careful setting up of the situation is important. It is the first time in

the film we have been away from the Corleone residence. We have no notion (assuming we do not recall the novel) of what is happening, who exactly Tom Hagen is, and what procedures are to be followed. But when Woltz responds to Tom's request for a role for Johnny and his threat of union problems if the request is not met by saying, "I don't care how many dago, guinea, wop, greaseball goombahs come out of the woodwork," we perceive immediately a difference in personalities. The Godfather's patriarchal wisdom and patience and Tom's diffident assertiveness are contrasted to Woltz's racist meanness (Tom says, "I'm German-Irish." "Well, let me tell you something my kraut-mick friend," answers Woltz).*

At the dinner Woltz gives for Tom, we see them first in a high shot from the stairway landing over the dining room, a camera angle that suggests foreboding. Why should we suddenly be at such an odd distance from the characters unless something unexpected is about to occur? It is the first time we have been so isolated. As the dinner proceeds, our anxiety is somewhat quieted, for Coppola begins to assemble the sequence by means of quite standard over-the-shoulder shots. In fact, Coppola uses this cutting pattern throughout the film, though in most instances he transcends its conventional nature by creating with it a sense of proximity and intimacy that goes far beyond its usual perfunctory qualities. In this particular sequence, the calming effect of the conventional cutting is shattered when Woltz launches into his tirade about Johnny and the starlet he ruined. The over-the-shoulder proximity ceases, and Woltz is isolated before us, momentarily threatening, but in fact sealing his doom. "Mr. Corleone is a man who insists on hearing bad news immediately," Tom says and departs. There is a closeup of Woltz and a dissolve from his face to a far shot of the house. Various shots of the house exterior dissolve to a tracking movement into Woltz's bedroom, over the bed, to Woltz asleep. Over this series of shots we hear nothing but the sound of crickets chirping. As the camera continues its track, the

---

* Earlier Don Corleone had made a reference to "Jew Congressmen." It is an offhand, almost natural comment coming from an old Italian of power. But it is the first indication of the deep racism inherent in many of the film's characters.

main musical theme appears on the sound track, a theme which from now on will signal or follow a major, usually bloody, event. The camera tracks close to and around Woltz as he awakes to discover blood; it tracks down to the foot of the bed as the horse's head is revealed. Woltz screams, there are various shots of him, a cut to the outside of the house again, screams continuing on the sound track, and on those screams a dissolve to a medium closeup of Don Corleone, eyebrows raised, talking to Tom. "You're not too tired, are you, Tom?" "No," answers Tom, "I slept on the plane."

We have seen the first manifestation of family power. It is surrounded by the gentleness of Don Corleone and his presence is within it. That presence is partly responsible for the perverse pleasure we take in it, a pleasure aided by Woltz's belligerent crudeness, which disengages from him any sympathy we might have. Most important, though, is the fact that the act of terror itself is done without our knowledge—without our seeing it and therefore with our complicity; only its results are shown to us, and only in terms of smug invitation. The camera tracking in on Woltz is the first major camera movement in the film since the opening shot. There the movement drew us into the mysterious heart of the family; here it is leading us, as it were, from that heart, the core of power, to its manifestation. The result, for us, is the innocent pleasure of seeing an unpleasant man get his comeuppance and the not-so-innocent pleasure of enjoying the individuals who are responsible for it.

Woltz is the only major character in *Godfather I* who is outside the world in which the family operates (though not for long, assuming that the horse's head will put him under the Don's control). This is a matter of some importance for the delicate game that keeps us intrigued by, and on the side of, the family. Great pains are taken to create a fictional environment in which the outside, everyday world never intrudes, is never seen in any detail. There are street scenes, of course, but they are brief and used mainly for transitional purposes. There are of course references to the outside world. During the meeting of the five families to settle the problems of drug trafficking, someone says, with a cynicism that could only come from the Don's rivals (Don Corleone is always thoughtful, never cynical), that they will restrict selling to "the coloreds . . . they're animals anyway, so let them lose their souls." When Clemenza teaches Michael how to use the gun to kill Sollozzo and McCluskey, he says, "I left it noisy. That way it scares any pain-in-the-ass innocent bystanders away." And, indeed, in the restaurant where the killings take place there are a few pain-in-the-ass innocent bystanders, as there are when Sonny beats up Carlo on the street. In *Godfather II,* as the power of empire expands and the closeness of family collapses, more of the outside world is seen: Havana, the Senate hearings, the assassination of Hyman Roth at the airport, Little Italy in the flashbacks. But in *Godfather I* the world is kept pretty much at a distance from us, and we, as observers, are thereby kept safe. Coppola works a combination of distance and engagement, feeding our fantasies of familial security while protecting us from the public suffering that is the result of that security. Everything is done to keep the ramifications of what the family does, and the details of how it does it, quiet, almost absent. We need not feel guilt, nor do we need to feel uncomfortable in wanting to share, in David Thomson's words, "its heroic purpose and its embattled unity."[8]

Therefore, when Vincent Canby writes that *"The Godfather* seems to take place entirely inside a huge smoky plastic dome, through which the Corleones see our real world only dimly," he has his colors, material, and point of view wrong.[9] The fictive characters of the film live in a richly dark, brown-and-gold world, and they see the "real world" very clearly. It exists for their control. It is we, as privileged attendants to their world, who are not permitted to see the "real world" clearly. By not doing so we are protected not only from feelings of guilt, but, more important, from feelings of being intruded upon. We are left free to admire and desire the protection and power offered by the family. This secure isolation, this dark center from which all power emanates as the Don merely raises an eyebrow or whispers in someone's ear, articulates the mythic realm I alluded to earlier. It is a phenomenon that clearly distinguishes *The Godfather* from its gangster-film ancestors. In comparing it to the classic form of the gangster genre (as outlined by Robert Warshow), William S. Pechter writes that *The Godfather* strips "the gangster of his mythic dimension and his tragic meaning for us . . . [and] converts him into only one more of those 'good husbands and fathers.' . . ."[10] He is missing the very point of the film. By creating Don Corleone as a good father and husband who mysteriously, surely, and unquestioningly exercises unlimited power, whose will is carried out swiftly and with a vengeance, Coppola gives him a mythic dimension that far outstrips the Ricos, Camontes, and Tommy Powerses of the conventional gangster film.

In *Bonnie and Clyde,* Penn removed self-centered pride and arrogance from his gangsters in order to make them more attractive and more vulnerable. Coppola, too, removes these qualities, so evident in the gangsters of the thirties, from the Corleones and gives it to the rival families. Unlike his cinematic progenitors, Don Corleone is not on the make; he has it made. The police (except for McCluskey, who works for a rival family) and the politicians are in his pocket. There is no major opposition to the Don's activities from the external world, and the little there is is quickly taken care of. The Don is far removed from those stupid little men of the early gangster films who pushed their way to the top by brute force and then fell when the police or a rival gang discovered their characterological or emotional flaw. The *Godfather*s in fact have less in common with the early cycle of gangster films than they do with a later cycle that began appearing in the late forties and early fifties, when "the mob" began to take prominence over the individual hood.[11] "Mr. Big" had often figured prominently in the gangster film, living in elegance, directing the activities of lesser hoods, taking under his wing Little Caesar or his like. But after the war and in the culture at large there seemed less and less likelihood of individual success, of someone moving to the top, within or without the law, by the force of individual will. Success was to be the result of group effort. In the gangster film Mr. Big became organized into a business, so the lone gangster became an employee, quietly and anonymously doing the killing so the business could succeed by careful accounting and by balancing its books. Vincent Sherman's *The Damned Don't Cry,* a Warner Brothers Joan Crawford vehicle of 1950, presents the transition clearly, as its hoodlum-turned-businessman eschews the "front-page tactics" of the twenties and thirties and hides his gangsterism in his bookkeeping. The independent hood, who wishes to go his own way, is either made to truckle under to the mob's authority or wiped out.

There are no independents in *Godfather I,* but neither is there the mean, gray bookkeeping mentality of the organized syndicate portrayed in earlier films. Rather, there is a large family business, rigidly codified, but genial nonetheless; dark and powerful, but warm and protective. The threats to it occur only from other families like it, and with this Coppola enlarges upon the insular, mythic qualities of his people and their environment. The Woltz episode is enough to indicate Don Corleone's reach into the world; the middle portion of the film, up to the ascendency of Michael, presents the intrusion not of the world but of the rival families into the heart of Don Corleone's power. As strong as the family is, it is vulnerable, and that vulnerability is an endearing quality, mitigating the fears that would otherwise occur if the Corleones were presented as insuperable. The result, again, is an extraordinary balance of insularity, strength, vulnerability, and weakness played out within the film and upon us, the points of view we assume, and the sympathies we offer.

The manipulative aspect of this cannot be denied, for Coppola carefully molds his narrative and its images to hold us for as long as possible in a state of attraction, understanding, and pity for the Corleones. No better example can be found than the murder of Luca Brasi by Tattaglia and Sollozzo, the second act of violence in *Godfather I.* Our introduction to Luca is at the wedding. He is a large, almost repulsively ugly man whom Kay Adams—Michael's girlfriend, and the only outsider allowed into the periphery of the family—finds scary, and who Michael himself indicates is a terrible person. Even the Don is not happy about having to see him. But this hulk is presented to us as a gentle giant. He sits alone and shy, rehearsing his little speech to the Don, blessing his daughter and her husband with brilliant Latin machismo: "May their first child be a masculine

168

child." Luca is later assigned to watch the rival Tattaglia family, who wish, against Don Corleone's best paternal advice, to enter the narcotics trade. We see Luca preparing for his assignment, putting on his bullet-proof vest, checking his gun, in a small room, framed by a doorway, and flooded with the golden light that often is present before a scene of great violence. Both the lighting and composition of this shot, even more than the scene of Luca sitting by the door during the wedding, emphasize both a loneliness and a strength. But because we have not seen any physical manifestation of that strength, we are impressed mostly by the quiet purposefulness of his activities and his isolation. He enters a luxurious art deco bar, and we see him through a glass partition decorated with fishes. The murder at the bar is swift and ugly. In a series of short shots, the greasy Sollozzo puts a knife through Luca's hand, pinning it to the bar. A shadowy figure strangles him with a rope from behind. There is a shot over Sollozzo's shoulder to a bug-eyed, gurgling Luca, sinking beneath the bar, a short insert of his hand pinned by the knife, and then a long shot from behind the fishes as Luca sinks to the ground. (The glass partition not only prepares for the pun on Luca sleeping with the fishes that occurs later when the Corleone family receives a fish wrapped in Luca's bullet-proof vest, but provides a match for the next shot, as the camera observes from behind a window Tom Hagen emerging from a department store.)

If the sequence of Woltz and the horse's head delighted us as a manifestation of the family's power, the murder of Luca Brasi appalls us as a manifestation of power against the family. By emphasizing Luca's isolation and Sollozzo's treachery, cutting the murder sequence itself so that we see its details close up, and then withdrawing discreetly so that we observe the scene from afar, Coppola allows us to be immediately horrified and then somewhat speculative about that horror. The speculation is short-lived, for the murder is part, really, of an extended sequence of attacks that includes the shooting of Don Corleone. It is a measure of Coppola's narrative skill that he rather rapidly indicates the family's vulnerability, having spent considerable time indicating its strength. And while he portrays the weakening of

Don Corleone's power, he simultaneously shows Michael's movement into the sanctum of the family. We, meanwhile, are toyed with, made ashamed that we laughed at an ugly man, made uncomfortable about the security we hoped to discover in the family, horrified by the shooting of the Don, and rapidly assured that the family's strength will continue.

The attack by the Tattaglia family on the Corleones is framed by two scenes in a warehouse. The first is the meeting of Don Corleone, Sonny, Tom, and Clemenza with Sollozzo in the Genco warehouse office. It is at this meeting that Sollozzo broaches the business of drugs and Sonny commits the deadly sin of speaking aloud the family's indecision. We know Sonny has done a bad thing not only because the Don stops him from talking, but because there is a series of short inserts of Clemenza, Tom, and Sollozzo reacting to Sonny's words—short takes of significant looks being conventional cinematic signs of a serious breach in conversation. The ramifications of Sonny's admission of a certain family insecurity do not become apparent for a while. For the sequence still shows Don Corleone in control, assuming an almost moral position, although his major objection to the narcotics business is that the politicians won't stand for it. In terms of surroundings, the dark browns that, along with the black and gold, make up the major tonalities of the film, are evident here, though somewhat colder than they were in his office at home; a change in tonality begins to indicate a change in situation.

The warehouse scene that follows the shooting of the Don is rather different: Sollozzo has taken Tom Hagen prisoner while the shooting is going on and tries to convince him to come over to his side. The place where they speak is dark and enormous. Their faces are in half light, and as they leave they are observed in a far shot, submerged in the dark. The lighting of this scene is very close to that of forties *film noir,* and Coppola is consciously re-creating the sense of reduced individuality, lost power, and vulnerability that the chiaroscuro lighting of so many forties films produces. This scene marks the nadir of the Corleones' fortune, the point where their power seems drained, and the choice of a dark and featureless area to play

Don Corleone (Marlon Brando) shot down in **Godfather I.**

it in is appropriate. It is especially appropriate to the shooting of the Don that precedes. The ambush follows closely on the murder of Luca Brasi, separated from that sequence by the kidnapping of Tom, and prepared for even earlier when, in the middle of Luca's preparations for combat, Coppola inserts a scene in which we are informed that Don Corleone's regular driver has not reported for work (a bit of information that should alert us to the fact that something unpleasant is about to happen).[12] The ambush itself presents the Don at his most domestic, and his most vulnerable, buying fruit outside his warehouse in Little Italy, undistinguished and unprotected. The short shots of unidentified men approaching him, inserts of their feet to indicate the Don's recognition of their direction and purpose, the guns in their

171

hands, and the Don's flight give way to a high shot of the shooting itself and the Godfather falling hopelessly over a car and into the gutter.

At this moment the interlocking structure of control and power, vulnerability and weakness, the structure that keeps us locked into the film and on the Corleones' side, is momentarily broken. The Don, it would seem, is dead, and therefore the heart of the family destroyed. To indicate this rupture, Coppola alters our perspective by cutting to the high-angle shot, typically employed by Hitchcock, usually at moments of extreme stress or crisis, just before or just after a physically or emotionally violent event. For Hitchcock this camera position helps create in the audience a complex response of helplessness and distance. Coppola cuts down on the Hitchcockian complexity a bit: we are separated from the felling of the Don, rendered helpless, in fact made to share, for a moment, the emotional space of Fredo, the bumbler, the weak son, who has dropped his gun and can only sob impotently in the face of his father's ambush. Unlike the opening shot of the film that moved us into the heart of the family, or the tracking shot to Woltz that engaged us in its potency, this static high shot of Don Corleone freezes us into a position of vulnerability, or at least a position that allows us to associate ourselves with the vulnerability of the situation. Rather than guilt, which is often suggested by the distance Hitchcock's use of this camera position creates, we are here asked to feel sorrow and discomfort at our helplessness.

But if this sequence of events makes us fear for the Corleones and their power, interconnected with it is another narrative pattern that will lead to a reestablishment of that power, but without the warmth and security we have heretofore experienced. That pattern constitutes the emergence of Michael, who has so far occupied, physically and emotionally, a space separate from the activities and travails of the family. At the warehouse narcotics meeting, Don Corleone gives Luca his instructions to watch Sollozzo. The scene is played with dark and foreboding music on the track. It fades to a Christmas scene of Michael and Kay walking out of a department store, with "Have Yourself a Merry Little Christmas" ironically accompanying their innocent pleasures.* After the murder of Luca and the shooting of Don Corleone we cut to Kay and Michael exiting from Radio City Music Hall, having seen Leo McCarey's sentimental film *The Bells of St. Mary's*. Kay sees the headline of the attack in the *Daily Mirror* (a scurrilous, sensational New York newspaper, now defunct), and Michael calls home. We see him next after the sequence in the dark warehouse where Sollozzo holds Tom. He is in his father's office with Sonny, Tom, Clemenza, and Tessio, photographed from behind Don Corleone's desk and empty chair. He is all but shut out of the family's attempt to reestablish order. We see him again, after Clemenza kills the Don's chauffeur (one of the funniest and most disturbing scenes in the film: an assassination in the marshland, the Statue of Liberty in the distance, Clemenza pissing in the weeds as his second shoots Paulie; Clemenza reminding him, "Leave the gun. Take the cannoli."). He helps Clemenza feed the men and puts off Kay when she calls him. He and she have dinner, a properly set, WASP dinner, in perfect contrast to the rough-and-tumble meals of the Corleone family and the larger family that constitutes their mob. And this is the last time we see the two outside of the presence of the family and the business. Michael consciously withdraws himself from Kay; his voice is beginning to harden; he is putting himself through his own rite of passage, out of the exterior bourgeois world and into the mysterious depths of the family, within which he will turn himself back into a domestic parody of the bourgeois family man.

In the hospital sequence, with its dark, empty corridors, its threatening isolation, Michael pledges devotion to the Don and protects his life. In the preparations for the killing of McCluskey and Sollozzo, Michael already demonstrates his ease. He sits almost comfortably in a chair, in a position that will become his most significant

---

* Coppola wisely removed a sequence of Michael and Kay in bed, talking of their marriage, followed by Michael calling home to tell them he will not be down for Christmas. This material, cut back in for television, breaks the rhythm of the film, adds a sexual element between Michael and Kay that is otherwise understated, and in general tells us more than we need to know.

one: half at ease, half cornered, simultaneously secure and insecure. The camera dollies in on him as he quietly decides to kill both men, a movement here of emphasis, indicative of a certain threat. Michael's bearing is already cold, too purposeful and unemotional. But at this point his actions are still part of his initiation, his killing of Sollozzo and McCluskey a kind of recapitulation of his father's killing the Black Hander Fanucci, or the old Don in Sicily (we can't know this until Part Two, of course, but when we do, a narrative symmetry becomes clear). It is an act of revenge, of purification, and of emergence. Michael's journey to Sicily is a further ritual, a reliving of the past and the violence of the past. It is presented almost as a dream of the Don's, introduced as a dissolve from the face of the bedridden Don Corleone to a pastoral scene of meadows and sheep (a dissolve from a face in bed is an old cinematic convention for dreaming). But it is no dream and Sicily is no pastoral land, but a country of power and death. The Sicily that Michael visits has a different politics than the one Vito Corleone left: a Communist Party poster is seen during Michael's walk through the town. But the signs of external change—unlike the events in Cuba in Part Two—have no direct bearing. Sicily is the place where the family originated and where the threats to their power intrude. Michael learns the decorum of the Old World, and marries. When his wife is blown up, he learns the vulnerability of his power and, presumably, the obsessive need for vigilance, protection, and the purging of enemies.

The narrative, from the Sicily episode on, essentially belongs to Michael. Earlier, sequences devoted to him were cut into more central narrative episodes; now the central episodes are his. Sonny's conflict with Connie's husband and Sonny's murder at the toll gate are intercut with scenes in Sicily. Don Corleone is given only one more moment of prominence, in the meeting with the five families. But it is a prominence tempered greatly by what has gone before. The meeting follows upon the bombing in Sicily that destroys Michael's wife. The threat of the rival families is almost inescapable. The calm control and security of the old ways are finished. At the meeting the Don is seen framed to the right of a portrait of a late-nineteenth-century gentleman. Standing under an electric candelabra, he is now a parody of elegance and authority, of a time passed. He asks, Lyndon Johnson style, for everyone to reason together. "We are all reasonable men here," responds Barzini. And he and the Don are right, for reason equals power and only those with power can exercise the control of reason (which is exactly what Johnson meant). The Don believes power can be shared; the other families, and Michael, know that power is only taken. The Don continues to recede from dominance.

When we see Michael returned from Sicily, he is walking with Kay, looking old and stiff, slightly ridiculous in his black coat and hat. He is already turning rigid and already being protected. As they walk down a tree-lined street, a black car follows them in the distance (the shot is slightly reminiscent of the opening of *The Rain People*). Michael expounds upon power to Kay. His father, he tells her, was like a senator or the president, in control, acting with authority. Kay accuses him of naiveté: "Senators and presidents don't kill people." "Oh," asks Michael, "who's being naive . . . ?" This sequence marks Michael's difference from his father, his stiffness, his humorlessness, his outwardly stated awareness of the means to power, his hypocrisy: what's important, he tells Kay, is life together and children. He lets on to Kay as much as he ever will about his "business" and then completely buries it in the cant of domesticity. It is our first indication of how Michael will turn the warm, unquestioning, familial closeness of Don Corleone into a rigid and destructive mechanism.

The old family ends with the Don's homey, comfortable death in the vegetable garden. Just before, there is a touching dialogue sequence between him and Michael. Coppola cuts the first part of this sequence into a series of the over-the-shoulder shots he has been using so well throughout the film. The Don warns Michael of assassination, of carelessness. "Women and children can be careless, but not men." He is calm and detached, a bit wandering. Michael tells him he has taken care of everything. Don Corleone moves closer to Michael, and Coppola begins a long two shot: the father is closer to the camera, on the right and looking slightly away from Michael. He talks of his life, his independence, his refusal to be a fool dancing on

175

the strings held by the big shots. He wants Michael to be as independent as he, to hold the strings, to be a senator. But it is not what is said that is important here; it is rather the comfort and closeness of Coppola's observation of them. That Michael is different from Don Corleone has already been established; that his exercise of power is more abrupt, more brutal will soon be clear. But this last, long look at them together has an emotional power that goes beyond the subject of a gangster passing on the reins of power to his son. It is an engaging observation of father and son in a last moment of serenity. It is, as well, the last time we will observe the heart of the family in its warmth and closeness. With the power transferred, a cold and alienating force will take over.

One motion disturbs the serenity of the sequence and indicates the change: Michael assures "Pop" that he will take care of the family's enemies and keep control; they embrace, and as Don Corleone gets up, Michael sinks back into his chair. It is a motion both of assuredness and of complacency, indicative, as are many of Michael's gestures and the way he holds his body, of a self-centered, retentive, secretive, even passive nature, for we rarely will see Michael do anything, though we will see the results of his will. This contradiction in character is made manifest in the baptism-slaughter montage that is the final set piece of *Godfather I*. It is in this montage that Michael reveals his ruthless presence by his absence; his satanic cruelty by his Catholic hypocrisy; the brutality of his world by the protected innocence of church and family. In its construction of opposing images, the baptism sequence comes close to the models of montage set forth by Eisenstein: a complex of opposing shots that affect us by the way they play off of each other. Their full meaning is created by means of their formal conflict.

The montage is based upon ironic visual and kinetic associations: as Kay and Michael unwrap the bonnet from the child's head, there is a cut to hands reaching for a gun. As the priest reaches for holy water and touches the child, there is a cut to a barber reaching for shaving foam for a customer who will soon shoot someone down. Another shot of the priest's hands is cut to hands removing a gun from a bag, which is cut to a killer, disguised as a policeman, mopping his face, which is cut to Clemenza, climbing stairs mopping his face. It is based as well on aural associations. Michael, as godfather to Connie's child, is engaged in question and response by the priest; he speaks for his godson. "Do you renounce Satan?"—A group of men in an elevator are gunned down by Clemenza. Michael responds: "I do renounce him"—Moe Green is shot through the eye. And so on, until, as the priest asks, "Will you be baptized?" we are given a montage of the bodies whose deaths constitute Michael's baptism into the kingdom of earthly power.

This may not be a particularly subtle bit of filmmaking, and is not so intended. It is meant to reveal brutality hiding under sanctity, and reveal it in a brutal way (it is also meant, of course, to be sensational, to excite and to appall the viewer). It is significant, for the narrative, in its clear presentation of Michael as a vicious man, willing to use ritual as a shield for his character. Michael renounces Satan only to emerge as a social-economic antichrist. At the same time, he emerges a hero. He has wiped out his enemies, and Coppola knows this is deeply appealing. Nowhere will Coppola allow us to engage in whole-hearted condemnation of Michael; he will allow us to pity and fear him, and in Part Two these conflicting emotions will be played upon almost to the point of making Michael into a tragic figure. A problem with the baptism montage is that, rather than reveal to us the horrible contradiction of murder sanctified or hidden by church ritual, it may merely make us smug and allow us to take pleasure in the ease with which Michael does lie, kill, protect himself, and remain clean. If we enjoy the spectacle of violence (as Kubrick suggests we do in *A Clockwork Orange*) we become accomplices; our own admiration of violence by proxy condemns us, perhaps, to the vicious and empty world that will be Michael's. Coppola is aware of this, and traps us with it. In the last sequence of the film, when Michael lies to Kay about his not being a murderer and shuts her out of the heart of the family, the inner sanctum, we, as observers, are placed in a peculiar situation. Kay leaves the room, and there is a long shot from her point of view down the corridor into the den. As she looks, we cut to a closer shot of the den, through the doorway, as Clemenza comes in and kisses Michael's ring. The door is closed, but before it shuts we cut to a reaction shot of Kay from within the sanctum, looking out at her as the door closes across her *and* us. We are not allowed to remain in Kay's position, sharing only in her removal from the mysterious space of the new Godfather and his minions. Rather, we are made to observe her as she is cut off, from the point of view of the inner sanctum itself. However, there is no reverse to this shot. In the opening of the film, as the camera drew us into the heart of the family, we are allowed a reverse shot that revealed the Don to us. Now the door is closed in Kay's face and in ours; we are trapped in the inside and in the dark. We get to see no more than Kay does, even though we look from the inside out. Our implication in Michael's world is both suggested and withheld. Almost as a warning, the film leaves us closed in the dark.

The reverse shot is finally given us as the opening of *Godfather II,* where we see Michael, some years later, in medium closeup, head tilted, a minion kissing his hand. We see the chair that belonged to Don Corleone, carrying a depression in its back from long, comfortable use. The scene fades to black and, after the main title, opens in Sicily at the beginning of the century. Coppola drops the linear narrative form of Part One to create in Part Two a counterpoint of rise and fall, of Vito Corleone's seemingly effortless and righteous rise to fortune and Michael Corleone's equally effortless and self-righteous fall to powerful aloneness. The result is an enormous interlocking narrative structure. *Godfather II* builds itself into a series of statements and counterstatements, a dialectic of rise and fall, profit and loss, warmth and coldness, and attempts not so much to clarify the situation and the history of its characters as to play off and contrast their past and present, their attitudes and positions. The narrative of *Godfather II* encompasses Part One and recalls it so that Part One also becomes part of its structure, through our memory. (When both films were edited together for television, this structural complexity and richness vanished.)

John Hess, in his brilliant reading of the film, states that Coppola fashioned its non-linear structure in order to create a distancing of the audience so that they might clearly perceive the socialist analysis of American culture and capitalism he is presenting.[13] It is an intriguing idea and one I want to pursue. But it must be clear that *Godfather II* is far from alienating, far from distancing the audience to the point where they *must* observe and analyze the contrast and counterpoint of two men and two families and two times. Because of his own narrative sense and commercial necessity, Coppola simply cannot afford the narrative dislocations practiced by some European and Third World filmmakers, nor the distancing effects employed by Kubrick, effects which force the spectator to look *at* the film rather than be engaged within it. The narratives of both *Godfather*s are enormous and complex, yet sealed and almost seamless, each sequence felicitously linking itself with another, permitting the audience easy access to the narrative flow (to be sure, there are some infelicitous and downright confusing sequences in Part Two—Pentangeli and the Rosato brothers, the assassination of Roth's bodyguard—but these are the results of insufficient editing time and only momentarily dislodge the continuity).[14] Coppola insists, as he does in *Godfather I,* that we be intrigued and tempted by the events he depicts. But in Part Two he does want us to be more reflective, to contrast Michael with his father and observe a difference in personalities and in lives. He wants us to observe the decline and calcification of the myth of the family, and so he directs us to past and present as a means of judging these differences and observing how something possibly good (familial strength) is corrupted by externalizing its heart into a protective shell that is used to hide a vicious wielding of power.

Formally, the interweaving of past and present is done with marvelous grace. The flashbacks are introduced with titles and with dissolves that effortlessly and touchingly match situations and positions. At one point, Michael, who is about to leave for his visit to Hyman Roth, says goodbye to his son, who asks him if he can help him with his business. "Someday," he answers, as he leans, screen left, over the boy. A slow dissolve introduces the young Vito Corleone (Robert De Niro) on screen right. Through Michael's head a bright lamp appears and Vito's wife enters into the frame. There is a title and a date; the shot dissolves again, showing Vito and his wife with Sonny as a baby. At a point where Michael's wife, Kay, has moved further away from him and where a question from his son about joining his business has frightening and ironic connotations, the slow movement back to the original family of mother, father, and child presents an irresistible comparison of cold and complicated present to warm and simple past. But the past, of course, is warm and simple in our fantasy only.

Each of the flashback sequences, no matter how simply it may begin, shows an advancement in Vito's life of crime and rise to power, which climaxes in his brutal killing of Fanucci. The flashback in which this event occurs is the most crucial in the film, a pivotal narrative moment for the events of both *Godfather I* and *II*. It occurs after Michael's return from Cuba, his hopes for owning the island ruined by the Revolution. He comes to his Las Vegas office, the old dark wood and golden light of its interior setting it off from the banal, sun-baked world that surrounds it. Tom informs Michael that Kay has lost their baby, and Michael, in a fit of hysteria, demands to know if it was a boy (the old family obsessions, the need for a "masculine child," overcome any other feelings he might have). He puts a cigarette to his mouth and there is a dissolve to Vito, hand placed on his mouth, standing under the image of Michael that dissolves out. Vito is looking at his baby, Fredo, sick with pneumonia, being cupped. (Michael has just learned in Cuba that Fredo betrayed him, so this association with Fredo's weakness is particularly apt: the helpless conditions of the baby and of the adult are put into pathetic contrast.) As the flashback continues, we learn that the Black Hander, Fanucci, is seriously blackmailing Vito, who has been thieving. Fanucci threatens to call the police and hurt Vito's family. At dinner with young Tessio and Clemenza, Vito plans to take care of Fanucci. It is to be his first act of vengeance and of consolidation. He insists his friends remember the favor he is about to do for them, saying, in one of his first utterances in English, "I'll take care of everything." The scene parallels Michael's decision to kill Sollozzo and McCluskey, though Vito is softer, more congenial than Michael. The murder itself echoes the baptism sequence of *Godfather I*. It occurs during a street festival in Little Italy. A band plays "The Star-Spangled Banner." The statue of a saint, obscenely plastered with dollar bills, is carried along. Intercut with the religious procession is Vito setting his ambush. When Fanucci appears at his apartment door, Vito shoots him in the chest, in the face, in the mouth. The towel wrapped around his gun to silence it catches fire, matching the fireworks of the festivities outside. It is a brutal and flamboyant act, and its flamboyance tends to mask its brutality. But with it Coppola tries to undercut the nostalgia, to disrupt our wholehearted endorsement of the heavily overdetermined conventions of familial innocence and paternal strength. After the killing, Vito returns to his wife and children. They sit on a stoop outside their tenement. Behind them a guitar player sings. This image of simple domestic immigrant bliss is almost hilarious in comparison to what has gone before. Vito picks up baby Michael and tells him he loves him very much. The central dialectic structure of the film, the unquestioning love of family and the brutal power that this love is used to shroud, is made apparent.

On this domestic tableau there is a fade to black and a fade in to the snow of Michael's Tahoe fortress. He is alone, scrunched in the corner of his car. The interior of his home is dark; Kay, alone in a room sewing, is distanced from him and does not acknowledge his presence. Intruding into this coldness is a scene at a Senate hearing, where the complicated criminal structure of the family is being revealed. Back at his home, Michael goes to his mother, isolated, alone, sitting by a fire, a relic of the old family. He worries aloud about losing his family. He is motionless, his face almost completely dark. On the opposite side of the screen, Vito's face appears, brightly lit, animated, wearing a moustache; he is now gaining full control of the neighborhood, at the start of his life of power. The symmetry of these sequences is hair-raising, for it is clear that the comparison of Vito's loving innocence and Michael's cold corruption is more apparent than real, that Vito's innocence is a facade and Michael's coldness a protective mask. Father and son differ in style only, and in time; the way they act and the acts themselves are determined by the time

The rise of Vito Corleone: future owner of America, flamboyant murderer, family man.

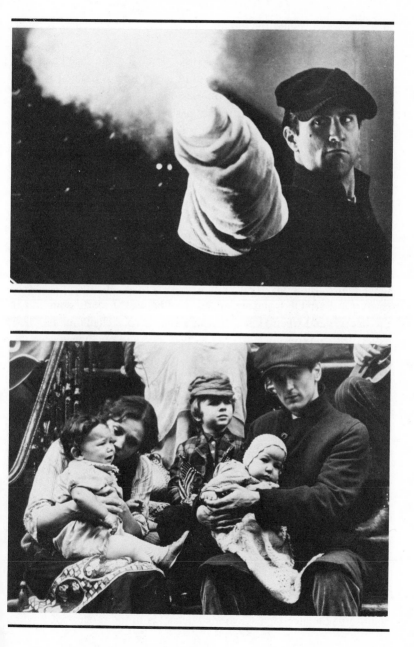

in which they live and the circumstances that surround them as much as by personality.

This is suggested in the contrast offered by the flashback that opens the film. Young Vito's arrival in New York is created with all the splendor of our nostalgic fantasies of the New World at the turn of the century. The camera tracks past rows of immigrants at Ellis Island in one of the most powerful re-creations of the past in recent film. Coppola has, in moving from the vicious confines of Sicily to the openness and vitality of Manhattan, allowed us to take the cliché of the "promised land" at full value. The shot that closes this first flashback, so often commented upon for its simple poignancy—little Vito, quarantined, sitting on a stool looking out the window and singing—contains a powerful dialectical force. Yes, the proto-Godfather, killer to be, is alone and showing great courage in his isolation. But the Statue of Liberty he looks out upon will soon be part of his domain and part of his cover ("I love America" are the first words spoken in Part One, and we recall the Statue of Liberty standing in the background when Don Corleone's treacherous chauffeur is killed. When Vito returns to Corleone to take revenge on Don Ciccio, he brings as a gift to his family a model of the Statue of Liberty). This image has a double meaning: little Vito the brave child, and little Vito the future proprietor of the American way.

The slow dissolve from this image to Michael's son, Anthony, receiving his Communion realizes the dialectic. The lonely foreigner has become the pampered bourgeois American child; the promise of power has become the aridity of power. The Communion and subsequent party play not only against the simplicity and courage in the flashback, but against the opening of *Godfather I* as well. The warm, closed, happy family wedding on Long Island in the forties has become the cold, open, tacky Communion party in Nevada in the late fifties. Earlier, the police were chased away; now they are served drinks in the parking lot. Michael has entered the modern world, assumed its trappings, its vulgarity, its lack of subtlety. But he tries, at the same time, to hold on to the old notions of the family. The loathsome Senator Geary, whom Michael is in the process of buying, tells him, "I despise your masquerade, the dishonest way you pose yourself—yourself and your whole fucking family." "Senator," responds Michael, "we're both part of the same hypocrisy, but never think it applies to my family." It is precisely this willful blindness that causes Michael's undoing. He insists that the "family" as it existed in Don Corleone's time is still alive. In fact it is only the myth, the abstract notion of that family, that exists, and its existence is only in Michael's head. It is so dead that it kills. In the name of the family and his loyalty to it, he kills his family.

In the scene with Geary, Michael and his attendants are shown, like his father in the beginning of Part One, within an inner sanctum, cut off from the outside. Like his father, Michael is behind his desk, against a window. The senator is in a corner, impotently toying with a paperweight in the shape of a cannon, pointing it at Michael. After the introduction of Frank Pentangeli, a family member from the old days—loud, abrupt, uncomprehending of Michael's new ways—and when we see Michael dealing with Johnny Ola, the representative of Hyman Roth, an arch-enemy whom Michael courts out of fear, pride, and greed, something unusual happens to the lighting and to the way Michael is treated visually. He begins to be swallowed by the dark. He retreats to a dark part of the room, and his face appears in half-light, as it will for most of the rest of the film. One of the first times the half-lighting on Michael's face is noticeable is after the baptism sequence in Part One when he fools Connie's husband into thinking he will not be killed. But the lighting effect is suggested at the very beginning of *Godfather I*. When Michael and Kay sit talking at the wedding, part of his face appears even then in shadow. The very first shot of Part Two shows Michael looking away, refusing to reveal his whole face. All through the narrative of the *Godfather*s, Michael emerges as a half-hidden figure, dissembling, obsessed. In Part Two he seems to disappear before our eyes. A man without a conscience, whose past exists in ritual without substance, and whose future seems to consist mainly of killing off opponents, he does not appear fully present before us. Michael is trapped between the myth of the past and his present actions; Michael exists as a perpetual threat to everyone around him; we never know him fully. His half-lit face is a continual reminder of these contradictions, indicating a character lost to himself and to us.*

At the beginning of Part One, we were invited into the dark inner world of the family and shown that within the darkness existed a warm golden world of security. That security proved tenuous, for throughout the film the golden light often augured violence against the family. The golden light is present within Michael's sanctum in Part Two, but here it offers only threat and no security (an assassination attempt is made on Michael in his own bedroom, an event unthinkable in the earlier film). The lighting on Michael presents a man half in the dark of the mysteries of his own life, its plots and counterplots, its scheming and betrayals, and half in a light that is itself a mocking reminder of a past whose security was illusory but which at least offered the hope of love and care. Michael wants to keep that security, but with the love and care replaced by brute authority and within a world different from his father's. For where Vito Corleone was a cottage industry, Michael is a multi-national corporation, and in building his vertical holdings he has had to divest himself of his family and of any possibility of trust.

In this sense, *Godfather II* is much closer to the conventional gangster film than was Part One. Michael's rise, like that of his filmic forebears, is inexorable and brutal, and it forces him to thrust away everyone around him. The rise of Vito Corleone may also have been brutal, but it is presented as not exactly inexorable and as having depended on his surrounding himself with friends and family. Michael moves toward a wretched aloneness, an aloneness which even the precipitous return of his sister Connie near the end of Part Two and

---

* An interesting bit of counterpoint occurs in one of the flashbacks discussed earlier. Just before Vito kills Fanucci, he meets with him in a café. In that scene, Vito is seen in half-light, almost as a signal of the threat he will become to anyone who goes against his will.

---

Michael (Al Pacino) in **Godfather II**, a half-hidden figure, dissembling, obsessed.

her affirmation of his strength as leader of the family, cannot change. Her return, in fact, is reminiscent of the end of Howard Hawks's *Scarface* (1932), when Tony Camonte's sister joins him in his bullet-proof fortress, declaring her love and devotion, only to have the police shatter everything: her, Camonte's pride and bravura, and his life. Connie's hysterical assumption of the role of family mother only points up her parody of the old family life and the empty power that is the fruit of Michael's aggression.

Of course, Michael does not die. Unlike his gangster ancestors he continues a life of power and ruthlessness. He destroys all his enemies, including his own brother, and is left entirely alone: no friends, no family, only the memories and distorted fantasies of the past (the flashbacks constitute both an objective commentary on present and past and a subjective reflection of Michael's wish-fulfilling fantasies, the content of the familial myth he carries with him). *Godfather II* then becomes a study of isolation, of the way power punishes those who acquire it, especially if the past is denied or used as an excuse to wield power without feeling. Michael almost seems to understand this, though his understanding falls just short of a tragic sense. We are made to understand the moral implications of Michael's aggression; he does not. We may decide that Michael has been punished for his ruthlessness by losing first his soul and then his wife and friends; Michael sees what happens to him only as punishment for being too strong, for trying too hard to remain faithful to the idea of a family created by his father.

It is at this point that contradictions inherent in the two films begin most clearly to manifest themselves. If we indulge in an analysis of the motives and feelings of the characters, we can easily turn the film (and our reactions to it) into melodrama, a form Coppola seems to want to avoid. In *Godfather I* he allows us to experience a certain awe of Don Corleone and his world and a temptation to be part of it; but we are never permitted "identification" with the characters or even a precise understanding of their emotions. Neither is there a manipulation of our emotions into the standard melodramatic curve of sympathy, sadness, and triumph. Or if there is, if we find

ourselves moved by the deaths of Sonny and Don Corleone and triumphant over Michael's revenge on the family's enemies, then we
are trapped in the very moral dilemma that destroys Michael in *Godfather II*. It is a trap Coppola sets and continues to bait in the flashbacks of Part Two, which do tend toward the melodramatic, furnishing
us with images to nurture our myths of the immigrant freely en-
terprising his way to power and fortune, supported by good friends,
a silent but strong wife, and a self-sufficiency that makes all opposition either fall to its knees or—only when necessary—die.*

We must ask whether the nostalgic grace of the flashback sequences, as well as the familial warmth and protection offered in
Part One, is canceled by the events of Part Two, betrayed by them,
or set up as a lost dream, a fantasy of something that never could
have existed. Do past and present exist in a balanced status of equal
worth and validity, each inevitably part of the other, a result of the
other? Has Coppola created not a linear structure, an epic of domestic
and criminal progress and decline, but, as John Hess suggests, a synchronic mythos of the squalid American dream? That is, do all the
parts, taken together, present a lesson about the inevitable corruption and murderousness inherent in capitalist acquisition and exploitation? The triumph of Vito Corleone is structured with our profoundest conservative themes. "Not since Andy Hardy," writes David
Thomson of *Godfather I* (and, by extension, the flashbacks of Part
Two), "had an American film shown such unshadowed love between
father and sons. All the treachery and bloodletting is devoted to one
object—reputedly close to the hearts of our silent majority—the defense of the old order, business stability, domestic virtues, and the
hope for decency."[15] But on the other side, the moral decline of Michael Corleone seems to be structured with some of our more recent

---

* Coppola seems to perceive the melodrama and at one point makes fun of it.
Vito first sees Fanucci at a vaudeville show in Little Italy, in which we see a
melodrama full of preposterous gesturings, rendings of the heart, and singing.
Backstage, Vito sees Fanucci threaten the actress who was in the play with a
knife and demand money from her father, with gestures similar to those in the
vaudeville act on stage.

revelations of the loathsomeness of the American legal and economic system, revelations which we have quietly assented to. "Michael, as 'America,' " writes Hess,

> embodies a basic contradiction in capitalism between the luminous bourgeois ideals of peace, freedom, opportunity, love, and community and the harsh, brutal realities of the irrational economic system which encourages these ideals and feeds off their unobtainability. . . . The film does not compare a success with a failure [Vito with Michael], but shows how the success leads directly and inevitably to the failure. The seeds of Michael's destruction lie in Vito's social and economic success, his rise to power.[16]

The points of view are in such opposition that it seems impossible to reach a compromise. The two films celebrate the myth of the family; they expose that myth as a mystification of power and ruthlessness. The two films comfort us with images of security and domestic order; they reveal to us the horrors that must be committed to keep up a semblance of security and order. Vito Corleone's life can be seen as made up of actions necessary to protect himself and his family. It can also be seen as a life of killing and manipulating those with less power, of raising and creating a family by murder and victimization, a "family" who in turn become killers, victimizers, and victims. Vito's "business" is threat, the exchange of favors, and the garnering of power. The religious protection that guides the family can be seen as a shield and a fraud: the baptism that covers Michael's slaughter of his enemies, the saint plastered with bills that is carried through the procession that covers Vito's murder of Fanucci indicate that rituals can be used, just as the myth of the family is used, to hide corruption. Finally, Michael himself, who believes in the church, in the family, in free enterprise, *and* in murder, power, and revenge, succumbs to his own acceptance of hypocrisy and his attempt to deny that hypocrisy at the same time. The figure of Michael seated in the chair at the end of *Godfather II,* enveloped in darkness, holding his face with his hands, is the figure of a man of power trapped by that power, trapped by the ways to that power, trapped by the confusions and contradictions of an ideology that holds up power as the best goal

190

of all free men (anyone can grow up to be president or a millionaire). It warns us that attaining power is a dangerous, lonely occupation.

But with that warning we need to pause, for we are suddenly confronted not with a political insight into the way capitalism destroys the soul, but with a much more conventional way of explaining our reaction to Michael. Although he does not die at the end of the film, like the conventional movie gangster, he does suffer a death of the spirit; he does, in some way, seem to suffer for his sins and elicit our pity. He seems to manifest the condition of all movie gangsters. Robert Warshow writes:

> . . . the gangster is doomed because he is under the obligation to succeed, not because the means he employs are unlawful. In the deeper layers of the modern consciousness, *all* means are unlawful, every attempt to succeed is an act of aggression, leaving one alone and guilty and defenseless among enemies: one is *punished* for success. This is our intolerable dilemma: that failure is a kind of death and success is evil and dangerous, is—ultimately—impossible.[17]

This statement defines a phenomenon deeply embedded in all of our cinema and which constitutes one of its profoundest lies. It is the idea that the rich and the powerful *must* somehow be guilty, unhappy, and lonely. Stated in its most clichéd form: "money and power can't buy happiness." Indeed, money and power almost guarantee unhappiness. Only the screwball comedies of the thirties responded to this with the notion that the rich could in fact be free and happy people. Otherwise, whether gangsters, businessmen, tycoons, those with wealth and power almost inevitably suffer, and we are (presumably) convinced that it is better not to be rich and powerful, for what such people lose in achieving their status is not worth losing. It is possible to read *Godfather II* in this simple light, as a narrative of personal failing rather than political reality. Don Corleone retained his happiness and his security because he did not overreach; he remained content with a moderate exercise of controlled power.[18] Michael loses his humanity because he is too arrogant, wants too much, forgets his friends and his family. He is concerned only with power in an abstract and total way. His punishment is his empty aloneness. He is a modern-day Charles Foster Kane.

Certainly Coppola at least questions these mundane equations of power and unhappiness. But we must see that he also uses them as way out of confronting more difficult problems. We may finally need to be satisfied with the small probings into matters of family integrity, bourgeois respectability, and political power that he undertakes and understand that these films are simply in no position openly to condemn the very economic system that made them possible. They may go a bit further in their analysis than other films in exposing the brutality and limitations of capitalism; but they hedge by allowing us simple responses to familiar categories.*

In this obscured light, even the Cuban episode of *Godfather II* is compromised. It could stand as one of the most hopeful moments of political insight in American film and the one clear expression of an alternative to the Corleone myth. Michael and Hyman Roth join with other corporate heads to buy the island and carve it up, literally, as Roth's birthday cake with its Cuban island icing is passed around to be consumed. But it is in Cuba that Michael is presented with the only threat to his power that he cannot overcome. The rebels are moving in. Michael is appropriately upset when he sees a guerrilla blow up himself and a policeman, destroy himself for a cause rather than for a payment. When the guerrillas take Havana, Michael is without recourse. He leaves, isolated in his car, the inhabitants of the city in their new freedom banging on its roof. This is the only time in both films that we have seen an unowned outside world in any detail, and, when we do see it, it moves with a strength and a power that the Corleones, the politicians in their pockets, and the ideology they all represent cannot resist or control. But there is nothing to prevent another reading of this episode. If an American audience is entrenched in the belief that the Cuban revolution was an evil event, and if an audience is convinced that, for all his mistakes, Michael is still a

---

* Coppola is no stranger to the double point of view. His screenplay for *Patton* is equally accessible to a sensibility that loathes the military and to one that admires and supports it.

figure of some nobility, even of pathos, then it is quite possible to see the episode not in political and social terms but as part of Michael's personal downfall, the concatenation of events partly of his own making, partly resulting from situations outside his control, that make him a sad, lonely rich man.

The *Godfather* films incorporate sentiment, fantasies of protection and vengeance, elements of *Bildungsroman,* family melodrama, and a suitable moral of the immorality and loneliness of power. At the same time they attempt to suggest a critical inversion of these themes, giving us the space to observe how the family and the accretion of power are deeply embedded, mutually destructive operations of our social, economic, and political life. We can therefore pull back and offer three possible judgments of the films: we can dismiss them as being ideologically in complete confusion; we can dismiss them as pandering to whomever wishes to read them in a certain way; or we can accept them as the only way, at the moment, insightful narratives about the contradictions of American culture can be made in American film and be successful. Coppola is quite possibly the great sleight-of-hand artist in American film of the seventies—and the great subversive.

What we cannot dismiss is his narrative power and his ability to weave the perceptions of his audience into and out of the film he creates. His control of the spectator's gaze, the precision with which he directs that gaze—even if it is in two directions at once—are considerable. And he is aware of this; aware, too, of the way perception can yield confusing information. The *Godfather*s are very much films that mean what a particular sensibility wants them to mean: glorification of the family; excoriation of American capitalism; melodrama of the loneliness of power. As if in response to the moral questions posed by such seemingly contradictory significations, Coppola makes, between *Godfather I* and *II* (almost in anticipation of the dilemma presented by the second part of his great narrative), a film that examines the phenomena of seeing, listening, and interpreting, of accepting or rejecting what is seen and heard, and of the morality of being either a passive or an active observer.

*The Conversation* is remarkably different in style and tone from the two monuments that surround it. Its images have none of their richness of color or texture: the black, browns, and golds are replaced by blues and grays; the lavish and detailed interiors replaced by spare, functional rooms and offices. There are few characters, and all are dominated by Gene Hackman's Harry Caul, a surveillance expert and a man so withdrawn and recessive, so expressionless and motionless, that he appears to create a stillness about him wherever he is. *The Conversation* is a still film, an introspective work about an individual, quite unlike any of the characters in the *Godfather*s, who attempts and fails to come to terms with what he sees and hears.

In the two *Godfather*s, our point of view and our relationship to the world of the films are large and encompassing. We are allowed a proximity to the characters that is enticing and provocative: we feel ourselves a part of their space. We are not, of course. Coppola insists we keep a certain objectivity; he presents a world we wish we could join, but may not. In *The Conversation,* he does everything to keep us away. The camera acts as a barrier between us and the events and the central character, refusing to reveal what we want to see or think we ought to see, revealing instead only the phenomenon and problems of observing. The slow, inviting, reverse track that pulls us into the heart of the family at the beginning of *Godfather I* becomes a long, slow zoom down from the sky, at an angle of almost ninety degrees to the ground, revealing a mime and a group of people walking around a city square. An inexplicable shot, from an inexplicable angle, with inexplicable, distorted sounds. It is a shot that seems to reveal something to us, but never does, for this is a film in which nothing is revealed, save for the frightened soul of an individual who traps himself by his own blindness and fear.

In the middle of the film, there is a party. It is given by Harry in his office (an office between metal cage partitions, tucked in the corner of a huge, empty expanse of warehouse) for his associates, who are attending a surveillance convention. It is a party at which he will be betrayed by his would-be partner Moran (Alan Garfield) and by the woman to whom he offers a rare expression of his feelings. At one point Harry is caught by the camera, alone, standing over his work desk, staring and blowing at a tag dangling from the ceiling. The tag reads "Turn Lights Off," but what it says has no real significance. Rather, the act of staring, the lonely fix Harry takes on an inanimate, unrevealing, mute object, and his ability to isolate himself with it in the midst of other people reveals a great deal not only about his character but about the essential nature of cinematic looking that Coppola is examining. Harry cuts himself off from his boisterous and boorish friends; but he is being observed, by us. Harry attempts to remain inviolate throughout the film; yet he is always observed. He is observed by us and by those he works for. And as he is observed, innocent of our gaze, so he observes two people innocent of his.

Earlier in the film, after he has bugged a couple in the park, Harry goes to his apartment. We see his room in a far shot. On the back wall are a long, vertical radiator and a chair. Everything is bright, barren, and colorless. With a static gaze, we see Harry leave the frame, walk into another room, return, move right and behind a partition and come back with a telephone. He leaves the frame again, this time going out to the left. The camera remains on the empty room for a moment, and then, almost as a second thought, pans left to pick up Harry sitting on his couch, against a window, speaking to his landlady on the phone. It is his birthday, and she has left a bottle of wine for him; he is beside himself that someone other than himself has access to his apartment. "I have nothing personal, except my keys," he tells her. During this conversation, he again gets up and leaves the frame—the camera remaining motionless—and then returns to the couch, where he continues his conversation and gets undressed. As we observe all of this, in one long shot, something else catches our attention. Behind Harry, out the window, something is moving: formless, silent, but *there* (on closer examination it turns out to be a construction crane, though identifying it in no way reduces its troubling presence). This sequence is again concerned with observation, with looking. Who is the author of the gaze? From whose point of view are we observing the privacy of this private man who invades others' privacy? Why is the gaze so distant and so offhand, allowing its object to disappear from sight? Why does the shot, more than anything else, seem to emphasize its own presence and the presence of the room, of Harry in it or out of it, the object moving unnoticed by him outside his window, the presence of the act of observation itself?

Of course, it is the function of film to look at people who are in the act of creating fictitious characters in a fictitious world and who are not meant to be conscious of the fact that they are being observed. In theater, the actors play to the house; in film, the "house," the audience, does not exist at the moment of creation for the actors, and, as I noted earlier, they may not even acknowledge the future presence of such an audience by looking at the camera. The gaze of actors in the space invented by a film is inward, to that space, and is surrounded by it. That space is, in conventional film narratives, closed, constituting a finished world which at the same time is open to us. If, as Dayan and Oudart say, the function of conventional film narrative is to "suture" itself, to seal any uncomfortable openings in its completeness, it also is at all times ruptured by our view. We are the buggers of the film fiction, which is made for our gaze, but pretends ignorance of it. Coppola plays with this contradiction and makes the study of the act of observation the subject of the film and of our viewing of the film. When we observe Harry in his moments of assumed privacy, we do to him what he does to others and what he never wants done to himself. But then we also do what is *expected* to be done to a character in a film. We invade his world with our gaze. The result is a simultaneously twice-viewed film: we are involved in the life of a fictional surveillance man and in our surveillance of the fiction.

Unlike Hitchcock, who morally implicates the audience in its voyeuristic role (*Rear Window* makes an interesting parallel to *The Conversation*), Coppola only alludes to our situation within and without the fiction. His particular moral scrutiny is focused upon Harry Caul's attempts to make himself invisible, unseen, protected by a mantle of grayness and quiet, so unobtrusive as to be non-existent, while he works at bringing into public existence the private worlds of other people. The result is that he creates for himself a dilemma and a trap. The more he tries to withdraw, the more he is seen by us, by someone else; and the more he attempts to look into the privacy of the couple he bugs, the more he traps himself in his guilt and his vulnerability. The couple in the park, who may or may not be planning murder, are the least important element in the film. How Harry interprets his information and how that interpretation opens him to observation and allows his own guilt to destroy him are the primary concerns. That is why there is no clarification as to who the couple are, what their relationship is to the "Director," the nameless character played by Robert Duvall who hires Harry to bug them, or the exact nature of the crime possibly planned, probably committed. For as much as we are cold observers of Harry, we also are made to share his perceptions—his aberrations, more appropriately. The film becomes a complex of first- and third-person perspectives.

We see Harry, and we see with Harry. Our surveillance of him in his room is also a sharing with him of a barren, frightened life. The discomfort we experience when we see the moving object outside the window foreshadows Harry's own discomfort when he discovers the people he works for are observing him. Harry's furtiveness and obsessiveness, the way he picks up a scrap of paper from the walk in front of his girl friend's house, the deliberate and delicate way he builds a full conversation out of the scrambled tapes and begins, finally, talking to the voices, anticipating them, convincing himself that murder is in the works, every bit of this character's self-destroying behavior is observed by us in two ways: distantly, as if through the eye of a surveillance camera, and subjectively, almost sharing Harry's fear and guilt. When Harry goes to confession, the priest's face on the other side of the screen looms dark and menacing: not an agent to cleanse the soul, merely another eavesdropper. When Harry calls from a phone booth, the blues and greens of the image are slashed by red neon, suggesting his vulnerability and a foreboding danger. Almost every shot in the film is carefully structured to create in us a sense of discomfort as well as a sense of being both with and beyond Harry in the knowledge of his failure to keep himself inviolable.

In some of its methods and objectives, *The Conversation* parallels Antonioni's *Blow Up*. But Antonioni is not as concerned with developing a moral focus through his photographer as he is in managing a perceptual gamesmanship in which the cinematic-photographic image of the world becomes a locus of existential dread. Coppola, much more in the tradition of American film, attempts to locate an individual *angst,* a localized suffering which, in this instance, may reflect a larger cultural situation. The appearance of the film at the climax of Watergate, as we were discovering that surveillance had become a governmental preoccupation, makes the complexity of its point of view all the more unnerving. Coppola could easily have presented a wholesale condemnation of his bugger; but in choosing to force us both to observe and to share Harry's anxieties, he implicates us in the act of surveillance and its consequences. It is easy for us to dismiss Harry's rival Moran (the guy who told Chrysler that Cadillac was getting rid of its fins; the guy whose surveillance was responsible for throwing an election) as a crude buffoon. It is impossible to dismiss Harry, whose protestations of moral uninvolvement in his work, whose guilt, and moral destruction do not allow us to withdraw judgment or remain ourselves unscathed. Coppola's refusal to cite Harry as an agent of evil and his refusal at the same time to allow us a subjective understanding of him denies us both pathos and outrage. We are, instead, urged to understand the destructiveness of the act of surveillance for all concerned.

Antonioni's photographer is lost in his perceptual puzzle; Harry Caul is trapped by his. In re-creating a conversation, he creates a murder plot (once before, we are told, murder had resulted from Harry's eavesdropping). He obsessively works and reworks his tapes, and as he does, we obsessively hear and see the couple he has taped, their intentions presumably becoming clearer the more their conversation is heard. He is like a filmmaker, putting together bits and pieces to make a whole. But what he puts together is the wrong movie. At one point he has a dream in which he "sees" the events he thinks he has uncovered—the Director is planning to kill the couple, or at least the woman (Cindy Williams) involved. His guilt over this imagined uncovering of the plot, his betrayal at the hands of the people who hired him to record the couple (they pursue him, set him up, and steal his tapes) force him to continue his eavesdropping in an attempt to clarify for himself what is going to happen. As he continues, he is encircled by his own fear and guilt, reduced finally to groveling beneath a toilet bowl in order to penetrate the secret with his electronic instruments. It is a squalid, humiliating image, this man forced by his obsessiveness to squat beneath a toilet and then to hide like a child beneath the blankets of the hotel-room bed when he hears the noise of murder and sees through a window the violent action in the next room. When he awakens from his almost catatonic state to examine that room, he finds it clean, its bathroom sparkling, the way Norman Bates made his bathroom sparkle after the shower murder in *Psycho* (the allusion is quite conscious). But its toilet bowl vomits blood and bloody rags over Harry. His debasement and his confusion are complete. What did he see and hear? The couple presumably murdered the Director, who originally purchased Harry's services. At least that is what Harry seems to see and hear in the hotel room. In a wretchedly confused attempt to put together the pieces in his mind, he fantasizes the murder of the Director, but the pieces are out of order. He hears and sees, in memory, the bugged conversation, and the words that originally prompted him to suspect that a murder would occur take on a new emphasis: "He'd kill *us* if he had the chance . . ." He thinks he has it right; he thinks he knows what happened; he can do nothing about it.

Coppola has been criticized for confusing the story of the murder.[19] But this misses the point entirely. He is uninterested in it. What may or may not have "happened" is important only in terms of Harry's perception of it, the way he thinks he has reconstructed it, and what happens to him as a result. For if Harry's perception determines the events as he experiences them, then he is in turn determined by them. It is the joke and the bitterness of the film that it does not permit the personal anguish of its central character to answer the

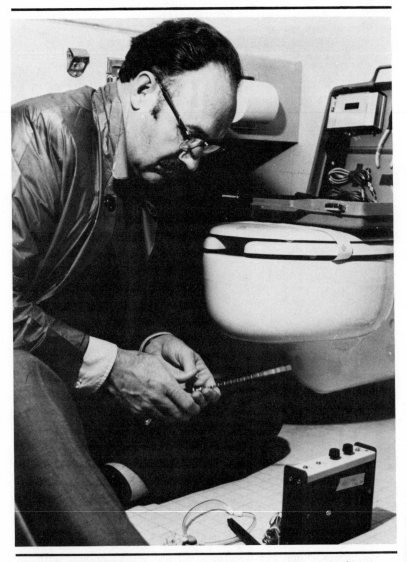

Harry Caul (Gene Hackman) forced by his obsessiveness and guilt to work beneath a toilet bowl in **The Conversation.**

questions the film raises (a risk run by *Godfather II*). We may not satisfy ourselves by attaching our emotions to a miserable, suffering character. Harry is subdued by his guilt and then by the very act, the very way of life, that created that guilt. The man who attempted to erase his personality now has that personality open to the eyes of a greater, more omnipotent surveillant, one not troubled by anxieties.

After he makes his "discovery" about the murder, he is called by the Director's office, called on the phone whose number no one is meant to have, and told that he is being observed. It is the final exposure of Harry's vulnerability. When he rips apart his apartment to discover how he is being bugged, the action is, at first, almost funny (we return, for a moment, to that far shot of the back wall of the apartment that we had seen earlier, and suddenly Harry comes stalking in with a machine that looks like a minesweeper, which is held against the wall to detect a bug). But as he obsessively tears apart each object in the apartment, first purposively, then indiscriminately, the activity becomes terrifying, climaxing in his ripping apart his rubber statue of the Virgin—violating his sacred object and himself. In this crescendo of destruction, as the camera pans the torn walls and floors, Coppola suddenly inserts one last flashback to the couple in the park. It is a tender moment, as the girl removes something from the man's eye, an act that seems to negate the violence that proceeded from their conversation and from Harry's discovery of it. This insert is followed by a high shot of Harry's apartment. It is torn to bits and Harry sits in a corner playing his saxophone. The situation is reminiscent of another Harry played by Gene Hackman, Harry Moseby in Penn's *Night Moves,* whom we last see from a high angle in the ocean, lying wounded in a boat that circles hopelessly around and around. Both Harrys are undone by the complexity of events that they attempt and fail to subdue. Both are impotent in the face of these events; both are themselves subdued and alone.

There is a major difference. The final observation of Harry Moseby in Penn's film is from a position of conventional superiority/diminution. The camera looks down at a lost soul, removing us from him, allowing us a feeling for his situation, but an escape as well. At first glance, this is also what the camera appears to be doing at the end of *The Conversation*. But there is something more: the camera pans from its superior position left across the rubble to Harry, moving almost past him; it then returns right, past Harry, back to the rubble of the apartment; then it begins once more to move left. It is observing the scene as would a surveillance camera. We have seen this before, in the sequence in Harry's apartment when he calls his landlady. And we recall the opening shot of the film, the long, slow zoom into the park where Harry originally records the conversation. The shot begins from a very high position and quietly but purposively enters the action, like a disengaged observer removed but present.[20] We are left in a position similar to those we have been forced to take throughout the film: observing, intruding, observing our intruding, removed and engaged at the same time. But this last shot, more than the others, also indicates powerlessness—not only Harry's, but our own.

To conclude from this that Coppola is telling us we are all being watched and are powerless to control it is possible, but it would be reductive. It would put *The Conversation* on the level of those paranoia films—*Three Days of the Condor, The Parallax View, The Domino Principle,* among others—that so matter-of-factly assume our impotence in the face of nameless governmental or corporate powers that they paradoxically relieve our fears by reinforcing them.* Coppola attempts to avoid the glibness of these films and instead to explore the very real terrors of the spirit that the phenomenon of surveillance can create. By dealing with a character who is a failure at hiding from himself the meaning of his work, and who by his work exposes himself to the prying he wants to avoid, Coppola is getting

---

* Gene Hackman plays a man set upon by complex, unknowable, and uncontrollable manipulators of power in Stanley Kramer's *The Domino Principle.* He seems well suited to roles of strong but ultimately undone figures, characters who struggle with their own powerful personalities and are diminished by personalities even more powerful than they. Compare the roles he plays in the films mentioned here with others, like *The French Connection,* particularly the second part, directed by John Frankenheimer, and even Jerry Schatzberg's *Scarecrow.*

at the fragility of the politics of surveillance through the fragility of his character. *The Conversation* is a political film; it speaks to myths of power, to our desires to control and our fears of being controlled. Unlike the *Godfathers*, it does not attempt to seduce us into the security power seems to offer; it does not comfort us with memories of a golden time when power and security might have been innocent; it does not caution us that power held without emotion will lead to a sterile unhappiness. It merely makes us observe that power destroys, that the attempt to achieve domination is an endless attempt that traps both the victim and the agent who wishes to control the victim. Harry Caul is a passive aggressor. He wishes to hold power furtively, negatively, by invisibly intruding upon people. He was once responsible for murder because of the work he did, and he is incapable of stopping another murder because of his anxieties over the work he does. He is almost like a Kubrick character with a conscience, unable to do anything about himself or his circumstances, and suffering because of it. He manipulates and is manipulated and comes up powerless and alone.

If Harry Caul is unlike the Corleones because he has no past to support him, he is like Michael because he has no future. If Michael is trapped in an empty past, Harry is trapped in a desolate present, a proper, Catholic—almost Dantesque—hell, where the sinner suffers eternally his own sins. (Harry, like Michael and Vito Corleone, uses the church to protect his own bad conscience; but it becomes an ironic protection. *The Conversation,* like the central portion of *Godfather I,* takes place at Christmas, and in both films the characters take no cognizance of, nor joy from, the season.) Like *Godfather I* and *II, The Conversation* is an essentially joyless work (though, like the two films which surround it, full of energy and a creative joy in its form and in the performances of its players). All three of the films address themselves to the impossibility of discovering security, of keeping affection, and of successfully promoting and maintaining the self in the world. Like the films of Penn and Kubrick, they persist in depicting a grim and violent life in which individuals are or become isolated, without human support or community, in a state of perpetual antagonism with their surroundings. The *Godfather*s, on their lowest level, play to fantasies of selfishness (which is an accurate reduction of the concept of family and the perpetuation of its rituals), revenge, and brute power, and they go forward to suggest how this selfishness results in isolation. *The Conversation* offers no comfortable fantasies. In the modernist tradition, it forces us to look down "on a scene of bondage, frustration, or absurdity."[21] The human being as prisoner seems to be a major image in contemporary Western art, the rueful dialectic to the romantic myth of the transcendent spirit.

Transcendence, in American film, has appeared as romantic melodrama or the bloody explosions of violence. In either case death seems the finest expression of the freed spirit, so that anyone who survives, at least in contemporary American film, is usually crippled, restrained, or diminished. Consider this montage of dissolves: the last image of *Godfather II,* Michael, alone, face in hand, peering into the darkness of his own bad conscience and memory; the impassive faces at the end of *Barry Lyndon,* as checks and accounts are passed from hand to hand; the imprisoned fetus adrift in the universe at the end of *2001;* the quiet survey of Harry Caul, trapped in the corner of a demolished room, playing a saxophone like a frightened child sucking a pacifier (like the young Vito Corleone singing in his Ellis Island quarantine, but, unlike Vito, without a future); the wounded Harry Moseby circling on a path of ocean at the end of *Night Moves;* the figure of Thornton, under the vultures, hunched against the wall of the blood-drenched Mexican fortress near the end of *The Wild Bunch;* Travis Bickle, locked in his cab, traveling down hallucinatory streets at the end of *Taxi Driver;* Jimmy Doyle, walking down an empty, rainy street at the end of *New York, New York;* McCabe dying alone in the snow while Mrs. Miller lies alone in an opium stupor. Separate from their individual narratives, we would still understand their meaning, for images of loneliness and helplessness are deeply impacted within our ideological apparatus. Their opposite, images of community, of hopeful struggle, are reduced to sentimental structures, low comedy, or the vigilante blowing to pieces his own or his community's individual enemies. Some recent films, like John

Avildson's and Sylvester Stallone's *Rocky* (1976) and Jonathan Demme's *Citizen's Band* (1977), place their notions of triumph on grounds so limited and circumscribed that they fall into dismissible structures of wish-fulfillment fantasy on the one hand or the small-town neighborliness that has been a movie myth for decades, on the other. Even the thoughtful comedy of Woody Allen depends on the creation of a persona essentially lost, out of touch, able to exercise power only in fantasies.

Coppola's success in fashioning complex and detailed narratives out of the contemporary images of loneliness must be admired, but it must be placed in the context of our contemporary image of ourselves as essentially impotent and removed from power. *Godfather I* and *II* in particular act to confirm this ideology of "dreadful nihilism," to use David Thomson's phrase. These films constitute a "model for a public placid about its own powerlessness to resist authorities." "To admire the Corleones . . . ," he writes, "is part of our cultural breakdown, and a symptom of our longing for some domineering conspiracy. It is a movie for those who prefer to live in darkness."[22] If, as is so often repeated, film can only reflect its audience, Coppola, and most of the filmmakers in this book, are doing the job well. Too well, perhaps, for their ingenuity at building their cinematic mirrors make us delight in rather than be appalled by the image we see.

# CHAPTER FOUR

# EXPRESSIONS
# OF THE STREETS

---

# Martin Scorsese

"I'm God's lonely man."

TRAVIS BICKLE

The careers of Martin Scorsese and Francis Ford Coppola have interesting parallels and more interesting divergences. They are both young. They are both, obviously, Italian. But Coppola is from a midwestern middle-class and Scorsese a New York working-class family. Both went to film school, Coppola to UCLA and Scorsese to New York University. Both did an apprenticeship at American International Pictures for Roger Corman, though Coppola did this early in his career, before he had established his own style and approach to filmmaking, while Scorsese had already made a feature of his own, *Who's That Knocking at My Door?* (1969), which, along with his student films, provided a foundation for the style that he would further develop in *Mean Streets* (1973). *Dementia 13* was, for Coppola, a learning exercise, the first move in a ten-year period of writing screenplays and making films before he established himself directorially and financially with *Godfather I. Who's That Knocking?* established Scorsese's direction straight off, though it did not situate him within the Hollywood production system. *Boxcar Bertha* (1972) was a Corman excursion. It gave Scorsese the opportunity to make use of greater technical resources than had been available to him on his first feature and to begin working through the formal concerns of camera movement and the contextual concerns of violence that have occupied him throughout his career.

That career has not been marked by the overwhelming success of Coppola's. *Alice Doesn't Live Here Anymore* (1974) and *Taxi Driver* (1976) did well, but were not blockbusters. *New York, New York* (1977) was, in terms of the kind of profit distributors like to see, a failure. Scorsese has therefore been able to keep himself from the trap in which Coppola and other young filmmakers (such as Lucas, Spielberg, and Friedkin) have caught themselves, of having to compete against themselves and each other not artistically but financially, by trying to make each successive film bigger in size and bigger in cost so that it can be bigger in financial returns. While Coppola has had to take on millions of dollars, his reputation, and the Pentagon to complete *Apocalypse Now,* Scorsese was able to follow the moderate financial failure of *New York, New York* with the moderate success of *The Last Waltz* (1978), a documentary of the rock group The Band.

There are, of course, important differences between the work of Coppola and Scorsese other than their economic situations. Coppola, in the *Godfather*s, establishes himself in the tradition of American narrative film, in which the viewer is carefully guided through a series of determined events, in sympathy with the central characters and with an assured emotional reaction. In *Godfather II* an attempt is made to implant within the narrative questions about that sympathy and to set up a dialectic that morally and politically alters our perception and understanding of events. But even the subversion that occurs in Part Two is integrated within the narrative so that, as I indicated, it is possible to react to it in melodramatic terms and to read the film merely as another caution on the excesses of power Coppola provides opportunities for the viewer to disengage from the narrative and observe its contradictions, but he does not force this disengagement. Scorsese, however, does not create narratives that are easily assimilable. The formal structure of his work is never completely at the service of the viewer or of the story it is creating. There is an unashamed self-consciousness in his work and a sense of kinetic energy that sometimes threatens to overtake both viewer and story, but always provides a commentary upon the viewer's experience and prevents him or her from easily slipping into a series of narrative events.

Scorsese does not have the stateliness of composition apparent in Coppola's work, nor the intellectual distance and rigor of Kubrick; he does not perform the radical experiments in cinematic space or indulge in the generic revisionism of Altman. He is, of the directors discussed here, closest to Arthur Penn, in the sense that, like Penn at his best, Scorsese is interested in the psychological manifestations of individuals who are representative either of a class or of a certain ideological grouping; he is concerned with their relationships to each other or to an antagonistic environment. Scorsese's films involve antagonism and struggle, and constant movement, even if that movement is within a tightly circumscribed area that has no exit. His work is like Penn's (and like that of most of the other filmmakers discussed here) in that there is no triumph for his characters. With the notable exception of *Alice Doesn't Live Here Anymore,* all of his characters lose to their isolation or their antagonism. Unlike Penn's his work shows a degree of stylization which eschews, for the most part, the sixties conventions of realism, defined primarily by location shooting and natural acting styles. In *New York, New York,* he moves indoors entirely, depending on studio sets to achieve an expressive artificiality. But even in the preceding films, where locations are used, there is a sense that the place inhabited by the characters is structured by their perceptions and by the way we see and understand their perceptions.

This brings us back to one of the central concerns of this study: the concern with point of view, with how and why a filmmaker allows us entry into the fiction he creates, and, once entered, with where we are permitted to stand and how we are permitted to observe. In Kubrick's work, there is always the sense that the entire *mise-en-scène* is commentary. It represents not a dwelling, a habitation, but what we must think or feel about that habitation. Kubrick does not so much construct places for his characters to live as he does an idea about how and why those characters live. Coppola encloses his characters in an environment expressive of their security, in *Godfather I* and the flashbacks of *Godfather II,* or their insecurity, as in the Michael episodes of *Godfather II* and throughout *The Conversation.* In the *Godfather* films he invites us to engage our fantasies of familial protection and our fantasies of power not so much with those of his characters as with the way those characters are situated within their world. In *The Conversation* we assume the role of uneasy observer parallel to the role assumed by the central character. Penn will often depict characters as emerging from or being formed by an environment that barely contains them: the Depression South in *Bonnie and Clyde* seems to call forth a rebellion against its barrenness; the dark, fragmented Chicago of *Mickey One* threatens its hero by echoing his state of mind.

Scorsese's *mise-en-scène* does something quite different. It is never accommodating; his characters do not have homes that reflect comfort or security. The places they inhabit are places of transition, of momentary situation. But these places are not Kubrick's abstract ideas of places. The Manhattan of *Taxi Driver,* the Little Italy of *Mean Streets,* even the Southwest of *Alice* are perfectly recognizable, almost too much so. The *mise-en-scène* of *Mean Streets* and *Taxi Driver* represent more than New York, a place of tough people, crowded streets, fights and whores. They represent, to borrow a notion of Roland Barthes', a New York-*ness,* a shared image of New York which has little to do with the city itself, but rather expresses what everyone, including many who live there, have decided New York should look like. At the same time—and this is where the difference with Kubrick occurs—the New York of *Mean Streets* and *Taxi Driver* is reflective of the energy of the characters, in the former, and of the anomie of Travis Bickle, in the latter, and these qualities are communicated to us by means of the ways we are made to see the *mise-en-scène.* Our own perceptions and preconceptions merge with the filmmaker's within the narrative and are then filtered through a third point of view, that of the character or characters created by the narrative, resulting in a rather complex perspective.

The complexity is heightened by the fact that, up until *New York, New York,* and beginning again in *The Last Waltz,* Scorsese's films create a tension between two opposing cinematic forms: the documentary and the fictional. The documentary aspect offers the possibility of a seemingly objective observation of characters, places, and events; the other demands a subjectivity of point of view which in Scorsese's work is so severe that the world becomes expressionistic, a reflection of a particular state of mind.*[1] Scorsese is close to Godard in understanding the arbitrary nature of these conventions, and he freely mixes them. There is the sense in most of his work of capturing a "reality" of places and events that might exist even without his presence. Until *Taxi Driver,* he employs the hand-held camera and the rapid, oblique editing which have become associated with a "documentary" and improvisational style. His actors (particularly Robert De Niro and Harvey Keitel) create their characters with an off-handedness and an immediacy that gives the impression of unpremeditated existence (as opposed to the carefully studied character-making obvious in the way Kubrick and Coppola direct their players). When these qualities are interwoven with the subjective impressions of the world communicated to us by the ways the characters see their environment and themselves, and when Scorsese modifies the location shooting we have come to take for granted in contemporary film with artificial sets and stylized lighting, a complex perceptual structure is created that demands careful examination.

Scorsese started his commercial career with a film strongly influenced by the New Wave. *Who's That Knocking at My Door?*—a finger exercise for *Mean Streets*—is inscribed in the hand-held, jump-cut, non-transitional style that many filmmakers took from the surface of the French films of the early sixties. Its *mise-en-scène* is partly neo-realist, partly documentary, mixed with the subjectivity of per-

* This is not a very original definition of documentary, and not a very thorough one either. The objective-subjective dichotomy in filmmaking has been a matter of controversy since film criticism began, and must be seen, finally, not as a dichotomy but as a dialectic.

ception and allusiveness that marks *Breathless* and *The Four Hundred Blows.*[2] *Who's That Knocking?* is an "experimental" film in all senses: formally, it begins trying out the camera strategies, the restless, foreboding movement, that will become one of Scorsese's major formal devices. Contextually, it prepares the way for *Mean Streets,* J. R. (Harvey Keitel) being an early version of Charlie in the later film—more of an oppressed Catholic than his later incarnation, less rooted in his environment, standing over and against New York rather than being enclosed within it as Charlie is.

Scorsese has not yet found in this early film a method of integrating the character with the space he occupies so that the two become reflections of each other. Nor has he yet discovered a way of incorporating his love of film, a love which manifests itself, as it does in the work of Godard, by references to film, within the narrative. Here the references stand out irrepressibly; the central character speaks Scorsese's obsession with his cinematic inheritance. J. R. and his girl friend (Zina Bethune) have a long discussion about westerns, John Wayne, and Ford's *The Searchers.* At a party, when a man shoots up a shelf of liquor bottles, there is a cut to a photograph of Wayne with a gun and a montage of stills from Hawks's *Rio Bravo.* This allusiveness will remain in Scorsese's later work, becoming more thoroughly woven into the pattern of his films, until in *New York, New York* a dialogue will occur not between characters, but between the film itself, other films, and our perception of and reaction to them.

*Who's That Knocking at My Door?* stands as a document of Scorsese's beginnings. Unlike Coppola's *Dementia 13,* and, perhaps, more like Kubrick's early films, it is less an impersonal generic exercise than an inquiry into the possibilities of subjective cinematic expression. But unlike Kubrick, and like Coppola, Scorsese needed the technical facility and formal restraints of commercial production to smooth out his approach. He never falls into the zero-degree style and simple generic repetitions that those restraints can cultivate, but, like other strong American filmmakers, uses them as a base to build upon, as a tradition to recognize and overcome. This base was provided by Roger Corman and American International Pictures.

*Boxcar Bertha,* a film totally different from *Who's That Knock-*

*ing?* and *Mean Streets,* still sets itself up as a link between them, if only by smoothing out the stylistic quirks apparent in the former and preparing for the consistent and assured approach of the latter. A violent film, situated in the seventies, late—*Bonnie and Clyde* mode of period evocation, it is a short, direct narrative which does little more than prepare for an enormous shoot-out at the end and a rather repulsive series of images in which David Carradine is nailed to the side of a freightcar which pulls out with the camera mounted on its top, looking down at the crucified body as a distraught Bertha (Barbara Hershey) runs after. The only inherent interest of the film is its mild pro-union, pro-left stand (the nominal subject is a radical union organizer of the railroads in the thirties). This is, I am certain, the work of its screenwriters, Joyce H. and John William Corrington, for it is a subject Scorsese otherwise shows no interest in. What Scorsese adds to the film is a further indication of his talent with the moving camera. Scattered throughout are shots in which the camera booms down upon a character or arcs around two people talking to each other, investing them with that sense of energy and tension that will be developed more fully in the films to follow. *Boxcar Bertha* is an important work not so much *by* Scorsese as *for* him; it permits him to work within the basic patterns of early-seventies film, its violence and its urgency, and to understand how those patterns can be worked together with the looser, more self-conscious and subjective elements of *Who's That Knocking?*

The integration occurs in *Mean Streets,* a film which can be seen as a "documentary" in the form of a carefully structured narrative fiction of four young men growing up on the fringes of society in New York's Little Italy, or as a subjective fiction of incomplete lives and sporadic violence in the form of a documentary of four young men in New York's Little Italy. I do not mean to be over-ingenious, but *Mean Streets* does keep altering its perspective on itself, combining what appears to be a spontaneous capturing of its characters' lives with carefully considered, formal arrangements of *mise-en-scène* and character point of view. It is not a confused or confusing alteration. On the contrary, Scorsese carefully integrates a double perspective in the film, a free-flowing observation and a carefully structured point of view of and from a central character. As opposed to the contained, highly structured lives of middle-class Italians developed by Coppola in a contained, highly structured narrative form, Scorsese investigates the almost incoherent street ramblings of disenfranchised men whose lives are defined by disorder, threatened by their own impulses, and, though confined by narrow geographical boundaries, paradoxically liberated by the turmoil of the bars, tenements, and streets that make up their confines. The central character of the film, Charlie (Harvey Keitel, who here and in *Who's That Knocking?* becomes a kind of alter ego for Scorsese, even sounding like him), is a further development of the character of J. R. in the earlier film. Less guilt-ridden than J. R., Charlie attempts to come to terms with his Catholicism, his future as a petty mafioso, and his odd, violent friend Johnny Boy. Johnny Boy (Robert De Niro, in the first of three films he made with Scorsese) is a saintly idiot, a character with no center, who destroys himself with his own inarticulate desire to be a free spirit.

But then none of the characters in the film, with the possible exception of Tony, the barkeeper, has the center or sense of direction that we have come to expect from characters in conventional film fictions, and it is the purpose of the film to observe them in their randomness and as part of an unpredictable flow of events. When we see Charlie on the streets, no matter how central he may be to the narrative moment, he is composed in the frame as one figure among many, standing off-center, next to a building, other people moving by him. Johnny Boy is continually "caught" in randomness. When we first see him (his name, like the names of the other characters who are introduced to us at the beginning, flashed on the screen, in imitation of the way David and Albert Maysles introduce the characters in their documentaries), he is at the end of a street. He pauses by a mailbox, throws something in it, runs up the street, looking back as the box explodes. In another sequence, he is up on a roof, shooting a gun at the Empire State Building uptown. Elsewhere he walks down the street, the camera rapidly tracking him from behind.

A kid bumps into him, and he proceeds to beat him up. Little violences, sporadic shootings, and fistfights punctuate the film as if they were parts of ongoing events, or as if they were moving toward some greater violence, which in fact they do. The end of the film is an explosion of gunfire and blood. The exasperated loan shark, Michael, pursues Johnny Boy, Charlie, and Charlie's girl friend, Teresa, in a car chase through rainy streets. Michael's henchman (played by Scorsese) shoots them up, horribly wounding Johnny Boy in the neck (as De Niro's Travis Bickle will be shot in the neck in *Taxi Driver*).

This random, violent flow of events is fed by the persistent uncertainty of Charlie's perception of them; his attempts to test his Catholicism; his attempts to justify his life: "You don't make up for your sins in church; you do it in the streets; you do it at home. The rest is bullshit, and you know it." These are the first words we hear in the film, and we hear them over a dark screen. At their conclusion, the first shot we see is movement: Charlie rising quickly from his bed (it is important for the rhythm to be established throughout the film that we do not see Charlie at rest and then observe him getting up, but cut into the movement that has already begun). A hand-held camera follows him to a mirror on the opposite wall; a crucifix is prominent behind him. A police siren is heard outside. Charlie goes back to bed, and as he lies down there are three rapid cuts, each one closer to his head. On the second cut, a loud rock song begins on the track. Without preparation or explanation, this carefully executed sequence creates the sense of nervous and purposeless energy that continues throughout. It creates too an immediate intensity and initial engagement, which is supplied by the kinetic closeup of Charlie's face. ". . . The simplest close-up is also the most moving," writes Godard; it can "make us anxious about things."[3] And a complex closeup, like that which opens *Mean Streets,* the intensity of which is magnified by our hearing its vocal component first, both voice and face unlocated temporally and spatially, forces our attention, makes us uneasy, and does not allow us to rest. A number of the films under discussion here—*Bonnie and Clyde, Godfather I, A Clockwork Orange*—use a similar method of entry: beginning on a closeup, without the conventional establishing shot. The face demands our attention; its lack of location makes us uncomfortable. The act of locating it, which is partially the job of the film, partially the job of our perception of the film, creates a tension between our expectations and desires to be comfortably situated within the narrative and, in the case of *Mean Streets,* the stubborn refusal of the narrative to meet those expectations and desires.

This stubbornness is apparent in Scorsese's refusal to allow his narrative to begin just yet. The jump cuts to Charlie's face are followed by, of all things, a shot of an eight-millimeter movie projector, which throws on a small screen scenes from the street, scenes of Charlie and Johnny Boy, flashing lights in the night, a church which suddenly fills the screen, giving way to shots of the San Gennaro Festival which will provide visual and aural background throughout the film. The scenes from the projector provide background for the credits and provide as well an active expression of the fiction/documentary tension I spoke of earlier. The immediacy and proximity of the opening shots are momentarily undercut by the projector, the home movies, the typewritten credits. Is the film we are about to see a version of Charlie's home movies? Are they somehow subjective projections of his memories? We *are* seeing a movie, and will be reminded of this throughout, as Scorsese intercuts scenes from his favorite films, integrating cinematic allusions into the narrative in a way he was unable to do in *Who's That Knocking?* Charlie and his friends go to see *The Searchers,* the film discussed at length by J. R. and his girl friend, the film that will have a perverse influence on *Taxi Driver.* Charlie and Johnny Boy go to see Corman's *The Tomb of Ligeia* (Scorsese, like Coppola, pays homage to his mentor). Outside the theater Charlie stands under a poster for *Point Blank* with Lee Marvin's gun pointing, forebodingly, at Johnny Boy's head. In the middle of the sequence in which Charlie and Johnny Boy are gunned down, we suddenly see Glenn Ford standing over his wife's body in the blown-up car of Fritz Lang's *The Big Heat* (it turns out to be a movie on television watched by Charlie's Mafia uncle, who is oblivious to what is happening to his nephew, but oddly close to it through the image on the screen). These intrusions and allusions, like a poet's allusions to other poems within his or her work, or a jazz musician's quotations from other melodies within the piece he or she is playing, serve a double or triple function. They constitute a celebration of the medium, an indication of a cinematic community; they enrich the work by opening it out, making it responsive to other works and making others responsive to it; and they point to the nature of the film's own existence. We are urged to observe the relation of film not to "reality" but to the reality of films and their influence upon each other. *Mean Streets* is a film, and by playing upon the various signs of its existence as film, it becomes a documentary not only of fictive events, but of itself.

The eight-millimeter projector is part of that self-documentation. It shows fragments of Charlie's world that *Mean Streets* as a whole shows in only a slightly less fragmented way. It alludes to the way Charlie sees himself in his world, and *Mean Streets* is a documentary of how its characters, Charlie in particular, see themselves. After the credit sequence, we are introduced to the major characters and then return to Charlie, observing him in church, observing the church from his point of view as he prays and comments upon his unworthiness. The camera tracks around him as he announces his desire to do penance for his sins. He comments on the pain of hell and puts his finger over a candle flame: "You don't fuck around with the infinite. There's no way you do that. . . ." "The pain in hell has two sides," he says, "the kind you can touch with your hand; the kind you can feel with your heart. . . . You know, the worst of the two is the spiritual." And with these words there is loud rock music and a cut to a slow-motion tracking shot down the glowing red bar that is the focal point of the group's activities.

The expectations created by montage would lead us to believe that the cut on these words from Charlie and the church candles to the drifting point of view in a fiery red bar, replete with go-go dancer, must indicate that this place is Charlie's hell. But unless Scorsese is adopting a literal Sartrean position, it is not hell, but merely the place where Charlie hangs out. The redness, the slow motion, the disrupting arcs around Charlie when he talks with the loan-shark Michael about Johnny Boy are all disturbing and portentous. More than anything else, they indicate to us Charlie's uncertainty of himself, his lack of faith in what and who he is. They allow us to share in the nascent violence of this and every situation Charlie is in (allow us to share because of the movement, the lack of rest, the lack of a stable eye-level gaze, the fistfight that breaks out behind him between two people who have nothing to do with him). If this is hell, it is eagerly embraced by Charlie, as a place to work out his conflicts, perhaps even a place to die in, but not as a place of suffering or torture. It is, rather, a place of great vitality, even of hilarity. The relationship of all concerned is loose and joking. The joke goes very sour at the end, and serious strains in Charlie's life keep emerging. But an apparent good-naturedness is kept up most of the way. When Johnny Boy comes into the bar, we hear Charlie saying to himself, in mock piety, "We talk about penance and you send this through the door. Well, we play by your rules, don't we? Well, don't we?" The camera booms into him and cuts to his point of view of Johnny Boy, walking down the bar in slow motion as the Rolling Stones sing "Jumping Jack Flash." Charlie's guilt, his burden, is a screwy kid whom he protects and who gets them both shot up. Charlie talks about suffering and about penance, but these are deeply internalized, and we see only a few profound signs of his suffering until it emerges directly from the barrel of a gun.

It is difficult to accept or to understand a film that does not have emotional turmoil as its subject but merely as a referent, and chooses instead to make its own action its subject. *Mean Streets* is not about what motivates Charlie and Johnny Boy, not about what they think and feel (although these are present), but about how they see, how Charlie perceives his world and Johnny Boy reacts to it. In none of his films will Scorsese opt for the psychological realism of explained actions, defined motivations, or identifiable characters. If his often-commented-upon Catholicism does appear in his work, it is in the form of a purgatorial sense of his characters' serving in the world, not looking for grace (if they do, they never, with the possible exception of Alice, find it), but attempting survival and barely making it. The world they inhabit is violent in the extreme, but it is a violence that is created by the characters' very attempts to make peace with it. From the point of view of the characters in *Mean Streets,* their world is perfectly ordinary, and Scorsese reflects this through the documentary nature of many of the images. But at the same time, we perceive a heightened sense of reality, a stylized, expressive presence most evident in the bar sequences, in the restless, moving camera, in the fragmentary, off-center editing.

Vitality and tension are apparent not only in the images, but in the dialogue (written by Scorsese and Mardik Martin) as well. Everyone in *Mean Streets* is a compulsive talker—not obsessive, like Cassavetes's characters, who appear driven to reveal themselves through their words at all moments and always on the brink of, or deeply in, hysteria, but using words as an extension of themselves, a sign of their vitality. Their language is rooted in New York working-class usage, profoundly obscene and charged with movement.[4] The slow, self-conscious, and reflective speech of Coppola's middle-class mafiosi is here replaced by an expressive thrust of endless words. In a great set piece of the film, Johnny Boy is attempting to explain to Charlie why he does not have the money to pay off Michael (the need to pay this debt is one of the few things that provides something like a conventional "plot," though it is less like a plot than like a motif). In a simple set-up located in the back room of the bar, against dark walls, punctuated by a bare light bulb hanging over Charlie, a sequence cut in simple shot/reverse shot, over-the-shoulder continuity, with an occasional far shot of the two men, De Niro tells the following story, a story whose telling serves to create the character who tells it:

> You don't know what happened to me. I'm so depressed about other things I can't worry about payments, ya know what I mean? I come home last Tuesday, I had my money, in cash, ya know . . . blah, blah, bing, bing, I'm comin' home, I ran into Jimmy Sparks. I owe Jimmy Sparks seven hundred, like for four months. I gotta pay the guy, he lives in my building, he hangs out across the street, I gotta pay the guy, right? So what happened? I had to give some to

The dialogue between Johnny Boy (Robert De Niro) and Charlie (Harvey Keitel) in **Mean Streets.**

my mother, then I wound up with twenty-five at the end of the week. And then what happened? Today, you ain't gonna believe, this is incredible, I can't believe it myself . . . I was in a game, I was ahead like six, seven hundred dollars, right?

CHARLIE: You gotta be kiddin'.

JOHNNY BOY: Yeah, on Hester Street. You know Joey Clams?

CHARLIE: Yeah.

JOHNNY BOY: Joey Scalla, yeah.

CHARLIE: I know him too, yeah.

JOHNNY BOY: Yeah, no, Joey Scalla is Joey Clams.

CHARLIE: Right.

JOHNNY BOY: Right.

CHARLIE: They're the same person (*smiles*).

JOHNNY BOY: Yeah!

CHARLIE: Hey!

JOHNNY BOY: Hey! So I was in there playing Bankers and Brokers. All of a sudden I'm ahead like six, seven hundred dollars. I'm really winnin'. All of a sudden some kid walks in and the kid yells that the bulls are comin', right? Yells that the cops are comin'. Everyone runs away, I grab all the money, I go in, it's an excuse, like, to get away . . . Ya know, and I give everybody the money back later, and that way I get out, I don't have to go into the game and get a losin' streak and all that. What happens? I come out in the yard. I don't know this buildin'. I don't know nothin', I couldn't get out, it was like a box, big, like this (*makes the shape of a box with his hands*). So I gotta go back in. Not only do I go back in, but this kid says it's a false alarm. Can you imagine that? I wanted to kill this fuckin' kid. I wanted . . . (*bites fingers in mock rage*). I was so crazy, man, I wanted to kill this kid. Meanwhile I gotta get back in the game, bing, bing, bing, I lose four hundred dollars. Meanwhile Frankie Bones is over there, Frankie Bones, I owe him thirteen hundred for like seven, eight months already. He's after me, I can't even walk on Hester Street without duckin' that guy. He's, he's like waitin' for me, like I can't move, ya know, and he sees that I'm losin', right, so like he's waitin' for me here, so he's tappin' me on the shoulder (*taps Charlie*), he says, "Hey," tappin' me like this, like a hawk, "hey, ah, get it up, you're losin', now give me some money." I says, "Hey, Frankie, come on, ya know, ya know, give me a break over here, let me win some back, ya know, I got debts, I mean·I'm in the big O." He says, "Never mind, give me the money." I says, "O.K. Frankie," so I give him two hundred dollars. Meanwhile I lose the deal, I go outside, I'm a little depressed . . . anyway I wanna cut this story short, 'cause I know you don't wanna hear all this, and I know, I know, I know. But . . . (*Charlie protests that it's all right*) to make a long story short, anyway, I went to Al Kaplan, gotta new tie, I got this shirt . . . like this shirt? . . . it's nice . . . This tie. . . .

De Niro's Johnny Boy is all nervous energy and self-delight, the opposite of the serious, unsmiling, self-contained Vito Corleone whom he creates for Coppola. The character makes himself from moment to moment, almost speaks himself into being. The result is that his language and that of the other characters plays a game with us similiar to that played by the film's images: it seems spontaneous, emerging from the moment—indeed a great deal of improvisation must have occurred in the creation of it. Yet it manifests rhythm and energy and concentration greater than could be expected were it merely made up and "overheard" on the spot (the notion of improvisation, introduced by Godard and brought into American narrative film by Cassavetes, Altman, and Scorsese, is one of the trickier elements in modern cinema, giving an effect of immediacy and spontaneity that is in fact created with craft and planning, the demands of shooting being too precise to allow for many on-the-spot changes and surprises). Like Abraham Polonsky, who in his 1948 film *Force of Evil* heightened to a poetic rhythm the diction and cadences of New York dialect, Scorsese, his co-writer, and his actors take the forms of the everyday language of a particular ethnic group, concentrate it and make it artificial, the artificiality creating the effect of the overheard and the immediate. The language of *Mean Streets* becomes a means of self- and group-definition, speaking of an unrooted life yet at the same time attempting to root that life in a community of shared rhythms and expressions. Of course the expressions themselves can be used as weapons against this community. Early in the film Michael, the loan shark, tells Charlie that Johnny Boy is a "jerk-off," a phrase that brings Charlie immediately to his friend's defense. At the film's end, Johnny Boy throws the same phrase back at Michael, which, with the empty gun he waves at him, puts Michael in a killing rage. Words which communicate not meaning but feelings are dangerous; but they are at least alive (compare the language of Kubrick's characters, which communicates rigid, unalterable ideas and is deadening). It is this tension of a dangerous vitality, friendships that become provocations, a restlessness that can't be satisfied, that makes up the structure of the film.

*Mean Streets* does not, finally, define itself as any one thing. Although it depicts the activities of a group of disenfranchised urban ethnics, it does not attempt to comment on a social and economic class. A film about volatile emotions, it seems uninterested in analyzing

The violent end of **Mean Streets** (the gun is held by Scorsese himself).

emotions or baring souls. Although it deals with gangsters, it does not reflect upon or examine the generic tensions of the gangster film, as do *Breathless, Bonnie and Clyde,* Kubrick's early films, or the *Godfathers.*[5] What it does reflect is Scorsese's (and hopefully our) delight in the film's capacity to capture a moment of communication, of interaction, and out of a series of such moments to fashion a sense of place and movement, energy and violence. It reflects Scorsese's growing control of point of view, his ability to shift from objective to subjective observation, often intermingling the two, until, in *Taxi Driver,* it is difficult to tell them apart.

*Mean Streets* is, more than anything else, a manifestation of vital filmmaking, with narrative subordinate to the pleasures of formal manipulations of image and dialogue. The film that follows it, *Alice Doesn't Live Here Anymore,* allows Scorsese to develop a more commercial narrative sense, to put his talents at the service of a "story."

In *Taxi Driver,* his most complex film to date, a meticulous sense of formal control and the ability to use this control to create a narrative of considerable power and mystery are joined. It is so much an extension of *Mean Streets* that I want to consider it in relation to that film, leaving discussion of *Alice* for later.

*Taxi Driver* is the inverted extension of *Mean Streets.* Where that film examines a small, isolated urban sub-community, *Taxi Driver* focuses on one isolated urban sub-individual. Where *Mean Streets* presents its characters in tenuous control of their environment, at home in their surroundings, *Taxi Driver* presents its character trapped by it, swallowed and imprisoned. More accurately, the objective-subjective points of view of *Mean Streets* that allow us to look both at and with the characters is replaced by a subjective point of view that forces us continually to see as the character sees, creating a *mise-en-scène* that expresses, above all, the obsessive vision of a madman. Finally, where *Mean Streets* celebrates urban life in its violence and its community (as opposed to Sam Peckinpah's celebration of violence as the only means to community), *Taxi Driver* rigorously structures a path to violence that is separate from community, separate from the exigencies of any "normal" life, separate from any rational comprehension, but only the explosion of an individual attempting to escape from a self-made prison, an individual who, in his madness, attempts to act the role of a movie hero.

One further connection exists between the two films. *Mean Streets* is a diffuse *film noir.* Its dark, enclosed, violent urban world recalls many of the *noir* conventions. But, despite its violent end, it escapes the total bleakness of *noir* precisely because of its sense of community. Even though its characters *are* trapped, they do not evidence the loneliness, dread, and anxiety manifested in *film noir.* Again, despite the cruelty that ends the film, the bulk of it emphasizes a friendship—albeit unstable—among its characters. *Taxi Driver,* however, renders the conventions of *film noir* in an immediate, frightening manner. Its central character lives completely enclosed in a city of dreadful night; he is so removed and alone that everything he sees becomes a reflection of his own distorted perceptions. Travis Bickle

223

(Robert De Niro) is the last *noir* man in the ultimate *noir* world: closed and dark, a paranoid universe of perversion, obsession, and violence. In the creation of this world, Scorsese goes to the roots of *film noir,* to certain tenets of German Expressionism that call for "a selective and creative distortion" of the world by means of which the creator of a work can represent "the complexity of the psyche" through a visual style that exposes the "object's internal life, the expression of its 'soul.' "[6] Scorsese does want to "expose" the inner life of his character, but not to explain it. The internal life of Travis Bickle remains an enigma throughout the film. It cannot be explained, even through the most dreadful violence, and a major concern of the film is to frustrate our attempts at understanding that mind. But Scorsese is very interested in communicating to us the way a world looks as it is perceived by such a mind, and he uses "a selective and creative distortion" of perception in extraordinary ways.

The focus of my analysis of *Taxi Driver* will be on the ways Scorsese creates an expressionist, *noir mise-en-scène* and the ways he asks us to observe it and deal with it. But before proceeding with that analysis, it is necessary to inquire briefly into the role of Paul Schrader, who wrote the script for the film, and who has received some attention from its critics. Schrader is an articulate man whose essay on *film noir* remains the best on the subject. It offers pertinent ideas for an understanding of the film. But most critics have chosen to look at his book, *Transcendental Style in Film: Ozu, Bresson, Dreyer,* to help explain *Taxi Driver* and the apparent disparity between what Schrader might have intended and what Scorsese executes. Of course without an original script to compare to the finished film, such speculation as to intentions remains speculation.[7] But it appears that some critics of the film wanted to see in it a study of Travis Bickle as a lost and insular but coherent and self-contained individual, in the manner of a Robert Bresson character who achieves a spiritual grace by the almost negative persistence of his activities. Certainly, if this was Schrader's intent, Scorsese has perverted it.[8] For Scorsese's character starts and ends without grace, persists in unmotivated fits and starts, and lives in a world so much his own creation—or, better, his own perception—that no salvation is possible, for there is no one to save and no one to do the saving. If Schrader intended *Taxi Driver* to be an inquiry into spiritual isolation and redemption, the loneliness and transcendence of the disenfranchised, the film itself presents us with no such transcendental material. Scorsese has rooted his film in the very earthbound context of the madness of a lonely, barely coherent individual who cannot make sane associations between the distorted fragments of his perceptions. The "salvation" he receives, the recognition he gains for gunning down a mafioso and freeing a young runaway from a brothel, is simply ironic. It is the result of other people's distorted perceptions, and in no way changes the central character or his inability to understand himself or his world. If anything, it aggravates it, for there is an indication at the film's end that Travis Bickle has some glimmering and fleeting recognition of his madness, but only enough to make him turn away from that recognition.

One problem does arise in the film when elements that attempt to give Travis more character and "motivation" than Scorsese wishes him to have seem to intrude. This intrusion appears in the diary— Schrader's invention—that the character keeps and reads in voice-over throughout the film. In discussing the use of voice-over commentary in the films of Bresson, Schrader writes that the "narration does not give the viewer any new information or feelings, but only reiterates what he already knows . . . ; it only doubles his perception of the event. Consequently, there is a schizoid reaction; one, there is the sense of meticulous detail which is a part of the everyday, and two, because the detail is doubled there is an emotional queasiness, a growing suspicion of the seemingly 'realistic' rationale behind the everyday."[9] Unfortunately, Schrader and Scorsese follow this Bressonian principle only sporadically. For example, we see Travis in his cab and, from his point of view, street after dismal street, populated solely by hookers. We hear Travis comment: "All the animals come out at night, whores, skunk pussies, buggers, queens, fairies, dopers, junkies." Here the voice-over does strongly double our perceptions of

Travis's one-dimensional view of his world. It emphasizes, along with the visuals, the selectiveness of his point of view and makes us "queasy" and "suspicious" over the relationship between Travis's "reality" and any we are likely to experience outside his gaze. But when, later, Travis suddenly uses words like "sick" and "venal" to describe the world he has chosen to see, or says of himself, "All my life needed was a sense of someplace to go. . . . I don't believe that one should devote his life to morbid self-attention. I believe that someone should become a person like other people," we come perilously close to the old convention of psychological motivation. It seems that Travis, in words quite above the diction level he usually uses (early in the film, talking to the manager of the cab company, he did not even know what "moonlighting" meant), is giving us reasons for his behavior. Scorsese is allowing the entry of language that gives an analytic cast to the character, unsupported by what we see. It is language that gives us hope that motivation and rationale, of the conventional kind, will allow us to "understand" and account for the character, and perhaps dismiss him as yet another tortured soul.

While Travis is speaking of himself in the words just quoted, what we see and what we hear on the music track lead us in another direction. For this sequence Bernard Herrmann provides a thudding sound almost like a heartbeat.* What we see is Travis lying expressionless in bed. His face is expressionless, but the camera, craning over and down to him, provides a commentary more eloquent than the words. Travis is a paralyzed being; what feelings he has come in abrupt, disconnected spurts. The movement of the camera is almost a lunge toward him, which expresses both an attempt to approach him (to carry our gaze close to a figure we feel we must understand) and a repulsion from him, for the angle of approach to the figure is too disorienting; we could never "normally" see a figure from this angle and with this approach. And it is just this tension of attraction

_____

* I wish it were possible to describe, in other than imprecise, impressionistic language, the facets of Herrmann's score for this film and the ways it models the various sequences. It is his last, and, after his music for *Citizen Kane, Vertigo,* and *Psycho,* his best.

and repulsion that the film depends upon to keep us at an appropriate distance from the character, to keep us from an explanation of who or why Travis Bickle is. His voice-over commentary at this point, as at others, is a distraction and a false clue to an enigma.

It would be fairer to the film and to Schrader and Scorsese to disregard the obviously abortive Bressonian influences (or simply to acknowledge their presence and how they do and do not work) and look rather at Schrader's concepts of the *noir* hero in order to under-stand Travis Bickle and his perverse universe. "The . . . final phase of *film noir*," Schrader writes of the period 1949–53,

> was the period of psychotic action and suicidal impulse. The *noir* hero, seemingly under the weight of . . . years of despair, started to go bananas. The psychotic killer, who had in the first period been a subject worthy of study . . . now became the active protagonist.
> . . . *Film noir*'s final phase was the most aesthetically and socio-logically piercing. After ten years of steadily shedding romantic conventions, the later *noir* films finally got down to the root causes of the period: the loss of public honor, heroic conventions, personal integrity, and, finally, psychic stability. The third phase films were painfully self-aware; they seemed to know they stood at the end of a long tradition based on despair and distintegration and did not shy away from that fact. . . . Because *film noir* was first of all a style, because it worked out its conflicts visually rather than thematically, because it was aware of its own identity, it was able to create artistic solutions to sociological problems.[10]

Certainly *Taxi Driver* is aware of its own formal identity, more so than the films of the period Schrader discusses. The film defines its central character not in terms of social problems nor by any *a priori* ideas of noble suffering and transcendent madness, but by the ways we see the character and the way he sees himself and his surround-ings. He is the climactic *noir* figure, much more isolated and very much madder than his forebears. No cause is given for him, no under-standing allowed; he stands formed by his own loneliness and trapped by his own isolation, his actions and reactions explicable only through those actions and reactions. I do not mean to be enigmatic, only to indicate that Scorsese has made a film that not only expresses insularity and psychosis, but is insular itself. In the tradition of *film noir,* the world created by *Taxi Driver* exists only within its own space, a space which is itself formed by the state of mind of its central character, in that strange double perception in which we see the world the way the character sees it, but see as well the character himself and therefore perceive and judge his perceptions.

*Taxi Driver* does suffer somewhat from a split between its screen-writing and its director's intentions.* But it is an important and still valid premise of the *auteur* theory that the director absorbs, or, better, re-creates the script into something else—the film itself, which is more than the script. If we assume that Schrader's notions of the formal integrity of *film noir* are valid, we can forget about Bresson and proceed to a close examination of this film about the "despair and disintegration" of a psychotic killer who is its active protagonist on its own terms. We can discover in its very first shot the methods of presentation that will be at work throughout. This shot is of the front end of a Checker cab emerging from smoke. This image is immediately

---

* Schrader's other work in film has been a brief history of mixed intentions and uncertain execution. Most of his material, with the exception of *Taxi Driver,* has been directed by indifferent filmmakers (e.g., *The Yakuza,* directed by Sidney Pollack). He has twice yielded to the necessities of Hollywood survival: he wrote *Obsession,* a version of Hitchcock's *Vertigo,* for Brian De Palma, a director who keeps trying to imitate Hitchcock without the slightest notion that there is more to Hitchcock than violence and bizarre events. AIP produced a Schrader script called *Rolling Thunder,* a version of the Vietnam-veteran-comes-home-to-be-abused-and-take-revenge subject, featuring William Devane having his hand put down a garbage disposal and partaking in a revenge shoot-out in a Mexican brothel, in the easily imitated Peckinpah manner. (To be fair to this film, directed by John Flynn, there is an excellent sequence in which another veteran, played by Tommy Lee Jones, has dinner with his family, dead in spirit and just managing the forms of its survival.) When Schrader finally directed his own material, the uncertainties and mixed intentions were almost overcome. *Blue Collar* (1978) is about workers, the rarest of subjects to be taken seriously by American film. It is a subdued and, for Schrader, remarkably violence-free examination of economic frustration and political powerlessness. *Blue Collar* is, visually, closest to Scorsese, while thematically it goes beyond Scorsese in its inquiry into an ideological situation. Unfortunately, the film, which featured Richard Pryor, Harvey Keitel, and Yaphet Kotto, was marketed as another black exploitation film and did not get proper exposure.

recognizable. The streets of New York often have steam pouring from their manhole covers, and such a sight, at night, illuminated by headlamps, is quite striking. Scorsese therefore begins with an image familiar to anyone who knows New York. But at the same time he instantly defamiliarizes it, makes it strange.* The smoke is yellowish, and the taxi that emerges from it is not so much moving as looming, viewed from a low angle and traveling at a speed too slow and regular for it to be an "actual" cab on the street. The music which accompanies this presence is percussive and slowly accelerates in tempo and loudness, not unlike a car engine starting in slow motion. This shot dissolves to a tight closeup of a pair of eyes, first tinted red, then normal in color, then red and white. The eyes move back and forth, scanning, blankly, something as yet unseen by us. A dissolve to the reverse shot (what the eyes are seeing) shows us the world through a wet and blurred windshield. The people and traffic seen through the windshield are hard-edged; their movements are multiplied and extended so that they leave trails of light and traces of their forms (this is, of course, a special effect, and therefore calls attention to itself as a specific filmic device as well as a perceptual aberration). The shot dissolves again to people going by on the streets, tinted red and blue, and moving through the smoke in slow motion; there is a dissolve back to the eyes looking left to right and then to the smoke with which the sequence opened.

Some critics have referred to this sequence, and the opening shot in particular, as an emergence from hell. This is an evocative analogy, but misses the point. It is precisely the lack of definition, the lack of knowable space, which has about it just the hint of the recognizable and the everyday that makes it so disturbing. The defamiliarizing of the familiar, the introduction of the blankly moving eyes (again, cinematic convention connects the title of the film, the shot of the cab, and the eyes, so that we assume they are the eyes of the driver—

---

* The notion of defamiliarization, "making strange," is a concept developed by the Russian formalist Shklovsky. He applied it to aesthetic creation and perception in general, but it seems particularly apt in accounting for the way we are forced to see things in a work like *Taxi Driver*.[11]

229

even if we might not recognize them as De Niro's), the strange movement of the people on the street (we may recall the slow-motion crowd in the bar sequence in *Mean Streets,* which indicated Charlie's detachment from what he sees), our gaze both at and from this foreboding car and its occupant, move us into a realm of distortion and threat in which we remain throughout the film. This credit sequence is also outside the narrative proper (in the sequence following this, Travis goes to a cab company to ask for a job driving) and is therefore out of time, a kind of perpetual state of mind that diffuses itself over the film.

As the smoke clears, we see Travis from behind entering the cab company to ask for work. His movement is accompanied by the crescendo of the main musical theme. As an exposition of plot, the ensuing sequence is simple. The antagonism between the cab owner and Travis offers a central notion of anger that envelops the film as a whole, and their dialogue supplies us with some minimal information about the character: he can't sleep at night; he goes to porn movies; he was in the Marines. But more than what is said and done, what is seen in this sequence, and the way it is seen, continue to provoke, almost subliminally, our discomfort and our perceptual dislocation. We observe Travis from behind as he stands over the cab owner. Opposite him, through an opening in the wall, we can see two men arguing. We barely hear them; they play no direct role in the sequence (on second viewing we can recognize one of the arguing men as Wizard [Peter Boyle], who will be one of Travis's cronies at the all-night cafeteria, and to whom Travis will attempt to disburden himself: "I got some bad ideas in my head"); but they form a focus of attention in the shot and literally reflect Travis, the angry, inarticulate man. The reverse of this shot, our look at Travis, places him low in the frame, too low and off-center, so that behind him a man seated on a stool seems too large for the perspective of the shot. A bit later, when asked about his license, Travis answers that it's clean, "real clean, just like my conscience." The cab owner blows up at him, and the camera booms up and forward, bringing Travis too close. The placement of the character in both of these shots and the movement toward him in the second is too portentous for the narrative function at the moment, and therefore the portent is greater than the immediate action and skews the reactions we expect from a covential expository dialogue sequence. The placing of a character in unexpected parts of the frame, particularly in closeups that are off-center or off-angle, is a device that Scorsese is here borrowing from Hitchcock, from whom he has learned the ability to load our perceptions, to give us something more than we expect and to prepare us, almost unconsciously, for events to come.

When Travis leaves the dispatcher's office, the camera follows him as he goes to the cab garage, but leaves him to pan across its dark space, following a totally peripheral character (Wizard, again), and picking up Travis as he walks back into the frame and out to the street. At first look, this seems a perfectly ordinary way to get a character from one point to another without cutting. But the question arises as to why the camera doesn't stay with him all the way rather than abandon him for an anonymous character. It is a curious shot, and it connects with an even more curious shot later in the film. Following Travis's disastrous date with Betsy (Cybill Shepherd), when he takes her to a porn movie only to have her walk out on him in outrage, he calls her from a public phone in an office building. We observe Travis at a distance, off-center, talking on the phone. His face is turned away from us. He is solicitous to Betsy and agonizingly simple-minded, concerned that she has the flu, wondering if she got the flowers he sent her (she says she didn't, and in the next sequence we see his room filled with dead flowers). Suddenly, the camera begins to move away from Travis, tracking to the right and coming to rest before a corridor that leads out to the street. It stays there as, off-screen now, Travis finishes the conversation. As he begins a voice-over comment on how Betsy refused to come to the phone on subsequent calls, he walks into the frame and down the corridor.

In a film that concerns a character who is radically displaced from his environment, and who perceives that environment empty of any "normal" articulations and filled with his own aberrations, we are allowed to share the spatial dislocations. We observe him in unconventional and uncomfortable placements within the frame. We also withdraw from him, when the camera indicates, unexpectedly and disconcertingly, the spaces around him, the neutral spaces of the taxi garage or the barren space of an office hallway, the highly significant spaces of his room, with its cracked walls, dead flowers, boxes of junk food. There are also the expressive possibilities of temporal distortion: I have indicated the way the narrative is enclosed within the timeless drift of the cab through the distorted streets, a drift that opens and closes the film and punctuates it throughout. There is the slow-motion movement of the people on those streets and the visual multiplication of their movements. And then there is this odd occurrence after Travis leaves the taxi garage in the sequence discussed earlier: the camera picks him up in a far shot walking up the street. Sunlight brightens the buildings behind him, but he is in shadow. There is, quite unexpectedly, a lap dissolve. But rather than moving us to another place and time, which is the conventional meaning of this device, it merely moves Travis a little closer forward in the shot and shows him taking a drink from a bottle in a paper bag. We are affected here not by any turn in the plot nor by a dramatic interchange, but simply by a cinematic device that works against our expectations and therefore disturbs us, setting up a complicated relationship with the character. The lap dissolve, as I said, is conventionally used to signify a lapse of time and/or a change of place. Here the effect is rather of a momentary lapse of consciousness, or of a drifting unbound by time, a perception by us of the character's state of mind. Scorsese will repeat the device during the "You talkin' to me?" sequence, as Travis accelerates his psychotic preparations for murder. In both instances it forces us to look at the character and disturbs that look at the same time. We observe him; we partake of his dislocation.* Our gaze at the character is continually disrupted, and

* Scorsese may have gotten the idea for the dissolve that plays against our expectations of its function from Bernardo Bertolucci. In *The Spider's Stratagem*, two characters have a conversation which is continually interrupted by fades to black—a transitional device similar to, though more emphatic than, the dissolve. But the fades do not actually interrupt anything, for when the scene fades back in, the conversation continues with no indication of change in time.

we are permitted neither sympathy with him nor comfortable distance from him. (In this context the shifts in diction between Travis's speech and his voice-over diary entries, which I earlier criticized, might be understood: they become further acts of dislocation, further denials of coherency in the character.)

We are made as well to share the gaze of the character himself, to see the world as he sees it. This is done immediately in the credit sequence through the appearance of the people in the street. It is done more forcefully, because more subtly, in our observation of the men arguing in the cab owner's office. It is done whenever Travis drives in his cab: whores and gangs inhabit every street, whores and their clients and would-be murderers are his fares. "Did you ever see what a forty-four magnum pistol can do to a woman's face?" asks a passenger (played by Scorsese) as he forces Travis to pull over to the curb and look with him at an apartment where, he says, his wife is having an affair with a black man. "I mean, it'll fuckin' destroy her. Just blow her right apart. . . . Now did you ever see what it can do to a woman's pussy? That you should see. . . . I know you must think I'm pretty sick. . . . I'm paying for the ride. You don't have to answer." And through it all, Travis remains impassive. He never looks at his passengers except through his rear-view mirror. He never reacts when his cab is spattered by a water hydrant or by garbage. A man walking down the street with his shirt pulled over his head or another yelling down the street over and over again, "I'll kill her" brings no reaction from him. Is it coincidence that the only people Travis sees are the mad and the disenfranchised, that the only streets he sees are the stews of the city? Why does the cafeteria frequented late at night by Travis and his cronies seem to be populated only by pimps and nodding drug addicts?

The answer is, simply, that these are the only people and the only places of which Travis is aware. They constitute the only things he perceives, and, since our point of view in the film is so much restricted to his perceptions, the only things *we* are permitted to perceive as well. The camera, therefore, does not, as Diane Jacobs suggests, appear "helpless to avert its gaze from the horrors that walk in its path," nor does it revel "secretly in the filth and the suffocation."[12] Rather it takes a very active role in transmitting to us a point of view which may itself be helpless to avert its gaze from filth and ugliness. Travis is prey to his own isolated and isolating gaze (a gaze that is infected with the myth of New York as a foul sewer—the "New York-ness" mentioned earlier), and we, in turn, are prey to it. *Taxi Driver* is not a documentary of the squalor of New York City but the documentation of a squalid mind driven mad by what it perceives.

*Taxi Driver* is the portrait of an obsessive, a passive obsessive, so oppressed by his isolation that when he does act, it is only upon

the dark and disconnected impulses triggered by his perceptions. There is, as I have noted, no analysis of, nor reasons given for, his behavior—none, at least, that make a great deal of rational sense. He can, perhaps, be viewed as a radically alienated urban castoff, a mutant produced by the incalculable dehumanization of our post-industrial society (the news continually makes us aware of the random murderers who keep appearing and disappearing in our culture). But the film withholds any political, social, or even psychological analysis. (The presence of a presidential candidate who becomes Travis's aborted target is used only to point out how terribly distant

God's lonely man (**opposite, below**): Travis Bickle (Robert De Niro) in **Taxi Driver.**

vulgar politics is from "the people" it professes to address.) However, after saying this, I must point out that the film does not neglect an analysis of the cultural aberrations that afflict Travis, and ourselves. Scorsese quietly, even hilariously, suggests one possible motivation for, or result of, Travis's psychosis. The more deeply he withdraws, the more he comes to believe in the American movie myths of purity and heroism, love and selflessness, and to actuate them as the grotesque parodies of human behavior they are. Travis Bickle is the legitimate child of John Wayne and Norman Bates: pure, self-righteous, violent ego and grinning, homicidal lunatic; each the obverse of the other; each equally dangerous.* Together they create a persona so out of touch with ordinary human experience that the world he inhabits and perceives becomes an expressionist *noir* nightmare: an airless and dark trap that its inhabitant escapes only by drawing everything into it with him. The final irony occurs when Travis's act of slaughter, which he believes is an act of liberation and purification, is taken as such by everyone else, and we discover that we have been trapped by the same aberrations as he, that the double perspective we are offered by the film fuses, and we momentarily accept the lunatic as hero.

Our closeness to the character's point of view and our distance from an understanding or comprehension of that character, put us in a confusing situation and make it difficult for us to see just how tightly the movements to destruction are drawn and how those movements are shaped by the various myths and ideological distortions that play upon the little that remains of the character's mind. Travis gets involved with two women, each not a character as much as a further creation of his aberrant sensibility. Betsy, the campaign worker for the clichéd liberal candidate, Charles Palantine (Leonard Harris), is, by Travis's own admission, a dream girl. She is a fantasy figure from a fifties movie, appearing to him as a woman in white who comes "like an angel" out of the "filthy mass" he sees himself living in. "They cannot touch her," he says, emphasizing each word. As

* By "John Wayne" I mean the collective persona of the John Wayne characters in film after film.

Travis spies on her from outside campaign headquarters, we see her with her fellow workers, a perfectly banal person involved in mindless conversation. Her ordinariness is played against Travis's stare, his impassive observation punctuated by strong camera movements which destabilize the space he occupies and make his presence a threat. When Travis invades Betsy's office, he speaks to her in the words of a movie hero: he says she's the most beautiful woman he has ever met, that he thinks she is lonely, that she needs a friend. He projects his own feelings on her in such sentimental terms that she can hardly help but react to them (why would a sane woman react at all to a weird man who has been staring at her and then greets her with a line out of a rotten movie? Is she fooled by his charm? Is it because this is really Robert De Niro talking to Cybill Shepherd? Is it, as Patricia Patterson and Manny Farber suppose, just bad scripting and improbable motivation and reaction?[13] Or is Scorsese allowing Travis's fantasy—and ours—to play out awhile? One of the things movies tell us is that it is not impossible for the most improbable boy to win the beautiful girl).

Scorsese is not entirely disinterested in the character of Betsy. He allows her to play with Travis, to indulge a kind of suburban curiosity about the freakish and the threatening. Once they begin talking—in a cafeteria sequence which is edited so that Betsy often appears in a shot over Travis's shoulder, but he almost always appears in a shot alone—it is clear how separate they are. Betsy says he reminds her of a song by Kris Kristofferson. "Who's that?" asks Travis. Betsy quotes from the song: "He's a prophet and a pusher, partly truth, partly fiction, a walking contradiction." This is perfectly meaningless to Travis. "You saying that about me? . . . I'm no pusher." "Just the part about the contradictions. You are that," says Betsy, who might as well be talking to no one. In the next sequence we see Travis buying the Kristofferson record, or more accurately, we see part of him, his arm, with a military patch that says "King Kong Company," through the window of the record store. Betsy is wrong. He is not a contradiction, but a thing of disconnected parts, any one of which can take momentary precedence until another disconnected part jars momentarily into place. The shuffling Andy Hardy romancer takes his white angel to a porn movie, and when she flees, condemns her to hell and says she is cold like all women. Cold "like a union," he says, drawing on a notion of people in groups, a notion totally repellent to this lonely man.

The second woman, or girl rather, is a twelve-year-old prostitute, who tries to get into Travis's cab and is pulled out by her pimp, who throws Travis a twenty-dollar bill. The event occurs midway between his first meeting with Betsy and his taking her to the porn movie, and just after he has picked up the candidate Betsy works for. It is a marvelously contrived series of coincidences (as most any movie plot is), and serves to echo the random, fragmentary nature of Travis himself. Betsy will put Travis over the edge; candidate Palantine will be his first object of violence; Iris (Jodie Foster), the baby whore, will catalyze the explosion. There is no real connection between them, except that they are all clichés, all the reflections of a junk-food mind to which women are either white angels or poor girls in distress, and presidential candidates clean, dashing men who, being clean, will clean up the mess that Travis is obsessed with. "The president should clean up this whole mess here," he tells a slightly astonished Palantine, "should flush it down the fuckin' toilet." If Palantine can salvage Travis's world, then Travis can save Iris from hers. Or, if no one can cleanse Travis's world, then he at least can save one person from it. Never mind that Iris is too stoned to know what Travis is talking about and is living in circumstances similiar to those of her would-be savior. Living, that is, under the oppression of clichés. In one of the few sequences of the film which does not encompass Travis's point of view, we see Iris and her pimp, Sport (played with outrageous menace and unctuousness by Harvey Keitel), alone in the red-orange light of their room. Sport plays out a strange ritual of seduction and ownership, holding Iris to him (she comes up to his chest) and dancing her about the room. "I depend on you," he says. "When you're close to me like this I feel so good. I only wish every man could know what it's like to be loved by you. . . . It's only you that keeps me together."

Iris is torn between two sets of platitudes, the concerned protective language of Travis and the cheap sentiment of Sport, whose words to her are like the junk food Travis is always eating, superficially filling but empty and finally destructive. Like junk food they are addictive, and therefore imprisoning. Hearing these words and seeing Iris's situation outside of Travis's perception sets up a peculiar tension: either Travis, in all his madness, is correct in wanting to "save" Iris from her situation because it is repulsive and inhuman, or he is blind to the ludicrousness of the situation of a little girl secure within a grotesque parody of affection stronger than he will ever know, and therefore his desire to help her is meaningless because she neither desires nor needs any help. Throughout the film, we have been perceiving the world as Travis does; now, briefly, we see it without him, and it appears hopeless, outrageously hopeless, but contains a suggestion that the loneliness that Travis sees and experiences everywhere can be mitigated. The mitigation is cruel and fraudulent, but it is something compared to nothing. The bourgeois solitude to which Iris is returned after she is "freed" by Travis, a solitude we hear about through the droning voice of her father, narrating a letter he has written to Travis, may be cleaner and more moral, but no less oppressive and sentimental.

It would be foolish to imply that the film is advocating teenage prostitution; that is not the question at hand. Scorsese is examining aspects of an ugly world, a non-bourgeois world that has adopted the other's clichés and revealed them as destructive. Travis is slowly destroyed by those clichés until, becoming the demonic parody of the avenging hero, he becomes a destroyer. In his dealings with Iris, he becomes nothing less than a parody of John Wayne's Ethan Edwards in Ford's 1956 film *The Searchers* (the film that obsesses Scorsese's alter ego, J. R., in *Who's That Knocking at My Door?* and that Charlie goes to see in *Mean Streets*). Ethan is himself a figure of neurotic obsession, who wants to rescue his niece from the Indians because of his hatred of miscegenation and his desire to purify and bring her back to white civilization (is Sport, in his hippie gear, meant to be a version of Ethan Edwards's rival, Chief Scar?). The equation—Travis Bickle as

Wayne's Ethan; Iris as Natalie Wood's Debbie; and Sport as the Chief—is perfect. Like Debbie, who becomes accommodated to the Indians before Ethan rescues her, Iris has accommodated to her world; it is an ugly accommodation, but it works on its own terms. Like Chief Scar, Sport attempts to protect his people, and like Ethan, Travis will overcome all odds, will risk his life, to save what is left of Iris's innocence. Travis believes in the rightness of his plan, as does his filmic forebear. What he does not see is that his whole notion of saving people is based on a movie cliché of heroic activity (which Ford himself questioned), a cliché that his madness seems to make valid. Iris passively submits to the clichés of squalid sentimentality; Travis submits to the clichés of violent action. (Betsy believes movie clichés, too; she is fooled by them until Travis attempts to draw her directly into his world, at which point she flees; the angel in white cannot exist in the dark hole of a porno house.) The different reactions of Iris and Travis to their predicament is presented in a strong montage that follows upon the sequence between Sport and Iris. As the pimp dances his whore away with loving words, shots are heard on the sound track. We cut to Travis, isolated in the square opening of a shooting gallery. As he shoots, the square leaps forward, persistence, threat, single-mindedness, madness confronting us directly.

The violence that Travis commits in his attempt to "save" Iris (or, more accurately, the violence that Scorsese creates on the screen) is the most problematic aspect of *Taxi Driver*. It is so enormous that it seems, on first viewing, to rupture an otherwise carefully restrained and thoughtfully constructed film, finally obviating that restraint by overwhelming it. It is impossible not to consider the sequence as one of the more cynical moments in recent American film. This needs a context: by 1976 the simulation of violence had reached a level of mindlessness and predictability that left only three alternatives: exaggerate it to more insane proportions in order to elicit a thrill from an audience dulled by endlessly exploding blood squibs and men careening backward from the force of a shotgun blast; show an actual death; or forget the whole thing, retire the various forms of brutality and consider some other manifestations of human behavior. Only in 1978 did the last option appear to be considered by some filmmakers. In 1976 there was some indication that the second alternative, the filming of an actual death, could be conceivable. The rumor and brief public appearance of "snuff" films (one of them was called *Snuff* and purported to show the actual dismemberment of a woman)[14] threatened to overturn every conventional relationship between film and its subject, film and its audience, and to destroy the possibility of narrative art by inverting its conventions. Were the "snuff" films "real" the contract of narrative film that states that what we see on the screen is a lie (does not *really* happen) would have to be rewritten. All distance between what is seen and what is understood by what is seen would be lost. It would no longer be a question of the viewer becoming prisoner to an illusion of reality, but being guilty of assenting to the actual event of murder. The only real meaning of such films would emerge from the moral choice of attending them or not.

The snuff films were probably lies (I did not see them, and I say they were lies out of a certain need for self-assurance and protection); they failed to gain an audience (surely a sign that we do need the protection of fiction); but it is impossible to downplay the significance of their appearance. They answered what appeared to be an insatiable hunger for death on the part of filmmakers. (Not, necessarily, on the part of audiences, who, if they went to the movies, had little choice as to what they saw. The fact that movie attendance fell off in the early to mid seventies may indicate that we did not like the lack of choice.)

The violence in *Taxi Driver* was another answer. It remains fiction (no one *really* gets hurt); it is, in fact, rather stylized. It is also enormous and insistent enough to create a very real nausea. Travis prepares to shoot down candidate Palantine at a rally. "My whole life has been pointed in one direction," he comments. "There never has been any choice for me." The obsessive decides that there is an object for his obsessiveness. Packed with weapons, his hair shaved like an Indian, he attends the rally, is spotted, and runs. (It is of interest to note that "freeing" Iris by violence is not the first act

Travis considers. Killing is his major impulse, and that urge connects itself to Iris only after the attempted assassination fails.) He returns home, drinks beer, and takes aspirin. At night he goes to Sport's apartment building in the East Village, where, after taunting Sport (who throws a cigarette butt at him), he shoots him in the stomach and goes off down the street to sit on a stoop. He returns to the building and enters, the dark interior appearing somewhat like the set of a German Expressionist film. The camera tracks through the corridors. An avuncular old man, whom we have earlier seen as the money collector for Sport's brothel, pursues Travis, who turns and shoots off a few fingers of the old man's hand (close up and in slow motion—reminiscent of the scene in *McCabe and Mrs. Miller* where the Reverend's hand is blown off by the gunman, Butler). Sport reappears and shoots Travis in the neck. Travis shoots Sport some more. The camera assumes a position above the stairs; we hear the sound of blood trickling, and there is a momentary calm, broken by Travis shooting more bullets into Sport and shooting and beating the old man, who starts running after him, yelling maniacally, "You crazy son of a bitch . . . I'll kill you. I'll kill you. I'll kill you."

At this point, in slow motion, a man opens the door of Iris's room. There is a cut to a shot of Travis being pursued by the old man, and a return to Iris's customer, who shoots Travis in the arm. The maniacal catapult that Travis has built to hold one of his guns and deliver it to his hand pops out and allows him to shoot the customer in the face (as De Niro's Vito Corleone shoots Fanucci in *Godfather II*). The old man, still yelling "I'll kill you," grabs Travis from behind as they enter Iris's room. They fight on the floor; Travis gets a knife he has concealed around his ankle, stabs the old man in the hand (the one that was not shot earlier), and then blows the old man's brains out, spattering the wall with blood (through all this, Iris's sobbing creates a counterpoint to the gunshots and the dripping blood). Travis now puts a gun to his throat and pulls the trigger, but it is empty. He sits down, and as the police enter (emissaries from the sane world who appear menacing as they first peer through the door, but soon bring a calming order to the scene), he puts a bloody finger to his head, works it like a gun, and, smiling, lays his head back. The camera cuts to a high, overhead shot, and, to a crescendo of music, tracks the carnage, down the blood-splattered stairway and, through a series of lap dissolves, over the bloody body of Sport and out the door, observing the police cars and the crowds, in slow motion, gathering.

I describe the sequence in detail partly to make a written record of the climax of screen violence in the mid-seventies and to see if the horror of the sequence can be recreated in verbal description. It cannot, of course; and I find that, in describing it, it is difficult to keep from either exaggerating the description or reflecting upon it verbally just enough to make it comic. And I wonder if beneath its horror there is not something of the comic, or at least the bizarre, attempting to be made manifest. Is it possible that this sequence, with all its doubling of shootings, fallings, and risings, its grotesque exaggerations, is meant to be a parody of screen violence? Early in the film, Travis drives by a movie house that is showing *The Texas Chain Saw Massacre*. The marquee is prominently in view as the cab drifts through the streets. It is interesting to speculate whether it suggests the influence of violent films on Travis, reflects his violent propensities, or alludes to cinematic violence that the big shoot-out will parody. I am suggesting that the shoot-out is another aberration of Travis's mind. It is not a fantasy; it "happens" as part of the fictional events of the film. But it happens the way everything else in the fiction happens, as an exaggerated expression of the way a madman perceives and acts upon his world, an expression doubled by our own perception of it as we view the film. In other words, it is another part of the inside/outside process of observation that Scorsese has followed throughout. So much so that Scorsese plays a little game with us. After the event, we see on the wall of Travis's room a newspaper clipping that shows an overhead diagram of the carnage—a sketch, in effect, of the high-angle shot that closed the sequence. It is a reflexive gesture on Scorsese's part: the "outside world" in the film (in this case the press) imitates the interior world of Travis. The film reflects its parts against each other and against our observation of them.

There is, too, something predestined about the shoot-out, pre-destined not merely because of the nature of Travis's mad self and the violent world he sees and absorbs until it becomes his reflection, but in the formal construction of the film. Throughout there are gestures made, compositional strategies set up, words said that pre-pare for the sequence. The second time we (and Travis) see Betsy, for example, she is bantering with a friend at campaign headquarters about a newsstand operator who has only one hand, and only two fingers on that hand. They speculate that the mob blew off his fingers. Travis does not hear this, and there is no suggestion that this ridic-ulous conversation suggests to him his treatment of the caretaker of Sport's brothel. It is simply a set-up and a contrast, the banal chatter of two people oblivious to the world in which Travis lives, words that will be ironically and grotesquely realized in the shoot-out and after. Reference to the Mafia turns up again when it is discovered that one of the men Travis kills was a mafioso. This is the event that, with the freeing of Iris, makes him a media hero.

Also in this sequence, when Travis approaches Betsy and makes his pitch to her, telling her how he sees all the people around her and all the work on her desk, there is suddenly a cut to a point-of-view shot from Travis to the top of her desk, which the camera pans, fol-lowing the sweep of Travis's hand. There is no reason for this shot; it adds nothing to the sequence and tells us little about either Travis or Betsy at this moment. However, the high angle, the movement across the clutter of the desk, *formally* predict the high-angle shot of the carnage later on. In fact we see such a high-angle shot twice before: once at the cab company, where there is a similiar point-of-view shot from Travis to the cab owner's desk, and then again at the candy counter of the porn movie theater Travis visits. This may, I am afraid, sound more than a bit overingenious. But in a film as carefully structured as *Taxi Driver,* every shot is made to count, to be meaning-ful immediately or to prepare us for something later in the work. This meaning need not be on a substantive level: form can refer to, or in this case foreshadow, form. A high-angle pan of a cluttered desk is contextually different from a high-angle track of a room full of bloody bodies, but formally similar: both are high-angle, and both move. A linkage is therefore set up that may not affect us consciously on first viewing, but remains part of the structural system of the film nevertheless.

Other foreshadowings are more apparent and direct: when Travis purchases guns from Andy, the gun fence, who sells his wares as if he were selling appliances, Travis holds one up and aims it through the window, the camera tracking along his arm to an anonymous couple on the street. Earlier, at the Belmore Cafeteria, when Travis takes Wizard aside in an attempt to tell him of the bad ideas in his head, a black cab driver looks up at him and points his finger at Travis as if it were a gun. There is a dolly back from this gesture, a shot from Travis's point of view, and then a reverse to Travis, who reacts with an odd look. Once outside the cafeteria, Travis attempts to unburden himself to Wizard, who cannot comprehend what he is saying. He calls him, with affection, "Killer." "Relax, Killer," he tells him, "you're gonna be all right"—words that will ironically ring true as Travis proceeds. Later, when Travis meets Sport for the first time, the pimp makes the same gun gesture with his hand at Travis. After the massacre, Travis repeats the gesture, at his own head.

Consideration of these events, along with Travis's killing of the robber in the delicatessen and the manic preparations and rituals he puts himself through, should make the main event less surprising and perhaps less gratuitous than it first appears. Unfortunately, no matter how much is revealed by such analysis, it remains an excrescence, a moment of grotesque excess in an otherwise controlled work. It damages the film, permitting it to be rejected as only one more entry in the list of violent exploitations rampant in the mid-seventies.[15] But even so damaged, the film is less cynical than many of its relatives, and no matter how much it may pander to the lowest expectations of an audience, it also holds back, tricks those expectations, and, save for those few minutes in which control is lost, remains a coherent, subtle work.

In its structuring of point of view, its reconsideration of the *noir* milieu, its intense observation of the character's relationship to himself within a carefully defined world that expresses his state of mind, and in its reticence in analyzing or seeking motivations for that character and his world, *Taxi Driver* sets up a closed narrative of loneliness and madness that proves, finally, to be quite responsible—responsible in the sense that it offers us, in a clearly defined form, the lack of clarity and the lack of definition that characterize solitude and madness, without falling into the trap that romanticizes madness as a redemptive experience. The film, in total, in presenting its character and his semi-life as simply *there,* implicates us and allows neither the character nor us to be removed from the consequences of events and of perception. It examines from the point of view of its character the clichés and the sentimentality that we have come to take for granted in films and television, conventions of masculine strength and feminine passivity that appear not merely banal but destructive in the context of this film and of an individual who takes them as meaningful when they are in fact only mad.

I spoke earlier of the use Scorsese makes of cinematic allusion, the way he follows the New Wave filmmakers in drawing upon, paying homage to, and in many instances changing the cinematic forms and conventions that precede his work. In *Taxi Driver* that allusiveness is carefully integrated into the film, making it rich and resonant. The Fordian lineage of Travis Bickle and his demonic recreation of the John Wayne persona in *The Searchers* has been mentioned. Even stronger and more conclusive is the film's homage to Hitchcock, and to *Psycho* in particular.*

What Hitchcock persistently examines in his best films are the ways an audience can be manipulated in and out of a moral situation, and made to react not so much to what is happening on the screen as

* There are allusions as well to the master of cinematic allusiveness, Jean-Luc Godard. Patterson and Farber point out the full-screen inserts of Travis's diary entries, a device Godard employs in *Pierrot le fou* and elsewhere, and the camera movement into a bubbling glass of Alka-Seltzer, an homage to the coffee-cup sequence in *Two or Three Things*.[16]

to what is happening to their reactions to what is happening. Hitchcock speaks to the power of images and sounds to manipulate us into reaction and counter-reaction, and, within the narratives constructed by these images and sounds, to the manipulative power of sexuality and domination and fear that one character can wield over another. Throughout the forties and into the fifties, Hitchcock cloaked this inquiry, sometimes almost hermetically, in romantic melodrama (*Notorious,* posing as a love story, is as frightening an exploration of sexual and emotional abuse and political manipulation as one can find in American film). In the fifties he slowly began to drop the generic pretenses, first in *The Wrong Man* and then in *Vertigo.* By the time he made *Psycho,* he was able to create a world that was the dialectic to that of melodrama, a dark, loveless, brutal world in which we are made emotional accomplices first to a petty thief and then to a homicidal maniac. The world of *Psycho* is a sub-division of *noir* territory, in which the isolation of a roadside motel takes the place of a barren urban landscape, and its parlor the reflection of a savage and savaged mind.

Taxi Driver becomes at many points an analogue to *Psycho.* (Tangentially, *Taxi Driver* is related to *Vertigo* as well, the relationships of Travis to Betsy and Sport to Iris being curious echos of Scottie's idealized and destructive relationship to Madeleine/Judy.) Both *Taxi Driver* and *Psycho* are studies of the impenetrability of madness, but where Hitchcock leads the audience by indirection, showing the effects of madness, bluffing the cause and withholding the source, Scorsese concentrates on the central figure, never denying us a concentrated gaze on a disintegrating mind. But in both cases, though by different means, we are allowed a degree of closeness to a character, reproved for that closeness, and made to feel horror and guilt because of it. Both Hitchcock and Scorsese play upon our desire to "identify," to sympathize with and understand a film's "hero." Both do this formally, through devices of framing and composition, through control of the *mise-en-scène;* so that as we tend to move toward the character, the way we see the character makes us move away, alienates our very desire to understand. Both films work through a sense of terrifying isolation: Norman Bates is completely removed from his world. Travis Bickle is removed *with* his world, half-seeing and half-creating it wherever he goes until it almost literally disappears into his own reflection. The sequence in which he looks at himself in the mirror—as if he were every antagonist he could ever fantasize—"You talkin' to me? . . . Who the fuck do you think you're talkin' to?"—signifies an almost total solipsism.

It is this solipsism that both *Psycho* and *Taxi Driver* attempt, finally, to delineate: a world and a state of mind so enclosed and so unknowable that we, as observers, are fooled for attempting to understand it. Hitchcock fashions his enigma through a major device of manipulation. Norman is discovered to be Norman's mother, a killer with knife and wig shrieking in the darkness. Our shock at this discovery is offered a palliative by means of a psychiatrist's rational explanation. In cold, deliberate tones, in the security of a police station, a doctor explains Norman's condition, placing it within the order of our known experience. By all expectations, this explanation should end the film, close it neatly and with the promise of comfort. But it is not meant to be closed comfortably, or at all. And after the psychiatrist's tidy words, we confront Norman himself, track slowly to him, in a cell, draped in a white sheet, his "mother's" voice telling us how she wouldn't hurt a fly; we approach his manic face until, beneath it, we barely see the grinning skull of mother, the two images punctured by the car in which Norman had buried his victims being pulled from the swamp. The face and the acts of madness, images of unexpected and uncontrollable violence, regain power over the psychiatrist's talk of complexes and psychoses. Rather than the security given us by explanation, we are left with the enigma of the irrational.[17]

The closing sequences of *Taxi Driver* similarly play on our desire to understand and to assimilate the unknowable. After the carnage, we gaze along the walls of Travis's apartment. We don't see him, but we see a version of him that has been created by his act: newspaper clippings announce his heroism: "Taxi Driver Battles Gangsters," "Reputed New York Mafioso Killed in Bizarre Shooting," "Taxi Hero to Recover." Over this we hear the voice of Iris's father: "You are something of a hero around this household." The anti-social lunatic killer has become savior; a combination of Clint Eastwood and Charles Bronson is born from the union of Norman Bates and John Wayne, with Kubrick's Alex acting as godfather. (What better off-spring than Dirty Harry Callahan and the urban vigilante of *Death Wish* in the person of that working-class philosopher, the cab driver?) The desperate search for heroes in recent cinema has thrown up some odd characters, who seem to insist that only viciousness and excesses of anti-social behavior can allow us to triumph in a society seemingly devoid of other means of self-expression. What prevents us from accepting Travis as another manifestation of such salvation? Nothing, except that he clearly manifests the psychotic nature that is hidden in the film heroes who are his antecedents. What we see in the clippings on Travis's walls, and hear in the voice of the father whose daughter he has returned, gives us permission momentarily to slip out of Travis's perception of the world. But if we take the opportunity to do so, we find that we are, on our own, capable of seeing the world in as mad a light as he, that we can find ludicrous heroes in unlikely places and indulge in fantasies as grotesque as his own.

This implication is allowed to continue in the following sequence, where we see Travis standing with his cronies in front of the St. Regis Hotel. It is the first time in the film that we see him in a setting not redolent of violence and perversity (although by this time his presence alone is sufficient to create the necessary aura). Betsy, the angel in white, gets into his cab, and Travis drives her to a leafy East Side street. The sequence continues the hero fantasy originated by the newspaper clippings and the letter from Iris's father. Travis is removed from Betsy, talking to her casually, not permitting her to pay the fare, playing the melodramatic role of the strong, rebuffed lover. Has he somehow been purified by his ritual act of destruction and its attendant glorification? Or does he think he has? We do not see Betsy for the duration of her ride, except as she is reflected through the rear-view mirror of the cab. When we do see her emerging, it is in a far shot. She has become even more of a ghostly image than she previously was, more of a projection of Travis's melodramatic

249

fantasies. But we are allowed to continue our momentary separation from him, our illusory reconsideration of his status. Is he, after all, a likable guy who just—as President Merkin Muffley says about Jack D. Ripper in *Dr. Strangelove*—went a little funny in the head? In truth, we are being set up in a manner analogous to the penultimate sequence in *Psycho,* given a false invitation to understand the character.

As Travis leaves Betsy, driving away, we see her through his rear window. The camera pans across the cab's interior, past Travis to his eyes, strangely lit, reflected in the rear-view mirror. He glances toward the mirror and there is a cut to a shot from behind it, looking at him. Suddenly, as if catching sight of his eyes, he makes a lunge, twisting the mirror toward him. As he does this, a loud squeak can be heard. We cut back to a shot from inside the cab, looking at the mirror and the street outside. We see Travis's hand push the mirror away and, as the credits come up, see the lights of the streets outside and reflected in the mirror. As the credits end, the percussive sound track rises, Travis's eyes briefly pass across the mirror, and outside we see the grainy night-time street, the people moving, as they did at the beginning of the film, in slow motion. Like the end of *Psycho,* the end of *Taxi Driver* returns us to the abysmal impossibility of understanding madness or accounting for its violence. What it adds is the suggestion that the carrier of this madness has some awareness of his state. Travis's avoidance of his eyes in the cab mirror refers back to his conversation with Iris. When he tells her that Sport is a killer, she responds, "Didn't you ever try looking in your own eyeballs in the mirror?" When he finally does, the recognition is for him what it is for us when we look into Norman's face at the end of *Psycho:* terror. New York's hero is still "God's lonely man," still a killer. He remains his own passenger, threatening to take others for a ride.

*Taxi Driver* has many more allusions to Hitchcock, although it is greater than the sum of these allusions and is certainly not diminished by being seen as an analogue to Hitchcock's work. The Hitchcockian reminders of the tenuousness of our physical and moral existence and of our willingness to believe lies and live them if they do not demand too much from us, are important enough to be seen and heard often in many forms. *Taxi Driver* is not as pure a statement as is the best Hitchcock and not as sure; but it is certainly as dark and as unremitting. It is, to date, Scorsese's best film, none of the others manifesting its care and intensity. *New York, New York,* which follows it, attempts ever so slightly to retune De Niro's character, essentially making Travis Bickle less crazy and dangerous but no less antisocial. Even more important, it attempts to extend the expressionist perception of *Taxi Driver* in ways that need some attention and analysis. *Alice Doesn't Live Here Anymore,* which precedes *Taxi Driver,* is a film so completely its opposite that it might be by another hand. And although it has great formal energy, it is more important for its subject than its execution.

*Alice* is a film of light, concerned with realizing personal energies and impressing those energies onto the world in a non-destructive way. It is one of the rare films of the late sixties and early seventies that offers a notion of optimism, "a small step forward," as Diane Jacobs says, out of the hatred and murder, passivity and manipulation that have informed most of our recent films.[18] But it remains only a step, and we seem more likely to retreat from it—as does Scorsese—than to follow it through. In the context of Scorsese's work, *Alice* stands apart, almost as a dialectic to the dark violence of *Mean Streets* and *Taxi Driver,* almost offering the possibility that the violence can be contained and subdued. The violent character of Harvey Keitel's Ben is seen in the film partially as an intrusion, partially as a mode of behavior that exists and must be attended to. It is not allowed, as is similar behavior in the other films, to encompass and diminish everything else. But it does exist, and there is a sense of brooding and nervousness in the camera movements throughout the film that seems to portend something other than what these movements are covering and that relates the film to the essential concerns of Scorsese's other works: threat always exists; energies are always ready to be expended. Here the threats are overcome and the energies directed joyfully.

*Alice* can be seen either as a comedy, a structure of outrageous and exaggerated incidents leading to a harmonious grouping of characters at the end, or as a feminist film that attempts to question and respond to the conventions of female behavior set by American film for decades. But neither of these approaches is consistent or easily definable within Scorsese's film. The feminist film has yet to be established in commercial American cinema, and probably will not be, considering the reaction to feminism in the culture at large and the cooptation of its most easily assimilable ideas and modes of expression by advertising and television. Comedy, on the other hand, while among the most established genres in film, is the most impure and unstable. There is no possibility of defining the generic bounds of comedy, as we can for the gangster film, or *film noir*, or even the broader form of melodrama. It is a genre whose definition is even more difficult since *Bonnie and Clyde*, which set the pattern for mixing conventions of comedy and melodrama and pathos within one film. To narrow the base somewhat and provide a model for comparison, I want to look at *Alice* from the perspective of the old form of screwball comedy, which does have certain definable elements.

These comedies of the late thirties provide some of the most delightful statements of liberation in our cinema. They are the films in which Cary Grant and Katherine Hepburn or Irene Dunne or Rosalind Russell fought for their independence and discovered it could be realized with each other. Screwball comedy was a comedy of class, of the wealthy (or, in the case of Lubitsch's *Trouble in Paradise*, the would-be wealthy), and it played against a major film convention, one we have met in the discussion of *Godfather II:* that the rich and powerful cannot be happy. Screwball comedy showed the rich as very happy and very free. It offered an alternate mode of perception to the Depression audience, not so much a perception that might make the viewer wish to be rich, but one that offered a model of behavior, perhaps not achievable, but desirable. These films were wish-fulfillment fantasies in the conventional sense: offering a means of escape to the audience, they did not attempt to fool the audience by offering the escape as a reality. Rather, they provided an alternative to melodrama, the notion that happiness and even sexual fulfillment were attainable without agony. While their celebration of wealth might appear rather cynical in the face of the Depression, their celebration of vitality was admirable and their notions of sexual liberation something that recent cinema has been unable to evoke.

Screwball comedy did not survive the early forties. Its vitality became compromised and its focus shifted from the upper to the middle and lower middle classes (the shift can be seen in George Cukor's *Holiday* [1938] and Preston Sturges's *Sullivan's Travels* [1942] and *Hail the Conquering Hero* [1944]). By the fifties it had degenerated into television situation comedy. Recently, some successful attempts at reviving the genre within a middle-class milieu have occurred, most notably in Melvin Frank's *A Touch of Class* (1973) and Ted Kotcheff's *Fun with Dick and Jane* (1977, written by Jerry Belson, Mordecai Richler, and David Giler). But, like all of Scorsese's films, *Alice Doesn't Live Here Anymore* is about working-class characters, and whatever remnants of screwball comedy it contains are therefore inverted. It is not about liberated and vital people, but about a woman who is unfamiliar with freedom trying it out. In screwball comedy, the equality of women was a premise that allowed the even match between male and female characters to occur. In fact, the male character was sometimes put at an emotional disadvantage to a stronger woman—confronted by her energy, as in Howard Hawks's *Bringing Up Baby,* and forced to be an equal.[19] This was not a situation the culture was, or is yet, very used to; neither was the compromise between individual energy and marriage that so many of the screwball comedies discovered. Nor did the culture seem able to emulate it. With the firm bourgeoisification of comedy in the fifties, the woman, while still strong, used her strength mainly to protect herself from the incessant sexual advances of the male, while coaxing him into a domestic life (most of the fifties Doris Day vehicles attest to the pattern). In the recent revivals of the screwball genre, the woman and the man again achieve a certain equality, but the balance is very tenuous. In *Alice* the balance is being sought and is never quite achieved.

Alice Hyatt (Ellen Burstyn) is not an independent figure. Her reach for liberation is the result of an accident and the memory of a fantasy. She moves out of the domestic order—the small, compacted, bleached world of a New Mexican suburb. Rather than seeking a man, she seeks escape from a world that has been dominated by one. It is not an active escape as in Coppola's *The Rain People,* where Natalie wrenches herself away from her husband's leaden embrace. Alice's husband dies, and his death allows a return of her desire to be a singer and a very real need to support herself. What is important in this movement is that neither Robert Getchell's script nor Scorsese's direction allows any attempt at analysis of Alice herself. She neither agonizes over her decision to move (though she feels sad about leaving her friend) nor voices any distinct understanding of it. If anything, the opening sequences of the film indicate she is rather out of touch with the realities of her situation, and subject to conflicting fantasies. The film opens with an artificial studio landscape, a farmhouse and a country road, lit in red and reminiscent of thirties film, of Dorothy's Kansas in *The Wizard of Oz* or a John Ford homestead. Alice's past is a movie past, a surrogate for real experience in a three-by-four screen ratio. It is personalized somewhat by being embodied in a tough, foul-mouthed little Alice, who insists she can sing better than Alice Faye. It is this fantasy past, the Monterey of her movie-made childhood, that Alice wants to rediscover in her escape from her domestic life. At the end, this sign of the past becomes a sign, literally. Alice and her son Tommy walk down a Tucson street, still uncertain about their future, and over them, against the hills, in a compressed, telephoto shot, is a roadside advertising sign that says "Monterey." One place is as good as another, if all places are divested of fantasy and invested with a secure sense of one's self. For as fantasy, the "Monterey" of Alice's past entraps her as much as her domestic life entraps her, and one of the areas the film investigates is whether a way out of any of these traps is possible.

Alice's married life, which booms into the movie fantasy of her past with a loud noise and rapidly moving camera, is the obverse of her childhood myth. Her son has his head clapped between two loudspeakers blaring rock, and Alice can only sing along while she sews. Her husband (Billy Green Bush) is a prostrate figure on the bed, yelling at the noise. When we finally see him, he appears a sulky, complaining, unresponsive man. In one rather touching and frightening shot, we look down at him and Alice in bed, she turned away, he hopelessly holding her from behind. Alice's "present" is sketched in with short but significant scenes. It seems to offer us an immediate, unpleasant reality that wipes out past dreams. It seems as well an exaggeration of what we have been told so often is bad about domestic life and the woman's place in it. The result of this exaggeration, and the stylized brevity of the sequence, is to make it play off of the fantasy sequence that precedes it. The one is presented in images that render the artificiality of an old movie set. The other is also artificial, even though it consists of images shot on location, in natural light, images that are comfortably "realistic" within the conventions of contemporary film. It is artificial because it is film, of course. But it is artificial as well because of its almost stylized expression of domestic brutality. Both the childhood fantasies that the opening sequence presents and the "reality" that the domestic sequence presents are experiences from which Alice must free herself. They reflect and exaggerate two regrettable situations and set up a potential for escape. (If a time comes when the domestic order is liberated and women are not oppressed and made passive by it, then the scenes with Alice and her husband may be recalled or recreated as images of a lost nightmare, much as the childhood sequence is presented at the beginning of the film as the recollection of a lost dream.)

Another result of the sketchiness of Alice's domestic life is the ease with which the husband can be removed. He is a brutish jerk whose death in his Coca-Cola truck is presented with a cold distance worthy of Godard. It is important that Scorsese not permit any emotional reaction to his death, because it is not central to the narrative, only a catalyst. His function is clearly to create a hopeless situation, and with him gone, Alice and the film are free to inscribe other patterns. The first man she meets on her travels is a slightly more complicated figure than her husband: Ben appears warm and gentle, only

Domestic life: **Alice Doesn't Live Here Anymore** (Billy Green Bush, Alfred Lutter, Ellen Burstyn).

to turn out to be a potential killer. (He makes the gesture that becomes so significant in *Taxi Driver,* of pointing his finger as if it were a gun—play violence preceding physical violence.) The sequences of their meeting and bedding down are well handled, Alice's resistance to his advances indicating her new strength and independence. The dissolve from her in bed with Ben to her and her son in bed, listening to a fight in the room next to theirs, prepares us for the violence to come, as does the nervous hand-held camera work that precedes the visit of Ben's wife and his breaking into Alice's motel room, threatening murder. The entire episode is somewhat cautionary. The woman alone is vulnerable (as vulnerable as the woman married), and the long far shot of the interior of the smashed-up motel room as Alice and Tommy leave after Ben's attack serves to isolate them and to emphasize the tenuous nature of their life alone on the road.

Her meeting with David (Kris Kristofferson) is the point where the film begins to fall back on conventional elements. Alice has taken a job as a waitress—a prime movie occupation for single working girls —and she meets a rancher who attempts to accommodate her independence and also disburden her of her fantasies of going to Monterey and becoming a singer. Scorsese and Getchell choose to give this affair melodramatic overtones and to deny the possibilities of vitality that have marked Alice's character up to this point. They opt for a sentimentality that has so far been missing from the film. Ellen Burstyn's character supplies too much energy suddenly to fall for the recessive machismo inevitably supplied by Kristofferson (who has become something of an axiom of recent American film, bland enough not to be threatening, rugged enough not to be completely boring). Alice's admission to her co-worker, Flo, in a very tender scene between the two women that takes place in a bathroom, that she is both afraid of not pleasing a husband and unable to live without a man, indicates that she remains burdened by old fantasies and cultural baggage. That she "falls" for David, even though she forces him to recognize her needs, betrays how far we have come from screwball comedy and how close we still are to the forties "woman's picture" in which a Bette Davis or a Joan Crawford character had strength only to hold on until the right man came along to be recognized as a figure of salvation. Few recent films that have pretended to focus upon women and consider them as individuals have succeeded in transcending the gravitational pull back into marriage and/ or a "fulfilling" relationship. The screwball comedies did not depict marriage as "fulfilling" in the sense that it determined a woman's role. Marriage was the end of most screwballs, but it was most often a celebration of battles continually to be fought and personalities continuing to be independent (it was often a placation of the Hays Office as well). *Alice* has disappointed many critics on this score, for it gives and takes away, depicts independence only to wind up back in dependence again. It ends with the termination of Alice's fantasies, but not with the termination of larger fantasies, those that insist that a tall and handsome stranger will protect the weak and dependent woman.

If the conclusions drawn by *Alice* are bright but less than radical, there are elements within it that do realize responses to old conventions in new ways. The most important of these is the friendship between Alice and Flo (Diane Ladd), Alice and her son (Alfred Lutter), and her son and Audrey (née Doris, played by Jodie Foster). In each of these groupings there is an evenness and equality that belie the manipulation or sentimentality that usually marks friendships, indeed relationships of any kind, in American film. Flo and Alice make up an almost unconventional pairing. In past films women have sometimes been allowed understanding companions, but the companionship had to retain a certain distance and inequality. Flo and Alice parallel the friendship between Joan Crawford and Eve Arden in *Mildred Pierce,* except that here the two women are equal and Flo presents a grounding, stabilizing component to Alice's dreams. The sequence in which the two of them sit and talk in the midday sun, observed in profile, faces raised to the warmth, an image which dissolves to a long shot in which we see them in the midst of the blowing sands of an unpleasant desert landscape, presents in almost symbolic fashion an image of two strong women trapped in unaccommodating circumstances, yet equal to themselves and what is demanded of them. All through the film, Scorsese quietly comments on the action with the placement and movement of his camera. The quiet energy of the tracks around Alice when she plays a piano, the nervous movement before Ben's attack, and the dissolve to what should be (but is not) an isolating far shot in the scene with Flo, all work to Alice's and our advantage, allowing us to perceive, with her, the movement, the danger, and the stability she finds and accepts. Obviously, if Alice sat alone in the arid sunlight, the shot would have very different connotations. Her ability to accept the friendship of an equal (which sounds perfectly trite, until one considers how few such female friendships exist in film) makes the space she occupies less inhuman than it would be otherwise.[20]

The humanizing quality exists more strongly in Alice's relationship with her son. A chapter in the history of American film could be written about its inability to come to terms with children: they exist either as small adults, as unconscionably cute, or as amazingly vicious. Only recently, particularly at the hands of Michael Ritchie in *Smile* and *The Bad News Bears,* have children been created with an independent character that bears up without extremes. Tommy and Audrey in *Alice* are further attempts to deal with children without laying upon them a predetermined notion of what their behavior should be. Even more, the characters are presented without any explanation of their behavior (except for the brief appearance of Audrey's prostitute mother) and therefore are unsentimentalized. Tommy and Alice exist in a free and equal interchange that provides a measure of companionship and support Alice does not get from strangers, as well as the major comic moments of the film. Every opportunity to exploit Tommy's loneliness or Alice's potential guilt for leaving him in a motel room while she works is avoided. Any profound concern that Tommy will start on a life of delinquency because of such treatment and because of his friendship with the tough Audrey is denied. This is done because the film is a comedy; though it is not an evasion merely for the sake of the genre, but part of an attempt to avoid psychologizing or moralizing that is, with the regrettable exception of the treatment of Alice and David, a mark of the film's success.

It is rare that a film, particularly when it takes the form of a journey, a road movie, leaves both us and its characters alone, without indicating momentous events and major change. Except for the event that sets Alice out (which is underplayed) and the violence of Ben (which Scorsese cannot avoid), *Alice* is content to observe possibilities of change and freedom, however limited, without forcing its characters to pay a price. No one dies (with the exception of Alice's husband), no one gets emotionally or physically hurt or scarred. It is perhaps one of the few films discussed in this book in which no character is seriously lonely, without recourse to community of some kind. Coming, as it does, between *Mean Streets,* in which the community is dark and volatile, finally destructive, and *Taxi Driver,* where there is no community and the isolated man explodes into madness, *Alice* indicates that the dialectic is not dead and that American film could, conceivably, survive with its characters talking to each other, listening, and responding. It stands, with all its flaws, as an important entry into that recent group of American films that attempts to come to terms with women in a way other than the conventional modes of melodrama. It perhaps fits as a middle link between Cassavetes's dark view of a husband and wife imprisoned in their own inarticulateness in *A Woman under the Influence* and Paul Mazursky's sentimentalizing of a rich divorcée in *An Unmarried Woman*. In it we see that, for all of his darkness, Scorsese is capable of making a film in which a character is permitted a modicum of freedom and joy. He does not, so far, seem interested in following up this possibility, at least not in his fiction films. He follows *Taxi Driver* with one of the odder experiments in recent American film, attempting a collation of genres that cannot mix and a design that becomes so self-enclosed it finally refers to nothing but itself.

In the three features before *New York, New York,* Scorsese shows a marked attraction to the obviously artificial. The opening of *Alice,* where the camera booms around a mock-thirties studio set; the carefully controlled lighting, framing, and movement (indeed the generally expressionist approach) in *Taxi Driver;* the red-lit bar sequences in *Mean Streets,* photographed in slow motion—all are part of Scorsese's desire to create a *mise-en-scène* that locates both his characters and our perceptions of them in a controlled space. Of all the directors discussed here, including Kubrick, Scorsese is the one who can be seen consistently moving away from the contemporary conventions of cinematic realism to images made in the controlled interior world of the studio set where no aspect of the design is left to chance. But unlike Hitchcock, who used studio interiors and process shots long after they had gone out of fashion, so that he could keep all aspects of the production under his control, Scorsese is not intent on making the artificial appear "real" but on drawing attention to the artificiality itself; he wants us to detect the unusual, the artificial, as such.*

* The issue is a bit more complicated than this. Hitchcock's "realism" is a tenuous affair; he constantly seeks to elicit a perception of the strange and

*New York, New York* contains no location shots. With the help of production designer Boris Leven and cinematographer Laszlo Kovacs, Scorsese builds an artificial world. The result is odd, and I am not certain that what we perceive is what was intended. The opening titles of the film, the painted city skyline, immediately refer us to a pastel evocation of the forties and early-fifties studio musical. But as the film proceeds, this intended evocation begins to disappear and be replaced by a consciousness of the *methods* of evocation. The forties interiors and the strange, almost abstract suggestiveness of the exteriors develop their own attraction; the control of the *mise-en-scène* seems to become more important than why that control is being exercised, so that form threatens to refer only to itself. The viewer becomes aware not of *why* the studio sets are there (to evoke the atmosphere of the studio musical), only that they *are* there. Not that they are not fascinating in themselves: Jimmy Doyle's ascent up the steps of the El, as he gazes upon a sailor and a girl doing a Gene Kelly ballet in an empty and undefined street below; a high-angle shot of Jimmy (Robert De Niro) playing his saxophone under a lamp in a deserted studio street; a meeting between Jimmy and Francine (Liza Minnelli) in the snow, with the silhouettes of cut-out trees behind them; a car driving off into a studio-red sunset, are all undeniably attractive. But they are only fascinating as aspects of design. And they are inconsistent. Most of the interiors, with the exception of an oddly lit motel room and a nightclub lit entirely in red neon, are conventionally "real." They look like interiors evocative of the forties, whereas the exteriors evoke not a time but the idea of studio sets.

Scorsese has confused two levels of realism: illusionary realism,

---

violent from the everyday. But it is true that he stuck to the studio long after studio sets and process shots, when compared to location shooting, began to look like the artifices they always were.

Scorsese (as well as Coppola) has expressed his admiration for the films of Michael Powell and Emeric Pressburger, who made *The Red Shoes* and *Stairway to Heaven* (among many others). Their films (at least those that I have seen) demonstrate a marked attraction to the artificial and the fantastic, even for their time. Their influence on Scorsese is an interesting item for further research.[21]

in which the cinematic space and its articulations create the illusion of a "real world," and a realism of form, in which the cinematic space points to its own existence, prevents the viewer from passing through the form into an illusion of reality, and uses that obstacle to create other levels of awareness. This is what Kubrick attains in *Barry Lyndon,* but through a consistency of spatial articulations which point both to their own artificiality and to the way that artificiality is the very content of the film. If Scorsese was consciously attempting to correct the phenomenon of "evocation" films that followed upon *Bonnie and Clyde* in the late sixties and early seventies by demonstrating that the evocation of the past in film is only the evocation of the ways film evokes the past, the inconsistency of exterior artificiality and interior "realism" compromises his attempt.

There is also an extraordinary mixture of genres in the film. It is primarily a romantic musical in the post-*Cabaret* style, in which the musical numbers occur as part of the narrative, as an actual stage performance—or, in one sequence, a film performance—rather than expanding out of the narrative and into another spatial plane, as was the convention from the Busby Berkeley Warner Brothers musicals through the Vincente Minnelli and Gene Kelly–Stanley Donen films for MGM in the late forties and early fifties. But here again Scorsese denies the tradition he apparently wants to celebrate, mixing a reflexivity that forces us to view the film as a self-conscious recreation not of a period but of a film of a period with a realism of quite recent origin. A film like Bob Fosse's *Cabaret* (which also stars Liza Minnelli) attempts to turn the musical into a "realistic" genre, a melodrama with music. *New York, New York* continues that attempt, but at the same time undoes it by attempting to evoke older musicals that had no pretense to that kind of realism and flaunting the unreality of its appearance. If that were not complicated enough, exteriors are so lit and photographed as to appear similar to the *mise-en-scène* of *Taxi Driver,* so that a claustrophobic, barren, and occasionally foreboding effect is achieved that saturates the film with the aura of *film noir.* This in itself is not novel, for some of the thirties Warner's musicals had a discomfiting darkness and despair about them. But it is not

Studio trees: Robert De Niro and Liza Minnelli in **New York, New York.**

clear what the darkness of *New York, New York* is reflecting, since the temporal overlays are so uncertain. The occasional despair about "putting on the show" or about personal and financial security that manifested itself in some thirties musicals grew out of the Depression, the time in which the films were made and the time they reflected. *New York, New York,* made in the seventies, is about the forties, and it is difficult to determine whether the *noir* elements of the film are merely part of the evocation of the forties *noir* style, an experiment in genre-mixing, or an attempt to create a setting for a romance that has its dark and anxiety-ridden moments.[22] With all of this, the film also has comedy and moments that recall the musical biography popular in the forties and fifties. Finally, these elements are placed at the service of the two major characters and their unromantic romance.

Here, too, an uncomfortable mixture of styles occurs. Liza Minnelli brings with her a persona full of vulnerability and almost masochistic passivity, fully in the tradition of her mother, Judy Garland (as well as her own past screen roles). De Niro, at least under Scorsese's direction, has developed a persona of barely restrained anger and violence. He has become a major figure of urban disenfranchisement, brooding, smirking, holding back, and very nervous. This persona creates curious reverberations. De Niro, in his screen persona, is the young Marlon Brando of the seventies (he of course plays a young Brando—Vito Corleone—in *Godfather II*), a repressed but articulate version of the fifties Brando and his mumbling energy. In the fifties, the rebellious, eccentric character had to be restrained by confusion and uncertainty, a looking inward that tempered outward bravura and threat. In the seventies, the rebellious male needs to be more self-effacing, more in control, more wise to his discontent, or at least more accepting of it. De Niro manifests more energy than most contemporary actors and, at the same time, more control. The conflict between the energy and the control results in explosion and violence—controlled violence in Coppola's hands, uncontrolled in Scorsese's—except in *New York, New York,* where the persona is restrained, and Scorsese attempts to domesticate it.*

Scorsese and screenwriter Earl Mac Rauch and Mardik Martin consciously attempt to play upon the conflict of "star" personalities. The result is that, with all the other tensions of the film generated by its clashing genres and its artificial *mise-en-scène,* we have as well the tensions created by two individuals whose existence is strongly determined outside the narrative impersonating two fictitious characters within it, who themselves are full of tensions. The film succeeds best when it focuses on the tensions of these characters as they attempt to live and work together as husband and wife and as performers. The body of the narrative traces Francine's falling under Jimmy's domination and yielding to his enigmatic isolation (a trait he shares with Travis Bickle and which is hilariously alluded to when we see

* The Brando/De Niro pairing becomes most interesting when the two actors are observed directed by the same individual: by Coppola, in the *Godfathers;* by Bertolucci, who directs Brando in *Last Tango in Paris* and De Niro in *1900;* and by Elia Kazan, who was Brando's best director in the fifties, and unsuccessfully attempted to manipulate De Niro in a romantic melodrama, *The Last Tycoon,* in the seventies.

him, in one shot, framed under a print of the *Mona Lisa*). He insists at one point, after he has stayed away from her, that she cannot understand his need to be alone: "No, you don't understand that. Don't tell me you do, 'cause you don't really understand it. But I had to do it, baby." To which she responds, "Well, I understand that I don't understand." And he agrees, "Okay, that's being better about it." Jimmy talks about himself either in romantic terms, or he bullies or withdraws. For her part, Francine can only withdraw, slip behind him and make her way and her career by default. Jimmy's aloneness is by his choice and need; Francine's results from this need. At the end of many of their scenes, Scorsese has Jimmy leave the frame or cuts to a closeup of Francine, holding it to indicate her isolation, or allows us to gaze at Jimmy, emphasizing his enigmatic character. Toward the end, when Francine begins her own career and attempts a reconciliation with her husband at a nightclub, Jimmy goes off to speak on the phone. We watch him, standing silently after his phone call, a very long, inarticulate gaze, on his part and ours, revealing nothing but his silence and his inability to come to terms with himself, and our inability to come to terms with him.

In his approach to the inarticulateness of the characters and to the somberness of their situation and surroundings, Scorsese avoids some of the glibness (but also the brightness) of *Alice Doesn't Live Here Anymore* and replaces its nervous energy with a slow, sometimes ponderous rhythm of emotional liberation emerging with considerable pain and uncertainty. But like *Alice,* this film does its best to avoid the melodrama and sentiment inherent in its subject, denying the emotional glut that might easily have been built up. Those sequences in which Francine begins to move on her own and in which Jimmy's separation from her is made complete are among the best indicators of Scorsese's control over the narrative movement. In the nightclub sequence just referred to, Francine attempts her reconciliation with Jimmy by singing with him on stage. He forces her off by upping the tempo, using the self-contained power of his music to drive her away. She waits for him in their car, where an enormous battle ensues. Jimmy drives and beats on the dashboard, and then beats on her. He attempts to express his feelings, but in so doing creates a nice inversion of expectations. Physically they are equals in the battle. Verbally, the emotions Jimmy expresses—his jealousy about their baby, his fears about being nothing on his own and nothing in relation to her—are feelings often reserved for the woman in a melodramatic situation, one that often dictates that it is the woman who must suffer in the face of an impassive man. Here we find that, once the man's impassiveness breaks down, he, too, suffers the fears and uncertainties that, in American film at least, are rarely allowed a man. But Scorsese is clever enough to have things both ways. If we are permitted to see a reversal in the relationship of man and woman, we are permitted as well to have our melodrama: the sequence ends, after much yelling and slapping, with the pregnant Francine going into labor.

This might provide the moment of reconciliation we hope for. But when she has her child, Jimmy walks out, because of his own frustration, his inability to conform to the passive paternal role, and because of her attempt to make him conform by naming the baby after him. He leaves the hospital, crying, refusing to look at his child. He walks behind a partition in the hospital corridor, and the camera remains on the partition for a long moment, providing a temporal and spatial transition to a recording studio, where Francine, her child now old enough to accompany her, is making the record that will bring her stardom. Again, the hospital sequence puts Jimmy in what is conventionally a feminine attitude. He feels used and hurt by Francine's control, over herself, over him—by naming his child without consulting him. And if his disappearance behind the partition is a bit obvious, it is important to recall that many of the film's sequences emphasize Francine's presence. Here, when the sequence ends on Jimmy, it ends on Jimmy's absence and his withdrawal. The separation is complete. Francine stays, endures, and succeeds. Jimmy withdraws, moves away, but—again denying the narrative direction that seems indicated—also succeeds. *New York, New York* is not to prove another version of *A Star Is Born,* where the husband fails as the wife triumphs.

The recording session begins on Francine alone, isolating her in the studio as she sings a song about broken dreams and perseverance and fate ("The World Goes Round"); as she gets absorbed in her singing and the camera tracks in toward her there occurs a montage of fan magazines, scenes in a movie studio, indicating, in the grand old Hollywood style, her rise to success. This ends with the appearance of her movie, *Happy Endings,* which Jimmy attends, watching, with us, her big production number on the screen. The movie is followed by a newsreel reporting Francine's triumphant return to New York, and the sequence ends with a shot of Jimmy in the audience, quiet, not applauding. By employing the "career montage," Scorsese again refers to the movie origin of his movie; but he denies it as well. His film is not to be about the rise of one person at the expense of another. Jimmy will have his as well: his success, and his own montage signifying his success, a montage that follows directly upon his attendance at Francine's movie and which shows us, via newspapers and record charts, the popularity of his song "New York, New York."

We are offered, finally, one more potential for melodramatic reversal as the narrative suggests the possibility of a reconciliation. Jimmy goes to see Francine perform her "big song." It is a moment when, once again, the complex of styles breaks apart. We watch not "Francine Evans," fictional character, but "Liza Minnelli" doing her nightclub routine, with a little more Garland than usual. The effect is not one of Brechtian distance; it rather makes us observe the collision of two fictions: the film fiction and the persona of Liza Minnelli in her "act." After the show, Jimmy joins her at a backstage party, where they almost quarrel. He leaves, but then calls her from outside to ask if she will join him for Chinese food (a De Niro character is at his best when he can think of nothing more complicated for a reconciliation dinner than Chinese food). She agrees; we raise our hopes. She looks out at the street from inside the stage door, hesitates, and turns back. There is a shot of Jimmy outside, a shot of her inside pushing the elevator button. We cut back to Jimmy, who quietly walks out of the frame. Inside, the elevator door closes on Francine. At this point, the film might have appropriately ended, but Scorsese needs more, and so he cuts back outside, to a high crane down on Jimmy on the street, down further to his shoes and umbrella, and then dissolves to a track of the empty, rain-slick, studio streets.

This final flourish reminds us again of a cinema where the artificial expressed the "real," where a studio street called forth a response to an *idea* of "streetness"—what an audience expected cinema streets to look like. But while the visual form evokes our reflection upon an older cinema, the narrative movement is taking us in another, perhaps newer, direction. The threatened reconciliation and its attendant melodrama do not appear. There is no violent provocation of our emotions, no happiness, no great unhappiness. The promise of domesticity has been broken and stays so, and the possibility of two people once together, now remaining apart is realized. In the tradition of the musical film, the ending is closer to those Warner Brothers musicals of the thirties, mentioned earlier, where a certain anxiety lurks about the success of the show. But the closure of *New York, New York* is not anxiety-ridden, merely a bit sad, at least if we want a couple to get back together. Alternately, it is a response to the conclusion of *Alice Doesn't Live Here Anymore*. For where that film emphasized the necessity and beneficiality of heterosexual bonding, *New York, New York* offers the possibility that such bonding is neither necessary nor always beneficial.

If we separate the narrative structure of *New York, New York* from its visual form, it takes its place among some other films that reexamine the conventions of romance and marriage, of male-female relationships. In the sporadic revivals of the screwball comedy genre, in films like Mazursky's *An Unmarried Woman,* in some of Cassavetes's recent work, in Claudia Weill's *Girlfriends,* in Altman and others, we find alternatives to the subject of the dominant male and subservient woman, the call for domestic order at any cost, subjects that have informed our cinema since its inception. The dialectic will always exist, and for every discovery of simple independence, as in *New York, New York,* there will be another Peckinpah film in which women are merely the objects of male aggression, or another sentimental romance where the woman yields to her man or discovers the inner strength to go on alone, or the male discovers the inner strength to go on alone, in one or another recombination of melodramatic excess.

It is difficult for American film to create a narrative that speaks to the immediate realities of people who do not and never will experience overwhelming insights and emotions, and to speak to these realities in a form that makes us understand them in a full social and political context. Cinema *can* do it: the films of Godard and Rohmer, of Alain Tanner and Rainer Werner Fassbinder prove that the cinematic imagination is more than able to work within valid emotional limits and a clear understanding of how people function in a world without heroism and emotional sacrifice. This is, of course, not within the American film tradition, and we must be content to observe and comment upon those films that at least question the tradition and offer other possibilities. Scorsese is rather unique among recent filmmakers in his ability to cover a full range of narrative possibilities, imitating, questioning, mocking them, sometimes all at the same time. If *New York, New York* fails to cohere because it attempts to do too much, its failure points to an ever greater success: the success of an active imagination, constantly probing and questioning, demanding that the forms of its art reveal and account for themselves.

Where Scorsese will go is difficult to determine. The film that follows *New York, New York—The Last Waltz* (1978)—is a documentary of a rock concert. But even as a documentary, it betrays Scorsese's inability to accept the conventions of any one form of filmmaking without seeing the dialectical possibilities of that form. The footage of the concert itself, though filmed in thirty-five millimeter by some of the best cinematographers working today, including Michael Chapman (who did *Taxi Driver*), Laszlo Kovacs (who filmed *New York, New York*) and Vilmos Zsigmond, betrays the restrictions and limitations of working in a large, crowded hall. So for a few numbers, Scorsese has The Band play in a studio, in a large, open set designed by Boris Leven (who did *New York, New York*), and there the camera moves with the grace and fluidity we have come to expect from Scorsese's films, in a smoky environment which at times is lit to resemble scenes from *Taxi Driver* and *New York, New York*. Once again the possible ways of perceiving reality cinematically are examined and questioned and recorded. The inquisitive eye keeps looking.

# CHAPTER FIVE

# RADICAL SURFACES

## Robert Altman

Altman tells a story about negotiating a project with Warner Brothers. After much talk and some compromise on the director's part, a Warner's executive became uncomfortable and pulled back, saying, "We don't want this to seem too much like a Robert Altman movie."[1] This recognition on the part of the money men that an individual may be responsible for and in control of a particular kind of film and that this kind of film and the control are not to their liking is terribly revealing of the state of American filmmaking today. In the studio days, a producer might have chosen a particular director for a particular kind of film, if he was known to have facility in one genre or another. John Ford made westerns at RKO and Fox. George Cukor made romantic comedies for Columbia and was adept at stage adaptations; Michael Curtiz was Warner Brothers' director of action films in the thirties and melodramas in the forties. The roles were never rigid, though, and most directors, whether they were independent or under contract, worked in many genres, sometimes revitalizing and even changing them with a particular style or point of view, like Ford; more often than not submerging themselves, like Curtiz, in the studio style. In fact the works of even the strongest Hollywood directors of the thirties and forties are really double or triple films existing simultaneously: they may represent an individual style; they will reflect the style of the studio at which they are made or the general style of the period; they express a particular ideological flux of the moment.

Now there are no studios, and therefore no studio styles; there are no contract directors, and filmmakers have no firm economic support. While directors get more critical attention than they did even ten years ago and are recognized as powerful forces by the financial backers of their films, their position remains tenuous. Audience recognition of directors remains poor (of the directors discussed here, I would guess only Kubrick and perhaps Coppola are names that have recognition among most movie-goers), and the ability of directors to find work consistently remains uncertain. With even minimum recognition comes maximum responsibility. Poor profit on a film means, more often than not, a poor chance to direct again.

But Robert Altman has, so far, been able to run counter to this pattern. He has made one "blockbuster," *M.A.S.H.* (1970), and that was largely accidental (it was, for one thing, an assigned project). Since then he has directed one, sometimes two, films a year, films made relatively inexpensively and returning relatively small profits. More important, they have been made entirely under his control and demonstrate a consistent approach and point of view. They are formally and contextually of a piece, so much so that, once Altman's style is understood, it can be recognized in almost any one part of any film he makes. This independence makes executives unhappy. Altman oversees his projects; he makes films that do not make the kind of money backers like to see; and, despite this, he continues to make the films he wants.

No better example can be found of this tenacity than his experience with *Buffalo Bill and the Indians, or Sitting Bull's History Lesson* (1976), which he made for Dino De Laurentiis. A big film with big stars—Paul Newman and Burt Lancaster—it turned out to be a dry and angry denunciation of the myths of show business and the distortions of people and history that those myths engender. Few people went to see it, and it could only have been taken as an insult by its producer, who cut it for European distribution. The whole affair resulted in the breakdown of a project Altman was planning, a film of E. L. Doctorow's best-selling novel, *Ragtime*. It was the kind of situation that could curtail the career of any filmmaker in the current economic situation. But within a year Altman came back with *Three Women,* a difficult, enigmatic film, and followed it, in 1978, with *A Wedding.*

One reason for Altman's survival is his ability to create around him a dependable community of production people and players, a mini-studio in which the logistics and complexities of his films are worked out among individuals who know and are comfortable with his methods and his approach. His associate producers, Scott Bushnell and Robert Eggenweiler, and assistant director, Tommy Thompson, have formed the nucleus of this group. Editor Lou Lombardo and production designer Leon Ericksen have worked on his best films, as have cinematographers Vilmos Zsigmond and Paul Lohmann. And, until they began branching out into their own careers, he had a stock company of players, including Shelley Duvall, Michael Murphy, Keith Carradine, René Auberjonois, John Shuck, and Bert Remsen. This group has helped provide security within an insecure environment and has made it possible for Altman to explore and expand upon his ideas from film to film, without having to start from zero each time.*

Given the extent of Altman's output and the relative consistency of his formal approach from film to film, I want, in the discussion that follows, to create something of an arbitrary division between form and content. I will first discuss the ways Altman alters conventions of

---

* He has had the opportunity as well of being a producer—of Robert Benton's *The Late Show* and Alan Rudolph's *Welcome to L.A.* Rudolph started as an assistant director for Altman and co-scripted *Buffalo Bill and the Indians* with him.)

cinematic space and narrative structure and will then examine the major films; though, since there are twelve of these, from 1969 to this writing, it will be impossible to give each the attention it deserves. This method will necessitate some doubling back and some fragmentation of exposition, but it seems the best way to encompass the scope of Altman's work, which itself encompasses nothing less than an inquiry into the images of contemporary America, as those images have been set by our films and our politics (among other forms of entertainment). His films, themselves engaging entertainments, continually reflect their origins and their status as films as they reflect from us and back to us the images we hold of ourselves and our culture. In creating these inquiries and reflections, Altman dissociates himself from the closed forms of classical Hollywood story-telling, turning the screen into a wide, shallow space (he uses the 2.35 to 1 anamorphic ratio almost exclusively), filled with objects and people, with movement, with talk and sounds and music woven into casual and loose narratives that create the appearance of spontaneity and improvisation. But it is only an appearance, for the apparent casualness is carefully intended, and the sense of arbitrary observation calculated to situate us in the narrative in specific ways.

Altman made two features in the fifties. One of them, a "documentary" on James Dean, employing stills and interviews, is an important artifact of the kind of sentimental myth-making he was to attack in the seventies. He did television in the early sixties and in 1968 a feature for Warner Brothers called *Countdown*. This potentially interesting work on astronauts, their jealousies and tensions, is filmed and cut in a frontal, static, eye-level mode which allows for little but a straightforward exposition of the story. It is in what could be called the Hollywood anonymous style: unobtrusive, linear, with no detail to detract from the headlong perpetration of plot. It gives no idea of what Altman was to do, though it does offer an example of the early work of two major seventies actors, James Caan and Robert Duvall. *Countdown* would hardly be worth mentioning were it not an example of the kind of formal structure that Altman and the other filmmakers discussed here are working against. It is a prepared text that the director has only to transfer to film; there is no space for his own style, the style that begins to appear in *That Cold Day in the Park* (1969).

The subject of a repressed spinster driven to murder by her activated but unrealized sexual desires seems at best a cliché, able to offer the opportunity for some conventional psychology and brooding, foreboding compositions, perhaps some shock cuts in the manner of an AIP horror film. Indeed, *That Cold Day* offers all of these, and, were it an isolated work, it could easily be dismissed by the reviewer's phrase "atmospheric." It is not isolated, however, and Altman's attempts to render the subjective states of a female consciousness, though crude here, will be refined in *Images* (1972) and fully realized in *Three Women* (1977). Most important is that Altman begins to develop in this film the opening of the aural-visual space of his narrative, diffusing its center by taking notice of the peripheries. The camera continually drifts away from the main action, zooming past a face into a window to pick up the out-of-focus light reflected on the glass, defining the central character and her state of mind by bringing to our attention the otherwise unnoticeable objects and minutiae that surround her. Dialogue shifts, too, away from the central speakers. In a bar, a diner, a doctor's office we pick up conversation to the side, almost off screen. When Frances Austen (Sandy Dennis) visits her gynecologist, she sits in the waiting room apart from the other women. Our attention is on her, but at the same time not on her. It is diffused by the fact that we observe her, through the length of the sequence, from outside a window, and further diffused by our being made to hear fragments of tantalizing gossip of the other women as they talk about sexual problems.

On the face of it, there is nothing unusual about one character set off against a group of strangers, those strangers speaking of matters that somehow reflect the main character's state of mind. Certainly a key development in American film of the sixties involved greater attention paid to peripheral action, a sense of life existing around the main focus of action (Penn's *Mickey One* is a good example). In conventional film narrative, our attention was concentrated on the central characters and their relationship. Sequences carefully moved from an establishing shot to a mid-shot and then to closeups of individuals or couples who spoke in turn, the dialogue and the cutting directing us to the central concern of the sequence. In a sequence that took place, say, in a nightclub or other public area, the "extras" were precisely that, extra to the sequence, filling the space rather than participating in the sequence. An exterior, such as a street scene, would be peopled by anonymous bodies, and, were any commentary on the main action needed from them, a closeup from the crowd would be cut in and quickly removed.

D. W. Griffith is the forerunner of this tradition of centralized, exclusionary screen space. He used the closeup to narrow the narrative field and concentrate attention inward, removing unwanted surroundings by inserting what he considered the center of those surroundings, the emotionally charged human face. Certainly an ideological force is operative in this: the focus in traditional American cinema on limited, concentrated areas, dominated by a few central characters, reflects our long-standing myths of individual potency as well as the pre-cinematic tradition in middle-class art that the only serious and engaging dramatic interests are those of the individual in conflict with himself or herself or another person. Responses to this narrative tradition in film did not begin with Altman or the other contributors to contemporary film but can be seen in the work of filmmakers as diverse as Eisenstein and Renoir.

Eisenstein's montage in his silent films creates a sense of constant movement from periphery to center and back again, from masses of people in action to the faces within those masses and the small events that make up the action. Cause and effect, action and reaction play against each other, the "center" of events occurring ultimately off screen, in the spectator's consciousness. Eisenstein, of course, is working out his filmic structures from an ideology more clear and immediate than Griffith's, and Griffith's films became a model for Eisenstein to work against. Jean Renoir's responses to the American narrative tradition in the thirties are less radical. His redefinitions of the visual field and the focus of individual sequences within a film are closer to what Altman will be doing in the seventies. *Grand Illusion* and *Rules of the Game* are structured with an acknowledgment that narrative blocks do not have to be built out of single, concentrated areas of activity. Renoir recognizes that the screen is capable of indicating an extension of space beyond what it frames rather than denying the existence of that space. Through deep-field composition and the use of the pan he extends the spatial limits of the shot, indicating that there is more to the space than is immediately depicted by continually showing additions to it. In the sequence in *Grand Illusion* where a soldier puts on a woman's costume while the other men stare at him, the pan of the men's faces not only indicates surprise, longing, and sadness, but also quantity. There are many men, in a large area, and they all share, at this moment, the same feelings. As the camera moves from face to face, the effect is incremental and expansive; we are allowed visually to embrace the physical presence and the emotions of the men. In *Rules of the Game,* Renoir orchestrates his characters and camera so that there is an expanding and contracting flow of spatial movement in response to the emotional and intellectual movement of the narrative, encompassing that movement and opening it out, permitting us observation of many activities and not allowing us comfortably to focus on any one character or point of view.[2]

As I said, since the sixties American cinema has taken more cognizance of peripheral activity. But with few exceptions this has not been in the manner of Renoir nor, certainly, in that of Eisenstein. The periphery recognized usually encompasses onlookers, and the sense is that of giving the extras a bit more work to do. With the rise of location shooting and the setting of action sequences within those locations, the possibility arose of counterpointing the central action against those observing the action but irrelevant to it. A source for this is Carol Reed's *The Third Man* (1949), whose post-war Vienna exteriors are punctuated by workers in the dark, barren streets, old faces observing speeding cars. The extension of this in recent film is the faces that are inserted into a sequence of a shooting or a car wreck—observers, commentators on the action who have nothing to

276

do with the "plot" or the central characters and their activities. Therefore, the suggestions of activity beyond the central character in *That Cold Day*—the women at the gynecologist's, for example—are a bit special. Altman is imposing peripheral action onto the central focus of the sequence, not merely indicating its presence but playing that presence over and against the main figure and her concerns, forcing us to take equal notice of both while at the same time removing us from both by shooting the sequence from the other side of a glass window. So, too, with the camera drifting off, away from the main character, and zooming to objects and blurred lights. Here Altman is using the zoom to capture a subjective sense of vagueness and disorientation; elsewhere he will use it to capture the particulars of a defined area, reorganizing the space of a given sequence by developing it as a place of inquiry rather than accepting it as a pre-existent whole. More than Renoir, Altman is launching an investigation of the ways we observe filmic constructions and the ways we read the narratives these constructions give form to.

The investigation moves forward rapidly in *M.A.S.H.*, the film Altman did not originate or choose, but which he was able to use both as a means to develop new formal approaches and, coincidentally, as a financial base upon which to build his future work. In *That Cold Day in the Park*, the shooting style is an extension of the basic horror-gothic approach. Most of the action takes place in the dark, heavy apartment of the main character, Frances Austen. Browns and blacks predominate; there is little red, so that the act of violence that concludes the film is all the more shocking because of the sudden appearance of blood. A standard focal length lens (which approximates the spatial relationships of the eye) seems to be used throughout, allowing Altman and cinematographer Laszlo Kovacs to explore the rooms and their shadows and the characters trapped within them. *M.A.S.H.* is shot largely out of doors, but the area is an isolated one, cut off. The men live in flimsy tents; they are pressed in by their situation, not only as a hospital unit stuck inside the war zone (this aspect is underplayed, for we never see or hear the war, only its casualties), but by the fact that their spirits are imprisoned by military order. To create the appropriate *mise-en-scène* of confinement, Altman employs two devices which effectively contradict each other. *M.A.S.H.* is photographed (by Harold E. Stine) in Panavision, whose great width is often used to suggest large horizons or actions. But Altman wishes to constrict the space of *M.A.S.H.*, and to this end he employs a telephoto lens for most of the sequences, which compresses space, making it flat. Unlike shallow-focus cinematography, which foregrounds the figures in focus, creating an undefined background (as opposed to the highly articulated depth of deep focus), telephoto cinematography tends to background everything, or at least to put foreground and background on the same plane. Within the extreme width of the Panavision screen and the compressed depth created by the telephoto lens, Altman fills the screen space with people and objects, all of which are drained of any bright colors, save for the spurting blood in the operating room, and observes them from a distance.

The result is visual conflict rendering an experience of claustrophobia, a sense, on the viewer's part, of being locked into an observation of a *mise-en-scène* which refuses to open up or to give way, to yield to the viewer's investigation of it. The visual denseness is supported and exacerbated, perhaps, by the sound track. There is not a silent moment in *M.A.S.H.*: dialogue, music, and announcements on a loudspeaker are continuous, sometimes at odds with, or in ironic counterpoint to, what is happening on screen, sometimes all things at once. Altman takes from Welles (and Howard Hawks) the notion of overlapping dialogue, people talking at the same time without waiting for a response. The effect is an aural space that parallels the decentralization of the visual space. By refusing to allow the comfort of pauses in the dialogue any more than he allows the comfort of simple visual orientation, Altman creates a demanding and busy visual and aural field. But the terms of his demands are not those that Bazin spoke about in his discussions of the long take and deep-focus cinematography, with their capability of opening the image to active participation on the part of the viewer. In *M.A.S.H.* and the films that follow, Altman rarely uses deep focus, and he cuts a great deal.

The visual structure of his films demands not that the viewer pick and choose among various visual and aural options but that he or she observe and understand the whole and integrate into the larger unit those parts of the whole that the director wishes to emphasize. What Altman creates is not the conventional structure of a whole that is analyzed into its parts, but a simultaneity of the whole *and* its parts, a simultaneity we must always attend to.

*M.A.S.H.* creates and sustains its busy, constricted, claustrophobic structure for about half its length, then dissipates itself as the action leaves the army camp for antics in Tokyo and on the football field. The spatial experimentation occurs only sporadically in the film that follows, *Brewster McCloud* (1970). Two sequences within this film—one in a police laboratory, the other a police investigation of a murder on the street—are constructed with large numbers of people talking all at once and at cross purposes, bad jokes weaving in and out of the conversations, no one element taking precedence over the others. These sequences tend to be isolated, for Altman is working out other problems of narrative structure. *Brewster McCloud* jokes around with itself, falls in love with its bird-shit jokes and the looney characters that fly and squawk around its demented assemblage. It is not until *McCabe and Mrs. Miller* (1971) that Altman realizes completely the possibilities of his spatial experiments and sees them through.

*McCabe and Mrs. Miller* is among the richest works of seventies cinema; form and content are so well integrated in it that a split is difficult to make, even for purposes of analysis. It will, however, bear talking about once in the context of its visual and narrative structure, and once again in terms of its genre and the way it responds to other westerns. In each case, it is helpful to see the film in the context of the work of John Ford.

In *The Man Who Shot Liberty Valance* (1962), Ford worked out the possibilities of an indoor western, eschewing wide-open spaces for the dark interiors of saloons and homes, a newspaper office and a meeting hall. Ford, near the end of his career, wanted to examine the transition of the frontier wilderness to the closed, law-bound community. He was saddened by this transition, though he realized its historic reality and inevitability. His film is an elegy for the past and an almost begrudging celebration of the change to the bourgeois security of a structured civilization. Altman has no stake in either part of the western mythos. A man with a late-sixties, early-seventies consciousness, with a certain left-liberal perspective, he sees the western, and most other film genres, along with the attitudes and ideology they embody, not as healing and bonding lies—which is the way Ford saw the western—but merely as lies. Like Ford, Altman realizes the elegiac element always latent in any myth of the past. But, unlike Ford, he does not mourn the passing of the frontier and boost the coming of law and order: he mourns rather the lost possibility of community and the enforced isolation of its members.

It is out of this paradox of community and the isolation it creates that Altman builds the *découpage* (the compositional and editing structure) of his film, working out of the reorientation of space and sound started in *M.A.S.H.*[3] Over the Warner Brothers logo at the beginning of the film are sounds of a harsh wind blowing. As the credits begin we see a man on horseback, heavily wrapped in furs, riding through the pine trees of a northern winter landscape. A sad lyric by Leonard Cohen accompanies the movement, a song about a gambling stranger. The space, as in *M.A.S.H.*, is enclosed, narrow, and flat, and the color is almost bichromatic: the greens of the trees standing out, barely, from a general blue haze. The man on horseback—as in so many westerns—enters a town. He pauses by a church, removes his furs, dismounts, mumbles something angry and incoherent. We begin to see some of the men in the town, and the concentration on McCabe (Warren Beatty) changes briefly to a concentration on them, standing about in the rain, looking, observing the stranger from a distance. We see McCabe again in a telephoto shot, from a vantage point inside a saloon; he is crossing a footbridge, moving toward the camera until his face is framed in the saloon window, looking in.

There is a cut to the interior of the saloon, dark, filled with low voices. The color, what little there is, is warmer than the exterior blue. Various faces are picked out. Through a barred partition we see the owner, Sheehan (René Auberjonois), lighting a candle under a statue of the Virgin and saying a blessing. We see more faces; Mc-Cabe asks for the back door. We can just hear various comments from the men in the saloon on his gun: "Is he wearing a gun? . . . Do you know what kind of gun that was . . . that was a Swedish . . . from Sweden . . . What the hell is he wearing a gun for? . . ." Those comments appear freely on the sound track, not assigned to any speakers we can directly see. McCabe returns with a tablecloth and spreads it out. Some people comment on the weather. A small fight breaks out over a chair. Again we see various faces. McCabe asks for a bottle. As they are about to begin playing cards, McCabe asks to go fifty-fifty with Sheehan, and as they talk of a business arrangement Sheehan lights a lamp, infusing the space with a warm golden light. There is talk of the game, of betting, a shot of hands dealing cards. McCabe's hand points to the table and his voice, off screen, says, "Jack off." With the accompanying laughter, the camera cuts to the whole group and then to a zoom to McCabe's face, smiling, revealing a gold tooth, cigar clenched happily.

For this verbal description of the film's opening sequence to work properly, I would somehow have to break the sentences up, slip some parts of them under others; still others would have to be bent sideways or placed at a diagonal. For in a more radical fashion than in *M.A.S.H.*, Altman has created in *McCabe* a tight and enclosed space, peopled with figures who, though contained in that space, seem unconnected to it and, even more, unconnected to each other. There is little eye contact between the various characters in this opening sequence. When McCabe looks, he doesn't get a direct look back. The camera rarely observes the characters squarely, at eye level, centered in the frame. They are rather picked out, seemingly at random, glanced at and overheard. The Panavision screen and telephoto lens serve, more than they did in *M.A.S.H.*, to inhibit our observation by compressing the screen space. The cutting and the sound mixing create a barely localized environment and a sequence of events that are just suggested.

Through it all, Altman produces a fine dialectical effect: the more random fragments of faces, figures, and conversation that are given, the more coherent the space becomes. It is undefined in the sense that we never are sure just where we are, or among whom we are, or even why we are observing the events. But the confusion itself becomes a coherent expression of this loose, unfocused community, existing in disorder, with its members operating not out of friendship but in a sort of mutual antagonism. And the less definition we are given, the less securely are we fixed in the narrative. We are offered the opportunity to help construct the proceedings from the interlocking fragments given us. To repeat what I noted earlier, this is quite a different phenomenon from what Bazin had in mind when he spoke of the filmmaker allowing the viewer to retrieve a range of information and experience from the image. Bazin's concept suggests an activating of the otherwise passive filmgoer; but this is only sometimes the case. The long deep-focus take may do little more than concentrate our attention and permit us to observe the details of the *mise-en-scène*. It may intensify our reactions by allowing them to build slowly rather than by commanding them through editorial direction. But Altman does direct our attention and our gaze. However, unlike the conventional *découpage* of American film, he does not order that gaze into, and then within, a determined and delimited space (as we have seen, for example, Coppola do at the beginning of *Godfather I*). He creates—or, more appropriately, allows us to create—an idea of place out of the visual and aural fragments he gives us.

The effect achieved is, again, reminiscent of Renoir: an extension of the screen space, the suggestion of rich and random activity of which the focus of narrative attention is only one part. Like Renoir, Altman attempts to indicate a wholeness, a continuum of space. Unlike Renoir he does it by cutting and by sound, rather than by panning and tracking. When movement occurs, it is most often executed by a zoom, which by its nature does not encompass space but narrows or extends it, depending on the zoom's direction. Like his cutting, Altman's use of the zoom offers more by showing us less. But it defines the relationship of a character and his or her surroundings, or the relationship between two characters, by directing our attention more coherently than would a direct cut. More gently too: Altman's zooms, at least in *McCabe,* invite us to regard faces and objects, to share a private moment or an intimate reaction on the part of a character. They reveal even a violent action without sensation and offer proximity without embarrassing us or the character. They inquire and connect.

Let me pick up the description of the early sequences in the film: the busy, rambling, off-centered gambling scene is brought to a small climax as the camera zooms into McCabe's smiling face, isolating it, accenting it, presenting us with an image of a man momentarily in control of his situation. But this zoom closeup is broken by a cut to a telephoto shot of the footbridge outside: we see the feet of a figure walking away from the camera, which pulls up and zooms back. The warm and embracing movement to McCabe is broken by the cold blue exterior from which we withdraw as soon as we see it. The figure on the footbridge turns out to be the minister of the town (which is named Presbyterian Church), the one person who cannot engage himself in the activities of the town and who, later, shares in McCabe's destruction by refusing him sanctuary in the church. In this instance the zoom serves to link us closely with McCabe, then to link McCabe with one of the individuals who will prove to be his nemesis, and to define sharply the two areas: the warm gold interior of the saloon and the cold blue exterior of the town. The act of linkage is most important: had Altman merely cut from the card game to the approach of the minister outside, only separation and opposition would have been implied. By first connecting us to McCabe by the means of the zoom to his face and then cutting to the footbridge and zooming back from that, Altman associates the places and the individuals and introduces important narrative tensions. In a later sequence, McCabe brings three ragged whores to town. It is the beginning of his entrepreneurial efforts. He shows them off to the men; a fight breaks out between the whores and the men; McCabe takes the women to their temporary, ramshackle quarters. He is deeply confused over what he has gotten himself into. "I've got to go to the pot," one of the whores tells McCabe, "and I don't think I can hold it." The camera zooms into her face and, in a reverse shot, zooms to McCabe, who looks distressed and uncertain. Out of a kaleidoscope of faces and events, the zoom isolates a moment, a relationship, a set of reactions. It does not necessarily bring the characters close to each other; in fact, the zooms to the whore and to McCabe indicate the extent of incomprehension between them. But the zooms indicate as well their forced proximity and the necessity of our dealing with that proximity.

The zoom for Altman is most often a means of attempting to understand, of a cautious but assured approach, of detail and of emphasis. It does not have the positive sense of space transgressed as does the tracking shot.[4] Rather—in Altman's hands, at least—it inscribes the parts and details of the visual field. With the zoom, and in conjunction with his editing, Altman can create a field of action and event that is detailed and particularized. The point of view given to the audience is that of discoverer and connector. The zoom functions as an offering to us, giving us perspective and detail, coaxing, leading, but never totally situating us or closing off the space that is being examined.

The visual and aural field created in *McCabe and Mrs. Miller* sets the pattern that Altman will build upon in the films that follow. As much as he alters the pattern to fit the needs of each film, the basic preoccupations remain: the urge to decentralize the incidents and the area in which those incidents are acted out; the use of the zoom to probe details and emotions. There remains, too, a reticence, a desire not to overwhelm the viewer (another quality Altman shares with Renoir), to show him or her some respect and to allow a comfortable distance. Even the violence in his films, often random, sometimes gratuitous, is not brutalizing, but a part of the abrupt changes and alterations that make up his narratives.

Only once does he alter the distance and demand that the audience be implicated in the *mise-en-scène*. The film is *The Long Goodbye* (1973), and in it Altman so radically and subtly manipulates our perception of the cinematic space before us that we become aware of this manipulation through a sense of discomfort and uneasiness. The film is an attempt to reexamine the figure of Philip Marlowe, Raymond Chandler's private eye, traditionally embodied for us in the figure of Humphrey Bogart in Hawks's *The Big Sleep*. Altman's Marlowe (played by Elliott Gould) is a puzzled, passive, deeply abused man, caught in an environment and a moral structure he cannot comprehend. To allow *us* a comprehension of Marlowe's dilemma, Altman and his cinematographer, Vilmos Zsigmond, uproot us, prevent us from resting in the security of stable, centered observation of the characters in their surroundings. Almost every shot in *The Long Goodbye* is either a very slow, never completed zoom into or out from the characters observed, or a slow, almost imperceptible, arc around or track across them.

In one sequence, Marlowe and Roger Wade (Sterling Hayden), the broken, drunken writer, sit by the ocean, talking, drinking aquavit from enormous cups. The dialogue is broken down into one shots of each of the participants, isolating them from each other visually as they are isolated from each other emotionally and by the misinformation each has about the other. The one shots are punctuated by shots of both together, but these only serve to emphasize their separation by showing their physical distance. This would be a fairly standard *découpage* of a dialogue between two mutually wary antagonists, except for the fact that they are never observed with a still camera. A slow zoom back from Wade is cut to a slow arcing of Marlowe, to a slow zoom back of both, to a leftward arc of Wade, to a right arc of Marlowe, and so on until, at the end of the sequence, the camera zooms in and past both to the ocean behind them. More than what is said by the characters in the sequence, we are affected by what the sequence says to us about the characters. Here and throughout the film, the movement comments, insists that there is more to be known, catches us up in an instability and an incompleteness. In a later sequence, Marlowe is in Mexico investigating the assumed death of his presumed friend, Terry Lennox. He speaks to an official and his aide while the camera observes them through the open window of a building. The dialogue, in which Marlowe is thoroughly lied to by both men, is created by a series of slow lateral tracks across the bars in front of this window. When Altman cuts to a closer shot of the group, the camera is still outside the bars and still tracking, yet near enough so that the bars are out of focus and barely visible. The combination of the telephoto lens, the proximity of the bars, and the slowness of the track gives an immediate appearance of a static shot, yet the sense of movement is inescapable, and the effect insidious. Like Marlowe, we are unable to be sure of what we see, and at the same time not certain that we are unable to be sure of what we see.[5]

*The Long Goodbye* is Altman's most extensive experiment in altering the spatial coordinates of the film narrative. I referred to it as being manipulative, but that is not the appropriate term. Like the *mise-en-scène* of *McCabe,* it asks a different perceptual response than a more conventional film would; it is more insistent in its demands and more unsettling than is *McCabe,* or indeed any other of Altman's films. But as in the others, suggestion takes precedence over direction, and the peripheries of action take on equal importance with the centers. In an important sense, Altman is a director of peripheries. The dislocation of space that makes up the visual world of his films is part of a wider dislocation that concerns him. That is, the well-made American film, with its steady and precise development of story and character, appears to Altman to be itself a dislocation and a distortion. By attending to different spaces, both visual and narrative, he can reorient the ways we look at films, the ways we understand them, and the ways they reflect our fantasies to us.

The narrative structure of Altman's films—from *M.A.S.H.* on—develops out of, or as part of, their spatial structure. The movement from center to periphery demands an abandonment of straightforward narrative development. Events on the edges gain equal importance with events in the middle: we see and hear more than we are used to. Throughout the offhand conversations that make up the first sequence of *McCabe,* Altman cuts away to the bar, where a running and finally anticlimactic conversation about a beard is taking place. McCabe wanders in and out of the saloon to look around, to urinate ("That man out there takin' a pee . . . ," says Sheehan the barkeeper, inventing a legend for McCabe that will help undo him, "is the man who shot Bill Roundtree"), and as he wanders, so does the conversation, in and out of what should be the main concern: Mc-Cabe's buying into the town and his reputation as a gunfighter. But nothing definitive is ever said and no direction given to the narrative. The sequence ends as it begins, gently, humorously, and indirectly. McCabe returns to the gambling table, he tells one of his endearing filthy jokes, and the camera quietly zooms past everyone to a fiddle being plucked in the background.

When, in *The Long Goodbye,* Marlowe gets off the bus in Mexico and wanders, incongruous in his jacket and tie, through the squalid town square, the camera quietly moves from him to zoom in on a pair of fornicating dogs, who wind up snarling at each other (surely the finest example of the often-mentioned improvisational methods of Altman's direction). As fortuitous, offhanded, and incongruous as this particular zoom is, it enhances a narrative of offhanded and incongruous movements and of casual, Southern-California couplings that lead to snarling and to death. Snarlings, fistfights, acts of violence continually break out in Altman's films, often at unexpected moments, always to punctuate the tenuous calm of any given scene and to indicate the disruption that underlies any situation.

People and events are always disrupted in an Altman film, as are our expectations and assumptions. We no more expect to have our attention drawn to a pair of fornicating dogs than to a Philip Marlowe who cannot tell lies from truth—and does not seem to care—or to a frontiersman who is only interested in being an entrepreneur, or to a Buffalo Bill who is nothing but a preening, fatuous racist, or to a boy who lives in the Houston Astrodome while he builds a pair of mechanical wings so that he can fly off to nowhere. It is not that Altman's films contain unexpected turns; they are unexpected turns. They are quiet attempts at a deconstruction of the narrative and generic truths that we have taken for granted in our cinema.[6] In dislocating their visual and narrative centers, they dislocate their generic centers as well, and begin to reveal to us some of the ways in which the smooth, undistracted, and unquestioning forms of cinematic story-telling have lied to us. Altman will no more construct alternative truths to the lies he perceives than will any other American film-maker; but the deconstruction is insightful, funny, sometimes angry, sometimes off the mark, and always respectful of uncertainty and plurality.*

*Brewster McCloud,* as imperfect as it is, is a good place to start an examination of the deconstruction process and to extend our investigation of Altman's use of space to the wider areas of narrative and generic inquiry. The very opening of the film indicates what Altman will be up to: we see the MGM logo, but instead of the lion's roar we expect, we hear a voice saying, "I forgot the opening line." The film cannot quite get itself started. No smooth entry into a story is promised. We see a rather strange man, a lecturer (René Auberjonois), who talks to us about birds, men, the dream of flight, and environmental enclosures. As he is about to speak of the latter, we see the Houston Astrodome and in it Margaret Hamilton, the wicked witch of *The Wizard of Oz,* attempting to lead a marching band of black musicians in the national anthem. The credits begin; Hamilton stops the band and attempts to get them to sing on key. The credits begin again, and the band breaks into gospel, completely out of control. This film, which will concern itself with the conflict of freedom and constraint, announces this conflict from its beginning, not only in its images, but in the difficulty it has in getting its images started. It parodies itself, its existence as a controlled formal structure, from the very start.

It parodies as well other films—*The Birds, Bullitt,* and *The Wizard of Oz*—while it intricately shuffles its elements—a boy training for flight in the bowels of the Astrodome, under the care of a moth-

---

* Altman's film *Quintet* (1979) appeared just as this book was completed. A cold and bare narrative about the frozen remnants of a future civilization who obsessively play a game of death, it is the first film since *Thieves Like Us* to be shot in a non-anamorphic ratio. Not only are its images less wide than those in the other films, but Altman diffuses them around the edges in every shot. More than any of its predecessors, it focuses our attention to the middle of the screen, and its sequences are shot and cut in a slow and measured rhythm. It is a marked change from the structure of Altman's work that I discuss here.

ering bird-woman; the deaths by bird droppings and strangulation of various bigoted and brutal characters; the posturings of an artificially blue-eyed "super-cop" named Frank Shaft (played by Michael Murphy, drawing on the absurd elements of an earlier character created by Steve McQueen but in name looking forward to the black cop John Shaft, who appeared a year later in a film by Gordon Parks, also made for MGM). All the while it playfully comments on its own silliness while refusing to face its serious intent. The film's individual parts—the complicated sound track of radio announcements; the voice-over of the lecturer, who comments on the bird-like endeavors of the various participants and slowly turns into a bird as the film progresses; the intricate intercutting of foolish police investigations with Brewster's dream-like isolation; the car chases; the touching connotations of dreams of flight, of Icarus, and of Oedipus—are successful, but only as parts. They refuse to yield up a coherent statement about the anger that informs them. *Brewster McCloud* is a film about sexuality, power, and freedom, and about how these fundamental personal and ideological components of our lives were being changed, questioned, repressed, and corrupted under the Nixon regime at the turn of the seventies ("Agnew: Society Should Discard Some People, A Certain Number Who Won't Fit In," reads a newspaper seen early in the film and rapidly covered with bird droppings.) Altman attempts to realize the transformations and distortions of these three forces within a doomed adolescent fantasy of freedom and flight. This fantasy is in turn enclosed by another fantasy, that of the super-hero policeman, that aberration of the heroic which our culture allowed to be foisted upon itself, in film and on television, in the late sixties and early seventies. But although Altman feels the tensions inherent in repression and the need to escape it, and understands the absurdity of the heroic images we choose to embody our desire to escape, he cannot bring the playful openness of the narrative to do more than suggest them. The crushed corpse of Brewster—whose flight to freedom, doomed from the start, ends in an agonizing fall—lying amid the characters who are prancing about in circus garb (the mock-Fellini ending of the film is about the most unfortunate thing Altman has ever done) further rends the fabric of the narrative, rather than mending it with an intended irony.

*Brewster McCloud* is a significant and successful failure. It lays out Altman's formal and thematic concerns (though sexuality, power, and freedom are themes so general that almost any film can be said to deal with them, they are specific to Altman in that they do inform most of his work and he consistently deals with their manifestations in our culture). *Brewster McCloud* is important also in that it shakes him free of the potential trap of *M.A.S.H.*, for *Brewster* examines some of the contradictions in the "youth rebellion" of the late sixties —its inherent aimlessness and dependence on the existing social-political order—whereas *M.A.S.H.* is merely a gratification, indeed a pacification, of that rebellion. *M.A.S.H.* feeds a given audience what it wants and shocks others in a perfectly acceptable and unthreatening way. While the compression of space, the crowded *mise-en-scène* and sound track, is important for what will come out of it in Altman's films, *M.A.S.H.* presents very little for an audience to deal with contextually. Its narrative is constructed from a series of episodic gags, each representative of the anarchic individual fighting against a restrictive order, with no analysis offered as to the nature of that order and why it should be fought against. It is held up as "bad," the heroes of the film as "good." Since the script (by Ring Lardner, Jr.) is not of Altman's doing, we can really only observe it as something he put on the screen that contains material he will later abjure. Most inimical to his later work is the way the film accepts its generic origins. *M.A.S.H.* is a war film—no more antiwar than *Paths of Glory,* or, for that matter, Lewis Milestone's celebration of selfless bravery in a Korean battle, *Pork Chop Hill* (1959). *M.A.S.H.* is anti-authority only, and with its happy band of committed surgeons substituting for the committed band of fighting men omnipresent in earlier war films and its substitution of operating room for battlefield, it merely teases us with an attitude of liberated non-conformity. The war is not really present in *M.A.S.H.* (the bleeding bodies have no faces and merely provide more foils for the antics of our heroes) and therefore need not be confronted. There is a smugness not merely in the characters but in the way the narrative allows them to prevail without forcing them to confront anything—such as a notion of why they are where they are.[7] *M.A.S.H.*, like *The Graduate,* that other hymn to the paradoxically passive rebellion of the sixties, is a gentle massage. While the happy surgeons prevail over military order, nothing is revealed about it. It remains unchanged and enduring. *Brewster McCloud,* though it also goes some way in depicting the stupidity of the prevailing order, indicates too how difficult it is to overcome it with infantile fantasies of evasion and escape. *Brewster* is therefore a much less happy film than its predecessor. Only in its refusal to take itself seriously does it manage to avoid being rather grim.

*M.A.S.H.*, despite its sense of self-parody, takes itself too seriously and perhaps the only way it can be saved is by regarding it not as an army comedy but as part of the sub-genre of POW films.[8] If the war were regarded as a prison and the surgeons of the M.A.S.H. unit as its captives, their hopeless rebellion might be seen as a kind of protection against the destruction of the spirit. This reading gives the film an aura of hopelessness that provides an otherwise absent dialectic. Without it the narrative is all flashy episodes, running jokes, and unexamined assumptions, a balm to the viewer who wants to believe that the structure of authority can be destroyed (or humiliated) by either laughing at it or ignoring it (and being good at your work). Altman's later films try to avoid or at least to confront such false assumptions. That too few such assumptions are confronted in *M.A.S.H.* and too many in *Brewster McCloud* indicates that Altman needed a way to stabilize his perspective, to integrate and control the visual and narrative experimentation that goes on in these early works. He finds that way in *McCabe and Mrs. Miller,* through organizing his film both within and in opposition to one of the most established of American film genres. Where *M.A.S.H.* parallels the war film, *McCabe* sets up an active analysis of the western. Where *M.A.S.H.* celebrates the community that exists in opposition to military authority, *McCabe* is an elegy to the loss of community and the isolation of the individual on the frontier. I said earlier that Altman, unlike Ford, does not see the transition of wilderness to civilization as somehow natural and preordained, incorporating the struggles of individual heroes into secure bourgeois enclaves of law and order. Rather, he sees the conquering of the West as part of the inevitable movement of capitalism, with its attendant brutality, betrayals, and selfishness. The town of Presbyterian Church is no frontier bastion, no Fort Apache or Dodge City. Its inhabitants are not upright citizens or gunfighters. They are merely rather dull and passive people trying to keep warm. The bumbling entrepreneur, John McCabe, has only to walk in to bring a semblance of order, via a gambling saloon and whorehouse. His enemies are not savage Indians or anarchic outlaws but the very passivity of the people, his own misplaced sense of heroism, and the agents of a mining company (who include a savage Indian and anarchic outlaw). He is undone by refusing a business deal and by believing he is a gunfighter.

Altman offers no one in the film, or watching the film, the comforts of convention, the easy assumptions that there are ideals worth dying for or communities worth preserving, at least as those communities are constituted in our movie myths. In *My Darling Clementine* (1946), Ford creates a sequence in which the townspeople hold a square dance within the unfinished frame of a church, with American flags flying and the wilderness of Monument Valley safely in the distance and effectively sealed off by the structures of the community. He creates it with no irony and no subtext, but as a pure symbol of human order controlling and impressing itself upon the wilderness.[9] In *McCabe,* the comforts of civilization are on a cash basis only and the church a place of denial. Its interior alone of all the buildings in town remains unfinished; its inhabitant is an antisocial, mean little man. But it does serve ironically as a place of congregation. When it catches fire, the townspeople flock to save what they have heretofore ignored, leaving McCabe alone in the snow, pursued by the mining company's gunmen. He acts the hero despite himself and dies—unlike most heroes we have been taught to admire in our films—for absolutely nothing. In an alternating montage sequence worthy of Griffith, we observe McCabe alone with the stalking gunmen while the townspeople gather to save a worthless building. Unlike Griffith's, however, the two parts of the montage never join. The community is left to its own devices; McCabe to his death.

The church fire and the gunfight in the snow continue and conclude a set of visual ironies set up early in the film. When Sheehan, on McCabe's arrival, lights the lamp in his saloon, it infuses the area with a warm and golden light that continues to bathe the interiors of gambling house and whorehouse throughout the film. It is the light of warmth and security, contrasted with the cold blue of the exteriors. But this is a film in which warmth and security are shown to be delusions and snares and community a fraud. Altman and cinematographer Zsigmond manipulate the warm-gold-interior and cold-blue-exterior light to warn us against false comfort. When the mining company gunmen ride into town, they are bathed in gold light; when McCabe first confronts their leader, the enormous Englishman Butler (who would expect a western gunman to speak with an English accent?) in Sheehan's saloon, the gold light is replaced with the cold blue of the exteriors. The simple glow of protection, security, and community is easily transferred and broken down. The church, conventionally associated with refuge and security (a convention Altman acknowledges early in the film when he photographs it against the sunset as its cross is placed on the spire—one of the most photographically beautiful shots in all his work), burns up. Golden warmth is replaced by destructive fire, destructive not merely to the church (which everyone has ignored previously), but to McCabe and the sense of community obligation. The gold light proves to be false, fooling us as it has the characters of the fiction. When we see it for the last time, in contrast to the blue cold in which McCabe dies, it is suffusing the opium den where Mrs. Miller (Julie Christie) has withdrawn. All connotations of security and community are stripped from it. It still expresses warmth, but it is the warmth of withdrawal, avoidance, and isolation. Mrs. Miller is looking within herself, able to see no further than the marble egg she turns in her hands.

The shots that end the film—Mrs. Miller's eyes and the marbled patterns those eyes see—seem to be in perfect opposition to the opening shots of McCabe's entry into the town. But if we recall those opening shots, the enclosed space they embrace, McCabe mumbling to himself when he dismounts from his horse, the vacant and directionless stares of the men hanging about in the cold, it is clear that Mrs. Miller's state of isolation and self-absorption is only an intensification of the state of things at the beginning of the film. If we realize, in retrospect, how the cutting of the film and its crowded but fragmented spaces and sounds create a sense of pervasive isolation in the midst of community, the end comes as little surprise.

Isolation and self-absorption are qualities Altman discovers in many of his characters and most of the places they inhabit. He finds the idea of a successful community difficult to imagine and the smaller units within communities—conventional romantic couplings

McCabe (Warren Beatty) after his first meeting with Mrs. Miller.

and domestic unions of the kind usually celebrated by American film —impossible. The relationship of Mrs. Miller and McCabe is indicative of difficulties Altman sees in romantic conventions. Their initial isolation from one another is a result of the business arrangement that determines their actions. McCabe wishes to be an independent businessman; "Partners is what I come up here to get away from," he tells Sheehan, asserting his independence in a scene that is punctuated by the brutal stabbing of a customer by one of the whores McCabe clearly cannot control by himself. As he attempts to break up the fight, the scene is once more broken by violence, this time the scream and smoke of a steam engine bringing Mrs. Miller into town.

Her intrusion into McCabe's life is not physically violent, but it is disrupting and complicating. She proves to him his lack of entrepreneurial knowledge, particularly when it comes to running a whorehouse; but more, she shows him how dumb he is trying to do business alone. This is a difficult thing for the hero of a western to hear, and from a woman especially. The shot that occurs after the initial dialogue between McCabe and Mrs. Miller at a table in the saloon, she eating an enormous meal, McCabe manfully downing his scotch and raw egg, is a slow reverse zoom of McCabe alone, in slight disarray, belching and farting. This is a rare little shot, not merely because one is not used to hearing a character break wind in a film, but because of its effect as an immediate response to the dialogue preceding it. McCabe is a lone man, and his aloneness has just been assaulted; the brief insert permits us a sort of offhanded observation of his confusion and his attempt to reassert himself, if only to himself. The fact that the camera zooms away from him rather than toward him implicates us in his solitude, his desire to be alone, and his feeling of having been violated.

We rarely see Mrs. Miller alone, except for the very last sequence. She is occasionally set off from her girls, once glimpsed just in the background at a birthday party for one of the whores. The few times that a sequence begins with just her, McCabe appears shortly, and their conversation inevitably involves business, and inevitably puts McCabe in a bad light. She is not alone because, unlike her

generic forebears, she is a woman of business and not the center of
a family. She is not the frontier wife nor the schoolteacher from the
East who domesticates the hero. She is a whore and the administrator
of a whorehouse, jobs she knows well and does well. She demonstrates no desire to be other than what she is. (There is little domesticity in the film as a whole: only two "families" exist: a black barber and his wife, who are rarely seen, and Coyle [Bert Remsen] and
his mail-order bride, Ida [Shelley Duvall]. Coyle is killed in one of
those flash brawls that punctuate the film, and Ida becomes one of
Mrs. Miller's girls.)

Constance Miller does not provide the romantic, domesticating
role we would expect. Curiously enough, McCabe does; he is, despite himself, a character with romantic pretensions. Unfortunately,
like his pretensions as a businessman, he cannot handle them. Mrs.
Miller won't let him handle them. In a very touching sequence that
denies all of our expectations of romance, McCabe comes to make
love to Mrs. Miller, full of bravura and tenderness: "You're a funny
little thing. Sometime you're just so sweet. . . ." Well, in this instance she is not sweet, but stoned. Her reaction to McCabe is to
hide coyly under the sheets and point to her money box. He dutifully
counts out his payment, and the camera zooms into Mrs. Miller's—
very literal—heart of gold.

The only time McCabe can express his feelings is when he is
alone. We see him at one point, so tied up in his own inarticulateness
and inwardness that he paces a room and faces the wall, drinking,
mumbling to an absent Mrs. Miller, "If just one time you could be
sweet without no money around. . . . If you just one time let me
run the show. . . ." "I got poetry in me," he says; "you're freezin'
my soul." McCabe sounds here like a pubescent rock balladeer and
is expressing himself from the same source of conventional, sentimental clichés that has fed movie lovers and songwriters for years.
In his hopeless innocence and aloneness he can only confront himself, and with language that reflects that very innocence and aloneness. He is at this point one with almost every melodramatic character ever created in cinema who cannot call upon any other mode of

discourse but that which expresses his own barely articulate, self-satisfying emotions. Since there is no one who cares to share these emotions, he winds up talking about himself to himself.

The threat to McCabe is not merely that Mrs. Miller will not return what he thinks is his love for her (she does, in fact, demonstrate—to herself—some concern and even some affection for him), but that she and everyone else in the film talk a different language than he does. And he cannot understand the language of others anymore than they can understand his sentimental gibberish or his mock-tough gibberish. He will pretend comprehension of other gibberish, if it seems to fit in with his own understanding of things. The lawyer, Clement Samuels, feeds McCabe a most atrocious line of half-liberal—half-conservative nonsense when McCabe consults him about the threat of the mining company. Samuels talks of protecting big enterprise and small, of busting up the trusts and monopolies. "I just didn't wanna get killed," says McCabe. "Until people stop dying for freedom," says the lawyer, in a line redolent of patriotic illogic, "they ain't gonna be free." Samuels convinces McCabe he can be a hero, that he can "stare 'em down and make 'em quake in their boots." In other words, that he must be Gary Cooper or Henry Fonda, or even John Wayne. Poor McCabe buys it.

Altman's fiction continually turns in on itself and its predecessors; it continually places itself in a critical perspective to history and to the myths of history propounded by other westerns. Certainly McCabe would like to fancy himself a hero, if not actually be a hero. When he parrots the lawyer's words to Mrs. Miller, her expression of concern for him and his stupidity is more than a bit tempered by her concern for her investment should he be killed. Altman unfailingly responds to any outpouring of romantic individualism on McCabe's part with one or another expression of economic self-interest. The West, Altman tells us, contrary to what we have been told in film after film, was not so much the testing ground of our culture's initiative as it was an outgrowth, or the outward growth, of the wielding of economic power. The initiative was taken by those with the power to initiate. Mrs. Miller seems to understand this, so that at every moment she denies whatever emotion she might have—she might even wish to have—in order to protect herself.

McCabe kills the three mining-company killers, and he does it alone, like a good gunslinger should (and unlike that weaker cowboy, the sheriff of *High Noon,* who had to depend on his wife to help him). Like their relatives in *High Noon,* the townspeople ignore his plight, not out of cowardice, particularly, but rather out of passivity and distraction; the church is burning down. Mrs. Miller deserts him; what could she do to help him? McCabe finally lives up to his nonexistent "big rep" (and, could we extend the fiction, probably creates a bigger rep in his wake). He is shot, and dies in the snow, buried, no more than a mound of white, his heroism unseen, unapplauded, and unwanted.

Like *The Conversation* and *Night Moves, McCabe and Mrs. Miller* denies absolutely the possibility of the individual triumphing, in fact or in spirit; and it could be criticized for reinforcing our ideology of defeat and powerlessness. It is saved, oddly enough, by its own lyricism and gentleness, its sense of process and suggestion of other modes of behavior. For while the film does immediately express hopeless activity and inevitable loss, it points to the possibility of the opposite. There is a distinct lack of despair in the film (a quality shared by all of Altman's films, with the possible exception of *Images*) and a suggestion that, perhaps between the adolescent romanticism of McCabe and the hardness of Mrs. Miller, love might possibly exist on terms other than the raucous sentimentality our movies insist upon. There is a suggestion too that a community might cohere on terms other than self-interest and a brutality that arises out of greed. The film suggests these alternatives, but only by their absence.[10]

Altman will not admit them openly; but he at least tempers his film with a softness that somewhat denies the hopelessness of what we see. This is not to suggest that the film is in any simple way "optimistic." Altman cannot easily slide into any one extremity of point of view and stay there long. The very pluralism of his visual and narrative form forbids it: there is too much happening, too much diversity for any one mood to dominate any other. In his other films the altera-

McCabe, alone as the townspeople fight the fire, flees the gunmen.

tions of mood are usually more extreme than they are in *McCabe,* where a sadness of lost opportunity is most persuasive. Our readiness to respond to configurations of lost love and blighted romance provides a tension with the film's political and ideological nuances. The hazy quality of the images and Leonard Cohen's songs (poor by themselves, yet very effective in combination with the images) also provoke an emotional response. The continual and ironic contrasts of cold exterior and warm interior work out an idea of needed protection and desired community which we respond to despite the fact that the film continually denies them, a denial that assures our regret over their loss. An effective balance is thus achieved between what we want to happen and what we see happening, a balance and a tension that keep us actively engaged and continually responsive. Tenderness is achieved out of its opposite as the film evokes in us a longing for the very attitudes it attempts to deny.

If *McCabe and Mrs. Miller* portrays the community as desolation and romantic love as individual fantasy determined, externally, by economic necessity, *Thieves Like Us* (1974) reverses this point of view, attempting to locate a possibility of love within a larger social and economic context, a love that attempts to counter that context but inevitably fails in the face of it. The film also establishes a different perspective on the idea of community. There are three communities in *Thieves:* the American heartland in the thirties, Depression-ridden, listless, barely cohesive; the three thieves, Bowie (Keith Carradine), Chicamaw (John Shuck), and T-Dub (Bert Remsen), who attempt to form a bond of friendship in necessity, rob banks because it is the only thing they know how to do, and protect each other because they are the only ones who will protect each other; and the lovers, Bowie and Keechie (Shelley Duvall), who remove themselves from the male group, attempt a community of two, sealed off from the larger world, isolate themselves, and are destroyed when Bowie is killed by the police.

The film is something of a departure for Altman. There is little of the ironic lyricism and spatial dislocation of *McCabe* or the psychological intensity of *Images,* and certainly none of the restrained hysteria of *The Long Goodbye,* the film that immediately precedes it. It is visually quite different from its predecessors. The only one of the major films until *Quintet* not shot in Panavision, it does not play off a horizontal width against a compressed interior space. Its framing is loose and casual, and Altman indulges in a deep-focus sequence for only the second time in his major work. The first such sequence appears in *Images,* as we observe the living room of Cathryn's house, with its smoking fireplace, while to the right and in the rear, she goes about work in the kitchen; in *Thieves,* we see Bowie, Chicamaw, and T-Dub sitting together in a living room, while to the right and in the rear, Keechie goes about her work in the kitchen. In both shots we find a woman in her "proper place," oblivious to some larger event occurring outside her observation. But despite the departures in the film's spatial construction and its casual, even kindly, treatment of its characters, it follows through with some of Altman's major concerns. It is a film of generic protest, and the genre it protests is of recent origin, for with *Thieves Like Us* Altman looks directly at *Bonnie and Clyde,* and with that look denies the heroic, even mythic status that Penn gives his characters.

Bonnie and Clyde attempt to control their world by asserting their energy and spirit upon it. The characters of *Thieves Like Us* are always controlled by their world, enjoying a tenuous freedom from it only when the three men are alone in a joking camaraderie, or the two lovers withdraw within themselves. But even in these instances the world is present, either in the newspaper accounts of the gang's exploits or in the radio programs that create a background to all of their activities. If the Barrow gang create their own community and briefly dominate their world, the thieves and the lovers of Altman's film are always dominated by a community that oppresses them in the form of the soap operas, gangster stories, cheap poetry, and political and religious speeches that dominate the film's sound track. When the three robbers take a bank, we are forced to watch from the outside, listen to "Gangbusters" on the radio ironically mocking their exploits (or see a Coca-Cola Queen selling her delights to children on the street). When we are permitted to see a robbery, it is a disaster: the gang is forced to kill, and it marks the end of their success. But on the sound track we hear FDR speaking on security, peace, happiness and the power of a democratic government to protect its citizens. When Bowie and Keechie make love, their closeness is punctuated by a radio soap-opera version of *Romeo and Juliet.* Over and over we hear, "Thus did Romeo and Juliet consummate their first interview by falling madly in love with each other." The radio commentary mocks the couple and makes their adolescent passion the more endearing at the same time. Even more, it refuses to let them alone. None of the characters are free from the authority of their world and its cheapening images. Like McCabe and Mrs. Miller, Bowie and

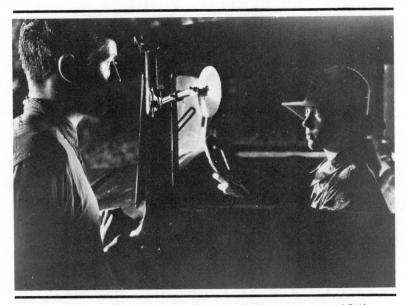

Two versions of Bowie and Keechie: **(above)** Farley Granger and Cathy O'Donnell in the **noir** world of Nicholas Ray's **They Live by Night; (opposite)** Keith Carradine and Shelley Duvall in the brighter world of Altman's **Thieves Like Us.**

Keechie are held down (within their fiction) by economic oppression and (outside their fiction) by the myths of their cinematic predecessors. They are oppressed by the demands of their culture. Its banality drains from them any possibility of heroic action. McCabe and Mrs. Miller inhabit a moment in history when that banality was just coming to be (its birth is witnessed in the characters of Eugene Sears and Ernie Hollander, emissaries from the mining company, who represent violence by wearing a bland face, and by the lawyer Clement Samuels, who mouths the clichés of free enterprise as if they were new truths). Bowie and Keechie are alive at its maturity. Bonnie and Clyde transcend for a moment the emptiness and banality of their culture; Bowie and Keechie merely sink beneath it.

If Altman refuses to indulge in the heroic lies of *Bonnie and Clyde* he also refuses to indulge in the total grimness of oppression and loss that Penn's myth-making leads to. He refuses as well the grimness that accompanies an earlier version of *Thieves Like Us,* Nicholas Ray's *They Live by Night* (1949), which was made from the same novel that is Altman's source. The two films offer a revealing comparison of style and temperament.[11] *They Live by Night* is a *film noir,* although it makes some important shifts in the *noir* structure by dealing with rural thieves rather than urban gangsters and private detectives. Ray's characters are trapped within their world, enclosed in a darkness that seals up their innocence like a coffin. His lovers are betrayed and humiliated; Altman's make at least an attempt to confront their situation, to work out the allegiances that Bowie has both to his friends and to his lover. In Ray's film, Bowie has to be physically coerced to stay with the gang; in Altman's film, he chooses to help Chicamaw escape from prison, though his friend proves so bitter and murderous that Bowie is forced to abandon him. At the end of both films, Bowie is killed and Keechie is left alone. But the different forms of the endings indicate an important change in points of view. In Ray's film, Keechie is left by Bowie's body. We are forced to observe her, with her eyes averted and her face full of hardness and despair, as she literally disappears into the darkness. Altman's Keechie watches her lover's death from a distance, restrained by Mattie, the woman who betrays Bowie to the police—explicitly in Ray's film, implicitly in Altman's. We observe Keechie behind a screen door, the bright red of a Coca-Cola icebox punctuating the blue haze, a romantic poem punctuating the sound track. As the police shoot to pieces the shack Bowie is in, we see Keechie smashing her omnipresent Coke bottle, violently screaming in slow motion (a nice reversal of the brutality forced upon us at the end of *Bonnie and Clyde*).[12] But Altman does not leave her there. After Bowie's body is carried out of the shack, we cut to the waiting room of a railroad station. We hear on the sound track Father Coughlin, the thirties radio evangelist, telling us to bear our burden in silence, like men. Keechie talks for a while to a woman (who is in fact Joan Tewkesbury, coauthor of the screenplay), telling her the child she carries will not be named after his father. Keechie then joins the crowd going up the stairs to the platform. We see one more shot of her impassive face and then cut to a far, slow-motion shot of the crowd disappearing up the stairs.

Where Ray ends in despair, Altman ends on a notion at least of a world in which some sad flow of life continues. He lifts the *noir* fatality that trapped Ray's characters, but diffuses it into a wider context, the larger trap of the world they inhabit. His Keechie endures, trapped as she is and strong as she is. She does not withdraw like Mrs. Miller, and she does not quite give in. She will exist ensnared in the promises of bourgeois comforts and security, ever-present in the radio shows she hears, promises negated by the narrow, disenfranchised life she must lead.[13] But at least some community, even the faceless, slow-motion crawl of a crowd in transit, exists, and no *film noir* offered even that much.

Out of *film noir,* Altman has made something that approaches *film lumière,* and which, like his western, indicates a potential of community as well as its inevitable dissolution. He indicates that neither male camaraderie nor heterosexual love is able to survive in a culture that denies the very security it promises to those who are unable to abide, for intellectual or emotional or economic reasons, by its rules. But he indicates as well that a kind of endurance is possible, albeit a passive, lonely endurance. Keechie's survival is in fact similar to Mrs. Miller's, similar as well to the survival of the crowd at the end of *Nashville:* isolated, with false comfort or none at all, unable or unwilling to change their situation. But Keechie at least moves on, and although it is a movement in sadness and resignation, it is more movement than Mrs. Miller's, and more certainly than any *noir* character can ordinarily make. Another kind of movement, more extreme, but no more hopeful, occurs in the film that precedes *Thieves Like Us,* a version of *film noir,* this time by way of the forties detective film: *The Long Goodbye.*

*The Long Goodbye* is at once a direct descendent and a powerful denial of its ancestry. The detective has fascinated Western culture since he was invented in the nineteenth century. An urban and urbane quester, he could descend into worlds the middle-class reader—and, later, viewer—could never approach. Even more, he could do what the reader and viewer could only dream of doing, gain control of complex situations through reason and perception and with a moral superiority that allowed him to be engaged in, but untouched by, the moral squalor around him. The detective was also the surrogate of the reader in the act of detection, an act that permitted an interplay, in the classical "whodunit," of many voices: the author, the criminal, the detective, and the reader/viewer, creating a complex discourse which, however, always promised that one voice would prevail, a voice that enunciated the pristine and integral solving of the problem.[14]

When, via Dashiell Hammett and Raymond Chandler, the detective entered (perhaps even created) the *film noir* world of the forties, changes occurred. He became less morally pure, less certain, less sure of his perceptions. The dark, oppressive *mise-en-scène* he worked in did not permit clear understandings and pristine solutions. The rich, devious perpetrators of criminal acts, their low and vicious henchmen, and the dark, treacherous women of the *noir* universe allowed for no easy comprehension and apprehension. The *film noir* detective was a sullied individual and almost always harmed morally and physically by his business. Yet he prevailed: Bogart's Sam Spade, in *The Maltese Falcon* (1941), had a sense of moral obligation and self-protection, as well as a sense of bluff and bravura, that allowed him some success. The various Philip Marlowes, especially Dick Powell's in *Murder My Sweet* (1944) and Bogart's in *The Big Sleep* (1946), had a strength of self-protective wit and cynicism that distanced them somewhat from the complexities and compromises of their work.[15] They also had, for the audience, at least, a recognizable *milieu* in which to operate. Now this would appear to be an immediate contradiction: the *film noir* world is dark and oppressive; yet the forties detective operates in a recognizable *milieu*. The contradiction arises from some curious results of convention. Forties *film noir* became so rapidly set in its visual forms that its threat was somewhat lessened because its images became almost comforting through repetition. The shadows and rain-soaked streets, dark nightclubs and narrow alleys, the half-lit faces and claustrophobic rooms with shadows of venetian blinds became instant icons of a quickly recognizable fictive world. This easy recognition, transmitted by an often stable, neutral camera, contradicted the amoral, indeed dreadful, vaguenesses of the world being created.

I am suggesting that *film noir* mitigated its own subversive potential by quickly giving its images and events a familiarity and a distance that protected the audience from them.* One need only look at

---

* Some early *films noirs,* like Wilder's *Double Indemnity* (1944) and Lang's *Scarlet Street* (1945), still have a desolation about them that belies the subsequent familiarity of their form and content.

Aldrich's *Kiss Me Deadly* and Welles's *Touch of Evil,* two late *noir* films deeply conscious of the way they are put together, to discover how disturbing the genre is when its forms are realized in a less conventional and recognizable manner than they were in the forties. *The Long Goodbye* continues this self-conscious reexamination of original *noir* forms. Its form, analyzed earlier, creates an unstable and unsettling perspective, a sense of disorder and lack of comprehension so extreme that it expresses as much or more in camera and lens movement than its forties predecessors did through chiaroscuro and the claustrophobic framing of their characters. If *Touch of Evil* is the last *film noir* in black and white, *The Long Goodbye* may be the first in color, eschewing the expressionism of the forties and of Welles (reintroduced by Scorsese in *Taxi Driver*) and replacing it with a drifting, unlocalized, uncertain perspective. Rather than being witnesses to a dark and doomed world, as we are in classic *film noir* (and as we are in that other seventies revision of the detective film, *Night Moves*), we share the point of view of a Marlowe so completely out of control of his world that there is no possibility of "detection," but only, perhaps, of accidental discovery. The "voices" woven into the text of detective fiction become here a confused mumble.

Many critics, some with outrage, have discussed how weak, fooled, and finally violent Altman's Marlowe is—particularly compared to his Bogart forebear in *The Big Sleep.* But a closer look reveals some interesting similarities, or at least extensions of Hawks's 1946 film. Hawks portrays a closed, dark, and curiously stable world over which Marlowe seems to exercise complete control. But Altman and his screenwriter, Leigh Brackett (who coscripted *The Big Sleep*), perceive that control to be tenuous at best, fraudulent at worst. The Hawks/Bogart Marlowe becomes, despite himself, deeply entangled in the world he enters, caught in the very morass he attempts to clear up. His control over things is apparent only in his wit and his ability to find momentary attachments based upon the least amount of mistrust. In fact, the Hawks/Bogart Marlowe is played for a fool by everyone and is reduced to committing murder as vicious as any committed by the various thugs, grifters, blackmailers, and rich young women who drift in and out of the film's complex narrative. *The Big Sleep* ends in a litter of corpses (dead of Marlowe's doing), with police sirens punctuating the night and sharply undercutting the apparent romantic calm Marlowe shares with Vivian Sternwood (Lauren Bacall).

In *The Long Goodbye,* Altman and Brackett merely strip away the security of the Bogart persona: his wit and his ability to stand back from a given situation in a posture of self-preservation. Their Marlowe is a man out of time. "I'm from a long time ago," he tells his police interrogators. He is a character without physical or emotional anchorage in the world: "Remember, you're not in here; it's just your body," he tells David Carradine, who happens, in one of those small, offhanded, tangential sequences of Altman's, to be sharing Marlowe's jail cell. He is a man whose every connection with the world is faulty and non-comprehending. The discourse he carries on with the world is barely coherent and neglectful of the basic logic even of conversation. As he passes on the ramp that separates his apartment from that of a group of girls who practice yoga in the nude (and go mostly unnoticed by Marlowe), the following interchange ensues. He asks them if they've seen his cat (who ran off the night before when Marlowe couldn't provide it with the proper brand of food). One girl answers, "I didn't even know you had a cat, Mr. Marlowe. . . ." Another girl emerges, saying, "Say you wanted a hat?" Marlowe replies, "No, no, you don't look fat." And as the verbal language drifts and glances in incoherent directions, so the camera—our gaze onto Marlowe's world—drifts and pans, zooms slowly in and out (never completing its motion), arcs and dollies until we are ourselves inscribed into an orderless, almost random series of interchanges and events.

The self-defensive Marlowe wit has turned into incomprehension. Mumbling passivity—Marlowe's key and favorite response is "It's o.k. with me"—is what has become of the Marlowe persistence and drive for moral order. And in his insular state Marlowe merely allows himself to be had. For no particular reason, he decides to refute the accusation that his friend, Terry Lennox, murdered his own

308

wife. It is as if this notion of trust and friendship that Marlowe irrationally holds somehow provides a center to his drifting world. In fact, it furthers the drift and results in terrible betrayals, that of Marlowe himself certainly being the worst. Friendship is always a difficult subject for Altman, and his films constantly probe the proximity of friendship to betrayal. Bowie, out of emotional necessity, betrays his friends when he goes off with Keechie in *Thieves Like Us*. McCabe is betrayed by Sheehan and eventually by the whole town. *Nashville* can be seen as a complex of betrayals, of people refusing to admit to each other's emotional validity and individual requirements, looking rather upon one another as objects to be used. Only in *California Split* does Altman see the possibility of two men (and it is interesting that it is two men and not a man and a woman) sharing a modicum of trust. But even here it is very tentative, and while no one is betrayed, nothing is very permanent.

Marlowe's unquestioning and irrational belief in his friend cuts him off from even the limited comprehension of things he may have had. It is just here that we can see how clearly Altman is changing the conventions of the detective film. His Marlowe does not "detect" anything, actively or passively. He attempts to prove wrong the charges against his friend, but in so doing accepts any lie that is thrown his way. The Bogart/Hawks Marlowe persists in an attempt at discovery, no matter how dark and futile the attempt may be (so too, for that matter, does Penn's Harry Moseby). Altman takes the inevitability of failure as a fact, and starts from there. He sees the *film noir* detective as a patsy and chooses not to have him struggle manfully to prove otherwise. (Interestingly, the core of Altman's revision may lie in a sequence in *The Big Sleep* where Marlowe, trapped in the shadows of a warehouse office, looks on helplessly and hopelessly as Lash Canino murders Harry Jones; Marlowe afterward reveals an unexpectedly sentimental attachment to little Jonesy.) Finally, Altman creates, out of the dialectical extension of the Philip Marlowe we have been brought up on, a perfect fictive surrogate of a major cultural phenomenon: the modern passive individual, who accepts everything, questions nothing, and is had continually by anyone less gullible than he. But this very passivity creates its own irrational activity, and deeply implicates Marlowe in the destruction of others.

One who loses because Marlowe cannot and will not act is the character Roger Wade. Wade is one of the more melodramatically powerful men that Altman has created. He is a precise and conventional rendering of the burned-out, alcoholic writer who has been part of our romantic mythology since the nineteenth century. His appearance in a film that otherwise denies conventional figures and acting styles (the kindly, vicious Jewish gangster, Marty Augustine—played by director Mark Rydell—is an example, along with Marlowe, of this unconventionality) makes him stand out as an immediately at-

Two versions of Philip Marlowe: (below) Humphrey Bogart in a noir warehouse office in Hawks's The Big Sleep; (opposite) Elliott Gould brought to bay by Mrs. Wade's dog in Altman's The Long Goodbye.

tractive figure. He stands out so clearly that Marlowe, a figure made up of anti-conventional unromantic elements, cannot even see him. "Looney Tunes" is Marlowe's response to Roger Wade. The romantic, boisterous loser, full of anger and sorrow, looks only mad to the modern, recessive, passive loser. With a just irony, Wade calls Marlowe "Marlboro Man," and both remain vulnerable and outside each other's spheres.

In a celebrated sequence, Marlowe goes out to the beach, while Roger and Mrs. Wade (Nina van Pallandt) argue, the writer expressing his passion to his cold wife (a *noir* woman, she is part of Terry Lennox's crime and uses Marlowe to push her husband to ruin and to further her escape to her murderous boyfriend Terry). We listen to and observe their conversation from outside the glass door of their beach house, the camera slowly zooming in on each and on both together. Marlowe, playing on the beach, is reflected in the window in front of the husband and wife (technically the sequence is more complicated than this, for it appears that one shot of Marlowe on the beach is superimposed on the window; therefore, when the camera zooms back from the window, there is a coordinated zoom back in the superimposed shot, doubling the spatial slipperiness and uncertainty). This complex spatial interraction serves as a metaphor for the film as a whole. We see the Wades, for much of the sequence, through the glass, which removes us from their conflict. The constant movement of the camera emphasizes this removal, this inability of ours to confront the action as we expect we have a right to. Marlowe, who is blind and deaf to what the Wades are going through and insensible to information that would go against his obsessive allegiance to his friend, is outside, dancing in the waves like a child. He is reflected on the same glass we look through, and because he is reflected, we see only his back, and from a considerable distance. Every participant in the sequence is cut off from every other, emotionally, physically, and in their mutual misunderstanding.

Later, after Wade is humiliated at a party by the slimy Dr. Verringer (Henry Gibson), he commits suicide by walking into the sea (like Norman Maine in *A Star Is Born*). Marlowe and Mrs. Wade are talking by the window, she misleading Marlowe by discussing Roger's affair with Mrs. Lennox, hiding her own connection with Marty Augustine, who has been pursuing Marlowe. Through the window that stands between them, we see in the darkness Roger walking to the ocean. The camera zooms past Marlowe, past Mrs. Wade, to the figure approaching the waves. It is not an urgent movement, merely another series of slow spatial drifts, not hurrying our gaze or theirs to this pathetic event, but merely alluding to their obliviousness to it. They do not react until a reverse shot is given, a slow zoom up to the window from outside (again, as so often in Altman's films, a window is used as a barrier to direct emotional contact). What follows is a scene of enormous energy for Altman. Marlowe attempts to save Wade from the ocean. It is his most active moment, and the noise of the surf, the darkness and confusion, Wade's dog running in the ocean with his master's cane, provide an engagement of the viewer with the action, and with the participants in the action, unlike anything else in the film. The problem is that this action and engagement are to no avail, for Wade is dead. The emotional peak the action creates and carries over to the investigation that follows reaches a level of hysteria that makes it impossible for either us or Marlowe to hear a policeman tell him that Wade could not have been responsible for Sylvia Lennox's death (as Mrs. Wade had said he was), information that further implicates Terry himself and further implicates Marlowe in his own stupidity and, because of his neglect of the facts, in the death of Roger Wade as well.

Altman is appropriately wary of highly emotional situations, of melodramatic crises and confrontations. These are the stock-in-trade of American film and represent a method of easily engaging the audience and, occasionally, obviating narrative difficulties. In television, even more than in classical Hollywood film, a sequence of overwrought feelings, of melodramatic hysteria, will be used to suture up narrative weakness, depending upon the audience's emotions to take the place of their perception. Altman refuses such orchestrated climaxes and prefers to dissipate emotional intensity by observing peripheral action. When he does create an emotional scene, like Wade's suicide and its aftermath, he uses it to indicate its deceptive qualities. Marlowe gets hysterical when he believes that Wade killed Sylvia Lennox; it is the highest emotional peak he reaches in the film, and it is based on lies. But neither he nor we (unless we listen very carefully, for the camera is on Marlowe when it is said) hear the police inspector say that Wade could not have done it.

Marlowe cannot hear or see; he is the detective as somnambulist. He is the bandaged mummy whom he meets in a hospital room in the penultimate sequence—his own double, as Jonathan Rosenbaum points out, who hands him a tiny harmonica that Marlowe will play as he skips off from his last encounter with Terry Lennox, the only encounter in the film in which Marlowe, his head momentarily cleared of lies, takes definitive and immediate action.[16] It is an action that has been found so distasteful that, when the film was recut for television, it was altered and rendered ambiguous. In the film Marlowe kills Terry, shoots him without hesitation. They confront each other in a series of slowly accelerating zooms. "So you used me," says Marlowe. "Hell," answers Terry, "that's what friends are for. . . . Nobody cares." The camera is on Marlowe's face as Terry offers this response, and it zooms in closer as Marlowe answers, "Yeah, nobody cares but me." For the first time in the film, spatial proximity with the character is achieved. It is still an isolating proximity, for we are not permitted to imagine that Marlowe is in touch with anything but a brief awakening of anger. We return to a shot of Terry and zoom in closer, faster on his face: "Well, that's you, Marlowe. You'll never learn, you're a born loser." The shot returns to Marlowe, zooms back— "Yeah, I even lost my cat"—and he pulls his gun and fires. In the network television version, the shot froze on the pulling of the gun and cut immediately to Marlowe walking down the road. But the fact is that Altman intends us to observe closely the result of Marlowe's action and his response. Terry falls into a pool, rolling in the water like the cowboy shot by the punk gunman in *McCabe,* or, in fact, the gunman himself when he is later shot by McCabe. The camera zooms in again on Marlowe's face as he watches Terry, spits, and leaves. He walks down the road, oblivious to Mrs. Wade, who passes him in a jeep, heading for her now dead lover. On the sound track, the musical theme of the film, which in parody of forties films has been repeated throughout, coming from every conceivable source—doorbell to Mexican marching band—is distorted and moaning: until Marlowe begins blowing the harmonica given him by the mummy. As he diminishes in size down the road, he begins dancing, and we hear on the track the music of "Hooray for Hollywood" that opened the film. The mummy comes to life, having activated himself by murder.

I detail the ending of *The Long Goodbye* because it is an unusually definitive one for Altman, though still highly diffuse and multivalent. The fact that neither Chandler's Marlowe, nor any of his forties film incarnations, could kill a friend coldly and unflinchingly is an element that Altman is directly responding to. The ultimate moral purity of Marlowe is a thing Altman cannot abide, and he detects the weakness and falseness of it. At the end of Hawks's *The Big Sleep,* Marlowe pushes Eddie Mars (toward whom he once felt friendship) out the door to meet the certain machine-gun fire of his henchmen. It seems a proper thing to do, for certainly Mars would have killed Marlowe, and anyway he is being forced into a death equal to his own viciousness. But Marlowe is responsible for the death nonetheless, as he was for the murder of Harry Jones by Lash Canino, a murder he passively observes. He is responsible for the death of Canino himself, whom he shoots out of revenge for Jonesy and out of a need to escape (at this point in the narrative Marlowe has no choice but to shoot his captor). The Bogart Marlowe is a killer whose killing is always morally accounted for. In Chandler's novel *The Long Goodbye,* Marlowe does not kill; he accepts Terry's having used him with sadness and understanding. The important thing for him is to remain true to an idea of friendship.

Altman cannot accept either the morally justified murders or the passive acceptance of abuse under the guise of loyalty. The act of his Marlowe is therefore a response to both, a murder as gratuitous as any shown on the screen and an action of a sleepwalker momentarily awake. There is undeniable satisfaction in Marlowe's act, for the vicarious pleasure felt when a narrative includes revenge is immediate.

There is particular satisfaction in that Marlowe finally does something, acts rather than being acted upon. Yet the act is repulsive, as repulsive as Marty Augustine smashing a Coke bottle in his girl friend's face to scare Marlowe ("Now that's someone I love, and you I don't even like"). It seems we must have the violence both ways: satisfying and repulsive. Peckinpah may insist that violence is a purgative; Penn may insist that it is the necessary result of defiant action; Kubrick and Scorsese may see it only appearing and disappearing, neither explained nor explicable, or, if explained, always something more than the explanation. For Altman, violence is not as vague as Camus's *acte gratuit,* but it is an inevitability as well as an erratic, unpredictable occurrence. And it hurts everyone concerned. After the killing, Marlowe is still a jerk, still unconnected to his world. McCabe is dead along with the three gunmen. After the assassination in *Nashville,* everyone remains gullible and manipulable, singing their great anthem of passivity: "You may say that I ain't free / But it don't worry me." No one is helped, ennobled, or purged by the violence that occurs in Altman's films, least of all the audience. If we applaud Marlowe's shooting of Terry, we must answer for its ramifications: is a person who has been played for a fool only able to rectify his or her passivity by murder? If we are appalled by this act, then why are we not appalled by other acts just like it in our cinema? Why is the futility of Bogart's Marlowe "heroic" and the futility of Gould's Marlowe repulsive?

That is why the "Hooray for Hollywood" theme opens and closes the film. Whatever its other qualities and faults, American film has helped make us as gullible and passive as poor Marlowe, unable to discriminate between the actions presented to us and our reactions to them, fudging the line between valid individual activity and destructive heroic fantasies. If Altman is not attempting to clarify our confusions, he is at least attempting to show us that we are confused, that our perceptions have become befuddled by false heroics and irrational acts that present themselves as being true to life, as believable, when all they are actually true to is conventions of behavior that can exist only in a film fiction. *The Long Goodbye* is not a goodbye to Hollywood. Altman's affection for it is too strong. He needs its conventions as material to deconstruct and reconsider. After the angry correctives applied by *The Long Goodbye,* he softens his approach in *Thieves Like Us,* still diminishing the heroic myth, but with more restraint and certainly a more kindly disposition to his characters.

*Thieves Like Us* is the closest Altman comes to a conventional film narrative. But it is only a momentary pause, for he follows it with one of his more ambitious reorganizations of narrative structure. *California Split* (1974) can be taken on one level as another entry into the sub-genre of buddy-buddy films, prevalent since the late sixties, which includes *M.A.S.H.* as well as such works as *Easy Rider, Midnight Cowboy, Scarecrow, Deliverance, Butch Cassidy and the Sundance Kid, The Sting,* and almost anything by Peckinpah. These films banish women from any major role and substitute a repressed or unstated homosexual relationship between two or more men engaged in extreme adventure.[17] *California Split* manages to escape some of the more uncomfortable sexual evasions and misogynistic attitudes of these films by keeping its emotional level low, by allowing, as few American films do, emotions and emotional relationships to be chancy, fleeting, non-destructive, unscarring. Unlike other buddy-buddy films, it gives its women characters equal status and equal strength. Though the Gwen Welles and Ann Prentiss characters are whores, they do not suffer and are not condescended to, nor are they any more oppressed by their situation than their male counterparts are by gambling. George Segal's Bill is sad a lot of the time, but mostly because he does not experience either the thrills or the agonies in gambling that so many other films on the subject have insisted one must feel. (Compare *California Split* with Karel Reisz's essay in metaphysical angst, *The Gambler:* Altman eschews completely the heavy masochism that Reisz sees as the motivating force of the compulsive gambler.)

Altman substitutes, in *California Split,* a sort of emotional *laissez-faire* for melodrama, and does so mainly by organizing not only the subject but also the narrative form of the film around gambling. The structure of *California Split* is that of a game of chance, a playful,

317

random, offhanded series of events full of accident, coincidence, and peripheral action brought to the center in a more extreme way than in the previous films. But the adjective is misleading: the film is not "extreme" in any way. If anything, it is extremely gentle and undemanding, requiring of us only that we enjoy its playfulness.

For example, there is a sequence in which a despondent, debt-ridden Bill enters a massage parlor, walks through it to a bedroom where some children are watching a cartoon of "Basketball Jones" on television, and passes by them to a poker game in a back room. Here Altman purposefully sidetracks, improvising upon not so much the acting or the story as our own expectations and responses. Each element of the sequence could be developed to major melodramatic proportions. A sad character in need of money to pay off gambling debts is reduced to the squalid comforts of a seedy brothel. No, he is visiting some wretched family forced to live on the very premises—surely the narrative will focus on this unhappy situation. No, they are ignored; the focus of the sequence must be on the card game in the back room. Certainly these must be a group of unpleasant gangsters, playing in a place like this. No, it is only a card game, and Bill loses, and leaves, and the place is never seen or referred to again, just as Sue and Barbara, Charlie's roommates, are never seen or referred to after a certain point. And what a coincidence that on the television set in the apartment in the massage parlor is a cartoon about basketball, a betting sport, a game that Charlie (Elliott Gould) will later hustle to get money for the big trip to Reno. A coincidence, too, that at a certain point in the film songs by Phyllis Shotwell, who will later appear as an entertainer in a Reno casino, suddenly begin to be heard on the sound track, commenting on the action. At one point, when Charlie is crossing a street in Reno, humming to himself, something he sings suddenly merges with a song on the sound track. The off-hand and out-of-hand keep occurring in sequence after sequence, with no climaxes, no directions. The film is carefully crafted to be open not to various interpretations but to various reactions to its juxtapositions and anomalies; it is made to be analogous to the wheel of fortune that closes the film, spinning and stopping where it will.[18]

This is, of course, not improvisation in the usual sense. Though much of the dialogue may have been made up in rehearsal and in preparation for shooting, the structure of chance and coincidence, the joking interplay of events in the film and the expectations of the viewer, would have to have been carefully planned. *California Split* holds an important place in Altman's work: experiment, joke, happy film, it also moves him a bit beyond the generic revisionism of *McCabe* and *The Long Goodbye* into a greater revision of narrative structure in general, of the ways movies tell their stories.

In *Nashville* he attempts to refine and enlarge upon the open structure of *California Split,* adding many more characters, each with his or her own small narrative to be worked out. Much more than its predecessors, *Nashville* has pretenses to being a grand cultural statement, a "metaphor for America," as at least one reviewer said. Unlike its predecessors, however, *Nashville* falls short of the notion of the open narrative, in which the viewer is asked to participate in, question, and respond to new forms of expression. The film loses its way, becomes ambiguous rather than responsible and attempts to hide its very real anger under a guise of geniality. It refuses to come to terms with itself, disingenuously pretending to encompass many attitudes and many points of view, when in fact its own perspective is rather restrictive. "All you need to do is add yourself as the twenty-fifth character," writes Joan Tewkesbury, in her introduction to her screenplay, "and know that whatever you think about the film is right, even if you think the film is wrong."[19]

Film, however, does not allow the spectator to become a participant on the same level as the fictions who inhabit its narrative. Even Altman cannot change the immutable status of an imaginative work as an object made separate from us and inviolable. As open and malleable as its structure of meaning might be, the elements that make up that structure—the immediate forms of what we see and hear—are permanent and removed from us. They may envelop us and make us assent to their presence (their "reality") or they may make themselves distant and recessive and demand that we approach them cautiously (the *Godfather* films, for example, do the former, *Barry Lyndon* the latter), but we may not become part of them. Furthermore, the fact that a narrative is made a certain way and that its characters say and do specific things (the same things, each time we see the film) makes it impossible for us to believe that *whatever* we think about them is right. We may change our attitudes on subsequent viewings, or even in our reflections upon a single viewing, but a certain structure and perspective remains. Altman, more than any other American film-maker, is making us view film as a process, as an observation of interacting details that cohere in sometimes non-directed ways. But cohere they must on some formal and contextual level, or narrative is impossible. If narrative is possible, then *some* basic meaning system is created.

I am trying to provide some limits to modernism and the notion of the open narrative. If Tewkesbury and Altman insist that any reading of their film is the right one, then no meaning exists, and the film's status as narrative disappears; it is merely an arbitrary arrangement of incoherent parts, mutually exclusive characters, and anomalous events (of course, if that were true, a very definite meaning system would emerge). *Nashville* is none of these: it is precisely located in time and place; it has many characters, but Altman takes great care to relate them, even if by apparent accident, and to define them; and even though it has no conventional story line, the various "stories" of the various characters move easily and neatly. The frame narrative—the organizing of a rally for candidate Hal Phillip Walker—easily holds the parts together. Structurally, *California Split* and *The Long Goodbye* are more complex and intriguing, for *Nashville* really only extends the parallel or alternate montage structure basic to American film. *Nashville* merely has more parallels and alternations.

As an experiment in smoothly integrating a number of narrative units into a whole, *Nashville* succeeds with much energy and a sense of delight in its scope. As an integration of the fragments that make up American culture in the mid-seventies, it remains close to *Brewster McCloud,* without that film's manic silliness, and *McCabe,* without its lyricism. Altman continues to be struck by the self-serving, passive nature of the culture, but adds here something more, a notion of hypocrisy and meanness that can be glimpsed in *McCabe* and begins to surface more in *The Long Goodbye* (it is present in *Thieves Like Us* but only as an envelope, as the false ideas and mean hopes foisted by the culture upon Bowie and Keechie, which they cannot possibly achieve). In *Nashville*, all the characters are fools, manipulated or manipulating, hurt or hurtful. Barbara Jean, perpetually in a state of nervous breakdown, is booed by her audience and shot down at a concert, but not before she is treated like a child by her husband-manager, Barnett, who is in turn insulted by Connie White and her manager. Tom, the pop singer, insults a poor soldier whose life is spent following Barbara Jean around and treats his women like things. Opal from the BBC uses everyone as a sequence in her non-existent documentary and insults Haven Hamilton's son Buddy and the chauffeur, Norman. Del Reese, Linnea's husband, cannot and will not comprehend his deaf children, helps Triplette organize his rally, and slaps the make on Sueleen after she has been first fooled and then humiliated into doing a striptease at Triplette's smoker. Linnea cheats on Del with Tom. Haven Hamilton condescends to everyone, but falls for Triplette's promise of political power. L. A. Joan refuses to visit Mrs. Green, thereby causing Mr. Green great pain. Triplette manipulates everyone into performing at his rally for Hal Phillip Walker, whose campaign is a load of meaningless rubbish. Kenny, the assassin, has the last word by shooting Barbara Jean, throwing everyone into chaos and revealing their inherent passivity.

The great difference between the humiliations here and those in *M.A.S.H.* is that we cannot share the victory over those who are hurt. Altman keeps us decidedly on the outside. In the very few instances where an emotional attachment threatens to break out, it is immediately squelched. Mr. Green learns of his wife's death in the hospital as the soldier, Kelley, is telling him how he watches over Barbara Jean for his mother's sake. We zoom in on Green as Kelley walks off saying, "You give my best to your wife." Green begins to cry, but, before we can indulge ourselves in this rare expression of emotion, Altman cuts to Opal and Triplette laughing, she giving him her theory of assassination. On that there is a significant cut to Kenny, the actual assassin, on the phone to his grasping, protective mother. (The other moments of emotional expression in the film are also compromised: Lady Pearl's feelings about the Kennedys are decidedly neurotic; Sueleen's shame at having to do a striptease is a result of her own self-delusion.)

The distance at which we are kept is an important part of Altman's narrative control, for it holds us in the position of discriminating observers. The problem, however, lies in the uncertainty of what and how we are to observe. The ugliness of the behavior of most of the characters is not dwelt upon nor commented upon, and it is easily dismissible as part of the "flow" of events. If it can be argued that Altman is somehow attempting an enormous "metaphor" of democracy, with all its flaws and all its attractions, it can be argued in return that what is shown is the very opposite of democracy: the great passive sink where those with some power manipulate those with less power and everyone sings a chorus of "You may say that I ain't free / But it don't worry me." Passivity and the alienation from power are a major subject of the film, from the opening speech of the invisible presidential candidate, Hal Phillip Walker, who denies our right to an apolitical stance, through the insistence of most of the characters throughout the film that they are apolitical. If Altman (correctly) perceives that the ideology of the apolitical is a trap that conveniently allows those with politics and power the ability to control, then he vitiates this perception by allowing his "candidate" to expose himself as just another political idiot and the political rally, toward which all the events and characters of the film lead, to be the arena of yet another senseless and unexplained assassination whose resulting trauma permits all the errant couples of the film to be rejoined and another talentless country and western singer to achieve stardom.

The pluralism of the film undoes itself—by condemning passivity while seeming to condone it, exposing the banal hypocrisy of country and western music while applauding its vitality, observing the vicious vacuity of "stars" while indicating that they're just folks, and giving everyone his or her due—and ends in ambiguity and evasion. A catastrophic event brings us all together, but in a devitalized state, ready to be herded and manipulated once again. No answers are offered; indeed, few questions are raised by the film, which ends in a most uncharacteristic camera movement for Altman, a movement away from the field of action up to the sky. It is a final evasion, and it needs a response. If *Nashville* suggests that America is divided into those who are in show business and those who passively watch the performance, it stops short of encouraging an analysis of this massive act of cultural manipulation. If everyone is at the mercy of everyone's lies, including their own, is there any meaning to individuality, is there any trust or any possibility of community?

Altman's basic answer is no. Although the terms of the answer vary from film to film, although some of his characters escape the lies and the manipulation by simply walking out on them, all are still trapped in one way or another. Altman's is a fundamentally desolate vision, all the more so because he sees the lies so clearly yet cannot find a response to them after they are revealed. Nowhere is this dilemma more apparent than in *Buffalo Bill and the Indians, or, Sitting Bull's History Lesson,* a film that stands as Altman's own response to *Nashville* and its evasive openness. It is an immediate, didactic, unambiguous, and closed essay on the substitution of personality for reality and the turning of history into lies. *Buffalo Bill* is a narrative about narrative, about making stories and assuming that these stories adequately account for our perceptions of the world. Ned Buntline, writer of dime novels, creates Buffalo Bill out of William F. Cody, and Buffalo Bill creates the Wild West in which the white man always and effortlessly triumphs over the savage Indian. America and its history is an enclosed compound of actors and producers who keep sucking the past into their arena and re-creating it into a banal and simple present. "Everything historical is yours, Bill," says one of the boss's toadies. "I'm going to Codyfy the world," promises Nate Salsbury (Joel Grey), producer-director of the Wild West. In the process the world is reduced to false assumptions of racial superiority, manifest destiny, and the complete gullibility of anyone not a party to the show.

Partly satire, partly farce, partly, as its sub-title states, history lesson, *Buffalo Bill* creates a set of exaggerated characters whose lives are devoted to exaggeration and to turning the false into the real. "Halsey doesn't mean a word he says," comments Buffalo Bill on Sitting Bull's interpreter. "That's why he sounds so real." Their words (in some of the best dialogue in Altman's work, dialogue written by Altman and his former assistant director, Alan Rudolph) constantly expose their own absurdity without their ever showing an awareness of what they are saying. Except for the somber and dignified Sitting Bull (Frank Kaquitts), Halsey (Will Sampson), and Burt Lancaster's Ned Buntline, who act as chorus, commenting sadly and ironically on the events, the characters stay enclosed within their world and their lies, feeding on each other and off Bill, who feeds off the image of himself created by Buntline and compounded by his show (Bill is played by Paul Newman, giving us the opportunity to observe one star of mythic dimensions play another who is playing the myth of himself that was created by someone else).[20]

The structure of the film is analogous to that of Kubrick's *Dr. Strangelove*. There is a similar use of language that signifies one thing to those inside the fiction and another thing to us on the outside; a similar blindness of the characters to the implications of their actions; and, like Kubrick's characters, the inhabitants of the Wild West are trapped in the logic of their lies, perpetuating an insulated and self-serving perception of the world that is destructive in its simplifications and assumptions. The film invites comparison as well with Penn's *Little Big Man*. But where Penn's picaresque narrative of a white man caught between his own corrupt world and the Indians' innocent and gentle culture suffers from special pleading, from an attempt to perpetuate another myth, that of the noble and gentle savage, Altman chooses another route. He is not concerned with the Indians *per se;* he realizes that their diminution and ruin is accomplished and irreversible (when the small and unprepossessing Sitting Bull first arrives at the Wild West, everyone mistakes Halsey for him—"That Injun's seven feet tall," someone says. "He's getting smaller every year," replies Buntline, aware that the myth cannot sustain itself). Rather, Altman speaks of the perpetuation of that ruin and of the self-deception that permits the perpetuation. Bill is in love with the image of himself (he looks in mirrors, gazes at his portrait), and that image is turned into an ideology of supremacy, of victory, of hegemony. When Bill dreams of the dead Sitting Bull, who appears, as always, silent, self-contained, private, and assured, he can only insist that this hegemony *must* be real, for, if it is not, he is alone and without value. "God meant me to be white," he says. "And it ain't easy. I got people with no lives livin' through me! . . . You see, in one hundred years I'm still going to be Buffalo Bill. Star! And you're still going to be the Injun." Gazing, yet again, at his portrait, Bill asks a question whose connotations pervade the film: "My God, ain't he ridin' that horse right? But if he ain't, then how come all of you took him for a king?"

Buffalo Bill and his Wild West *must* be right. Everyone assents to him and his myths. No one has ever questioned him. The mystical dreams and humane demands of Sitting Bull result only in his humiliation and defeat (the last thing we see of him is a charred bone). Buffalo Bill lives on in power and victory. These must be real. In the last sequence of the film, Bill "fights" Sitting Bull in the arena of the Wild West as hundreds cheer. The Sitting Bull he fights is actually Halsey, the tall Indian who everyone figured must have been Sitting Bull when they first rode into the Wild West together. Everyone was right after all. "When the legend becomes fact, print the legend," says the newspaper man at the end of Ford's *The Man Who Shot Liberty Valance*. Ford was quite serious. His conservative nature demanded assent to cultural myths. Altman is both amused and appalled by the ease with which the myths prevail. Buffalo Bill has his own way. He fights the Indian everyone expected him to fight, and he beats him by merely pushing him to the ground. He stands in phony triumph over his phony captive, and the fraud is climaxed by the camera pulling far away to a high shot of the Wild West arena surrounded by the wilderness. We are given a shot that indicates entrapment. Bill and his company are alone and isolated by their lies. But it is a troubling point of view, for it is not very clear to whom it belongs. Is it meant to indicate our new-found superiority to the lies of "the Show Business"? Having seen this film, do we now see clearly how we are abused by our cultural myths? The answer is moot. If in fact we are becoming more aware of the fraudulence of movie heroism and the white male supremacy it has insisted is our heritage, that knowledge does not yet seem to have brought us to any new strengths, any new notion of the power or control we might have over our lives. Quite the opposite. We seem, as a culture, content to remain in another kind of passivity, the passivity of disenchantment and disengagement. If our heroes are dead, if heroism is itself a fraud but no other alternatives seem possible, we seem quite prepared simply to bemoan the fraud and mourn the death.

Altman seems quite ready to encourage the passivity that grows out of awareness without corrective. *Buffalo Bill* offers no response to the old myths and ancient lies after it exposes them. Yet, within its limits, it is a brave film, and it must have been an affront to its producers, Dino De Laurentiis and David Susskind, and to any audience member who came to it expecting a Paul Newman western. It is very funny, but it is also bitter, angry, and very straightforward. It has little of the visual complexity of the earlier films, and the gold haze that warmed, however ironically, certain sequences in *McCabe* has here become a general and jaundiced yellow.

If Altman were as consistent and as politically committed as Jean-Luc Godard, *Nashville* might be considered his *Weekend* and *Buffalo Bill* his *Le Gai Savoir,* his farewell to narrative and his beginning of a new kind of cinema. Altman may be the closest analogue to Godard in American cinema, but he is not Godard. *Buffalo Bill* does not mark a move to didactic filmmaking, nor does it mark the beginning of a clear political stand on Altman's part. It is a political film (as are all of his works) in the general sense, as an investigation of power, of the creation of an ideology that manipulates history and substitutes simple images for the more complex realities of American history. As such the film studies and reveals a way of speaking about the world, in which the speaker satisfies himself that what is said, thought, and seen is the true reflection of that self, a self already predetermined by itself to be the owner, the beginning and end, and the hero of history.[21] *Buffalo Bill* stands as an indictment of this ideology, one stated in a clear and unambiguous form. But it does not, as I said, present anything other than the indictment. It does not have an alternate set of images or alternate ideology by means of which the one it attacks can be reorganized. The main advance of *Buffalo Bill* over Altman's previous films is that narrative is here subordinated to argument, the discourse deconstructs itself by reflecting on itself, with the words and actions of the characters manifesting their own lies and their own attempt to re-create history in their image: "I'm going to Codyfy the world."

*Buffalo Bill* gives and takes away. Its form is highly unusual, but its "content" falls into the very acceptable mode of "startling the bourgeoisie." We dearly love to be shown our faults, to be told how dreadful we are. It is a situation, perhaps even a trap, Altman seems increasingly unable to avoid. *A Wedding* furthers the explorations and revelations of hypocrisy, duplicity, manipulation, and humiliation that began in *Brewster McCloud* and continued through *Nashville* and *Buffalo Bill*. Here the subject of attack is the ritual that constitutes the institutionalizing of love in our culture,[22] and the film shows many of Altman's concerns: the interaction of large numbers of people, the breakdown of community, the difficulties—indeed the impossibilities—of romantic engagement. It is, in many instances, a clever and funny film. It is as well, in most instances, a film that denies itself and us an engaged perception of its subject. It is flippant and evasive. Every cut, every zoom, introduces us to further banalities and embarrassments without seeking to reveal the root causes of the banalities or to explain why they are so ridiculous. A senile priest, a pubescent bride with braces, her sexually promiscuous sister, a pompous lesbian wedding coordinator (played by Geraldine Chaplin, who merely expands a bit on her character in *Nashville*), a mother addicted to heroin, a love-sick in-law—these and other caricatures appear and reappear to be laughed at or degraded. We are shown that the rich are foolish and the *nouveaux riches* superficial and uncaring. We are offered neither insight nor concern. The emotional and intellectual engagement that informs *Buffalo Bill* and *Three Women,* the two films that precede *A Wedding,* is nowhere to be found.

It is difficult not to be angry at the film. Its cleverness always threatens to become smugness, a smugness that is always at the expense of its characters, and finally at ours. The vacuous prudery of the Brenners, the *nouveau riche,* middle-American, middle-class family who marry their daughter into a monied family—part old-line American wealth, part immigrant mafiosi—guarantees conflict. When each member of each family is portrayed as either slightly mad, slightly repressed, alcoholic, drug addicted, gay, or simply helpless, the contrivance becomes less than satire and perhaps worse than farce. When the farce is turned upon us, when we are led to believe that the newlyweds are killed in a car wreck, the manipulation becomes too extreme. When it is revealed that it was not the newlyweds who were killed, but another young couple, a rather attractive man and woman somewhat less odious than the others who populate the film, the manipulation of our emotions becomes too facile. We are asked suddenly to reflect on the situation, to be horrified by the fact that the parents of the newlyweds are oblivious to the death of the other couple when they discover that their own children are safe. It is the final shame visited upon them in their exposure to us, and we are invited to cheer when Luigi Corelli (Vittorio Gassman), the patriarch who has been held down by his wife's money, leaves them all behind for freedom.

It is precisely the leaving behind that is the problem. As with the high shot that ends *Buffalo Bill,* we are given permission to withdraw and to dissociate ourselves. *A Wedding* does not have the sense of anger found in *Buffalo Bill,* the insight into the sources of hypocrisy and self-delusion. Neither does it contain the lyrical lament for missed chances that is present in *McCabe and Mrs. Miller.* It is instead a stony gaze at a pack of unattractive people, a gaze like that of the statue in the garden to which Altman's camera is occasionally drawn: blank and uncomprehending. It is a gaze that allows us a privileged position, a position of safety and superiority. *Buffalo Bill* attempts at least to make us comply with its demythification, to make us see some of the foundations of our cultural lies. *A Wedding* only makes us smirk. In the end both characters and viewers are left alone, a situation by now familiar to us.

So much contemporary American film exposes or condemns and then stops, refuses to reintegrate us into some other moral or political structure that might offer amelioration rather than isolation. Perhaps it is too much to demand that Altman, who promises so much in his reexamination of the form, content, and conventions of American film, deliver more than he does. *Buffalo Bill and the Indians* may fall short of being revolutionary cinema, but it does go part of the way; it at least indicates how some work, bordering on the subversive, can be done from inside the commercial system. If Altman seems unwilling or unable to go further, he at least appears able to move around, to try various means of realizing the insights he does have. In between the angry satire of *Buffalo Bill* and the social farce of *A Wedding* is an extremely private film. *Three Women* is an almost hermetic work, more European than American in temperament, though at the same time very much American in its images of lower-middle-class Southern California life in the seventies. *Three Women* also continues a particular concern of Altman's, an attempt to examine female consciousness from a social and psychological perspective, an attempt begun in *That Cold Day in the Park* and *Images* (1972).

There are some problems here. It is impossible for a man to explore feminine consciousness from anything but a male perspective (whether the reverse is true is difficult to determine, for in commercial narrative film, at least, there has been little done about men by women), and therefore the trilogy made up by *That Cold Day, Images,* and *Three Women* is about women from the point of view of a particular male. Second, Altman finds it difficult, in these three films, to escape from some old Hollywood conventions of rendering psychological states: strained camera angles and odd point-of-view shots, dreams, hallucinations, and eerie music. He is not entirely successful with these devices, as is Scorsese in *Taxi Driver*. Unlike Scorsese, who managed an almost creditable film about a woman in *Alice Doesn't Live Here Anymore* by avoiding psychology, Altman gets caught in a dilemma: his attempts to define states of mind in novel ways are compromised by his use of old conventions. None of the films of the trilogy is therefore as successful in terms of narrative inquisitiveness and formal playfulness as are his other films, which explore character and event from the outside, choosing to avoid psychological analysis and defining character by what the character does and what is done to him or her.

*That Cold Day in the Park,* as I noted earlier, is important as an indication of Altman's beginning attempt at reorganizing the spatial centers of his narrative. Thematically, its attempt to present the old cliché of the sexually repressed spinster who can only take out her repressions in deviant behavior would hardly be worthy of comment, were it not for the respect that Altman shows for the character of Frances Austen and the skepticism shown toward the boy (Michael Burns) she brings in from the cold. She mothers, attempts to seduce, imprisons, and procures for him, and then kills the whore she has procured. Both Frances and the boy are presented as being equally repressed: she traps herself in the accouterments of old age, surrounds herself with old people; he is a passive onlooker to the sexuality of others. Both of them can be seen as the first of Altman's passive characters, acted upon, in this case, by their repressions and their environments—the gloom of Frances's apartment and the shallow brightness of the streets the boy wanders. Their environments help to define them, but they are at the same time set off from these worlds they inhabit. A sense of isolation and inwardness is achieved by the shots that zoom away from Frances in her apartment to a wall of glass bricks or the lights of the street seen out of focus through the window.

This movement is Altman's central attempt at rendering an internal state: a lack of emotional anchorage, a sense of surroundings precariously or incompletely grasped. He uses similar techniques in *Images* and *Three Women,* and in all three cases his use of the zoom is unlike that in the other films where it is used to accent a face, pick out a detail, indicate the extension of space. In *The Long Goodbye,* the zoom, along with the arc and the tracking shot, is used to create an unstable space, but that space is not merely reflective of the internal state of the central character; rather it indicates an almost universal instability of understanding. In *That Cold Day,* movement is to blurred or reflected objects; in *Images* to a wind chime, which becomes a kind of fetish, an instrument that is insistently played upon, but is itself passive, an apt reflection of the central character.

Like *That Cold Da*y (indeed, like *The Long Goodbye* and *Nashville*), *Images* is about a passivity that turns to the destruction of someone else. Rendered in the most extreme subjective terms—we see most of the time only what the character sees—this passivity results in the breakdown of the character's perception of the "real" world and a withdrawal into an interior, surrogate world. The character, Cathryn (Susannah York), redefines the exterior world by the interior one and sees it in those terms. Altman does something very clever here. *Images* contains his sharpest images (photographed by Vilmos Zsigmond). There is little apparent tinkering with the color (the "flashing" technique, a method of pre-exposing the film that renders the gold and blue in *McCabe,* the blue-green haze of *The Long Goodbye,* and the jaundiced yellow of *Buffalo Bill*) and a greater use than in the other films of deep-focus cinematography. By unlocalizing the place of the film (it was shot in Ireland, but the locations are never named) and then rendering that unnamed location in bright, hard, deep images, Altman makes Cathryn's hallucinatory world very immediate and very vague simultaneously. There is little narrative byplay in the film; the events are precisely focused among only five characters who become interchangeable in Cathryn's mind.\* In short, *Images,* in appearance and in narrative construction, is one of Altman's clearest films, and he takes great delight in playing that clarity and immediacy against a sense of the deranged and incoherent state of his main character.

In retrospect (the film was not well received or understood in

---

\* The name of each actor is given to another actor's character: Susannah York is Cathryn, Cathryn Harrison is Susannah, Hugh Millais—who plays the killer, Butler, in *McCabe*—is Marcel, Marcel Bozzuffi is René, and René Auberjonois is Hugh.

1972), it is also very clear and immediate in its statement about a particular kind of withdrawal and passivity. Cathryn is trapped by a dilemma basic to many women: how to reconcile the demands of the self with the demands of domesticity, of being a dutiful wife to—in this case—a meticulously bourgeois husband. Both in rebellion against and withdrawal from this conflict Cathryn retreats and then exterior-izes her other, a sexual being with lovers and with strong demands. She fears this other and the sexuality she represents. Her conflict undoes her, and she "kills" in "fantasy" her former lover, René, with a shotgun and stabs her husband's lecherous friend, Marcel (René is actually already dead when he appears to Cathryn's imagination, and Marcel reappears quite well and happy after she stabs him). In a final hallucinatory attempt to confront and destroy her other self, she kills her husband "for real." The "plot" of this film is in fact rather silly; the conclusion, in form and in content, sillier still. But Altman is attempting to come to terms, cinematically, with the possi-bilities of manifesting madness and, in turn, of showing madness as a manifestation of a particular social-political phenomenon, in this case the cultural oppression of women. He is perhaps more successful when he comes to the problem from the outside, as observer, than as analyst. Mrs. Miller is a better creation of a woman attempting to be free, and Keechie of a woman oppressed by her helplessness, than Cathryn is of either. *Images* may suffer from being too clear, too sim-ple, and too much centered on its main character. Altman needs to work with a rich and cluttered field of images and sounds from which he can appear casually to pick and choose, defining his character by indirection.

For this reason, *Three Women* is the most successful film of the trilogy because it attempts to combine the two approaches: to work simultaneously from the inside out—from the characters' minds to the world beyond them—and from the outside in—from the contemporary, nightmare landscape of Southern California to the people that land-scape defines. To this he adds a third element: mediating the interior and exterior worlds is the continual presence of a group of grotesque murals painted by one of the characters. These murals depict three reptilian women: one shows them at each other's throats; another shows two under the domination of the third; and both show all of them diminished by an enormous male figure. The result of the interplay of interior states, exterior landscape, and the bizarre murals that punctuate the film at strategic moments is an expressionism of sorts. It is not the almost classical expressionism of *Taxi Driver,* in which the external world is seen by way of an agonized mind, but rather an expressionism created through the counterpointing of the world in its physical and ideological presence with reflections of that world in the emotional states of the characters. The world of *Taxi Driver* is terribly concrete and immediate. The world of *Three Women* seems an appendage to the world of ordinary experience: not quite real, not quite nightmare, not even a fully articulated "world," but a realm of existence that combines parts of each and whose most distinguishing feature is aridity and banality. It is all but empty of anything but the bizarre and the commonplace.[23] At one point, Millie Lammoreaux (Shelley Duvall) is driving her roommate Pinky's parents to her apartment. The camera observes the mother through the windshield of the car as she says, "Sure doesn't look like Texas." The camera pans away to reveal a featureless desert landscape that could be Texas, Southern California, Arizona, New Mexico, anywhere that is dry and hot and without features or human habitation. Pinky's mother sees a difference where there is none, attempts to give meaning to that which is barren of meaning. She brings a present for her daughter, a plaque with a gruesomely oppressive rhyme: "In this kitchen, bright and cheery, daily chores I'll never shirk. So bless this kitchen, Lord, and bless me as I work." "It's for the kitchen," she says. In *Three Women* everyone is trapped by clichés, by an inability to speak beyond the ordinary and the commonplace, their minds rendered sterile by having nothing to think about, nothing to feel, nothing to say, nothing to see.

Throughout his films, Altman has shown a painful sensitivity to the banal and an awareness of its destructive capabilities. *Three Women* takes the banal as its subject. Its characters, Millie, Pinky Rose (Sissy Spacek) and Willie (Janice Rule), as well as everyone

Millie and Pinky (Shelley Duvall and Sissy Spacek) in the arid landscape of **Three Women.**

who surrounds them, are ciphers, empty vessels in an empty land-scape. They are filled by whatever floats by. Millie ("I'm known for my dinner parties"—which exist without benefit of any unprocessed food) is filled with the language of women's magazines and so insu-lated by its dehumanizing jargon that she seems oblivious to the fact that she is ignored by everyone. Pinky is filled by Millie, for she has no self at all. We first see her when the camera zooms to her face, wide-eyed and blank, staring through a window at the health spa for old people where she has come to work. Later, at the spa, when she talks incessantly about Millie and how she misses her, the camera slowly and deliberately zooms to and past her face—achieving an effect akin to having her face slide slowly off the side of the Pana-vision screen—to the bright windows behind her, which go out of focus. There is an immediate cut to a metered television set on the wall of Pinky's dark, close room. It is on, but there is nothing on it, and the camera pulls back from the bright empty screen (which suddenly goes off) to Pinky lying asleep. This movement and cut accomplish what Altman was trying to do in *That Cold Day* and *Images:* find a visual surrogate for a subjective state. Pinky is as blank as a curtained window or a television screen, a creature without a personality, without thought. The third woman, Willie, is less detailed. She is pregnant, and finally delivers a still-born baby, a barren birth into a barren world. She is an artist. She creates the murals of reptilian women (one of whom is pregnant) and the monstrous male who controls them. She is married to Edgar, a parody of a macho male, an ex-stuntman and gun-toting buffoon who sleeps with Millie (the only man who will) and is the analogue to the male figure in Willie's mural. Willie is mostly silent, seemingly removed from the banality around her, yet constantly commenting on the terror of that banality in her art.

The great problem that Altman has with these figures and their world is integrating them within a coherent design. As I said, he attempts to create a modified expressionist point of view, indicating states of mind by the faces and the surroundings of those faces. The early sequences in the health spa, with the silent old people being walked about by Millie and her colleagues; the first sequence in Millie's yellow apartment and Edgar's dilapidated bar where she hangs out, with motorcyclists and target shooters in the back and Willie painting her murals in an empty swimming pool; Millie's early relationship with Pinky; the sequence in which Millie enters her bedroom to find Pinky's decrepit parents locked in a sexual embrace— all form a complex point of view that oscillates between a recognizable world and a frightening, disengaged, disorienting one in which identities are uncertain because unformed and unformed because there is no sense of self or of location.

Our own point of entry into the film, however, is uncertain: there is no possible "identification" and little sense of understanding, on a rational level, this discourse of absent personalities. It is possible that Altman is attempting to split our perceptions, remove their foundations, as the characters are split and unfounded. In the sequence where Willie gives birth to her dead child we are placed just outside the doorway of this gruesome scene of pain and loss, but forced at the same time to share the point of view of Millie inside, helping Willie, and Pinky outside, frozen in terror. Here and throughout the film, we are caught in a forced perspective where the immediacy of the event and its detached and disorienting structure conflict. The result is a sense of being unanchored, like the characters, perhaps, but finally with no knowledge greater than the characters have: we tend to see and understand no more than they do.

Altman cannot seem to help overmystifying the narrative, or, perhaps more accurately, overdetermining it with expressions of mystery and a forced sense of the portentous. There is none of the playfulness present even in the most serious of his other films. The exchange of identities between Millie and Pinky is an excellent idea, but it is managed with a strained sense of profundity. Altman had toyed with it in *Images,* where Cathryn and her young friend Susannah are seen reflected together in mirrors, and finally with their faces superimposed in a window, suggesting that Susannah, as a woman, will follow Cathryn's path of madness. The more explicit exchange between Millie and Pinky (who says her name is really Millie) seems an inevitable result of the emptiness of their personalities. But Altman cannot disengage himself from the Bergmanesque pretentiousness of the situation. Certainly he does not infuse the situation with the metaphysical vaguenesses of *Persona;* he is too much in touch with the immediate presence of our culture. The world is present in *Three Women,* and we sense its influence on the characters. But that influence remains diffuse. The *idea* of interchanging identities is itself diffuse, too fanciful and too abstracted from the otherwise concrete and immediate indicators of barren souls in a barren world.

The tension between abstract and concrete is strongest in the final sequences of the film, as Altman attempts to re-anchor the psychological transformations of character back into the environment they came from. When Pinky absorbs Millie's personality, she expresses it in a spirit of meanness and coldness, without her host's cliché-ridden vocabulary and without the pathetic quality that vocabulary lent her. Millie buckles under Pinky's meanness, her passive nature submitting to Pinky's new-found and misdirected strength. But another change occurs after Pinky's nightmare—perhaps the most portentous, if not pretentious, sequence in the film, in which all the faces appear doubled or in violent and distorted form and the events of Willie's still-birth are foreshadowed. After the nightmare, Pinky is more docile; her fear brings her to Millie for mothering, she wants to sleep with her, and Millie comforts her, placing her hand on her face. A new relational complex is forming, which will be completed after the horrendous sequence of Willie bearing her dead boy.

During the still-birth, Millie acts with a strength she has never before demonstrated. Pinky is frozen in fear, unable to call for a doctor. After Millie emerges from the house, hands bloodied and shaking in front of her, as she had appeared to Pinky in the dream, she slaps her, again demonstrating a hitherto unrealized sense of power and control. The sequence ends on Pinky's face, bloodied by Millie's hand, which has in effect transferred to her the sign of Willie's agony. From Pinky's face a cut is made to a long, far shot of a desert road, barren and hot, power lines marking the background. A yellow Coca-Cola truck comes into view (yellow is the bright, bland color that Millie chooses for everything: her apartment, her dress, her car). It pulls into the "Dodge City" bar that Edgar owned and that was Millie's hangout. Pinky is behind the bar, chewing gum, reading a magazine. When the delivery man asks to have his Coca-Cola signed for, Pinky says she'll call her "mom," who turns out to be Millie. In the dialogue with the delivery man, we find out that Edgar has been shot, "a terrible accident, we're all grieved by it." Millie orders Pinky to the house to fix dinner. At the house Willie sits on the porch, telling of a dream she had and cannot remember. The camera zooms back from the house; we hear Millie ordering Pinky about, Willie asking why she has to be so mean to her. The camera pans to a pile of old tires, the last image of the arid landscape. The shot dissolves to the mural of the three reptilian women bent to the ground. The enormous male figure has one of the females by the tail; he raises his other hand

337

in a fist. One of the female figures points up to an occult symbol, a cross in a circle, around which emerge four snakes.

The film concludes with Altman's most bitter observation of domination and passivity, of assent to ritual and assumption of cultural myths. The three women, ridding themselves of men (Willie's child was male and is born dead; and the suggestion is clear that the women shot Edgar—"I'd rather face a thousand crazy savages than one woman who's learned to shoot," he has said earlier), proceed to reenact a family structure with one dominant member, now maternal rather than paternal, and two passive members. The enclave they form in the garbage-strewn desert is a parody of the male-dominant society reflected in Willie's mural. But not merely male-dominant, for Altman sees domination spread through all relationships. Millie and Pinky are dominated by the hard and thoughtless doctors who run the health spa, and they in turn manipulate the old people as if they were children. Millie is controlled by the prose of female exploitation in women's magazines. Pinky allows herself to be manipulated by Millie, briefly exchanges roles to become the dominating one, and in turn becomes a compliant daughter to her. Willie, Millie, and Pinky are all controlled by Edgar, and with Edgar gone, they can only exist in an isolated reenactment of power and passivity.

This is a structure, finally, that can be perceived in most of Altman's films. It is a structure of the controllers and the compliant: those like McCabe, who think they are in control, only to discover their own impotence and die; or like Marlowe, who discovers his impotence and kills; or the gallery of characters in *Nashville,* who attempt to outdo each other in humiliation and manipulation; or Buffalo Bill, who sees the entire history of America as his domain. But there is an extraordinary dialectic that operates in the films. They may take as their subject our cultural propensity toward passivity, our willingness to be oppressed by manufactured images that we accept as historical realities. But the images manufactured by Altman to inscribe these subjects refuse to dominate us. The open narrative construction—the flow, the sense of process and accident that his films achieve—attempts to deconstruct the very subject they announce. It is as if two distinct voices were speaking these filmic discourses, one enunciating the inevitability of defeat through the blind yielding to domination, the other enunciating a freedom of perception, and therefore a control over what is seen, understood, and interpreted. However, the dialectic can become mere contradiction: we are given an open narrative structure, and therefore freedom in our response to what we see; but if, no matter how great the openness, our only liberty is to consider the varieties of our lack of freedom, then the form of Altman's films is itself dominated by the voice that speaks of our inevitable passivity and lack of control.[24]

Still the films are at least energetically involved in the conflict. The other directors I have discussed seem determined to match narrative form and content, to deploy images of loneliness and entrapment, isolation and fear to reinforce that desperate perception we have of ourselves. If any of their characters prevail, it is for a while only, and they seem only to prevail in order to make their fall all the more hard. Altman is basically trapped in this same ideology of losing, of gaining and then losing, of profit and loss; he has, though, more generosity, more sense of the possibility (if not the probability) of breaking the model. If he can show the plurality of space, its fullness and variety, we *may* remain constricted within it, fooled, humiliated, and owned, but there is at least the opportunity offered of our seeing more, of overcoming the prison that our contemporary cinema seems dead set on insisting we inhabit. And there is in Altman's work always the hope, and sometimes the reality, that someone, perhaps someone just heard outside the screen space, will call out loud and clear—"Bullshit!"

# NOTES

## INTRODUCTION

1. Some of the ideas for the decline of Hollywood production values in the late forties were developed with David Parker. An excellent summary of the changes in Hollywood from the late forties through the sixties—from which much of the information in this section is drawn—can be found in Robert Sklar, *Movie-Made America: A Cultural History of American Movies* (New York: Random House, 1975), pp. 249–304. See also Gordon Gow, *Hollywood in the Fifties* (New York: A. S. Barnes, 1971); John Baxter, *Hollywood in the Sixties* (A. S. Barnes, 1972); Axel Madsen, *The New Hollywood: American Movies in the Seventies* (New York: Crowell, 1975). Other sources are cited in the chapter on Francis Ford Coppola.
2. See Michael Rosenthal, "Ideology, Determinism, and Relative Autonomy," *Jump Cut,* No. 17 (April 1978), 19–22.
3. See James Monaco, *The New Wave* (New York: Oxford University Press, 1976), pp. 3–12. Monaco's is the best study of the French movement and has served as something of a model for this book.
4. In the late seventies, filmmaking in France has fallen on hard times. The initial cohesion is gone, and while critical commitment remains

strong, production is in disarray. (See David L. Overby, "France: The Newest Wave," *Sight and Sound* 47 [Spring 1978], 86–90.)

5. Many people have been examining the phenomenon of film effacing its existence as film. Two out of many possible references are Colin Mac-Cabe, "Realism and the Cinema: Notes on Some Brechtian Theses," *Screen* 15 (Summer 1974); Christian Metz, "The Imaginary Signifier," trans. Ben Brewster, *Screen* 16 (Summer 1975). For the idea of fiction as lie and substitution see Umberto Eco, *A Theory of Semiotics* (Bloomington and London: Indiana University Press, 1976), pp. 6–7.

6. Rosalind Coward and John Ellis, *Language and Materialism* (London: Routledge & Kegan Paul, 1977), p. 67. On the same page, the authors quote a definition of ideology by Louis Althusser remarkable for its use of a cinematic metaphor: *"ideologies* are complex formations of montages of notions—representations—images on the one hand, and of montages of behaviours—conducts—attitudes—gestures on the other. . . ."* Althusser also defines ideology as "the 'lived' relation between men [and women] and their world, or a reflected form of this unconscious relation. . . ." (*For Marx*, trans. Ben Brewster [New York: Random House, Vintage Books, 1970], p. 252.) For a direct application of ideological theory to cinema studies, see: Jean-Luc Comolli and Jean Narboni, "Cinema/Ideology/Criticism," in Bill Nichols, ed., *Movies and Methods* (Berkeley and Los Angeles: University of California Press, 1976), pp. 23–30; Editors of *Cahiers du Cinéma*, "John Ford's *Young Mr. Lincoln*," in *ibid.*, pp. 493–529. The April 1978 issue of *Jump Cut* (No. 17) has an excellent series of essays summarizing the issue.

7. Rosenthal, *op. cit.*

8. James Linton, "But It's Only a Movie," *Jump Cut*, No. 17 (April 1978), 16.

## 1. ARTHUR PENN

1. Cf. Diane Jacobs, *Hollywood Renaissance* (South Brunswick, N.J., and New York: A. S. Barnes, 1977), pp. 35–37.

2. Robin Wood, *Arthur Penn* (New York: Frederick A. Praeger, 1969), p. 44.

3. Paul Schrader, "Notes on Film Noir," *Film Comment* 8 (Spring 1972), 8.

4. What follows is a general summary of the *noir* movement. A great deal has been written about it; Schrader's article remains the best.

Other works include the November–December 1974 issue of *Film Comment*, with essays by Raymond Durgnat, Stephen Farber, Alfred Appel, Jr., Paul Jensen, Mitchell S. Cohen, and Richard T. Jameson; Larry Gross, *"Film Après Noir," Film Comment* 12 (July–August 1976), 44–49; Charles Higham and Joel Greenberg, *Hollywood in the Forties* (New York: Paperback Library, 1970), pp. 19–55; J. A. Place and L. S. Peterson, "Some Visual Motifs of Film Noir," *Film Comment* 10 (January–February 1974), 30–35, reprinted in Nichols, *op. cit.,* pp. 325–38; Robert G. Porfirio, "No Way Out: Existential Motifs in *The Film Noir," Sight and Sound* 45 (Autumn 1976), 212–17; John Tuska, *The Detective in Hollywood* (Garden City, N. Y.: Doubleday and Co., 1978), pp. 339–42. For a thorough, cross-indexed filmography, see John S. Whitney, "A Filmography of Film Noir," *Journal of Popular Film* 5 (1976), 321–71. For background on the technological changes that made *noir* possible, see Barry Salt, "Film Style and Technology in the Thirties," *Film Quarterly* 30 (Fall 1976), 19–32, and "Film Style and Technology in the Forties," *Film Quarterly* 31 (Fall 1977), 46–57.

5. Wood, *op. cit.,* pp. 44–45.
6. *Dreams and Dead Ends: The American Gangster/Crime Film* (Cambridge, Mass.: MIT Press, 1977), pp. 288, 303–4. It is important to note that Shadoian does not approve of this self-consciousness.
7. John G. Cawelti, "The Artistic Power of *Bonnie and Clyde,"* in Cawelti, ed., *Focus on Bonnie and Clyde* (Englewood Cliffs, N. J.: Prentice-Hall, 1973), p. 57. Cawelti's is a major essay on the film and there are some parallels with what is discussed here, the most important of which are noted. For another view of sexuality in the film, particularly for the sympathy aroused by Clyde's impotence, see Wood, *op. cit.,* pp. 84–86.
8. Cawelti, *op. cit.,* pp. 59–60.
9. Many writers have addressed themselves to the vitality of the characters as against the barrenness of the landscape they inhabit (see, for example, Stephen Farber, "The Outlaws," *Sight and Sound* 37 [Autumn 1968], 174–75). Some have found their situation revolutionary and praised it (Peter Harcourt, "In Defense of Film History," John Stuart Katz, ed., *Perspectives on the Study of Film* [Boston: Little Brown and Co., 1971], pp. 266–69) or condemned it (Charles Thomas Samuels, in Cawelti, ed., *Focus on Bonnie and Clyde,* pp. 85–92). As should become clear, I do not see the film as a call to revolution, but, to the contrary, as a warning against being too free.
10. Richard Burgess brought this to my attention.

11. Cawelti, *op. cit.*, p. 79.
12. *Ibid.*, p. 82.
13. For the car as icon in gangster films, see Colin McArthur, *Underworld USA* (New York: Viking Press, 1972), pp. 30–33.
14. Robert Warshow, "The Gangster as Tragic Hero," in *The Immediate Experience* (Garden City: Doubleday and Co., 1962), pp. 127–33. See also my article, "Night to Day," *Sight and Sound* 43 (Autumn 1974), 236–39.
15. Shadoian, *op. cit.*, p. 1–6.
16. Cawelti, *op. cit.*, pp. 79–84.
17. Michael Walker, *"Night Moves," Movie,* No. 22 (Spring 1976), 37–38.
18. *Ibid.*, p. 38.

## 2. STANLEY KUBRICK

1. John Russell Taylor, *Directors and Directions: Cinema for the Seventies* (New York: Hill and Wang, 1975), p. 132.
2. I have not seen *Fear and Desire.* Description and some analysis of Kubrick's earlier work can be found in the three book-length studies of his films: Norman Kagan, *The Cinema of Stanley Kubrick* (New York: Holt, Rinehart and Winston, 1972); Gene D. Phillips, *Stanley Kubrick: A Film Odyssey* (New York: Popular Library, 1977); Alexander Walker, *Stanley Kubrick Directs* (New York: Harcourt Brace Jovanovich, 1971). Each of these books, and Walker's in particular, have been of great help for the study that follows. Walker's discussion of Kubrick's use of space is a special influence.
3. Walker, *op. cit.*, pp. 55–66.
4. Welles himself refers to his work as labyrinthine. Although Kubrick has mentioned Max Ophuls as an influence on his moving camera (see *ibid.*, p. 16), the influence of Welles is much more evident (see Terry Comito, "Touch of Evil." *Film Comment* 7 [Summer 1971], 51–53).
5. Quoted by Dilys Powell in Peter Cowie, *A Ribbon of Dreams: The Cinema of Orson Welles* (South Brunswick, N. J., and New York: A. S. Barnes, 1973), pp. 27–28.
6. So great is the communal need in Ford that in his later films the individual who is asocial by his nature and inclination—Ethan Edwards in *The Searchers,* Tom Doniphon in *The Man Who Shot Liberty Valance* (both characters played by John Wayne)—removes himself so the communal unit may survive. (See Joseph McBride and Michael

Wilmington, "Prisoner of the Desert," *Sight and Sound* 40 [Autumn 1971], 210–14).

7. Cf. Walker, *op. cit.,* p. 84; Kagan, *op. cit.,* p. 65.

8. Walker, *op. cit.,* p. 112, emphasizes the enclosed, geometric situating of the figures in the courts martial.

9. Cf. Kagan, *op. cit.,* pp. 64–66. For an excellent discussion of the "end of ideology" syndrome, see Roland Barthes, "Neither-Nor Criticism," in *Mythologies,* trans. Annette Lavers (New York: Hill and Wang, 1972), pp. 81–83.

10. Walker, *op. cit.,* pp. 160–62.

11. *Sade, Fourier, Loyola,* trans. Richard Miller (New York: Hill and Wang, 1976), pp. 33–34.

12. Gerald Mast, *The Comic Mind* (Indianapolis and New York: Bobbs-Merrill Co., 1973), pp. 317, 319. See also F. A. Macklin, "Sex and *Dr. Strangelove,*" *Film Comment* 3 (Summer 1965), 55–57.

13. "Kubrick's films have always dealt with characters who mechanized themselves. . . ." Don Daniels, "A Skeleton Key to 2001," *Sight and Sound* 40 (Winter 1970–71), 32. The mechanization of human behavior has been long recognized as a major element in Kubrick's work.

14. *Anatomy of Criticism* (Princeton: Princeton University Press, 1957), pp. 224–25. Most commentators on the film have seen it as satire. What follows is an attempt to clarify the details of the generic form.

15. The film reviewer John Simon recognized the film's demand for a strong moral response; cf. Kagan, *op. cit.,* p. 134.

16. *Signs and Meaning in the Cinema* (Bloomington: Indiana University Press, 1972), p. 164 and *passim.* See also Roland Barthes, *S/Z,* trans. Richard Miller (New York: Hill and Wang, 1974), pp. 10–11.

17. Kagan, *op. cit.,* pp. 161–62.

18. *Op. cit.,* pp. 129–32.

19. "This Typeface Is Changing Your Life," *Village Voice,* June 7, 1976, pp. 116–17.

20. *Expanded Cinema* (New York: E. P. Dutton and Co., 1970), pp. 140–46.

21. "Fascinating Fascism," in Nichols, *op. cit.,* p. 40.

22. Cf. Jonathan Rosenbaum, "The Solitary Pleasures of *Star Wars,*" *Sight and Sound* 46 (Autumn 1977), 209.

23. For the ending of *Star Wars,* see *ibid.;* for a more detailed analysis of the politics of Spielberg's film (which came to my attention after the above was written), see Robert Entman and Francie Seymour, "*Close Encounters of the Third Kind:* Close Encounters with the Third Reich," *Jump Cut,* No. 18 (August 15, 1978), 3–5.

24. François Truffaut, *Hitchcock*, trans. Helen G. Scott (New York: Simon and Schuster, 1967), p. 211.
25. Cf. Robert Hughes, "The Decor of Tomorrow's Hell," *Time* (December 27, 1971), p. 59.
26. Anthony Burgess, *A Clockwork Orange* (New York: W. W. Norton & Co., 1963), p. 158. My thanks to Richard Simmons for helping me connect the names.
27. For another, more favorable reading of the film, which attempts to fit it into a pattern within Kubrick's work, see Hans Feldmann, "Kubrick and His Discontents," *Film Quarterly* 30 (Fall 1976), pp. 12–19.
28. Mark Crispin Miller, "*Barry Lyndon* Reconsidered," *Georgia Review* 30 (Winter 1976), 843.
29. Cf. Michael Dempsey, "*Barry Lyndon*," *Film Quarterly* 30 (Fall 1976), 50.
30. "Kubrick's *Barry Lyndon*," *Salmagundi* (Summer–Fall, 1977), 204.
31. Cf. Miller, *op. cit.*, pp. 834–35. Feldmann, *op. cit.*, p. 14, discusses the ritual of eating in *2001*.
32. *Op. cit.*, p. 199.
33. Feldmann, *op. cit.*, p. 17.
34. *Op. cit.*, p. 206.
35. Cf. Feldmann's analysis, *op. cit.*, p. 18. Spiegel, *op. cit.*, p. 201, fully analyzes the symmetrical repetitions in the film.
36. Cf. Feldmann, *op. cit.*, p. 17.
37. Cf. Andrew Sarris, "What Makes Barry Run," *Village Voice*, December 29, 1975, pp. 111–12.

## 3.  FRANCIS FORD COPPOLA

1. For a summary of his early career and the work of American Zoetrope and the Directors Company, see Robert K. Johnson, *Francis Ford Coppola* (Boston: G. K. Hall, 1977), pp. 19–41, 86–88, 128–29; Jacobs, *op. cit.*, pp. 97–99. Jacobs points out Coppola's debt to Hitchcock and Bertolucci.
2. See William Paul, "Hollywood Harakiri," *Film Comment* 13 (March–April 1977), 40–43, 56–63; "Inside Hollywood," *Newsweek*, February 13, 1978, pp. 70–76; Stephen M. Silverman, "Hollywood Cloning: Sequels, Prequels, Remakes, and Spinoffs," *American Film* 3 (July–August 1978), 24–30.
3. Christian Metz, *Film Language: A Semiotics of the Cinema*, trans. Michael Taylor (New York: Oxford University Press, 1974), pp.

117–33. Barry Salt has pointed out some antecedents to Porter; see "Film Form, 1900–1906," *Sight and Sound* 47 (Summer 1978), 148–53.

4. Barry Salt, "Statistical Analysis of Motion Pictures," *Film Quarterly* 28 (Fall 1974), 13–22.

5. Daniel Dayan, "The Tudor-Code of Classical Cinema," in Nichols, *op. cit.*, pp. 439–51; Nick Browne, "The Spectator-in-the-Text: The Rhetoric of *Stagecoach*," *Film Quarterly* 29 (Winter 1975–76), 26–38. The Dayan article is based on the work of French critic Jean-Pierre Oudart. It has generated considerable controversy.

6. Bazin's central essays are in the two volumes of *What Is Cinema?*, trans. Hugh Gray (Berkeley and Los Angeles: University of California Press, 1967, 1971).

7. The notion of an enigmatic structure (code) is based loosely on Barthes, *S/Z*.

8. "The Discreet Charm of *The Godfather*," *Sight and Sound* 47 (Spring 1978), 79.

9. "*The Godfather*," in David Denby, ed., *Film 72–73* (Indianapolis and New York: The Bobbs-Merrill Company, 1973), p. 4.

10. "Keeping Up with the Corleones," in *ibid.*, p. 8.

11. McArthur, *op. cit.*, pp. 53–55.

12. Pechter, *op. cit.*, p. 7.

13. "*Godfather II:* A Deal Coppola Couldn't Refuse," in Nichols, *op. cit.*, pp. 82–90.

14. See Stephen Farber, "L. A. Journal," *Film Comment* 11 (March–April 1975), 2, 60–62.

15. *America in the Dark: Hollywood and the Gift of Unreality* (New York: William Morrow and Co., 1977), p. 188.

16. *Op. cit.*, p. 85.

17. *Op. cit.*, p. 133.

18. Cf. Pechter, *op. cit.*, p. 7.

19. By David Denby, in an otherwise excellent essay: "Stolen Privacy: Coppola's *The Conversation*," *Sight and Sound* 43 (Summer 1974), 131–33.

20. Cf. Jacobs, *op. cit.*, pp. 115–16.

21. Frye, *op. cit.*, p. 34.

22. *Op. cit.*, p. 80.

## 4. MARTIN SCORSESE

1. In her review of *Taxi Driver* in the *New Yorker* (February 9, 1976), Pauline Kael briefly notes these seemingly conflicting strains in Scorsese's work.
2. Jacobs, *op. cit.,* p. 124.
3. *Godard on Godard,* trans. Tom Milne (New York: The Viking Press, 1972), pp. 21, 28.
4. David Denby, "Mean Streets: The Sweetness of Hell," *Sight and Sound* 43 (Winter 1973/74), 50.
5. *Ibid.,* 48–49.
6. Lotte Eisner, *The Haunted Screen,* trans. Roger Greaves (Berkeley and Los Angeles: University of California Press, 1973), pp. 23–24.
7. I have not examined the original, but the description of Travis Bickle that appears in a script extract published in *Film Comment* 12 (March–April 1976), 12, does present him in extravagantly romantic terms, very different from the character created by Scorsese and De Niro in the film. See also Schrader's comments on his script in the same issue of *Film Comment.*
8. See Michael Dempsey, "Taxi Driver," *Film Quarterly* 29 (Summer 1976), 37–41; Jacobs, *op. cit.,* pp. 143–44.
9. *Transcendental Style in Film: Ozu, Bresson, Dreyer* (Berkeley and Los Angeles: University of California Press, 1972), p. 72.
10. "Notes on *Film Noir,*" pp. 12, 13. Colin Westerbeck notes the *noir* influence via Schrader in "Beauties and the Beast," *Sight and Sound* 45 (Summer 1976), 138.
11. See Frederick Jameson, *The Prison-House of Language* (Princeton: Princeton University Press, 1972), pp. 50–53.
12. Jacobs, *op. cit.,* p. 146. Jacobs does speak of the camera reflecting Travis's state of mind.
13. Patricia Patterson and Manny Farber, "The Power and the Gory," *Film Comment* 12 (May–June, 1976), 29.
14. See Peter Birge and Janet Maslin, "Getting Snuffed in Boston," *Film Comment* 13 (May–June 1976), 35, 63.
15. The view of Patterson and Farber, *op. cit.,* p. 30.
16. *Ibid.,* p. 27.
17. Cf. Robin Wood, *Hitchcock's Films* (New York: Paperback Library, 1970), pp. 132–33; Raymond Durgnat, *Films and Feelings* (Cambridge: MIT Press, 1971), pp. 217–18.
18. Jacobs, *op. cit.,* p. 34.

19. See Molly Haskell, *From Reverence to Rape* (New York: Holt, Rinehart and Winston, 1974), pp. 126–30. For an opposite view of the screwball comedy see Tom Powers, "His Girl Friday: Screwball Liberation," *Jump Cut* (April 1978), 25–27.
20. Jacobs, *op. cit.*, pp. 141–42, 128, covers some of the points discussed here.
21. See Kevin Brownlow, "Telluride," *Sight and Sound* 47 (Winter 1977–78), 27.
22. In *Film Comment* 14 (September–October, 1978), 64, Scorsese refers to *My Dream Is Yours* and *The Man I Love,* two forties musical *films noirs* that influenced *New York, New York.*

## 5. ROBERT ALTMAN

1. Gary Arnold, "Filmmaker Robert Altman—Back in the Swim," *Washington Post,* May 8, 1977, p. E4.
2. The ideological differences between Eisenstein and Griffith were most clearly articulated by Eisenstein himself. See his essay "Dickens, Griffith, and the Film Today," in *Film Form,* trans. Jay Leyda (New York: Harcourt Brace Jovanovich, 1969), pp. 195–225. Cf. Noel Burch, *Theory of Film Practice,* trans. Helen R. Lane (New York: Praeger Publishers, 1973), pp. 17–30; André Bazin, *Jean Renoir,* trans. W. W. Halsey II and William H. Simon (New York: Simon and Schuster, 1973), pp. 87–91. For a wide-ranging, speculative essay on the problems of screen space, see Stephen Heath, "Narrative Space," *Screen* 17 (Autumn 1976), 68–112. A number of critics have indicated the Renoir influences on Altman.
3. For a fuller analysis of *The Man Who Shot Liberty Valance,* see William Luhr and Peter Lehman, *Authorship and Narrative in the Cinema* (New York: G. P. Putnam's Sons, 1977), pp. 45–84. The notion of *découpage* comes from Burch, *op. cit.*, p. 4.
4. See Paul Joannides, "The Aesthetics of the Zoom Lens," *Sight and Sound* 40 (Winter 1970–71), 40–42.
5. For a detailed description of the camera work in *The Long Goodbye* see Michael Tarantino, "Movement as Metaphor: *The Long Goodbye,*" *Sight and Sound* 44 (Spring 1975), 98–102. In the same issue, Jonathan Rosenbaum's essay "Improvisations and Interactions in Altmanville" (pp. 91–95) considers the narrative dislocations in the film.
6. I borrow the notion of "deconstruction" very loosely from Jacques

Derrida, Cf. *Of Grammatology*, trans. Gayatri Chakravorty Spivak (Baltimore and London: The Johns Hopkins University Press, 1976).

7. Cf. Jacobs, *op. cit.*, p. 71.
8. As a student of mine, anxious to love the film, once suggested.
9. See Stefan Fleischer, "A Study Through Stills of *My Darling Clementine*," *Journal of Modern Literature* 3 (April 1973), 243–52.
10. Michael Dempsey sees the hope for community more positively stated than I do. See his essay "Altman: The Empty Staircase and the Chinese Princess," *Film Comment* 10 (September–October 1974), 14–17.
11. For a detailed comparison, see my article "Night to Day."
12. Jacobs, *op. cit.*, p. 66.
13. I owe this insight to John Pacy.
14. See the analysis of detective fiction by Tzvetan Todorov, in *The Poetics of Prose*, trans. Richard Howard (Ithaca, N. Y.: Cornell University Press, 1977), pp. 42–52.
15. Two excellent essays review the history of Marlowe on the screen: James Monaco, "Notes on *The Big Sleep*, Thirty Years After," *Sight and Sound* 44 (Winter 1974–75), 34–38; Charles Gregory, "Knight Without Meaning?" *Sight and Sound* 42 (Summer 1973), 155–59. The following analysis is indebted to them.
16. *Op. cit.*, p. 95.
17. The best discussion of this phenomenon is in Joan Mellon, *Big Bad Wolves: Masculinity in the American Film* (New York: Pantheon Books, 1977), pp. 311–25.
18. Cf. Rosenbaum, *op. cit.*, p. 91.
19. *Nashville* (New York: Bantam Books, 1976), p. 3.
20. Karen Stabiner, *"Buffalo Bill and the Indians,"* *Film Quarterly* 30 (Fall 1976), 55. Joan Mellon has a good discussion of the myths of male supremacy that are attacked in the film; *op. cit.*, pp. 339–41.
21. Cf. Barthes, *Mythologies*, pp. 109–59.
22. Margot Kernan helped develop this argument.
23. For a discussion of the film as dream, see Marsha Kinder, "The Art of Dreaming in *Three Women* and *Providence:* Structures of the Self," *Film Quarterly* 31 (Fall 1977), 10–18.
24. For a parallel argument, see Leonard Quart, "On Altman: Image as Essence," *Marxist Perspectives* 1 (Spring 1978), 118–25.

# FILMOGRAPHY

A listing of major theatrical features.

## ARTHUR PENN

1958    THE LEFT-HANDED GUN
Script: Leslie Stevens, from the play by Gore Vidal.
Direction: Penn.
Photography: J. Peverell Marley.
Editing: Folmar Blangsted.
Music: Alexander Courage.
Ballad: William Goyen and Alexander Courage.
Art direction: Art Loel.
   Cast: Paul Newman (*William Bonney*), Lita Milan (*Celsa*), John
Dehner (*Pat Garrett*), Hurd Hatfield (*Moultrie*), James Congdon
(*Charlie Boudre*), James Best (*Tom Folliard*), Colin Keith-Johnston
(*Tunstall*), John Dierkes (*McSween*), Bob Anderson (*Hill*), Wally
Brown (*Moon*), Ainslie Pryor (*Joe Grant*), Marten Garralaga (*Sa-val*), Denver Pyle (*Ollinger*), Paul Smith (*Bell*), Nestor Paiva (*Max-well*), Jo Summers (*Mrs. Garrett*), Robert Foulk (*Brady*), Anne
Barton (*Mrs. Hill*).

Produced by Fred Coe (Harroll Productions) for Warner Bros. 102 min.

## 1962   THE MIRACLE WORKER

Script: William Gibson, from his play.
Direction: Penn.
Photography: Ernest Caparros.
Editing: Aram Avakian.
Music: Laurence Rosenthal.
Art direction: George Jenkins, Mel Bourne.

Cast: Anne Bancroft (*Annie Sullivan*), Patty Duke (*Helen Keller*), Victor Jory (*Captain Keller*), Inga Swenson (*Kate Keller*), Andrew Prine (*James Keller*), Kathleen Comegys (*Aunt Ev*), Beah Richards (*Viney*), Jack Hollender (*Mr. Anagnes*).

Produced by Fred Coe (Playfilms) for United Artists. 106 min.

## 1964   MICKEY ONE

Script: Alan Surgal.
Direction: Penn.
Photography: Ghislain Cloquet.
Editing: Aram Avakian.
Music: Eddie Sauter, improvisations by Stan Getz.
Production design: George Jenkins.

Cast: Warren Beatty (*Mickey*), Alexandra Stewart (*Jenny*), Hurd Hatfield (*Castle*), Franchot Tone (*Ruby Lapp*), Teddy Hart (*Breson*), Jeff Corey (*Fryer*), Kamatari Fujiwara (*the artist*), Donna Michell (*the girl*), Ralph Foody (*police captain*), Norman Gottschalk (*the evangelist*), Dick Lucas (*employment agent*), Benny Dunn (*nightclub comic*), Helen Witkowski (*landlady*), Mike Fish (*Italian restaurant owner*).

Produced by Arthur Penn (A Florin/Tatira Production) for Columbia. 93 min.

## 1966   THE CHASE

Script: Lillian Hellman, based on the novel and play by Horton Foote.
Direction: Penn.

Photography (Technicolor, Panavision): Joseph LaShelle and (uncredited) Robert Surtees.
Editing: Gene Milford.
Music: John Barry.
Production design: Richard Day.

    Cast: Marlon Brando (*Sheriff Calder*), Jane Fonda (*Anna Reeves*), Robert Redford (*Bubber Reeves*), E. G. Marshall (*Val Rogers*), Angie Dickinson (*Ruby Calder*), Janice Rule (*Emily Stewart*), Miriam Hopkins (*Mrs. Reeves*), Martha Hyer (*Mary Fuller*), Richard Bradford (*Damon Fuller*), Robert Duvall (*Edwin Stewart*), James Fox (*Jake Jason Rogers*), Diana Hyland (*Elizabeth Rogers*), Henry Hull (*Briggs*), Jocelyn Brando (*Mrs. Briggs*), Steve Ihnat (*Archie*).

    Produced by Sam Spiegel (Lone Star/Horizon) for Columbia. 135 min.

## 1967    BONNIE AND CLYDE

Script: David Newman and Robert Benton.
Direction: Penn.
Photography (Technicolor): Burnett Guffey.
Editing: Dede Allen.
Music: Charles Strouse, Flatt and Scruggs.
Art direction: Dean Tavoularis.
Costumes: Theadora van Runkle.
Special consultant: Robert Towne.

    Cast: Warren Beatty (*Clyde Barrow*), Faye Dunaway (*Bonnie Parker*), Michael J. Pollard (*C. W. Moss*), Gene Hackman (*Buck Barrow*), Estelle Parsons (*Blanche*), Denver Pyle (*Frank Hamer*), Dub Taylor (*Ivan Moss*), Evans Evans (*Velma Davis*), Gene Wilder (*Eugene Grizzard*).

    Produced by Warren Beatty (A Tatira-Hiller Production) for Warner Bros. 111 min.

## 1969    ALICE'S RESTAURANT

Script: Venable Herndon and Arthur Penn, based on the recording "The Alice's Restaurant Massacree" by Arlo Guthrie.
Direction: Penn.
Photography (Technicolor): Michael Nebbia.

Editing: Dede Allen.
Music: Arlo Guthrie, Woody Guthrie, Joni Mitchell, Gary Sherman.
Musical supervision: Gary Sherman.
Art direction: Warren Clymer.

Cast: Arlo Guthrie (*Arlo*), Pat Quinn (*Alice*), James Broderick (*Ray*), Michael McClanathan (*Shelly*), Geoff Outlaw (*Roger*), Tina Chen (*Mari-Chan*), Kathleen Dabney (*Karin*), Police Chief William Obanhein (*Officer Obie*), Seth Allen (*evangelist*), Monroe Arnold (*Blueglass*), Joseph Boley (*Woody*), Vinnette Carroll (*lady clerk*), M. Emmet Walsh (*group W sergeant*), Judge James Hannon (*himself*), Graham Jarvis (*music teacher*).

Produced by Hillard Elkins and Joe Manduke (A Florin Production) for United Artists. 111 min.

## 1970 LITTLE BIG MAN

Script: Calder Willingham, from the novel by Thomas Berger.
Direction: Penn.
Photography (Technicolor, Panavision): Harry Stradling, Jr.
Editing: Dede Allen.
Music: John Hammond.
Production design: Dean Tavoularis.

Cast: Dustin Hoffman (*Jack Crabb*), Faye Dunaway (*Mrs. Pendrake*), Martin Balsam (*Allardyce T. Merriweather*), Richard Mulligan (*General Custer*), Chief Dan George (*Old Lodge Skins*), Jeff Corey (*Wild Bill Hickok*), Amy Eccles (*Sunshine*), Kelly Jean Peters (*Olga*), Carol Androsky (*Caroline*), Robert Little Star (*Little Horse*), Cal Bellini (*Younger Bear*), Ruben Moreno (*Shadow That Comes in Sight*), Steve Shemayne (*Burns Red in the Sky*), William Hickey (*historian*), Thayer David (*Rev. Silas Pendrake*), Ray Dimas (*young Jack Crabb*), Alan Howard (*adolescent Jack Crabb*).

Produced by Stuart Millar (Hiller Productions, Stockbridge Productions) for Cinema Center Films/National General Pictures. 150 min.

## 1975 NIGHT MOVES

Script: Alan Sharp.
Direction: Penn.

Photography (Technicolor): Bruce Surtees.
Editing: Dede Allen, Stephen A. Rotter.
Music: Michael Small.
Production design: George Jenkins.

Cast: Gene Hackman (*Harry Moseby*), Jennifer Warren (*Paula*), Edward Binns (*Joey Ziegler*), Harris Yulin (*Marty Heller*), Kenneth Mars (*Nick*), Janet Ward (*Arlene Iverson*), James Woods (*Quentin*), Anthony Costello (*Marv Ellman*), John Crawford (*Tom Iverson*), Melanie Griffith (*Delly Grastner*), Susan Clark (*Ellen Moseby*).

Produced by Robert M. Sherman (Hiller Productions/Layton) for Warner Bros. 99 min.

## 1976   THE MISSOURI BREAKS

Script: Thomas McGuane.
Direction: Penn.
Photography (DeLuxe Color): Michael Butler.
Editing: Jerry Greenberg, Stephen Rotter, Dede Allen.
Music: John Williams.
Production design: Albert Brenner.

Cast: Marlon Brando (*Lee Clayton*), Jack Nicholson (*Tom Logan*), Kathleen Lloyd (*Jane Braxton*), Randy Quaid (*Little Tod*), Frederick Forrest (*Cary*), Harry Dean Stanton (*Calvin*), John McLiam (*David Braxton*), John Ryan (*Si*), Sam Gilman (*Hank*).

Produced by Elliott Kastner and Robert M. Sherman for United Artists. 126 min.

# STANLEY KUBRICK

## 1953   FEAR AND DESIRE

Script: Howard O. Sackler.
Direction, photography, editing: Kubrick.

Cast: Frank Silvera (*Mac*), Kenneth Harp (*Corby*), Virginia Leith (*the girl*), Paul Mazursky (*Sidney*), Steve Coit (*Fletcher*).

Produced by Stanley Kubrick for Joseph Burstyn. 68 min.

## 1955   KILLER'S KISS

Script: Kubrick, Howard O. Sackler.
Direction, photography, editing: Kubrick.
Music: Gerald Fried.
Choreography: David Vaughan.

Cast: Frank Silvera (*Vincent Rapallo*), Jamie Smith (*Davy Gordon*), Irene Kane (*Gloria Price*), Jerry Jarret (*Albert*), Ruth Sobotka (*Iris*), Mike Dana, Felice Orlandi, Ralph Roberts, Phil Stevenson (*hoodlums*), Julius Adelman (*mannequin factory owner*), David Vaughan, Alec Rubin (*conventioneers*).

Produced by Stanley Kubrick and Morris Bousel (Minotaur) for United Artists. 61 min.

## 1956   THE KILLING

Script: Kubrick, based on the novel *Clean Break* by Lionel White.
Additional dialogue: Jim Thompson.
Direction: Kubrick.
Photography: Lucien Ballard.
Editing: Betty Steinberg.
Art direction: Ruth Sobotka Kubrick.
Music: Gerald Fried.

Cast: Sterling Hayden (*Johnny Clay*), Jay C. Flippen (*Marvin Unger*), Marie Windsor (*Sherry Peatty*), Elisha Cook (*George Peatty*), Coleen Gray (*Fay*), Vince Edwards (*Val Cannon*), Ted de Corsia (*Randy Kennan*), Joe Sawyer (*Mike O'Reilly*), Tim Carey (*Nikki*), Kola Kwariani (*Maurice*).

Produced by James B. Harris (Harris-Kubrick Productions) for United Artists. 83 min.

## 1957   PATHS OF GLORY

Script: Kubrick, Calder Willingham, Jim Thompson, based on the novel by Humphrey Cobb.
Direction: Kubrick.
Photography: George Krause.
Editing: Eva Kroll.
Music: Gerald Fried.

Art direction: Ludwig Reiber.

Cast: Kirk Douglas (*Colonel Dax*), Ralph Meeker (*Corporal Paris*), Adolphe Menjou (*General Broulard*), George Macready (*General Mireau*), Wayne Morris (*Lieutenant Roget*), Richard Anderson (*Major Saint-Auban*), Joseph Turkel (*Private Arnaud*), Timothy Carey (*Private Ferol*), Peter Capell (*Colonel Judge*), Susanne Christian (*German girl*), Bert Freed (*Sergeant Boulanger*), Emile Meyer (*priest*), John Stein (*Captain Rousseau*).

Produced by James B. Harris (Harris-Kubrick Productions) for United Artists. 86 min.

## 1960    SPARTACUS

Script: Dalton Trumbo, based on the novel by Howard Fast.
Direction: Kubrick.
Photography (Technicolor, Super Technirama-70): Russell Metty.
Additional photography: Clifford Stine.
Editing: Robert Lawrence, Robert Schultz, Fred Chulack.
Music: Alex North.
Production design: Alexander Golitzen.

Cast: Kirk Douglas (*Spartacus*), Laurence Olivier (*Marcus Crassus*), Jean Simmons (*Varinia*), Charles Laughton (*Gracchus*), Peter Ustinov (*Batiatus*), John Gavin (*Julius Caesar*), Tony Curtis (*Antoninus*), Nina Foch (*Helena*), Herbert Lom (*Tigranes*), John Ireland (*Crixus*), John Dall (*Glabrus*), Charles McGraw (*Marcellus*), Joanna Barnes (*Claudia*), Harold J. Stone (*David*), Woody Strode (*Draba*).

Produced by Kirk Douglas and Edward Lewis (Bryna) for Universal. 196 min.

## 1961    LOLITA

Script: Vladimir Nabokov, based on his novel.
Direction: Kubrick.
Photography: Oswald Morris.
Editing: Anthony Harvey.
Music: Nelson Riddle, Bob Harris.
Art direction: William Andrews.

Cast: James Mason (*Humbert Humbert*), Sue Lyon (*Lolita Haze*), Shelley Winters (*Charlotte Haze*), Peter Sellers (*Clare Quilty*), Diana Decker (*Jean Farlow*), Jerry Stovin (*John Farlow*), Suzanne Gibbs (*Mona Farlow*), Gary Cockrell (*Dick*), Marianne Stone (*Vivian Darkbloom*), Cec Linder (*physician*), Lois Maxwell (*Nurse Mary Lore*), William Greene (*Swine*).

Produced by James B. Harris (Seven Arts/Anya/Transworld) for MGM. 153 min.

## 1963 DR. STRANGELOVE, OR HOW I LEARNED TO STOP WORRYING AND LOVE THE BOMB

Script: Kubrick, Terry Southern, Peter George, based on George's novel *Red Alert*.
Direction: Kubrick.
Photography: Gilbert Taylor.
Editing: Anthony Harvey.
Music: Laurie Johnson.
Production design: Ken Adam.
Special Effects: Wally Veevers.

Cast: Peter Sellers (*Group Captain Lionel Mandrake, President Merkin Muffley, Dr. Strangelove*), George C. Scott (*General Buck Turgidson*), Sterling Hayden (*General Jack D. Ripper*), Keenan Wynn (*Colonel Bat Guano*), Slim Pickens (*Major Kong*), Peter Bull (*Ambassador de Sadesky*), Tracy Reed (*Miss Scott*), James Earl Jones (*Lieutenant Lothar Zogg, bombardier*), Jack Creley (*Mr. Staines*), Frank Berry (*Lieutenant H. R. Dietrich, D.S.O.*), Glenn Beck (*Lieutenant W. D. Kivel, navigator*), Shane Rimmer (*Captain Ace Owens, copilot*), Paul Tamarin (*Lieutenant B. Goldberg, radio operator*), Gordon Tanner (*General Faceman*).

Produced by Kubrick (Hawk Films) for Columbia. 94 min.

## 1968 2001: A SPACE ODYSSEY

Script: Kubrick, Arthur C. Clarke, based on Clarke's story "The Sentinel."
Direction: Kubrick.
Photography (Metrocolor, Super Panavision): Geoffrey Unsworth.
Additional photography: John Alcott.

Editing: Ray Lovejoy.
Music: Richard Strauss, Johann Strauss, Aram Khachaturian, György Ligeti.
Production design: Tony Masters, Harry Lange, Ernie Archer.
Costumes: Hardy Amies.
Special photographic effects design and direction: Kubrick.
Special photographic effects supervision: Wally Veevers, Douglas Trumbull, Con Pederson, Tom Howard.
Cast: Keir Dullea (*David Bowman*), Gary Lockwood (*Frank Poole*), William Sylvester (*Dr. Heywood Floyd*), Daniel Richter (*moonwatcher*), Douglas Rain (*voice of HAL 9000*), Leonard Rossiter (*Smyslov*), Margaret Tyzack (*Elena*), Robert Beatty (*Halvorsen*), Sean Sullivan (*Michaels*), Frank Miller (*Mission Control*), Penny Brahms (*stewardess*), Alan Gifford (*Poole's father*).
Produced by Kubrick for MGM. 141 min.

## 1971   A CLOCKWORK ORANGE

Script: Kubrick, from the novel by Anthony Burgess.
Direction: Kubrick.
Photography (Warnercolor): John Alcott.
Editing: Bill Butler.
Music: Walter Carlos.
Production design: John Barry.
Cast: Malcolm McDowell (*Alex*), Patrick Magee (*Mr. Alexander*), Anthony Sharp (*Minister of the Interior*), Godfrey Quigley (*prison chaplain*), Warren Clarke (*Dim*), James Marcus (*Georgie*), Aubrey Morris (*Deltoid*), Miriam Karlin (*Cat Lady*), Sheila Raynor (*Mum*), Philip Stone (*Dad*), Carl Duering (*Dr. Brodsky*), Paul Farrell (*tramp*), Michael Gover (*prison governor*), Clive Francis (*lodger*), Madge Ryan (*Dr. Branom*), Pauline Taylor (*psychiatrist*), John Clive (*stage actor*), Michael Bates (*chief guard*).
Produced by Kubrick for Warner Bros. 137 min.

## 1975   BARRY LYNDON

Script: Kubrick, from the novel by William Makepeace Thackeray.
Direction: Kubrick.
Photography (Metrocolor): John Alcott.

Editing: Tony Lawson.
Music: J. S. Bach, Frederick the Great, Handel, Mozart, Paisiello, Schubert, Vivaldi, The Chieftains.
Music adaptation: Leonard Rosenman.
Production design: Ken Adam.
Costumes: Ulla-Britt Soderlund, Milena Canonero.

Cast: Ryan O'Neal (*Barry Lyndon*), Marisa Berenson (*Lady Lyndon*), Patrick Magee (*the Chevalier*), Hardy Kruger (*Captain Potzdorf*), Marie Kean (*Barry's mother*), Gay Hamilton (*Nora*), Murray Melvin (*Reverend Runt*), Godfrey Quigley (*Captain Grogan*), Leonard Rossiter (*Captain Quinn*), Leon Vitali (*Lord Bullingdon*), Diana Koerner (*German girl*), Frank Middlemass (*Sir Charles Lyndon*), Andre Morell (*Lord Wendover*), Arthur O'Sullivan (*highwayman*), Philip Stone (*Graham*), Michael Hordern (*narrator*).

Produced by Kubrick and Jan Harlan for Warner Bros. 185 min.


# FRANCIS FORD COPPOLA

## 1963 DEMENTIA 13

Script and direction: Coppola.
Photography: Charles Hannawalt.
Editing: Stewart O'Brien.
Music: Ronald Stein.
Art direction: Albert Locatelli.

Cast: William Campbell (*Richard Haloran*), Luana Anders (*Louise Haloran*), Bart Patton (*Billy Haloran*), Mary Mitchell (*Kane*), Patrick Magee (*Justin Caleb*), Eithne Dunn (*Lady Haloran*), Peter Reed (*John Haloran*), Karl Schanzer (*Simon*), Ron Perry (*Arthur*), Derry O'Donovan (*Lillian*), Barbara Dowling (*Kathleen*).

Produced by Roger Corman for Filmgroup Inc./American International. 81 min.


## 1967 YOU'RE A BIG BOY NOW

Script: Coppola, from the novel by David Benedictus.
Direction: Coppola.
Photography (Eastmancolor): Andy Laszlo.

Editing: Aram Avakian.
Music: Bob Prince.
Songs: John Sebastian (sung by The Lovin' Spoonful).
Art direction: Vassele Fotopoulos.
Choreography: Robert Tucker.

Cast: Peter Kastner (*Bernard Chanticleer*), Elizabeth Hartman (*Barbara Darling*), Geraldine Page (*Margery Chanticleer*), Julie Harris (*Miss Thing*), Rip Torn (*I. H. Chanticleer*), Tony Bill (*Raef*), Karen Black (*Amy*), Michael Dunn (*Richard Mudd*), Dolph Sweet (*Policeman Francis Graf*), Michael O'Sullivan (*Kurt Doughty*).

Produced by Phil Feldman (Seven Arts) for Warner-Pathé. 97 min.

## 1968   FINIAN'S RAINBOW

Script: E. Y. Harburg, Fred Saidy, based on their musical play (music: Burton Lane; lyrics: E. Y. Harburg).
Direction: Coppola.
Photography (Technicolor, Panavision, presented in 70 mm): Philip Lathrop.
Editing: Melvin Shapiro.
Music direction: Ray Heindorf.
Production design: Hilyard M. Brown.
Choreography: Hermes Pan.

Cast: Fred Astaire (*Finian McLonergan*), Petula Clark (*Sharon McLonergan*), Tommy Steele (*Og*), Don Francks (*Woody*), Barbara Hancock (*Susan the Silent*), Keenan Wynn (*Judge Billboard Rawkins*), Al Freeman Jr. (*Howard*), Brenda Arnau (*sharecropper*), Avon Long, Roy Glenn, Jerster Hairston (*Passion Pilgrim Gospellers*), Louis Silas (*Henry*), Dolph Sweet (*sheriff*), Wright King (*district attorney*).

Produced by Joseph Landon for Warner Bros./Seven Arts. 144 min.

## 1969   THE RAIN PEOPLE

Script and direction: Coppola.
Photography (Technicolor): Wilmer Butler.
Editing: Blackie Malkin.
Music: Ronald Stein.

Art direction: Leon Ericksen.

Cast: James Caan (*Kilgannon*), Shirley Knight (*Natalie*), Robert Duvall (*Gordon*), Marya Zimmet (*Rosalie*), Tom Aldredge (*Mr. Alfred*), Laurie Crews (*Ellen*), Andrew Duncan (*Artie*), Margaret Fairchild (*Marion*), Sally Gracie (*Beth*), Alan Manson (*Lou*), Robert Modica (*Vinny*).

Produced by Bart Patton and Ronald Colby (Coppola Company Presentation) for Warner Bros./Seven Arts. 101 min.

## 1972  THE GODFATHER

Script: Mario Puzo, Coppola, based on Puzo's novel.

Direction: Coppola.

Photography (Technicolor): Gordon Willis.

Editing: William Reynolds, Peter Zinner, Marc Laub, Murray Solomon.

Music: Nino Rota (conducted by Carlo Savina).

Production design: Dean Tavoularis.

Art direction: Warren Clymer.

Costumes: Anna Hill Johnstone.

Cast: Marlon Brando (*Don Vito Corleone*), Al Pacino (*Michael Corleone*), James Caan (*Sonny Corleone*), Richard Castellano (*Clemenza*), Robert Duvall (*Tom Hagen*), Sterling Hayden (*McCluskey*), John Marley (*Jack Woltz*), Richard Conte (*Barzini*), Diane Keaton (*Kay Adams*), Al Lettieri (*Sollozzo*), Abe Vigoda (*Tessio*), Talia Shire (*Connie Rizzi*), Gianni Russo (*Carlo Rizzi*), John Cazale (*Fredo Corleone*), Rudy Bond (*Cuneo*), Al Martino (*Johnny Fontane*), Morgana King (*Mama Corleone*), Lenny Montana (*Luca Brasi*), John Martino (*Paulie Gatto*), Salvatore Corsitto (*Bonasera*), Richard Bright (*Neri*), Alex Rocco (*Moe Greene*), Tony Giorgio (*Bruno Tattaglia*), Vito Scottia (*Nazorine*), Tere Livrano (*Theresa Hagen*), Victor Rendina (*Philip Tattaglia*), Jeannie Linero (*Lucy Mancini*), Julie Gregg (*Sandra Corleone*), Ardell Sheridan (*Mrs. Clemenza*), Simonetta Stefanelli (*Apollonia*), Angelo Infanti (*Fabrizio*), Corrado Gaipa (*Don Tommasino*), Franco Citti (*Calo*), Saro Urzi (*Vitelli*).

Produced by Albert S. Ruddy (Alfran Productions) for Paramount. 175 min.

## 1974   THE CONVERSATION

Script and direction: Coppola.
Photography (Technicolor): Bill Butler.
Editing: Walter Murch, Richard Chew.
Music: David Shire.
Production design: Dean Tavoularis.
Technical advisers: Hal Lipset, Leo Jones.

Cast: Gene Hackman (*Harry Caul*), John Cazale (*Stan*), Allen Garfield (*Bernie Moran*), Frederic Forrest (*Mark*), Cindy Williams (*Ann*), Michael Higgins (*Paul*), Elizabeth MacRae (*Meredith*), Harrison Ford (*Martin Stett*), Mark Wheeler (*receptionist*), Teri Garr (*Amy*), Robert Shields (*mime*), Phoebe Alexander (*Lurleen*), Robert Duvall (*the Director*).

Produced by Coppola and Fred Roos (Coppola Company) for Paramont. 113 min.

## 1974   THE GODFATHER, Part II

Script: Coppola, Mario Puzo, from Puzo's novel.
Direction: Coppola.
Photography (Technicolor): Gordon Willis.
Editing: Peter Zinner, Barry Malkin, Richard Marks.
Music: Nino Rota (conducted by Carmine Coppola).
Additional music: Carmine Coppola.
Production design: Dean Tavoularis.
Art direction: Angelo Graham.
Costumes: Theadora van Runkle.

Cast: Al Pacino (*Michael Corleone*), Robert Duvall (*Tom Hagen*), Diane Keaton (*Kay Adams*), Robert De Niro (*Vito Corleone*), John Cazale (*Fredo Corleone*), Talia Shire (*Connie Corleone*), Lee Strasberg (*Hyman Roth*), Michael V. Gazzo (*Frankie Pentangeli*), G. D. Spradlin (*Senator Pat Geary*), Richard Bright (*Al Neri*), Gaston Moschin (*Fanucci*), Tom Rosqui (*Rocco Lampone*), B. Kirby, Jr. (*young Clemenza*), Frank Sivero (*Genco*), Francesca De Sapio (*young Mama Corleone*), Morgana King (*Mama Corleone*), Mariana Hill (*Deanna Corleone*), Leopoldo Trieste (*Signor Roberto*), Dominic Chianese (*Johnny Ola*), Amerigo Tot (*Michael's bodyguard*), Troy Donahue (*Merle Johnson*), John Aprea (*young Tessio*), Joe

Spinell (*Willi Cicci*), Abe Vigoda (*Tessio*), Tere Livrano (*Theresa Hagen*), Gianni Russo (*Carlo Rizzi*), Maria Carta (*Vito's mother*), Oreste Baldini (*Vito Andolini as a boy*), Giuseppe Sillato (*Don Francesco*), Mario Cotone (*Don Tommasino*), James Gounaris (*Anthony Corleone*), Fay Spain (*Mrs. Marcia Roth*), Harry Dean Stanton (*first FBI man*), David Baker (*second FBI man*), Carmine Caridi (*Carmine Rosato*), Danny Aiello (*Tony Rosato*), Carmine Foresta (*policeman*), Nick Discenza (*barman*), Father Joseph Medeglia (*Father Carmelo*), William Bowers (*Senate committee chairman*), Joe Della Sorte, Carmen Argenziano, Joe Lo Grippo (*Michael's buttonmen*), Ezio Flagello (*impresario*), Livio Giorgi (*tenor in "Senza Mamma"*), Kathy Beller (*girl in "Senza Mamma"*), Saveria Mazzola (*Signora Colombo*), Tito Alba (*Cuban president*), Johnny Naranjo (*Cuban translator*), Elda Maida (*Pentangeli's wife*), Salvatore Po (*Pentangeli's brother*), Ignazio Pappalardo (*Mosca*), Andrea Maugeri (*Strollo*), Peter La Corte (*Signor Abbandando*), Vincent Coppola (*street salesman*), Peter Donat (*Questadt*), Tom Dahlgren (*Fred Corngold*), Paul B. Brown (*Senator Ream*), Phil Feldman (*first senator*), Roger Corman (*second senator*), Yvonne Coll (*Yolanda*), J. D. Nichols (*attendant at brothel*), Edward Van Sickle (*Ellis Island doctor*), Gabria Belloni (*Ellis Island nurse*), Richard Watson (*customs official*), Venancia Grangerard (*Cuban nurse*), Erica Yohn (*governess*), Theresa Tirelli (*midwife*), James Caan (*Sonny Corleone*).

Produced by Coppola (A Coppola Company Production) for Paramount. 200 min.

## MARTIN SCORSESE

### 1969    WHO'S THAT KNOCKING AT MY DOOR?

Script and direction: Scorsese (additional dialogue by Betzi Manoogian).
Photography: Michael Wadleigh, Richard Coll, Max Fisher.
Editing: Thelma Schoonmaker.
Art direction: Victor Magnotta.
Cast: Zina Bethune (*the young girl*), Harvey Keitel (*J. R.*), Anne

Collette (*young girl in dream*), Lennard Kuras (*Joey*), Michael Scala (*Sally Gaga*), Harry Northup (*Harry*), Bill Minkin (*Iggy*), Phil Carlson (*the guide*), Wendy Russell (*Gaga's small friend*), Robert Uricola (*the armed young man*), Susan Wood (*Susan*), Marissa Joffrey (*Rosie*), Catherine Scorsese (*J. R.'s mother*), Victor Magnotta and Paul De Bionde (*waiters*), Saskia Holleman, Tsuai Yu-Lan, Marieka (*dream girls*), Martin Scorsese (*gangster*), Thomas Aiello.

Produced by Joseph Weill, Betzi Manoogian and Haig Manoogian (Trimrod) for release by Joseph Brenner Associates. 90 min. Earlier versions known as *Bring on the Dancing Girls* (1965) and *I Call First* (1967). Also released as *J. R.*

## 1972   BOXCAR BERTHA

Script: Joyce H. Corrington, John William Corrington, from the book *Sister of the Road* by Boxcar Bertha Thompson as told to Ben L. Reitman.
Direction: Scorsese.
Photography (DeLuxe color): John Stephens.
Editing: Buzz Feitshans.
Music: Gib Guilbeau, Thad Maxwell.
Visual consultant: David Nichols.

Cast: Barbara Hershey (*Bertha*), David Carradine (*Bill Shelley*), Barry Primus (*Rake Brown*), Bernie Casey (*Von Morton*), John Carradine (*H. Buckram Sartoris*), Victor Argo and David R. Osterhout (*The McIvers*), "Chicken" Holleman (*Michael Powell*), Grahame Pratt (*Emeric Pressburger*), Harry Northup (*Harvey Hall*), Ann Morell (*Tillie*), Marianne Dole (*Mrs. Mailer*), Joe Reynolds (*Joe*), Gayne Rescher and Martin Scorsese (*brothel clients*).

Produced by Roger Corman for American International. 88 min.

## 1973   MEAN STREETS

Script: Scorsese, Mardik Martin.
Direction: Scorsese.
Photography (Technicolor): Kent Wakeford.
Editing: Sid Levin.
Visual consultant: David Nichols.

Cast: Harvey Keitel (*Charlie*), Robert De Niro (*Johnny Boy*), Amy Robinson (*Teresa*), David Proval (*Tony*), Richard Romanus (*Michael*), Cesare Danova (*Giovanni*), Victor Argo (*Mario*), George Memmoli (*Joey Catucci*), Lenny Scaletta (*Jimmy*), Jeannie Bell (*Diane*), Murray Mosten (*Oscar*), David Carradine (*drunk*), Robert Carradine (*young assassin*), Lois Walden (*Jewish girl*), Harry Northup (*Vietnam veteran*), Dino Seragusa (*old man*), D'Mitch Davis (*black cop*), Peter Fain (*George*), Julie Andelman (*girl at party*), Robert Wilder (*Benton*), Ken Sinclair (*Sammy*), Catherine Scorsese (*woman on the landing*), Martin Scorsese (*Shorty, the killer in the car*).

Produced by Jonathan T. Taplin (Taplin-Perry-Scorsese) for Warner Bros. 110 min.

## 1974　ALICE DOESN'T LIVE HERE ANYMORE

Script: Robert Getchell.
Direction: Scorsese.
Photography (Technicolor): Kent Wakeford.
Editing: Marcia Lucas.
Original music: Richard LaSalle.
Production design: Toby Carr Rafelson.

Cast: Ellen Burstyn (*Alice Hyatt*), Kris Kristofferson (*David*), Alfred Lutter (*Tommy*), Billy Green Bush (*Donald*), Diane Ladd (*Flo*), Lelia Goldoni (*Bea*), Lane Bradbury (*Rita*), Vic Tayback (*Mel*), Jodie Foster (*Audrey*), Harvey Keitel (*Ben*), Valerie Curtin (*Vera*), Murray Moston (*Jacobs*), Harry Northup (*Joe and Jim's bartender*), Mia Bendixsen (*Alice aged 8*), Ola Moore (*old woman*), Martin Brinton (*Lenny*), Dean Casper (*Chicken*), Henry M. Kendrick (*shop assistant*), Martin Scorsese and Larry Cohen (*diners at Mel and Ruby's*), Mardik Martin (*customer in club during audition*).

Produced by David Susskind and Audrey Maas for Warner Bros. 112 min.

## 1976　TAXI DRIVER

Script: Paul Schrader.
Direction: Scorsese.
Photography (color): Michael Chapman.

Editing: Marcia Lucas, Tom Rolf, Melvin Shapiro.
Music: Bernard Herrmann.
Art direction: Charles Rosen.
Creative consultant: Sandra Weintraub.
Visual consultant: David Nichols.

Cast: Robert De Niro (*Travis Bickle*), Cybill Shepherd (*Betsy*), Jodie Foster (*Iris*), Harvey Keitel (*Sport*), Peter Boyle (*Wizard*), Albert Brooks (*Tom*), Leonard Harris (*Charles Palantine*), Diahnne Abbott (*concession girl*), Frank Adu (*angry black man*), Vic Argo (*Melio*), Gino Ardito (*policeman at rally*), Garth Avery (*Iris's friend*), Harry Cohn (*cabbie in Belmore*), Copper Cunningham (*hooker in cab*), Brenda Dickson (*soap opera woman*), Harry Fischler (*dispatcher*), Nat Grant (*stick-up man*), Richard Higgs (*tall Secret Service man*), Beau Kayser (*soap opera man*), Vic Magnotta (*Secret Service photographer*), Robert Maroff (*mafioso*), Norman Matlock (*Charlie T.*), Bill Minkin (*Tom's assistant*), Murray Moston (*Iris's timekeeper*), Harry Northup (*doughboy*), Gene Palma (*street drummer*), Carey Poe (*campaign worker*), Steven Prince (*Andy, gun salesman*), Peter Savage (*the john*), Martin Scorsese (*passenger watching silhouette*), Robert Shields (*Palantine aide*), Ralph Singleton (*TV interviewer*), Joe Spinell (*personnel officer*), Maria Turner (*angry hooker on street*), Robin Utt (*campaign worker*).

Produced by Michael and Julia Phillips (Bill/Phillips production) for Columbia. 112 min.

## 1977 NEW YORK, NEW YORK

Script: Earl Mac Rauch, Mardik Martin, from a story by Rauch.
Direction: Scorsese.
Photography (Technicolor): Laszlo Kovacs.
Production design: Boris Leven.
Original songs by John Kander and Fred Ebb ("Theme From *New York, New York*," "There Goes the Ball Game," "But the World Goes 'Round," "Happy Endings").
Musical supervisor and conductor: Ralph Burns.
Choreography: Ron Field.
Supervising film editors: Irving Lerner, Marcia Lucas.

Editing: Tom Rolf, B. Lovitt.

Costumes: Theodora van Runkle.

Hair designs for Liza Minnelli: Sydney Guilaroff.

Sound editing: Michael Colgan, James Fritch.

Saxophone solos and technical consultant: Georgie Auld.

Cast: Liza Minnelli (*Francine Evans*), Robert De Niro (*Jimmy Doyle*), Lionel Stander (*Tony Harwell*), Barry Primus (*Paul Wilson*), Mary Kay Place (*Bernice*), Georgie Auld (*Frankie Harte*), George Memmoli (*Nicky*), Dick Miller (*Palm Club owner*), Murray Moston (*Horace Morris*), Lenny Gaines (*Artie Kirks*), Clarence Clemons (*Cecil Powell*), Kathi McGinnis (*Ellen Flannery*), Norman Palmer (*desk clerk*), Adam David Winkler (*Jimmy Doyle, Jr.*), Dimitri Logothetis (*desk clerk*), Frank Sivera (*Eddie di Muzio*), Diahnne Abbott (*Harlem club singer*), Margo Winkler (*argumentative woman*), Steven Prince (*record producer*), Don Calfa (*Gilbert*), Bernie Kuby (*justice of the peace*), Selma Archerd (*wife of justice of the peace*), Bill Baldwin (*announcer in Moonlit Terrace*), Mary Lindsay (*hatcheck girl in Meadows*), Jon Cutler (*musician in Frankie Hart's band*), Nicky Blair (*cab driver*), Casey Kasem (*D. J.*), Jay Salerno (*bus driver*), William Tole (*Tommy Dorsey*), Sydney Guilaroff (*hairdresser*), Peter Savage (*Horace Morris's assistant*), Gene Castle (*dancing sailor*), Louie Guss (*Fowler*), Shera Danese (*Doyle's girl in Major Chord*), Bill McMillan (*D. J.*), David Nichols (*Arnold Trench*), Harry Northup (*Alabama*), Marty Zagon (*manager of South Bend ballroom*), Timothy Blake (*nurse*), Betty Cole (*charwoman*), De Forest Covan (*porter*), Phil Gray (*trombone player in Doyle's band*), Roosevelt Smith (*bouncer in Major Chord*), Bruce L. Lucoff (*cab driver*), Bill Phillips Murry (*waiter in Harlem club*), Clint Arnold (*trombone player in Palm Club*), Richard Alan Berk (*drummer in Palm Club*), Jack R. Clinton (*bartender in Palm Club*), Wilfred R. Middlebrooks (*bass player in Palm Club*), Jake Vernon Porter (*trumpet player in Palm Club*), Nat Pierce (*piano player in Palm Club*), Manuel Escobosa (*fighter in Moonlit Terrace*), Susan Kay Hunt, Teryn Jenkins (*girls at Moonlit Terrace*), Mardik Martin (*well-wisher at Moonlit Terrace*), Leslie Summers (*woman in black at Moonlit Terrace*), Brock Michaels (*man at table in Moonlit Terrace*), Washington Rucker, Booty Reed (*musicians at hiring hall*), David Armstrong, Robert Buckingham, Eddie Garrett, Nico Stevens (*reporters*), Peter Fain (*greeter in Up Club*), Angelo Lamonea (*waiter in Up Club*), Charles A. Tamburro, Wallace Mc-Clesky (*bouncers in Up Club*), Ronald Prince (*dancer in Up Club*), Robert Petersen (*photographer*), Richard Raymond (*railroad conductor*), Hank Robinson (*Francine's bodyguard*), Harold Ross (*cab driver*), Eddie Smith (*man in bathroom at Harlem club*).

Produced by Irwin Winkler and Robert Chartoff for United Artists. 137 min.

## 1978  THE LAST WALTZ

Direction: Scorsese.

Photography (DeLuxe color): Michael Chapman, Laszlo Kovacs, Vilmos Zsigmond, David Myers, Bobby Byrne, Michael Watkins, Hiro Narita.

Editing: Yeu-Bun Yee, Jan Roblee.

Production design: Boris Leven.

Concert producer: Bill Graham.

Concert music production: John Simon. (Audio production: Rob Fraboni.)

Music editor: Ken Wannberg.

Treatment and creative consultant: Mardik Martin.

The performers in order of appearance: Ronnie Hawkins, Dr. John, Neil Young, The Staples, Neil Diamond, Joni Mitchell, Paul Butterfield, Muddy Waters, Eric Clapton, Emmylou Harris, Van Morrison, Bob Dylan, Ringo Starr, Ron Wood.

Poems by Michael McClure, Sweet William Fritsch, Lawrence Ferlinghetti.

Interviewer: Scorsese.

The Band: Rick Danko (bass, violin, vocal), Levon Helm (drums, mandolin, vocal), Garth Hudson (organ, accordion, saxophone, synthesizers), Richard Manuel (piano, keyboards, drums, vocal), Robbie Robertson (lead guitar, vocal).

Produced by Robbie Robertson for United Artists. Executive producer: Jonathan Taplin. Filmed on location at Winterland Arena, San Francisco, November 1976, and MGM Studios, Culver City, and Shangri-La Studios, Malibu, thereafter. 119 min.

# ROBERT ALTMAN

## 1957 THE DELINQUENTS

Script and direction: Altman.
Photography: Charles Paddock (or Harry Birch).
Editing: Helene Turner.
Music: Bill Nolan Quintet Minus Two.
Song: Bill Nolan, Ronnie Norman ("The Dirty Rock Boogie"), sung by Julia Lee.
Art direction: Chet Allen.
Cast: Tom Laughlin (*Scotty*), Peter Miller (*Cholly*), Richard Bakalyn (*Eddy*), Rosemary Howard (*Janice*), Helene Hawley (*Mrs. White*), Leonard Belove (*Mr. White*), Lotus Corelli (*Mrs. Wilson*), James Lantz (*Mr. Wilson*), Christine Altman (*Sissy*), George Kuhn (*Jay*), Pat Stedman (*Meg*), Norman Zands (*Chizzy*), James Leria (*Steve*), Jet Pinkston (*Molly*), Kermit Echols (*barman*), Joe Adleman (*station attendant*).
Produced by Altman (Imperial Productions) for United Artists. 72 min.

## 1957 THE JAMES DEAN STORY

Script: Stewart Stern.
Direction: Altman, George W. George.
Photography: 29 various cameramen (stills: Camera Eye Pictures).
Music: Leith Stevens.
Song: Jay Livingston, Ray Evans.
Production design: Louis Clyde Stoumen.
Narrator: Martin Gabel.
Cast: Marcus, Ortense, and Markie Winslow (*Dean's aunt, uncle, and cousin*), Mr. and Mrs. Dean (*his grandparents*), Adeline Hall (*his drama teacher*), Big Traster, Mr. Carter, Jerry Luce, Louis de Liso, Arnie Langer, Arline Sax, Chris White, George Ross, Robert Jewett, John Kalin, Lew Bracker, Glenn Kramer, Patsy d'Amore, Billy Karen, Lille Kardell (*his friends*), Officer Nelson (*highway patrolman*).

Produced by Altman and George W. George for Warner Bros. 83 min.

## 1968   COUNTDOWN

Script: Loring Mandel, based on the novel *The Pilgrim Project* by Hank Searls.
Direction: Altman.
Photography (Technicolor, Panavision): William W. Spencer.
Editing: Gene Milford.
Music: Leonard Rosenman.
Art direction: Jack Poplin.
Set decoration: Ralph S. Hurst.
Cast: James Caan (*Lee*), Robert Duvall (*Chiz*), Joanna Moore (*Mickey*), Barbara Baxley (*Jean*), Charles Aidman (*Gus*), Steve Ihnat (*Ross*), Michael Murphy (*Rick*), Ted Knight (*Larson*), Stephen Coit (*Ehrman*), John Rayner (*Dunc*), Charles Irving (*Seidel*), Bobby Riha, Jr. (*Stevie*).
Produced by William Conrad (Productions) for Warner Bros. 101 min.

## 1969   NIGHTMARE IN CHICAGO

Script: Donald Moessinger, from the novel *Killer on the Turnpike* by William P. McGivern.
Direction: Altman.
Photography (color): Bud Thackery.
Music: Johnny Williams.
Cast: Charles McGraw, Robert Ridgely, Ted Knight, Philip Abbott, Barbara Turner, Charlene Lee, Arlene Kieta.
Produced by Altman for Roncom/Universal. 81 min. (Release version of the TV movie *Once Upon a Savage Night,* expanded with out-takes from an original 54 min. to 81 min. Shorter version first televised on 2 April 1964.)

## 1969   THAT COLD DAY IN THE PARK

Script: Gillian Freeman, from the novel by Richard Miles.
Direction: Altman.
Photography (Eastmancolor): Laszlo Kovacs.

Editing: Danford Greene.
Music: Johnny Mandel.
Art Direction: Leon Erickson.

Cast: Sandy Dennis (*Frances Austen*), Michael Burns (*the boy*), Susanne Benton (*Nina*), Luana Anders (*Sylvie*), John Garfield, Jr. (*Nick*), Michael Murphy (*the rounder*).

Produced by Donald Factor and Leon Mirell (Factor-Altman-Mirell Films) for Commonwealth United Entertainment, Inc. 115 min.

## 1970    M*A*S*H

Script: Ring Lardner, Jr., from the novel by Richard Hooker.
Direction: Altman.
Photography (DeLuxe color, Panavision): Harold E. Stine.
Editing: Danford B. Greene.
Music: Johnny Mandel.
Song: Johnny Mandel and Mike Altman ("Suicide Is Painless").
Art direction: Jack Martin Smith, Arthur Lonergan.
Set decoration: Walter M. Scott, Stuart A. Reiss.

Cast: Donald Sutherland (*Hawkeye Pierce*), Elliott Gould (*Trapper John McIntyre*), Tom Skerritt (*Duke Forrest*), Sally Kellerman (*Major Hot Lips*), Robert Duvall (*Major Frank Burns*), Jo Ann Pflug (*Lt. Dish*), René Auberjonois (*Dago Red*), Roger Bowen (*Col. Henry Blake*), Gary Burghoff (*Radar O'Reilly*), David Arkin (*Sgt. Major Vollmer*), Fred Williamson (*Spearchucker*), Michael Murphy (*Me Lay*), Kim Atwood (*Ho-Jon*), Tim Brown (*Corporal Judson*), Indus Arthur (*Lt. Leslie*), John Schuck (*Painless Pole*), Ken Prymus (*Pfc. Seidman*), Dawne Damon (*Capt. Scorch*), Carl Gottlieb (*Ugly John*), Tamara Horrocks (*Capt. Knocko*), G. Wood (*General Hammond*), Bobby Troup (*Sgt. Gorman*), Bud Cort (*Private Boone*), Danny Goldman (*Capt. Murrhardt*), Corey Fischer (*Capt. Bandini*), J. B. Douglas, Yoko Young.

Produced by Ingo Preminger for Aspen/Twentieth Century-Fox. Associate producer: Leon Ericksen. 116 min.

## 1970    BREWSTER McCLOUD

Script: Brian McKay (uncredited), Doran William Cannon.
Direction: Altman.

Assistant director: Tommy Thompson.

Photography (Metrocolor, Panavision): Lamar Boren, Jordan Cronenweth.

Editing: Lou Lombardo.

Music: Gene Page.

Songs: Francis Scott Key, Rosamund Johnson and James Weldon Johnson, John Phillips, sung by Merry Clayton, John Phillips.

Art direction: Preston Ames, George W. Davis.

Wings designed by Leon Ericksen.

Cast: Bud Cort (*Brewster McCloud*), Sally Kellerman (*Louise*), Michael Murphy (*Frank Shaft*), William Windom (*Haskel Weeks*), Shelley Duvall (*Suzanne Davis*), René Auberjonois (*lecturer*), Stacy Keach (*Abraham Wright*), John Schuck (*Lt. Alvin Johnson*), Margaret Hamilton (*Daphne Heap*), Jennifer Salt (*Hope*), Corey Fischer (*Lt. Hines*), G. Wood (*Capt. Crandall*), Bert Remsen (*Douglas Breen*), Angelin Johnson (*Mrs. Breen*), William Baldwin (*Bernard*), William Henry Bennet (*band conductor*), Gary Wayne Chason (*camera shop clerk*), Ellis Gilbert (*butler*), Verdie Henshaw (*Feathered Nest Sanatorium manager*), Robert Warner (*camera shop assistant manager*), Dean Goss (*Eugene Ledbetter*), Keith V. Erickson (*Prof. Aggnout*), Thomas Danko (*color lab man*), W. E. Terry, Jr. (*police chaplain*), Ronnie Cammack (*Wendell*), Dixie M. Taylor (*nursing home manager*), Pearl Coffey Chason (*nursing home attendant*), Amelia Parker (*nursing home manageress*), David Welch (*Breen's son*).

Produced by Lou Adler (Adler-Phillips/Lion's Gate) for MGM. Associate producers: Robert Eggenweiler, James Margellos. 105 min.

## 1971    McCABE AND MRS. MILLER

Script: Altman, Brian McKay, from the novel *McCabe* by Edmund Naughton.

Direction: Altman.

Assistant director: Tommy Thompson.

Photography (Technicolor, Panavision): Vilmos Zsigmond.

Editing: Lou Lombardo.

Music: Leonard Cohen.

Production design: Leon Ericksen.

Art direction: Phillip Thomas, Al Locatelli.

Cast: Warren Beatty (*John McCabe*), Julie Christie (*Constance Miller*), René Auberjonois (*Sheehan*), Hugh Millais (*Butler*), Shelley Duvall (*Ida Coyle*), Michael Murphy (*Sears*), John Schuck (*Smalley*), Corey Fischer (*Mr. Elliott*), William Devane (*Clement Samuels*), Anthony Holland (*Ernie Hollander*), Bert Remsen (*Bart Coyle*), Keith Carradine (*cowboy*), Jace Vander Veen (*Breed*), Manfred Shulz (*Kid*), Jackie Crossland (*Lily*), Elizabeth Murphy (*Kate*), Linda Sorenson (*Blanche*), Elizabeth Knight (*Birdie*), Maysie Hoy (*Maysie*), Linda Kupecek (*Ruth*), Janet Wright (*Eunice*), Carey Lee McKenzie (*Alma*), Rodney Gage (*Sumner Washington*), Lili Francks (*Mrs. Washington*).

Produced by David Foster, Mitchell Brower for Warner Bros. Associate producer: Robert Eggenweiler. 121 min.

## 1972    IMAGES

Script and direction: Altman (with passages from *In Search of Unicorns* by Susannah York).
Photography (Technicolor, Panavision): Vilmos Zsigmond.
Editing: Graeme Clifford.
Music: John Williams (with sounds by Stomu Yamash'ta).
Art direction: Leon Ericksen.

Cast: Susannah York (*Cathryn*), René Auberjonois (*Hugh*), Marcel Bozzuffi (*René*), Hugh Millais (*Marcel*), Cathryn Harrison (*Susannah*), John Morley (*old man*).

Produced by Tommy Thompson for Lion's Gate Film/The Hemdale Group/Columbia. 101 min.

## 1973    THE LONG GOODBYE

Script: Leigh Brackett, from the novel by Raymond Chandler.
Direction: Altman.
Assistant director: Tommy Thompson.
Photography (Technicolor, Panavision): Vilmos Zsigmond.
Editing: Lou Lombardo.
Music: John Williams.

Cast: Elliott Gould (*Philip Marlowe*), Nina van Pallandt (*Eileen Wade*), Sterling Hayden (*Roger Wade*), Mark Rydell (*Marty Au-*

*gustine*), Henry Gibson (*Dr. Verringer*), David Arkin (*Harry*), Jim Bouton (*Terry Lennox*), Warren Berlinger (*Morgan*), Jo Ann Brody (*Jo Ann Eggenweiler*), Steve Coit (*Detective Farmer*), Jack Knight (*Mabel*), Pepe Callahan (*Pepe*), Vince Palmieri (*Vince*), Pancho Cordoba (*doctor*), Enrique Lucero (*Jefe*), Rutanya Alda (*Rutanya Sweet*), Tammy Shaw (*dancer*), Jack Riley (*piano player*), Ken Sansom (*colony guard*), Jerry Jones (*Detective Green*), John Davies (*Detective Dayton*), Rodney Moss (*supermarket clerk*), Sybil Scotford (*real estate lady*), Herb Kerns (*Herbie*).

Produced by Jerry Bick and Elliot Kastner (Lion's Gate Films) for United Artists. Associate producer: Robert Eggenweiler. 112 min.


## 1974  THIEVES LIKE US

Script: Calder Willingham, Joan Tewkesbury, Altman, from the novel by Edward Anderson.
Direction: Altman.
Assistant director: Tommy Thompson.
Photography (DeLuxe color): Jean Boffety.
Editing: Lou Lombardo.
Visual consultants: Jack DeGovia, Scott Bushnell.
Radio research: John Dunning.

Cast: Keith Carradine (*Bowie*), Shelley Duvall (*Keechie*), John Schuck (*Chicamaw*), Bert Remsen (*T-Dub*), Louise Fletcher (*Mattie*), Ann Latham (*Lula*), Tom Skerritt (*Dee Mobley*), Al Scott (*Capt. Stammers*), John Roper (*Jasbo*), Mary Waits (*Noel*), Rodney Lee, Jr. (*James Mattingly*), William Watters (*Alvin*), Joan Tewkesbury (*lady in train station*), Eleanor Matthews (*Mrs. Stammers*), Pam Warner (*woman in accident*), Suzanne Majure (*Coca-Cola girl*), Walter Cooper and Lloyd Jones (*sheriffs*).

Produced by Jerry Bick and George Litto for United Artists. Associate producers: Robert Eggenweiler, Thomas Hal Phillips. 123 min.


## 1974  CALIFORNIA SPLIT

Script: Joseph Walsh.
Direction: Altman.

Assistant director: Tommy Thompson.
Photography (Metrocolor, Panavision): Paul Lohmann.
Editing: Lou Lombardo, assisted by Tony Lombardo and Dennis Hill.
Production design: Leon Ericksen.
Cast: Elliott Gould (*Charlie Waters*), George Segal (*Bill Denny*), Ann Prentiss (*Barbara Miller*), Gwen Welles (*Susan Peters*), Edward Walsh (*Lew*), Joseph Walsh (*Sparkie*), Bert Remsen (*"Helen Brown"*), Barbara London (*lady on the bus*), Barbara Ruick (*Reno barmaid*), Jay Fletcher (*robber*), Jeff Goldblum (*Lloyd Harris*), Barbara Colby (*receptionist*), Vince Palmieri (*first bartender*), Alyce Passman (*go-go girl*), Joanne Strauss (*mother*), Jack Riley (*second bartender*), Sierra Bandit (*woman at bar*), John Considine (*man at bar*), Eugene Troobnick (*Harvey*), Richard Kennedy (*used-car salesman*), John Winston (*tenor*), Bill Duffy (*Kenny*), Mike Greene (*Reno dealer*), Tom Signorelli (*Nugie*), Sharon Compton (*Nugie's wife*), Arnold Herzstein, Marc Cavell, Alvin Weissman, Mickey Fox, Carolyn Lohmann (*California Club poker players*), "Amarillo Slim" Preston, Winston Lee, Harry Drackett, Thomas Hal Phillips, Ted Say, A. J. Hood (*Reno poker players*).
Produced by Altman and Joseph Walsh (Won World/Persky Bright/Reno) for Columbia. Executive producers: Aaron Spelling, Leonard Goldberg. Associate producer: Robert Eggenweiler. 109 min.

## 1975   NASHVILLE

Script: Joan Tewkesbury.
Direction: Altman.
Assistant directors: Tommy Thompson, Alan Rudolph.
Photography (color, Panavision): Paul Lohmann.
Editing: Sidney Levin, Dennis Hill.
Political campaign: Thomas Hal Phillips.
Songs: "200 Years" (lyrics by Henry Gibson, music by Richard Baskin), "Yes, I Do" (lyrics and music by Richard Baskin and Lily Tomlin), "Down to the River" (lyrics and music by Ronee Blakley), "Let Me Be the One" (lyrics and music by Richard Baskin), "Sing a Song" (lyrics and music by Joe Raposo), "The Heart of a Gentle Woman" (lyrics and music by Dave Peel), "Bluebird" (lyrics and music by Ronee Blakley), "The Day I Looked Jesus in the Eye"

(lyrics and music by Richard Baskin and Robert Altman), "Memphis" (lyrics and music by Karen Black), "I Don't Know If I Found It in You" (lyrics and music by Karen Black), "For the Sake of the Children" (lyrics and music by Richard Baskin and Richard Reicheg), "Keep a Goin' " (lyrics by Henry Gibson, music by Richard Baskin and Henry Gibson), "Swing Low Sweet Chariot" (arrangements by Millie Clements), "Rolling Stone" (lyrics and music by Karen Black), "Honey" (lyrics and music by Keith Carradine), "Tapedeck in His Tractor (The Cowboy Song)" (lyrics and music by Ronee Blakley), "Dues" (lyrics and music by Ronee Blakley), "I Never Get Enough" (lyrics and music by Richard Baskin and Ben Raleigh), "Rose's Cafe" (lyrics and music by Allan Nicholls), "Old Man Mississippi" (lyrics and music by Juan Grizzle), "My Baby's Cookin' in Another Man's Pan" (lyrics and music by Jonnie Barnett), "One, I Love You" (lyrics and music by Richard Baskin), "I'm Easy" (lyrics and music by Keith Carradine), "It Don't Worry Me" (lyrics and music by Keith Carradine), "Since You've Gone" (lyrics and music by Garry Busey), "Trouble in the U.S.A." (lyrics and music by Arlene Barnett), "My Idaho Home" (lyrics and music by Ronee Blakley).

Cast: David Arkin (*Norman*), Barbara Baxley (*Lady Pearl*), Ned Beatty (*Delbert Reese*), Karen Black (*Connie White*), Ronee Blakley (*Barbara Jean*), Timothy Brown (*Tommy Brown*), Keith Carradine (*Tom Frank*), Geraldine Chaplin (*Opal*), Robert Doqui (*Wade*), Shelley Duvall (*L.A. Joan*), Allen Garfield (*Barnett*), Henry Gibson (*Haven Hamilton*), Scott Glenn (*Pfc. Glenn Kelly*), Jeff Goldblum (*tricycle man*), Barbara Harris (*Albuquerque*), David Hayward (*Kenny Fraiser*), Michael Murphy (*John Triplette*), Allan Nicholls (*Bill*), Dave Peel (*Bud Hamilton*), Cristina Raines (*Mary*), Bert Remsen (*Star*), Lily Tomlin (*Linnea Reese*), Gwen Welles (*Sueleen Gay*), Keenan Wynn (*Mr. Green*), James Dan Calvert (*Jimmy Reese*), Donna Denton (*Donna Reese*), Merle Kilgore (*Trout*), Carol McGinnis (*Jewel*), Sheila Bailey and Patti Bryant (*Smokey Mountain Laurel*), Richard Baskin (*Frog*), Jonnie Barnett, Vassar Clements, Misty Mountain Boys, Sue Barton, Elliott Gould, Julie Christie (*themselves*).

Produced by Altman (ABC Entertainment) for Paramount. Associate producers: Robert Eggenweiler, Scott Bushnell. Executive producers: Martin Starger, Jerry Weintraub. 161 min.

## 1976 BUFFALO BILL AND THE INDIANS, OR SITTING BULL'S HISTORY LESSON

Story and script: Alan Rudolph, Altman, based on the play *Indians* by Arthur Kopit.
Direction: Altman.
Assistant director: Tommy Thompson.
Photography (color, Panavision): Paul Lohmann.
Music: Richard Baskin.
Production design: Tony Masters.
Editing: Peter Appleton, Dennis Hill.
Costumes: Anthony Powell.

Cast: Paul Newman (*the Star*), Joel Grey (*the Producer*), Kevin McCarthy (*the Publicist*), Harvey Keitel (*the Relative*), Allan Nicholls (*the Journalist*), Geraldine Chaplin (*the Sure Shot*), John Considine (*the Sure Shot's Manager*), Robert Doqui (*the Wrangler*), Mike Kaplan (*the Treasurer*), Bert Remsen (*the Bartender*), Bonnie Leaders (*the Mezzo-Contralto*), Noelle Rogers (*the Lyric Coloratura*), Evelyn Lear (*the Lyric Soprano*), Denver Pyle (*the Indian Agent*), Frank Kaquitts (*the Indian*), Will Sampson (*the Interpreter*), Ken Krossa (*the Arenic Director*), Fred N. Larsen (*the King of the Cowboys*), Jerry and Joy Duce (*the Cowboy Trick Riders*), Alex Green and Gary MacKenzie (*the Mexican Whip and Fast Draw Act*), Humphrey Gratz (*the Old Soldier*), Pat McCormick (*the President of the United States*), Shelley Duvall (*the First Lady*), Burt Lancaster (*the Legend Maker*). With people from the Stoney Indian Reserve.

Produced by Robert Altman for Dino De Laurentiis Corporation/Lion's Gate Films, Inc./Talent Associates Norton Simon, Inc. United Artists. Executive Producer: David Susskind. Associate producers: Robert Eggenweiller, Scott Bushnell, Jac Cashin. Filmed entirely on the Stoney Indian Reserve, Alberta, Canada. 123 min.

## 1977 THREE WOMEN

Script and direction: Altman.
Photography (DeLuxe color, Panavision): Chuck Rosher.
Editing: Dennis Hill.
Art direction: James D. Vance.

Visual consultant: J. Allen Highfill.

Music: Gerald Busby.

Murals: Bodhi Wind.

Cast: Shelley Duvall (*Millie Lammoreaux*), Sissy Spacek (*Pinky Rose*), Janice Rule (*Willie Hart*), Robert Fortier (*Edgar Hart*), Ruth Nelson (*Mrs. Rose*), John Cromwell (*Mr. Rose*), Sierra Pecheur (*Ms. Bunweill*), Craig Richard Nelson (*Dr. Maas*), Maysie Hoy (*Doris*), Belita Moreno (*Alcira*), Leslie Ann Hudson (*Polly*), Patricia Ann Hudson (*Peggy*), Beverly Ross (*Deidre*), John Davey (*Dr. Norton*).

Produced by Robert Altman for Lion's Gate Films, Inc. Twentieth Century-Fox. Associate producers: Robert Eggenweiler and Scott Bushnell. 124 min.

## 1978  A WEDDING

Script: John Considine, Patricia Resnick, Allan Nicholls, Altman, from a story by Considine and Altman.

Direction: Altman.

Assistant director: Tommy Thompson.

Photography (DeLuxe color, Panavision): Charles Rosher.

Editing: Tony Lombardo.

Music: John Hotchkiss, sung and played by the Choir of St. Luke's Episcopal Church, Evanston, Illinois, the Chicago Brass Ensemble, Ruth Pelz (organ).

Song: "Bird on a Wire" by Leonard Cohen.

Bridal consultant: Carson, Pirie, Scott & Co., Chicago.

Cast: The Groom's Family: Lillian Gish (*Nettie Sloan*), Ruth Nelson (*Beatrice Sloan Cory*), Ann Ryerson (*Victoria Cory*), Desi Arnaz, Jr. (*Dino Corelli, the groom*), Belita Moreno (*Daphne Corelli*), Vittorio Gassman (*Luigi Corelli*), Nina van Pallandt (*Regina Corelli*), Virginia Vestoff (*Clarice Sloan*), Dina Merrill (*Antoinette Sloan Goddard*), Pat McCormick (*Mackenzie Goddard*), Luigi Proietti (*Little Dino*).

The Bride's Family: Carol Burnett (*Tulip Brenner*), Paul Dooley (*Snooks Brenner*), Amy Stryker (*Muffin Brenner, the bride*), Mia Farrow (*Buffy Brenner*), Dennis Christopher (*Hughie Brenner*), Mary Seibel (*Aunt Marge Spar*), Margaret Ladd (*Ruby Spar*),

Gerald Busby (*David Ruteledge*), Peggy Ann Garner (*Candice Ruteledge*), Mark R. Deming (*Matthew Ruteledge*), David Brand, Chris Brand, Amy Brand, Jenny Brand, Jeffrey Jones, Jay D. Jones, Courtney MacArthur, Paul D. Keller III (*the Ruteledge children*).

The Corelli House Staff: Cedric Scott (*Randolph*), Robert Fortier (*Jim Habor, gardener*), Maureen Steindler (*Libby Clinton, cook*).

The Wedding Staff: Geraldine Chaplin (*Rita Billingsley*), Mona Abboud (*Melba Lear*), Viveca Lindfors (*Ingrid Hellstrom*), Lauren Hutton (*Flo Farmer*), Allan Nicholls (*Jake Jacobs*), Maysie Hoy (*Casey*), John Considine (*Jeff Kuykendall*), Patricia Resnick (*Redford*), Margery Bond (*Lombardo*), Dennis Franz (*Koons*), Harold C. Johnson (*Oscar Edwards*), Alexander Sopenar (*Victor*).

The Friends and Guest: Howard Duff (*Dr. Jules Meecham*), John Cromwell (*Bishop Martin*), Bert Remsen (*William Williamson*), Pamela Dawber (*Tracy Farrell*), Gavan O'Hirlihy (*Wilson Briggs*), Craig Richard Nelson (*Capt. Reedley Roots*), Jeffry S. Perry (*Bunky Lemay*), Marta Heflin (*Shelby Munker*), Lesley Rogers (*Rosie Bean*), Timothy Thomerson (*Russell Bean*), Beverly Ross (*Nurse Janet Schulman*), David Fitzgerald (*Kevin Clinton*), Susan Kendall Newman (*Chris Clinton*).

The Musicians: Ellie Albers (*gypsy violinist*), Tony Llorens (*at the piano-bar*), Chuck Banks' Big Band with Chris La Kome (*in the ballroom*).

Produced by Robert Altman for Lion's Gate Films, Inc. Twentieth Century-Fox. Executive producer: Tommy Thompson. Associate producers: Robert Eggenweiler, Scott Bushnell. Filmed on location in the suburbs of Chicago. 124 min.

## 1979  QUINTET

Script: Altman, Frank Barhydt, Patricia Resnick, from a story by Altman, Resnick, Lionel Chetwynd.
Direction: Altman.
Assistant director: Tommy Thompson.
Photography (DeLuxe color): Jean Boffety.
Editing: Dennis Hill.
Music: Tom Pierson.
Production design: Leon Ericksen.

Cast: Paul Newman (*Essex*), Fernando Rey (*Grigor*), Bibi Anderson (*Ambrosia*), Vittorio Gassman (*St. Christopher*), Nina van Pallandt (*Deuca*), Brigitte Fossey (*Vivia*).

Produced by Altman for Lion's Gate Films, Inc. Twentieth Century Fox. Associate producer: Allan Nicholls. 118 min.

# INDEX

Aldrich, Robert, 17, 22, 307
*Alice Doesn't Live Here Anymore,*
207–9, 222, 251–60, 265, 268,
330
*Alice's Restaurant,* 18, 19, 28, 55–
57, 64
Allen, Dede, 27, 39
Allen, Woody, 205
*All the President's Men,* 59
Alternate montage, 150, 292, 320;
*see also* Montage
Altman, Robert, 6, 18, 58, 61, 66,
103, 153, 208, 221, 268, 270–339;
visual structure in films of, 279;
improvisational methods of, 287;
narrative, aural-visual space of,
274, 277–86; women in films of,
330
American cinema: conventions of,
67; cultural themes in, 44, 45;

*découpage* in, 282; narrative traditions in, 275; violence in, 48,
54–55; *see also* American film
American film, 228n, 259–60, 268,
295, 316; children in, 358–59;
changes in, 17; classical approach
to, 9; country vs. city in, 42;
editing structure of, 151–52; foreign perspective on, 17; generic
patterns of, 8; melodramatic
crises in, 313; myths, 236; narrative, 207, 221; reality in, 11; relationships in, 258; sexual and
emotional abuse in, 247; strength
of, 8; traditions of, 269; visual
components of, 158; women in,
252, 258–60; *see also* Genres;
Ideology; Production
American filmmaking, state of,
270–71